Java Programming with JBuilder

Java Programming with JBuilder

Steven Holzner

M&T BOOKS

M&T Books
A Division of MIS:Press, Inc.
A Subsidiary of Henry Holt and Company, Inc.
115 West 18th Street
New York, New York 10011
http://www.mispress.com

Copyright © 1997 by Steven Holzner

Printed in the United States of America

All rights reserved. No part of this book may be reproduced or transmitted in any form or by any means, electronic or mechanical, including photocopying, recording, or by any information storage and retrieval system, without prior written permission from the Publisher. Contact the Publisher for information on foreign rights.

Limits of Liability and Disclaimer of Warranty

The Author and Publisher of this book have used their best efforts in preparing the book and the programs contained in it. These efforts include the development, research, and testing of the theories and programs to determine their effectiveness.

The Author and Publisher make no warranty of any kind, expressed or implied, with regard to these programs or the documentation contained in this book. The Author and Publisher shall not be liable in any event for incidental or consequential damages in connection with, or arising out of, the furnishing, performance, or use of these programs.

All products, names and services are trademarks or registered trademarks of their respective companies.

First Edition—1997

Library of Congress Cataloging-in-Publication Data

```
Holzner, Steven
   Java programming with JBuilder/ by Steven Holzner
      p.      cm.
   ISBN 1-55851-507-0
     1. Java (Computer program language) 2. JBuilder 3. I. Title.
   QA76.73.J39H65        1997
   005.2'762--dc21                                         97-16387
                                                               CIP
```

MIS:Press and M&T Books are available at special discounts for bulk purchases for sales promotions, premiums, and fundraising. Special editions or book excerpts can also be created to specification.

For details contact: Special Sales Director
                      MIS:Press and M&T Books
                      Subsidiaries of Henry Holt and Company, Inc.
                      115 West 18th Street
                      New York, New York 10011

10 9 8 7 6 5 4 3 2 1

Associate Publisher: *Paul Farrell*

Executive Editor: *Shari Chappell*
Editor: *Michael Sprague*
Copy Edit Manager: *Karen Tongish*

Production Editor: *Natalie Fortin*
Technical Editor: *Jonathan Lipkin*
Copy Editor: *Bert Shankle*

DEDICATION

To my sweetie, Nancy Conner, the editor extraordinaire (and the most beautiful too!)

ACKNOWLEDGEMENTS

A book like the one you hold in your hands is the result of the hard work of many people. I'd especially like to thank Michael Sprague, Paul Farrell, Natalie Fortin, Kitty May, and Maya Riddick.

Chapter 4: Check Boxes and Radio Buttons 133

Using Check Boxes 134
    Connecting Check Boxes to Code 135
Handling Radio Buttons 144
    Using Check Box Groups 145
Putting Check Boxes and Radio Buttons Together 154
Retailer2 166
    Customizing the retailer2 Application 170

Chapter 5: Lists, Choices, Popups, and Scroll Bars 187

Using Lists 188
    Filling a List Control with Items 191
    Getting the User's Selection 191
Using Choice Controls 196
    Filling a Choice Control with Items 198
    Getting the User's Selection 198
Using Popup Menus 203
    Placing Items in a Popup Menu 204
    Displaying the Popup Menu 206
    Getting the User's Selection 207
Scroll Bars 215
    Using Panels 216
    Using the Border Layout 216
    Determining User Actions 220

Chapter 6: Windows, Menus, and Dialog Boxes 231

Creating Frame Windows 232
    Creating a New Frame Window 233
    Adding Controls to a Window 235
    Overriding Window Methods 236
    Displaying and Hiding a Window 237

Using Menus 246
    Adding a Menu Bar 247
Full Menus 259
    Adding Menu Separators 262
    Adding Check Menu Items 262
    Adding Grayed Menu Items 262
    Adding Submenu Items 263
Using Dialog Boxes 274
    Sending Data from Dialog Box to Applets 277

Chapter 7: Graphics: Image Handling and Text 287

Using the Image Class 288
Scaling Images to Different Sizes 295
    Scaling an Image 296
Using the Image Control 299
The Writer Applet 304
    Setting the Writer Applet's Flags 305
    Using the Mouse in Writer 308
    Reading Keystrokes 310
    Selecting a Font and Drawing Text 313
Justifying Text 328

Chapter 8: Graphics: A Mouse-Driven Paint Program ..339

Handling the Mouse 340
    The MouseEntered Event 344
    The MouseDragged Event 346
    The MousePressed Event 346
    The MouseReleased Event 347
    The MouseExited Event 348
A Mouse-Driven Paint Program 356
    Designing the Painter Program's User Interface 360
    Handling the Mouse in Painter 364

Drawing Lines 367
Drawing Ovals 372
Drawing Rectangles 374
Drawing 3D Rectangles 376
Drawing Rounded Rectangles 377
Drawing Freehand Objects with the Mouse .379

Chapter 9: Making It Move — Graphics Animation 395

Using Image Controls for Animation 396
   Making Applets Multithreaded 397
   Starting a Thread 400
   Stopping a Thread 401
   Running a Thread's Code 402
   Drawing the Image 405
Creating Graphics Animation 409
   Animating Our Images 412
   Drawing the Images 414
Reducing Screen Flicker 419
Double-Buffering 424
   Drawing a Buffered Image 428

Chapter 10: JBuilder Advanced Topics 437

Using More Than One Thread 437
   Keep Threads Separate 440
Synchronizing Multithread Functions 449
   Setting Up the Threads 453
   The Synchronized1 Application's run( ) Method 454
   Synchronizing Data Access 457

Index 467

Introduction

Welcome to the JBuilder

Welcome to the world of Java and JBuilder. Java has been making a tremendous splash in the programming world, and we'll see why in this book. People are very excited about the power of this package and what it can do, both for Web pages and in creating stand-alone applications. In this book we're going to embark on a guided tour of the world of Java, and JBuilder will be our guide.

Until now, if you wanted to work with Java, you had to use the command-line version of the Java compiler, javac. However, it struck people inside Sun Microsystems—the creators of Java—as odd that you had to use a command-line program to create Java programs which are targeted to purely graphical environments. That was fixed with the release of the JBuilder, which allows us not only to edit our Java programs in a windowing environment, but also to develop, compile, build, test, and debug them. With the arrival of the JBuilder, Java can reach out to a tremendous new audience.

In this book, we're going to see how far Java can take us, and that is very far. Have you ever thought that Web pages could pop their own windows on the screen (and even move those new windows around)? Or that such windows could support menus and dialog boxes? Or that Web pages could become multitasking entities filled with animation? All this, plus the more usual Web page techniques of animation and clickable imagemaps, are part of this book. We'll see them and more in our guided tour.

Introduction

What's in this Book

There is a great deal of programming power in Java, and we are going to put it to work for us. Some of the topics we'll see in our tour include:

- Using JBuilder
- Creating JBuilder projects
- Java applets and applications
- Java classes and objects
- TextFields
- Buttons, radio buttons, checkboxes
- List controls
- Image controls
- Opening new windows
- Font handling
- Menus
- Popup menus
- Scroll bars
- Dialog boxes
- Multitasking
- Java layouts
- Graphics animation
- Interactive animation
- Image handling
- Popup menus

Java is an exceptionally strong and simple programming language, and we're going to see it at work for us. That's the emphasis of this book—seeing it work. We're not going to start with programming theory; instead, we'll start with ideas of what we want to do and let the abstract concepts come in only when they are needed and their introduction makes sense. That's why you won't see chapters entitled "Program Flow Control" or "Calling Frame Structure" in this book. Instead, you'll see chapters like "Graphics Animation," or "TextFields and Buttons," or "Drawing Lines, Circles, Rectangles and More"—topics organized around what Java programmers want to create in their Web pages. Our guided tour is studded with literally dozens of examples, and that's the way it works best: seeing bite-sized examples that are clear and to the point. That's our approach—seeing Java at work and putting it to work for us with JBuilder.

What You'll Need

You'll really only need the JBuilder to use this book. Although the code developed here is mostly targeted at the Internet, it can be run on your machine at home (this is because JBuilder has a built-in browser, allowing you to preview your Web pages). However, most people will also want to have an Internet Service Provider (ISP) which will host their Web pages and Java applets so that other people may download and use them. That's all you need, so let's get started without further delay.

Since Java is primarily used in Web pages today, our first chapter will be a review of exactly that—creating Web pages, the normal environment of Java applets. In this chapter, we'll review the language of Web pages (Hypertext Markup Language, or HTML), giving us a place to install the Java applets we create. If you feel confident of your HTML abilities, you might want to skip this chapter; otherwise, let's begin our guided tour now as we turn to Chapter 1.

CHAPTER 1

Handling HTML

Welcome to our book on JBuilder! In this book, we'll see how to create some very powerful Java programs: programs that display more than static information; programs that can interact with the user, ask questions, change their appearance, and support many unique interactions with the user. JBuilder offers us the best of two worlds—Java programming that is both powerful and simple to create. In this book, we're going to explore what JBuilder has to offer to us, and we'll see it all at work.

It's no secret that the Internet has taken-off these days, and Java is a big part of that. Just about all Web browers are Java-enabled. Even so, programming with Java can be difficult, especially if you're just starting out. With JBuilder however, the process is almost a breeze. JBuilder has the most advanced Java programming tools available today. As we'll see in this book, it's a remarkable package.

We'll be able to design the look of our programs right in JBuilder, seeing it as it will appear when it runs, and placing buttons, check boxes, and more in our programs just where we want them. JBuilder itself will write a great deal of code for us, connecting the various parts of our progams together automatically. Anything you can do in Java—and there's just about no limit there—can be designed with JBuilder.

Much Java programming is aimed at the World Wide Web, and in fact, we will start with a review of working with Web pages in this chapter. Here, we'll review Hypertext Markup Language (HTML), the langage of Web pages. This information will be important when we create our own Web pages using the Java programs we create in this book.

After we review HTML, we'll proceed with JBuilder itself in Chapter 2. If you're an HTML expert, there's no reason that you can't skip on to the next chapter immediately. If you're not an HTML expert, however, you might want to read through the following material to brush up.

… Chapter 1

Our First Web Page

Our first task will be to see what goes into a Web page. It's important to remember that a Web page at its most basic is really just text that can be interpreted by a Web browser. Although you can open many different types of files with Web browsers these days (especially if you have a number of helper applications) such as .avi movie files or .zip compressed files, Web pages themselves are written in text (even though they include HTML statements). With all the different possible formats, how does a Web browser know what kind of file it is working on? That's based on the file's extension—and if that extension is .html, such as review.html, the Web browser expects a file written in HTML. Note that because of MS-DOS's three letter file extension limit, many Web browsers also assume that files with the extension .htm are also written in HTML.

The Shortest Web Page

Because the text in a Web page is interpreted based on the file's .html extension, we can write a Web page that is extraordinarily short, something which might contain only this line, for example:

```
Hello, world!
```

as long as we give the Web page's file the html extension. In this case, we might put the above text into a file named hello.html, and Web browsers would treat it as a Web page:

hello.html file

```
Hello, world!
```

In fact, we could have a Web page as short as a single character, as long as we gave the file containing it the html extension (this also assumes that you install the Web page in your Internet Service Provider as discussed below).

That's all it takes to write a Web page, although we should note that the text in a Web page's .html file is just straight text, and on PCs that usually means ASCII text. If you are using a word processor like Microsoft Word for Windows 95, you must save your files in plain text format (i.e., as can be displayed on the screen with the TYPE command).

In addition, we're going to assume that you are familiar with the basic steps of installing a Web page on the Web. That usually means having an Internet Service Provider (ISP) with a computer that runs constantly so your Web page is always accessible, and that uploads your Web page properly. The actual uploading details vary from machine to machine; uploading can mean using special uploading software that will upload Web pages at the click of a mouse button, or using a FTP (File Transfer Protocol) program to transfer the Web page and any graphics files you want to include to a specially designated area of your ISP, then using UNIX commands to set the page's protections so no one but you can modify them. The default name for a Web page is *index.html,* which is what a Web browser will look for at a given Web site if you do not specify the name of a file to open.

Our "Hello, world!" Web page isn't really all that exciting (unless you want to prove to your friends how easy it is to create a Web page), so let's start designing a more typical Web page now, building it up part by part during the rest of this chapter until it's functional at the end. We'll start our example Web page with the <HTML> tag:

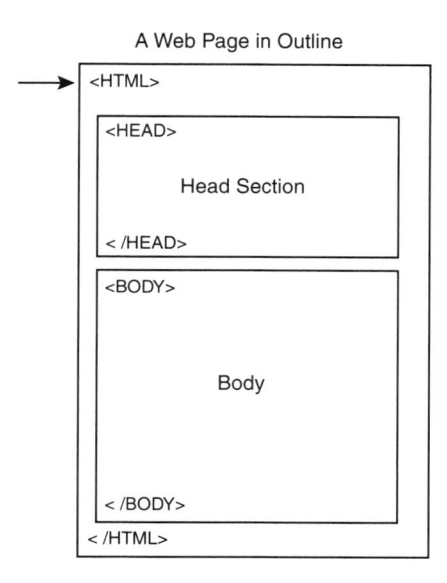

A Web Page in Outline

```
→ <HTML>
    <HEAD>

            Head Section

    </HEAD>
    <BODY>


            Body



    </BODY>
  </HTML>
```

The <HTML> Tag

Usually, Web pages include both text that you want to display and HTML commands to Web browsers. Those commands are enclosed in *tags*, which are surrounded by the < and > characters. For example, the usual first line in a Web page indicates that the Web page is written in HTML with a HTML tag this way:

```
<HTML>
    .
    .
    .
```

A Web browser can tell that what is to follow is written in HTML, although, as mentioned, that information is usually gotten from the Web page file's extension.

The <!> Comment Tag

Since we want to make it clear what's going on in our first Web page, we will add comments to it with comment tags. Such a tag simply begins with a !, and Web browsers will ignore the comments that follow. (You have to be careful here—early versions of some browsers had problems when you include a tag, such as <HTML> inside a comment, which is why we enclose the tags we are talking about in quotes in our comments here.)

```
<HTML>
<!—START THE PAGE with an HTML tag (a tag is an HTML command, and
    HTML tags appear between angle brackets) We use "HTML" to indicate this
    document is in HTML, which is the language of Web pages.>
    .
    .
    .
```

Here we indicate what the <HTML> tag is all about in our comment. Adding comments this way can help you recall what's going on in your own Web pages and help understand what's going on in others' Web pages. Keep in mind that your whole Web page has to be downloaded into someone's Web browser before they can see it, and that means your comments will be downloaded as well. For that reason, comments (which most people surfing the Web will never see) should probably be kept to a minimum. Some professional Web page writers keep a commented version of Web pages and then run software to strip the comments out of the copy they actually install. In this case, however, we'll comment our first page heavily.

The <HEAD> Tag

Web pages consist of both a head and a body:

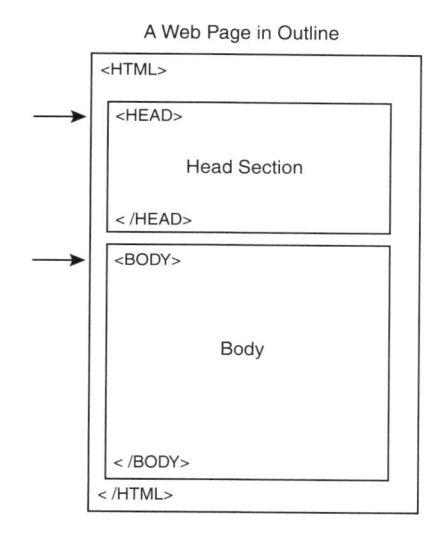

```
                    A Web Page in Outline
            ┌─────────────────────────────────┐
            │ <HTML>                          │
            │   ┌─────────────────────────┐   │
         →  │   │ <HEAD>                  │   │
            │   │                         │   │
            │   │      Head Section       │   │
            │   │                         │   │
            │   │ </HEAD>                 │   │
            │   └─────────────────────────┘   │
         →  │   ┌─────────────────────────┐   │
            │   │ <BODY>                  │   │
            │   │                         │   │
            │   │         Body            │   │
            │   │                         │   │
            │   │ </BODY>                 │   │
            │   └─────────────────────────┘   │
            │ </HTML>                         │
            └─────────────────────────────────┘
```

A Web page's head section is defined with the <HEAD> tag, and in this section we can add text that explains more about the Web page. In the past, the head section was used more often—these days, Web pages usually only have a title for the Web page in the head section (see the <TITLE> tag, coming up next). It is worth noting, however, that certain advanced tags, like <BASE> and <RANGE>, can only function in the head section of a Web page (<BASE> is an interesting and unusual tag, since it allows you to specify a page's "base location" and all other references to subdirectories and so on will be taken from that base. This allows you to move a page to another directory entirely to work on it, while the images and so on embedded in it will still be found properly). We start our page's head section with the <HEAD> tag this way:

```
<HTML>

<!—The HEAD section of the Web page includes text about the page,
    although usually this section only includes the title.>
```

Chapter 1

```
<HEAD>              <--
    .
    .
    .
```

The <TITLE> Tag

Although Web page programmers often skip the <HEAD> tag, they rarely skip <TITLE>. That's because a Web page's title counts; it's the text that most Web browsers will enter into the list of favorites or bookmarks when someone likes your page and wants to remember it for later. Also, it's the text that usually appears in the title bar of the Web browser when it's displaying your page, like this *THIS IS THE TITLE OF MY PAGE! — Microsoft Internet Explorer*. In this case, we'll give our new Web page the title *Welcome to JBuilder* using the <TITLE> tag. In addition, tags come in pairs in HTML, and we indicate that we are finished with the title by using the tag </TITLE> and also finished with our Web page's head section with the tag </HEAD> :

```
<HTML>

<!--A PAGE'S TITLE is how a browser will refer to it if someone saves
    it in their Favorites or Bookmarks menu. Note that we also indicate
    we are done defining the title with "/TITLE". This second tag
    matches the first tag, "TITLE", and as mentioned, HTML tags
    always come in pairs, like the following one, which indicates that
    we are done with the page's header.>

<HEAD>                                      <--
<TITLE>Welcome to JBuilder</TITLE>          <--
</HEAD>                                     <--
    .
    .
    .
```

Usually, for each tag <TAG>, there is a corresponding closing tag, </TAG> (although that is not true for some tags, such as the line break, <BR>, tag). While making sure you have as many </TAG>s as <TAG>s may sometimes not be necessary in HTML (Web browsers are very forgiving), it is good form to make sure you do. In fact, this is one of the first things that Web page *val-*

Handling HTML

idators (programs on the Web that will check your page for errors—just do a Web search for "validator") check for.

Now we've completed the head section of our Web page, and we're ready to turn to the body itself:

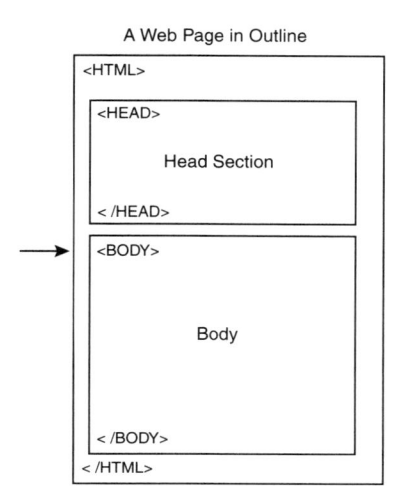

```
A Web Page in Outline
<HTML>
    <HEAD>
        Head Section
    </HEAD>
    <BODY>   ←
        Body
    </BODY>
</HTML>
```

The <BODY> Tag

The body follows a Web page's head section, and makes up the remainder of the document (i.e., this is where the action is). We can declare the body simply with the <BODY> tag, as follows:

```
<HTML>

<HEAD
<TITLE>Welcome to JBuilder</TITLE>
</HEAD>

<BODY>   <—
    .
    .
    .
```

Chapter 1

There's much more that we can do with the `<BODY>` tag. Here, for example, is where we set up some options. These options will indicate how we want our entire Web page to appear—what color text we want, what color to use for hyperlinks, what color hyperlinks that the person viewing our page (the user) has already been to should look like, and so on.

In this example, let's make the text yellow, hyperlinks red, and hyperlinks that the person viewing our page has already visited yellow although they will still appear underlined, hyperlinks that have already been visited will no longer stand out in red). This, of course, brings up the question: how do we define colors in HTML?

Setting Web Page and Text Colors

Recent Web browsers (such as Microsoft Internet Explorer and Netscape) have a set of predefined colors that you can use if you like. The names of these colors are Aqua, Black, Blue, Fuchsia, Gray, Green, Lime, Maroon, Navy, Olive, Purple, Red, Silver, Teal, Yellow, and White. However, older Web browsers have no idea what these words are supposed to mean and ignore them, so we will not use them either (there are many people out there with older Web browsers). Instead, we will specify color using color values, which is a six digit number in hexadecimal.

Color values are defined in the following way: *rrggbb*, where *rr* is the red color value, *gg* the green color value, and *bb* the blue color value. Each of these color values is a two-digit hexadecimal value from 0 to ff—that is, from 0 to 255 in decimal (hexadecimal digits go from 0 to f). In this way, we could specify pure red as "#ff0000", pure blue as "#0000ff", bright yellow (a combination of red and green) as "#ffff00", and bright white as "#ffffff", while black is simply "#000000". Of course there are intermediate values as well, such as a more muted green, which might look like this: "#00aa00", grey is "#888888", as well as combinations of colors like a powder blue, which is set up this way: "#aaaaff".

We'll add some color values to our `<BODY>` tag now. In this example, we intend to make the text yellow (using the TEXT keyword), hyperlinks red (using the LINK keyword), and hyperlinks that the person viewing our page has already visited yellow (using the VLINK keyword). In addition, we can specify that as the user clicks a link, it should be displayed momentarily in white (using the ALINK keyword), to indicate that we are jumping to that location. All that looks like this in our `<BODY>` tag:

Handling HTML

```
<HTML>

<HEAD>
<TITLE>Welcome to JBuilder</TITLE>
</HEAD>

<!—BODY OF PAGE starts with the following "BODY" tag. COLOR VALUES
   are "#rrggbb" (red, green, and blue) in hexadecimal (0-255 = 0-ff);
   for example pure red is "#ff0000", pure green #00ff00" and yellow
   is "#ffff00". Here we start the Web page's body, indicating we want
   yellow text, hyperlinks to be red, hyperlinks to turn white when
   pushed, and links that the user has already clicked to be
   yellow.>
<BODY TEXT  = "#ffff00" LINK  = "#ff0000" ALINK = "#ffffff" VLINK = "#ffff00">
   .
   .
   .
```

In addition, we can specify the background color of the Web page with the BGCOLOR keyword if we wished (for example, we could make the background color white this way: <BODY BGCOLOR = "#ffffff">). For this example, however, let's use a graphics file for the background; the Web browser taking a look at our Web page will use this graphics file to "tile" the background of our Web page, which can produce some pleasing effects—you may have seen Web pages whose background mimics various cloth or paper textures or even looks like marble. We'll use a graphics file named, say, back.gif to show how this works, and that file appears in Figure 1.1—simply a white dot on a black background.

Figure 1.1 Our first Web page's graphics background.

Chapter 1

We can install back.gif as our Web page's background with a new **<BODY>** tag and the BACKGROUND keyword like this:

```
<HTML>

<HEAD>
<TITLE>Welcome to JBuilder</TITLE>
</HEAD>

<BODY TEXT = "#ffff00" LINK = "#ff0000" ALINK = "#ffffff" VLINK = "#ffff00">

<!—BACKGROUND PICTURE (which is optional) is tiled on the page's
   background. Here, we indicate we want the Web browser to use the
   graphics file back.gif, which is in our www/gif directory (see
   explanation, below).>
<BODY BACKGROUND = "gif/back.gif">        <—
   .
   .
   .
```

Since back.gif is a small file, Web browsers will use it repeatedly to tile the background of our Web page, so the background will appear as a series of white dots.

This, however, brings up the subject of graphics—how did we produce back.gif? Where do we store it? We'll take a look at that topic now, because graphics are a large part of Web page programming.

A Little About Graphics

There are a few things to review about graphics before we proceed. For example, the usual graphics file formats used in Web pages are .gif format and .jpg (or .jpeg) format—which is better? (The Internet Explorer can handle .bmp format, but many other browsers can't.) It depends on your needs: .jpg format files can indeed be smaller, which translates to faster download times, but compared to .gif format, there is some loss of data, and consequently images can look less sharp. The best thing to do, of course, is to give it a try both ways: the Microsoft Internet Explorer can load images in .bmp, .gif, and .jpg format, and lets you save them in any of these formats as well, so you can easily convert images between formats this way. You can even

Handling HTML

use the Windows Paint program to design your graphics (although of course there are far more powerful graphics programs out there), save your work in .bmp format, and use the Microsoft Internet Explorer to re-save the file in .gif or .jpg format.

Besides graphics you draw, there are other sources of graphics files—scans of photos, for example. If you don't have your own scanner, you can often get this done commercially at a copy center. Ask for the standard 72 dots per inch (dpi) resolution (which is as good as screens get) and make your graphics file a reasonable size (of course, if you expect people to download your file and print it on very high resolution laser printers, you can ask for better scan resolution). Another possible source of graphics are the Web pages already out there, and that can be very tempting. However, before simply copying what somebody else has done, you should be aware that such work may be copyrighted, and ask first.

When we insert graphics into a Web page such as the one we're designing, we'll need to know the width and height of the image in pixels (the background .gif or .jpg file is an exception) so the Web browser can fit the page together while leaving space for our graphics. If you have a scan done, you can ask the people who scanned the photo for you what the image size is in pixels; otherwise, you can use a program like Windows Paint, which will tell you your image's dimensions. (Windows Paint displays the current location of the mouse in pixels, so you only have to move the mouse cursor to the lower right of the image to get the image's height and width.)

Where do we store our images? It is customary to set up a separate directory for image files in your ISP. If you store your HTML files in a directory named *www*, you might want to create and store your images in a subdirectory named, say, *www/gif*; such a directory can be created with the **mkdir** command on UNIX machines. We will store back.gif in a subdirectory named gif. When we want to reference a file in that directory, such as back.gif, we do it by indicating the correct path to that file, gif/back.gif (note that since the files reside in the ISP's computer, we use the UNIX convention of many ISPs, which is to use forward slashes to separate directories, not backward slashes as is the IBM PC convention):

```
<HTML>

<HEAD>
<TITLE>Welcome to JBuilder</TITLE>
</HEAD>

<BODY TEXT = "#ffff00" LINK = "#ff0000" ALINK = "#ffffff" VLINK = "#ffff00">
```

Chapter 1

```
<!—BACKGROUND PICTURE (which is optional) is tiled on the page's
   background. Here, we indicate we want the Web browser to use the
   graphics file back.gif, which is in our www/gif directory (see
   explanation, below).>
<BODY BACKGROUND = "gif/back.gif">         <—
     .
     .
     .
```

It is not necessary to use a separate directory for your image files, and many Web sites do not. Your ISP can give you site-specific requirements.

At this point, we've installed our background image from back.gif. The next step is to add some text to our Web page, since nothing appears there yet but the background dots. We might add a heading that says *Welcome to JBuilder* like this—this is the first time we see what our new Web page will look like:

> Welcome to JBuilder

The <Center> and Header Tags

To add a header to our Web page, we can use the header tags, `<H1>` to `<H6>`. `<H1>` creates the largest-font header, and we can use that here:

```
<HTML>

<HEAD>
<TITLE>Welcome to JBuilder</TITLE>
</HEAD>
```

Handling HTML

```
<BODY TEXT = "#ffff00" LINK = "#ff0000" ALINK = "#ffffff" VLINK = "#ffff00">

<BODY BACKGROUND = "gif/back.gif">

<!—HEADERS. Now we are going to place a header of the largest size in
    our page, so we use the "H1" tag, as well as the "CENTER" tag.
    "CENTER" simply makes sure the following text or image is centered.
    Note that all HTML tags come in pairs—to turn off centering, we
    use "/CENTER" at the end of our header's specification.>
<H1>Welcome to JBuilder</H1>         <—
    .
    .
    .
```

Now our header will appear in the text color we have chosen (yellow) in the largest header style. In addition, we center our header in our page with the <CENTER> and </CENTER> tags as follows:

```
<HTML>

<HEAD>
<TITLE>Welcome to JBuilder</TITLE>
</HEAD>

<BODY TEXT = "#ffff00" LINK = "#ff0000" ALINK = "#ffffff" VLINK = "#ffff00">

<BODY BACKGROUND = "gif/back.gif">

<!—HEADERS. Now we are going to place a header of the largest size in
    our page, so we use the "H1" tag, as well as the "CENTER" tag.
    "CENTER" simply makes sure the following text or image is centered.
    Note that all HTML tags come in pairs—to turn off centering, we
    use "/CENTER" at the end of our header's specification.>
<CENTER>                             <—
<H1>Welcome to JBuilder</H1>
</CENTER>                            <—
    .
    .
    .
```

Chapter 1

In this case, our header will appear in large yellow letters, centered on our Web page, as shown in Figure 1.2. Note that we did not have to use the `<CENTER>` tag; instead, we could have specified an alignment for our header in the `<H1>` tag as `<H1 ALIGN = alignment>`, where alignment can be `LEFT`, `RIGHT`, or `CENTER`.

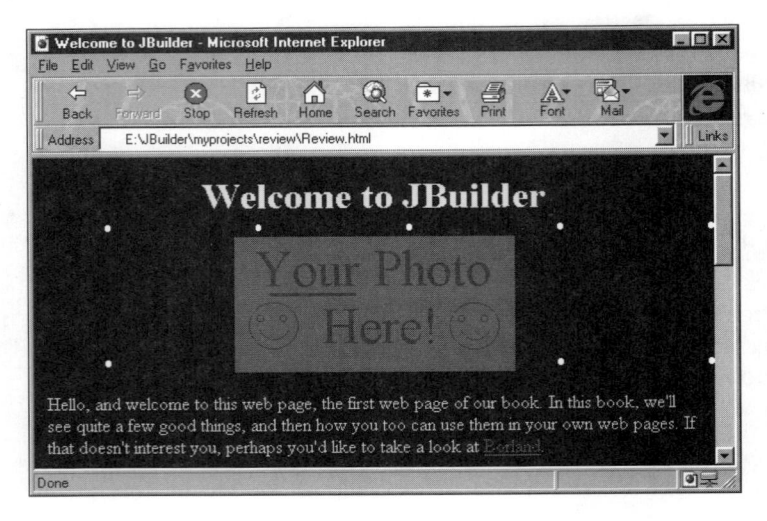

Figure 1.2 Our first Web page.

At this stage, our Web page has just started appearing—we've set up the background image and the header text. Next, we review how to space things appropriately.

The `<BR>` Tag

The next step is to leave some space after the header and before adding any images. We do that with the line break tag, `<BR>`. That looks like this:

```
<HTML>

<HEAD>
<TITLE>Welcome to JBuilder</TITLE>
</HEAD>
```

Handling HTML

```
<BODY TEXT  = "#ffff00" LINK  = "#ff0000" ALINK = "#ffffff" VLINK = "#ffff00">
<BODY BACKGROUND = "gif/back.gif">
<CENTER>
<H1>Welcome to JBuilder</H1>
</CENTER>
<!—LINE BREAKS. To space things vertically, we use "BR" and "/BR"
    to
    skip a line.>
<BR>                            <—
    .
    .
    .
```

Let's add some graphics next. For example, this might be a photo of yourself, yourgif.gif:

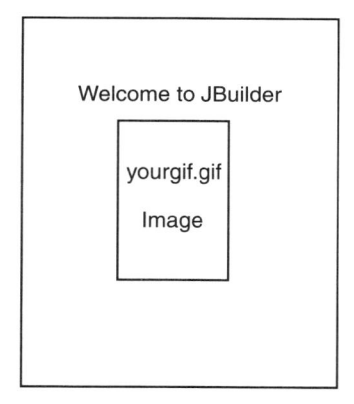

```
┌─────────────────────────────┐
│                             │
│     Welcome to JBuilder     │
│                             │
│       ┌───────────┐         │
│       │ yourgif.gif│        │
│       │           │         │
│       │   Image   │         │
│       │           │         │
│       └───────────┘         │
│                             │
│                             │
└─────────────────────────────┘
```

Graphics images are inserted with the <IMG> tag, which we'll review next.

The <IMG> Tag

At this point in our Web page, we will insert the image file yourgif.gif. We can center that image with the <CENTER> tag, and actually perform the insertion with the <IMG> tag. To do this, we indicate the dimensions of the image with the WIDTH and HEIGHT keywords. We also have to indicate where the image file is to be found by indicating its path as well as its name with the SRC (for Source) keyword, making our <IMG> tag look like this:

Chapter 1

```
<HTML>

<HEAD>
<TITLE>Welcome to JBuilder</TITLE>
</HEAD>


<BODY TEXT  = "#ffff00" LINK  = "#ff0000" ALINK = "#ffffff" VLINK = "#ffff00">
<BODY BACKGROUND = "gif/back.gif">

<CENTER>
<H1>Welcome to JBuilder</H1>
</CENTER>

<BR>
<!—IMAGES. We display an image, which will appear centered because of

   the "CENTER" tag, with the "IMG" tag, adding the width and height
   in pixels. Here, we display our GIF file yourgif.gif from the GIF
   directory, but this is where a photo of you could go.>
<CENTER>                                                         <—
<IMG WIDTH=236 HEIGHT=118 SRC="gif/yourgif.gif"></IMG>           <—
</CENTER>                                                        <—
     .
     .
     .
```

If you want to have text appear in the space the image will take up on the Web page while that image is being loaded, you can add that with the ALT keyword to the IMG tag (and this text is all that will appear in text-only Web browsers):

```
<IMG WIDTH = 236 HEIGHT = 118 ALT = "A photo of the Web page author as a young man." SRC="gif/yourgif.gif">
```

And that's it—now yourgif.gif appears in the Web page, as shown in Figure 1.2. It's that easy to add images to our Web page.

Now that we've added our first picture, let's put in some text next in our developing Web page:

Handling HTML

```
┌─────────────────────────────────┐
│                                 │
│      Welcome to JBuilder        │
│                                 │
│         ┌─────────┐             │
│         │  Image  │             │
│         └─────────┘             │
│                                 │
│      ┌───────────────────┐      │
│      │ A paragraph of text│     │
│      └───────────────────┘      │
│                                 │
└─────────────────────────────────┘
```

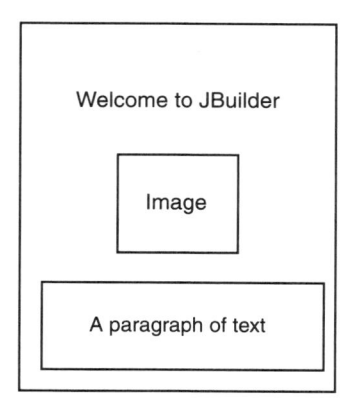

The <P> Tag

To start off our text, which will introduce the Web page to the user, we can use the <P> paragraph tag. This tag moves us to the next line and starts a paragraph of text (note that it is not necessary to use the <P> tag when inserting text). We might place this text in our Web page at this point, simply by typing it to follow the <P> tag; note that we will set up a hyperlink to borland.com at the very end of the paragraph:

```
Hello, and welcome to this Web page, the first Web page of our
book. In this book, we'll see quite a few good things, and then how
you too can use them in your own Web pages. If that doesn't
interest you, perhaps you'd like to take a look at [borland.com].
```

In our Web page, we simply place the text directly into the .html file, like this:

```
<HTML>
<HEAD>
<TITLE>Welcome to JBuilder</TITLE>
</HEAD>
<BODY TEXT = "#ffff00" LINK = "#ff0000" ALINK = "#ffffff" VLINK = "#ffff00">
<BODY BACKGROUND = "gif/back.gif">
<CENTER>
<H1>Welcome to JBuilder</H1>
</CENTER>
<BR>
```

Chapter 1

```
<CENTER>
<IMG WIDTH=236 HEIGHT=118 SRC="gif/yourgif.gif"></IMG>
</CENTER>
<!—PARAGRAPHS of text start with "P".>
<P>
—> Hello, and welcome to this Web page, the first Web page of our
—> book. In this book, we'll see quite a few good things, and then how
—> you too can use them in your own Web pages. If that doesn't
—> interest you, perhaps you'd like to take a look at
              .
              .
              .
```

And that's it—now our paragraph of text appears, as shown in Figure 1.2.

The `<P>` tag has one keyword: `ALIGN`. You can align text using these keywords: `ALIGN = LEFT`, `ALIGN = RIGHT`, and `ALIGN = CENTER`. In this way, we have some modest control over the formatting of our text paragraph. In addition, we can use the `<B>` tag to make displayed text bold, and the `<I>` tag to make it appear italicized.

We still have not made our hyperlink to borland.com at the end of the paragraph active. Let's do that next, introducing a link into out .html file with the `<A>` tag.

The <A> Tag

We add hyperlinks using the `<A>` (**Anchor**) tag, used together with the `HREF` keyword. In particular, we will add a link to borland.com's Web page at the end of our paragraph of text. For that, we need the page's World Wide Web address, or URL (Universal Resource Location), and that is: "http://www.borland.com". We don't want to give that as the name of the link, however—we'll just display this link as "Borland" in the color for hyperlinks we've chosen (red). That looks like this with the `<A>` tag in our Web page:

```
<HTML>

<HEAD>
<TITLE>Welcome to JBuilder</TITLE>
</HEAD>
```

Handling HTML

```
<BODY TEXT = "#ffff00" LINK = "#ff0000" ALINK = "#ffffff" VLINK = "#ffff00">
<BODY BACKGROUND = "gif/back.gif">

<CENTER>
<H1>Welcome to JBuilder</H1>
</CENTER>

<BR>

<CENTER>
<IMG WIDTH=236 HEIGHT=118 SRC="gif/yourgif.gif"></IMG>
</CENTER>

<!—PARAGRAPHS of text start with "P".>
<!—LINKS. We add a hypertext link with the "A" tag, using the HREF
   keyword. In particular, we add a link to borland.com's Web page
   at http://www.borland.com below. This means that the text
   "Borland" will appear underlined and in the standard link color
   (which we've set to red); when the user of your page clicks that
   text, they will jump to borland's home page.>
<P>
   Hello, and welcome to this Web page, the first Web page of our
   book. In this book, we'll see quite a few good things, and then how
   you too can use them in your own Web pages. If that doesn't
   interest you, perhaps you'd like to take a look at
   <A HREF="http://www.borland.com">Borland</A>.    <—
<BR>
<BR>
</P>
   .
   .
   .
```

When someone takes a look at our Web page, this paragraph of text will appear yellow, while the word "Borland" at the end will appear in red and underlined, indicating it is a hyperlink. When clicked, this hyperlink will take us to borland.com. If we had wanted to use an image as a hyperlink, we would have simply used an <IMG> tag instead of the text "Borland".

Chapter 1

Now we've added text and hypertext to our Web page. Next, let's take a look next at getting the format of things right. All we've done so far is to place text or images into our page and, at most, centered them. There is much more we can do, and we'll take a look at the process of setting up text and images to be right next to each other. In our Web page, that might look like this:

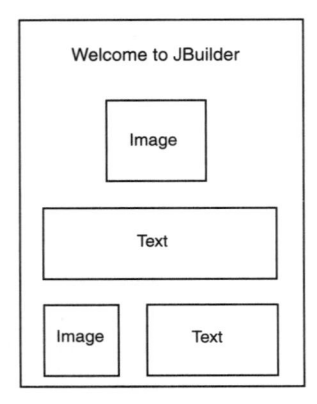

Aligning Images and Text

We've already reviewed how to put images and text into our Web page separately; now we will combine them, placing an image on the left and text on the right. This is actually accomplished very easily—all we have to do is to use the ALIGN keyword in the <IMG> tag. For example, if we want to add a new image named, say, sidebar.gif—which appears in Figure 1.3—on the left of our page, we would just specify that its alignment be LEFT (as opposed to CENTER or RIGHT):

```
<HTML>

<HEAD>
<TITLE>Welcome to JBuilder</TITLE>
</HEAD>

<BODY TEXT = "#ffff00" LINK = "#ff0000" ALINK = "#ffffff" VLINK = "#ffff00">
<BODY BACKGROUND = "gif/back.gif">
```

Handling HTML

```
<CENTER>
<H1>Welcome to JBuilder</H1>
</CENTER>

<BR>

<CENTER>
<IMG WIDTH=236 HEIGHT=118 SRC="gif/yourgif.gif"></IMG>
</CENTER>

<P>
   Hello, and welcome to this Web page, the first Web page of our
   book. In this book, we'll see quite a few good things, and then how
   you too can use them in your own Web pages. If that doesn't
   interest you, perhaps you'd like to take a look at
   <A HREF="http://www.borland.com">Borland</A>.
<BR>
<BR>
</P>

<!--ALIGNING PICTURES AND TEXT is done with the ALIGN keyword used in
   the IMG tag. In this case we just have to indicate that we want the
   graphics to appear on the left with ALIGN = LEFT. We also change
   the text color to green temporarily with a "FONT" tag ("FONT" only
   works in recent browsers).>
<IMG WIDTH=141 HEIGHT=126 SRC="gif/sidebar.gif" ALIGN=LEFT>      <--
      .
      .
      .
```

Figure 1.3 Sidebar.gif, the image that appears next to text on our Web page.

Chapter 1

Now we're ready to add our text on the right. To do that, we just type it in; since the image is on the left, the text will automatically fill the space on the right. To make it a little more interesting, let's switch the color of our text from our default of yellow to green. We do that with the <FONT> tag.

The <FONT> Tag

The <FONT> tag is not supported in early versions of Web browsers like Netscape (i.e., in the 1.n versions), so you have to be a little careful when relying on <FONT> tags. Nonetheless, most Web browsers support it now, so we'll put it to work here. To switch the color of our text to green, we just use the <FONT> tag with the COLOR keyword this way:

```
<IMG WIDTH=141 HEIGHT=126 SRC="gif/sidebar.gif" ALIGN=LEFT>
<FONT COLOR = "00ff00">                <—
    We can even do green text next to graphics. This text appears next
    to the graphics on the left, allowing you to intersperse your words
    with pictures. When you take a look at the HTML for this Web page,
    you'll see how this and more is done.
</FONT>                                <—
</IMG>
    .
    .
    .
```

Note that to restore the text's default color, we also used a </FONT> tag. And that's it—now our text appears next to the sidebar image we used, as shown in Figure 1.4.

Handling HTML

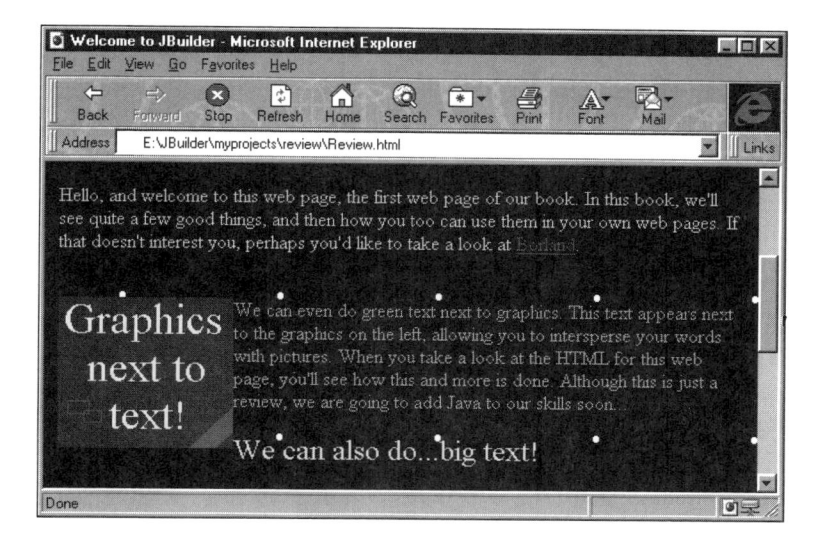

Figure 1.4 Setting up text next to images.

Besides changing the text's color, we can also change its size with the <FONT> tag and the SIZE keyword; for example, let's increase the size of our text temporarily so that it appears larger, as also shown in Figure 1.4. We might do that with this line in our .html file:

```
<IMG WIDTH=141 HEIGHT=126 SRC="gif/sidebar.gif" ALIGN=LEFT>
<FONT COLOR = "00ff00">
    We can even do green text next to graphics. This text appears next
    to the graphics on the left, allowing you to intersperse your words
    with pictures. When you take a look at the HTML for this Web page,
    you'll see how this and more is done.
</FONT>
</IMG>


<!—FONT SIZE is also done with the "FONT" tag; here, we set the
    size of our text temporarily to 5, a large size.>
<FONT SIZE = 5>                     <—
We can also do...big text!          <—
</FONT>                             <—
```

23

Chapter 1

```
<BR>
<BR>
.
.
.
```

The result appears in Figure 1.4. In addition, using the <FONT> tag with the FACE keyword, you can set the typeface used for your text, like Courier or Arial—assuming that the font you select is installed on the machine running the Web browser. (If you list a number of typefaces, the first one that is available will be used.)

Now that we've worked started to review some formatting of our Web page, let's continue that a little more. Take a look at how to put up a table in our page:

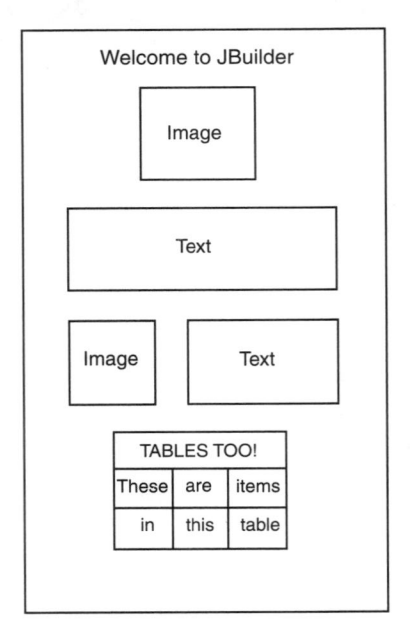

Making Tables

Setting up a table is not very difficult, even though the resulting HTML is not very readable. To continue our review, we might aim for this table, in which we have three rows (one of which is the table's header), three columns, text centered in each table cell, and a header reading *TABLES TOO!* that spans all three columns:

TABLES TOO!			
These	are	items
in	this	table

We start our table with the <TABLE> tag. Here, we can indicate that our table should have a border with the BORDER keyword. In addition, we'll use the CELLPADDING keyword to add some padding around our text to improve its appearance and readability—say 4 pixels like this:

```
<TABLE BORDER CELLPADDING = 4>
    .
    .
    .
```

In setting up a table, we work row by row. To set up a row, we use the <TR> tag. Here, we can align the text in our table's rows with the ALIGN keyword this way:

```
<TABLE BORDER CELLPADDING = 4>
<TR ALIGN = CENTER>                 <—
    .
    .
    .
```

We want our table's header—which we set up with the <TH> tag—to span all three columns and to read *TABLES TOO!*, so we set that up like this, using the COLSPAN keyword:

```
<TABLE BORDER CELLPADDING = 4>
<TR ALIGN = CENTER>
<TH COLSPAN = 3>TABLES TOO!         <—
</TH>                               <—
    .
    .
    .
```

Chapter 1

That finishes off this row, so we use the `</TR>` tag:

```
<TABLE BORDER CELLPADDING = 4>
<TR ALIGN = CENTER>
<TH COLSPAN = 3>TABLES TOO!
</TH>
</TR>     <--
    .
    .
    .
```

The next step is to start the next row, and we'll use the `<TR>` tag, aligning text in the center again, like this:`<TR ALIGN = CENTER>`. Now we have to set up our data for the three columns in this row, and we do that with the `<TD>` tag. In this case, we want to set up the columns like this:

TABLES TOO!		
These	are	items
in	this	table

To do that, we use `<TD>` and `</TD>` pairs, one for each column:

```
<TABLE BORDER CELLPADDING = 4>
<TR ALIGN = CENTER>
<TH COLSPAN = 3>TABLES TOO!
</TH>
</TR>
<TR ALIGN = CENTER>
<TD>These</TD>           <--
<TD>are</TD>             <--
<TD>items</TD>           <--
</TR>                    <--
    .
    .
    .
```

Handling HTML

Note that at the end, we use `</TR>` to finish the table row. The last step is to set up the third and final row:

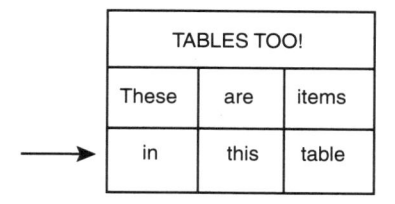

TABLES TOO!		
These	are	items
in	this	table

And we do that much as we did with the previous row, this way:

```
<TABLE BORDER CELLPADDING = 4>
<TR ALIGN = CENTER>
<TH COLSPAN = 3>TABLES TOO!
</TH>
</TR>
<TR ALIGN = CENTER>
<TD>These</TD>
<TD>are</TD>
<TD>items</TD>
</TR>
<TR ALIGN = CENTER>      <—
<TD>in</TD>              <—
<TD>this</TD>            <—
<TD>table!</TD>          <—
</TR>                    <—
```

That's how we set up the table; at the end of the table specification, we just include the `</TABLE>` tag to indicate we are done:

```
<HTML>

<HEAD>
<TITLE>Welcome to JBuilder</TITLE>
</HEAD>
    .
    .
    .
```

Chapter 1

```
<!—TABLES. Tables are not so hard; just use the "TABLE" tag; here
    we indicate we want our table to have a border and to add space
    "padding" around the text in each cell. You don't have to worry
    about cell widths or heights—that's done automatically by Web
    browsers. The "TH" tag sets up a table's header (and here we
    indicate we want that header to span all three columns of our
    table), the "TR" tag sets up a table row, and we just include
    entries for each column with the "TD" tag—if you want more
    columns, just add more "TD" tags in each table row.>
<CENTER>
<TABLE BORDER CELLPADDING = 4>
<TR ALIGN = CENTER>
<TH COLSPAN = 3>TABLES TOO!
</TH>
</TR>
<TR ALIGN = CENTER>
<TD>These</TD>
<TD>are</TD>
<TD>items</TD>
</TR>
<TR ALIGN = CENTER>
<TD>in</TD>
<TD>this</TD>
<TD>table!</TD>
</TR>
</TABLE>            <—
</CENTER>
    .
    .
    .
```

That completes our table; the result appears in Figure 1.5. Tables enable us to organize our data in one way, but there are other ways. For example, we can set up a list, which displays items vertically this way:

Handling HTML

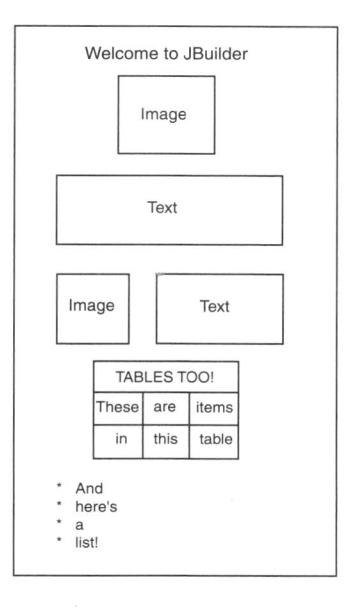

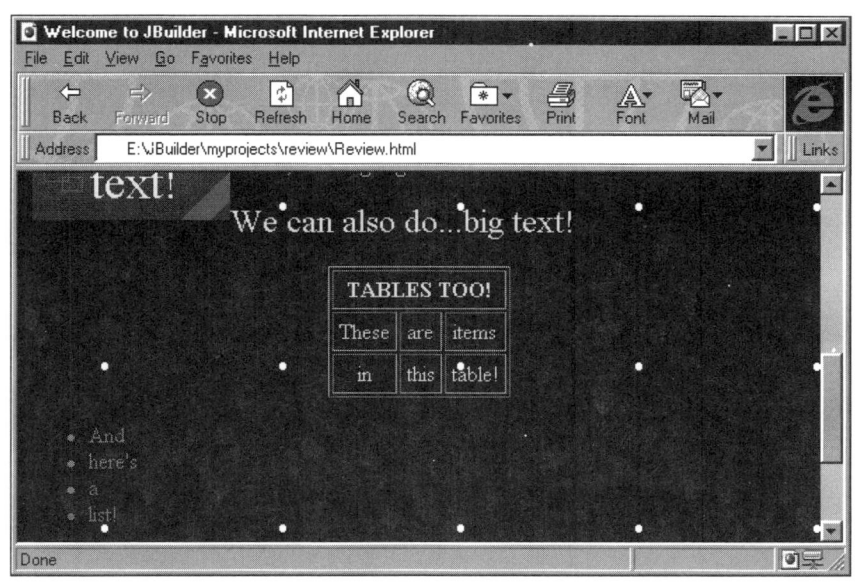

Figure 1.5 Our Web page with a table and list.

Chapter 1

Let's review the process of setting up a list next.

Making Lists

The list we want might just have four items in it, this way:

```
* And
* here's
* a
* list!
```

There are four kinds of lists: unordered (bulleted) lists, ordered (numbered) lists, directory lists (can be arranged into columns), and menu lists (plain lists without bullets or numbers). Here we'll set up a bulleted list with the <UL> tag. To make it a little more interesting visually, we can first change the color of our list to light blue with a <FONT> tag. Next, we start the list with <UL>:

```
<FONT COLOR = "#aaaaff">
<UL>
    .
    .
    .
```

Now we simply indicate what items we want in our list with the list item tag, <LI>, like this:

```
<FONT COLOR = "#aaaaff">
<UL>
<LI> And              <—
<LI> here's           <—
<LI> a                <—
<LI> list!            <—
    .
    .
    .
```

Finally, we finish our list with </UL>:

Handling HTML

```
<FONT COLOR = "#aaaaff">
<UL>
<LI> And
<LI> here's
<LI> a
<LI> list!
</UL>
</FONT>
    .
    .
    .
```

The result appears in Figure 1.5—that's all it took to add a list to our Web page.

Another very popular item in Web pages is to allow people who look at your Web page to email you, and that will be the last item in our HTML review.

Enabling Email

To enable email, we simply use an anchor tag with the HREF keyword, but instead of referencing an URL here, we use the MAILTO keyword. For example, to let the person viewing your Web page email the address **username@server.com**, you would do this:

```
<!—EMAIL. We let the user of our Web page email us by using an HREF
   tag with the MAILTO keyword. When the user of your page clicks on
   the underlined MAILTO address, their email program will open and
   they can write email directly to you.>
E-mail username: <A HREF="MAILTO:username@server.com">   <—
   username@server.com</A>                                <—
```

In this way, we've enabled email, as shown in Figure 1.6.

Chapter 1

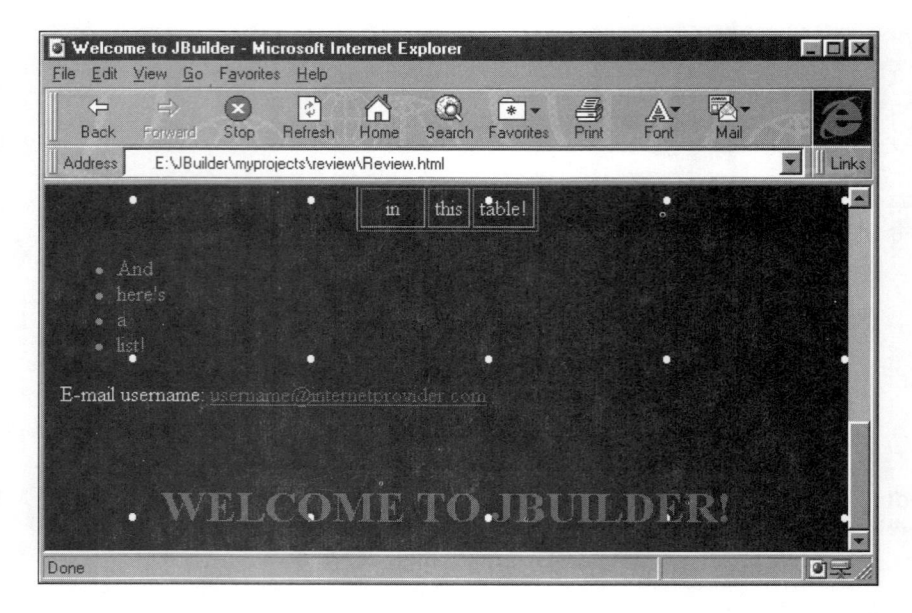

Figure 1.6 Our first Web page, with email capability.

That's It

That's it for our review and that's it for our first Web page—we finish it with the message *Welcome to Visual Basic Internet Programming!* in large type like this:

```
<!-EMAIL. We let the user of our Web page email us by using an HREF
   tag with the MAILTO keyword. When the user of your page clicks on
   the underlined MAILTO address, their email program will open and
   they can write email directly to you.>
E-mail username: <A HREF="MAILTO:username@server.com">
   username@server.com</A>
<BR>
<BR>

<BR>
<FONT COLOR = "#ff0000">
<CENTER>
```

Handling HTML

```
<H1>Welcome To JBuilder Programming!</H1>      <—
</CENTER>
</FONT>
     .
     .
     .
```

The very last step is to finish the body of our Web page with the `</BODY>` tag and finish the HTML file itself with the `</HTML>` tag:

```
<!—EMAIL. We let the user of our Web page email us by using an HREF
   tag with the MAILTO keyword. When the user of your page clicks on
   the underlined MAILTO address, their email program will open and
   they can write email directly to you.>
E-mail username: <A HREF="MAILTO:username@server.com">
   username@server.com</A>
<BR>
<BR>

<BR>
<FONT COLOR = "#ff0000">
<CENTER>
<H1>Welcome To JBuilder Programming!</H1>
</CENTER>
</FONT>

</BODY>                              <—
</HTML>                              <—
```

Our Web page is now ready to be installed in our ISP. The result appears in Figure 1.6; our first Web page is a success, and we've included many popular HTML items in it. The HTML for our review Web page, review.html, appears in Listing 1.1.

Listing 1.1 review.html

```
<!—START THE PAGE with an HTML tag (a tag is an HTML command, and
   HTML tags appear between angle brackets) "HTML" to indicate this
   document is in HTML, which is the language of web pages.>
<HTML>
```

Chapter 1

```
<!—A PAGE'S TITLE is how a browser will refer to it if someone saves
    it in their Favorites or Bookmarks menu. Note that we also indicate
    we are done defining the title with "/TITLE". This second tag
    matches the first tag, "TITLE", and as mentioned, HTML tags
    always come in pairs, like the following one, which indicates that
    we are done with the page's header.>
<HEAD>
<TITLE>Welcome to JBuilder</TITLE>
</HEAD>

<!—BODY OF PAGE starts with the following "BODY" tag. COLOR VALUES
    are "#rrggbb" (red, green, and blue) in hexadecimal (0-255 = 0-ff);
    for example pure red is "#ff0000", pure green #00ff00" and yellow
    is "#ffff00". Here we start the web page's body, indicating we want
    green text, hyperlinks to be red, hyperlinks to turn white when
    pushed, and links that the viewer has already clicked to be
    yellow.>
<BODY TEXT = "#ffff00" LINK = "#ff0000" ALINK = "#ffffff" VLINK =
"#ffff00">

<!—BACKGROUND PICTURE (which is optional) is tiled on the page's
    background. Here, we indicate we want the web browser to use the
    graphics file back.gif, which is in our www/gif directory (see
    explanation, below).>
<BODY BACKGROUND = "gif/back.gif">

<!—HEADERS. Now we are going to place a header of the largest size in
    our page, so we use the "H1" tag, as well as the "CENTER" tag.
    "CENTER" simply makes sure the following text or image is centered.
    Note that all HTML tags come in pairs—to turn off centering, we
    use "/CENTER" at the end of our header's specification.>
<CENTER>
<H1>Welcome to JBuilder</H1>
</CENTER>

<!—LINE BREAKS. To space things vertically, we use "BR" and "/BR"
    to
    skip a line.>
<BR>
```

```
<!—IMAGES. We display an image, which will appear centered because of
    the "CENTER" tag, with the "IMG" tag, adding the width and height
    in pixels. Here, we display our GIF file yourgif.gif from the GIF
    directory, but this is where a photo of you could go.>
<CENTER>
<IMG WIDTH=236 HEIGHT=118 SRC="gif/yourgif.gif"></IMG>
</CENTER>

<!—PARAGRAPHS of text start with "P".>
<!—LINKS. We add a hypertext link with the "A" tag, using the HREF
    keyword. In particular, we add a link to borland.com's web page at
    http://www.borland.com below. This means that the text "borland" will
    appear underlined and in the standard link color (which we've set
    to red); when the viewer of your page clicks that text, they will
    jump to Borland's home page.>
<P>
    Hello, and welcome to this web page, the first web page of our
    book. In this book, we'll see quite a few good things, and then how
    you too can use them in your own web pages. If that doesn't
    interest you, perhaps you'd like to take a look at
    <A HREF="http://www.borland.com">Borland</A>.
<BR>
<BR>
</P>


<!—ALIGNING PICTURES AND TEXT is done with the ALIGN keyword used in
    the IMG tag. In this case we just have to indicate that we want the
    graphics to appear on the left with ALIGN = LEFT. We also change
    the text color to green temporarily with a "FONT" tag ("FONT" only
    works in recent browsers).>
<IMG WIDTH=141 HEIGHT=126 SRC="gif/sidebar.gif" ALIGN=LEFT>
<FONT COLOR = "00ff00">
    We can even do green text next to graphics. This text appears next
    to the graphics on the left, allowing you to intersperse your words
    with pictures. When you take a look at the HTML for this web page,
    you'll see how this and more is done. Although this is just a
    review, we are going to add Java to our skills soon...
</FONT>
</IMG>
```

Chapter 1

```
<BR>
<BR>

<!—FONT SIZE is also done with the "FONT" tag; here, we set the
    size of our text temporarily to 5, a large size.>
<FONT SIZE = 5>
We can also do...big text!
</FONT>
<BR>
<BR>

<!—TABLES. Tables are not so hard; just use the "TABLE" tag; here
    we indicate we want our table to have a border and to add space
    "padding" around the text in each cell. You don't have to worry
    about cell widths or heights—that's done automatically by web
    browsers. The "TH" tag sets up a table's header (and here we
    indicate we want that header to span all three columns of our
    table), the "TR" tag sets up a table row, and we just include
    entries for each column with the "TD" tag—if you want more
    columns, just add more "TD" tags in each table row.>
<CENTER>
<TABLE BORDER CELLPADDING = 4>
<TR ALIGN = CENTER>
<TH COLSPAN = 3>TABLES TOO!
</TH>
</TR>
<TR ALIGN = CENTER>
<TD>These</TD>
<TD>are</TD>
<TD>items</TD>
</TR>
<TR ALIGN = CENTER>
<TD>in</TD>
<TD>this</TD>
<TD>table!</TD>
</TR>
</TABLE>
</CENTER>
```

Handling HTML

```
<!--LISTS. Bulleted lists are also easy, using the "UL" tag. Just
    use the "LI" tag for each list item as follows.>
<FONT COLOR = "#aaaaff">
<UL>
<LI> And
<LI> here's
<LI> a
<LI> list!
</UL>
</FONT>

<!--EMAIL. We let the viewer of our web page email us by using an HREF
    tag with the MAILTO keyword. When the viewer of your page clicks on
    the underlined MAILTO address, their email program will open and
    they can write email directly to you.>
E-mail username: <A HREF="MAILTO:username@internetprovider.com">
    username@internetprovider.com</A>
<BR>
<BR>
<BR>
<FONT COLOR = "#ff0000">
<CENTER>
<H1>WELCOME TO JBUILDER!</H1>
</CENTER>
</FONT>
</BODY>
</HTML>
```

That completes our first Web page, and our review of HTML. If you don't feel comfortable with what we've done so far, you should turn to a book on writing Web pages before proceeding. On the other hand, if all this is old hat to you, then it's time to dig into JBuilder itself and start writing some Java, as we turn to Chapter 2.

CHAPTER 2

JBuilder: Running Our First Programs

In this chapter, we'll start seeing some Java and start creating programs with JBuilder.

Java programs come in two types: *applets* that you run in Web pages, and *applications* that can run by themselves. We'll concentrate on the more popular applet form first, and see them at work at once. Instead of working through a lot of theory, we're going to put JBuilder to work for us as fast as we can. In this chapter, we're going to see how to create an applet using JBuilder, and then see exactly what makes that applet work.

We'll also start seeing how to add a new text field to an applet —a text field (also called a *text box* or *edit control*) displays text that the user can edit. In our example, we'll place some text in our text field ourselves. Items like text fields, buttons, check boxes, and so on are called *controls*, and we'll see how to add controls to a Java applet in this chapter. All in all, there's a great deal going on in this chapter, so let's start now with our first applet.

Just What Is an Applet?

Just what is an applet? It's a Java-created binary file that has the extension .class, and which we can embed in our Web pages with the <APPLET> tag. When run in a Web page, Java applets are downloaded automatically and run by the Web browser. They can do anything from working with graphics to displaying animation to handling buttons and check boxes. Using applets makes your Web pages active, not passive, and that, of course, is their main attraction.

Chapter 2

The process goes like this: you create a new applet project in JBuilder first. Next, you design and write your new applet's Java code, placing it in a file named, say, **myApplet.java**. You then use the tools in the JBuilder to compile myApplet.java into myApplet.class, which is a file of *bytecodes*—binary bytes that Java-compatible Web browsers interpret to run your applet.

When you have your myApplet.class file, you upload it to your Internet Service Provider (ISP) and (usually) store it in the same directory as your HTML files. You can embed the new applet in a Web page with the <APPLET> tag, indicating the name of the .class file for the applet—myApplet.class—as well as telling the Web browser how much space (in pixels) to leave for the applet:

```
<HTML>

<BODY>

<CENTER>
<APPLET CODE = "myApplet.class" WIDTH = 300 HEIGHT = 200>      <—
</APPLET>
</CENTER>

</BODY>
</HTML>
```

In this case, we set up a centered 300 × 200 pixel space in our Web page in which to display our applet, and tell the Web browser to load the myApplet.class file from your ISP and run it. The <APPLET> tag includes these keywords, where the optional keywords are in brackets:

```
<APPLET
    [ALIGN = LEFT or RIGHT or TOP or TEXTTOP or MIDDLE or
             ABSMIDDLE  or BASELINE or BOTTOM or ABSBOTTOM]
    [ALT = AlternateText]
    CODE = AppletName.class
    [CODEBASE = URL of .class file]
    HEIGHT = AppletPixelsHeight
    [HSPACE = PixelSpaceToLeftOfApplet]
    [NAME = AppletInstanceName]
    [VSPACE = PixelSpaceAboveApplet]
```

```
        WIDTH = AppletPixelsWidth
    >
    [<PARAM NAME = Parameter1 VALUE = VALUE1]
    [<PARAM NAME = Parameter2 VALUE = VALUE2]
              .
              .
              .
    </APPLET>
```

Note in particular the `<PARAM>` tag, used to pass parameters to our applet for initialization, indicating the name of the parameter and the value it should have, like this:

```
<HTML>

<BODY>

<CENTER>
<APPLET CODE = "myApplet.class" WIDTH = 300 HEIGHT = 200>
    <PARAM NAME = MonthsInYear VALUE = 12>        <--
    <PARAM NAME = DaysInWeek VALUE = 7>           <--
</APPLET>
</CENTER>

</BODY>
</HTML>
```

Note also that JBuilder uses Java 1.1, so you'll have to use a browser that supports Java 1.1 to see your applet at work (we'll use JBuilder's built-in applet viewer in this book).

What does the Java language itself look like? It's a language very close to C++. Our goal in this book is to use JBuilder to write our Java language programs, then compile them to create the corresponding .class file which you can embed into your Web pages with the `<APPLET>` tag. Let's start that process now, as we create our first working applet.

Chapter 2

Our First Applet

In our first applet, we will keep things simple, just printing out a message of welcome like this in our applet:

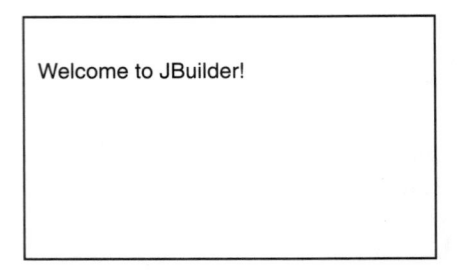

> Welcome to JBuilder!

Let's get this started now. Open JBuilder as shown in Figure 2.1.

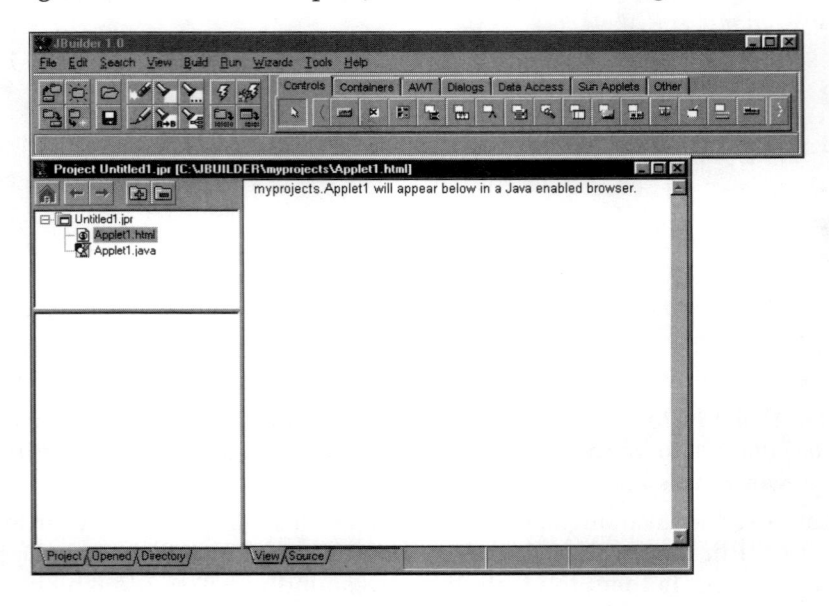

Figure 2.1 The JBuilder environment.

We see two separate windows in Figure 2.1—JBuilder itself (at the top of the figure) and a project window underneath.

JBuilder organizes tasks into projects, and it has already set up a default project for us. A *project* keeps track of the files associated with a given

JBuilder: Running Our First Programs

applet or application. In the case of an applet, that's two files: an .html file for the Web page HTML code, and a .java file for the actual Java code. JBuilder assumes your project will be an applet (although we will also see how to create Java applications), and it has added two files to the current project, Applet1.html and Applet1.java, as shown in Figure 2.1.

Now we'll use one of the JBuilder wizards—special tools that help you write code—to create our first applet.

Writing an Applet with the Applet Wizard

To start, we'll need to name our first project, and we'll call it Hello. To name the project, select the entry **Untitled1.jpr** (.jpr is the extension for JBuilder projects) in the project window with the mouse, highlighting that entry. If you don't see **Untitled1.jpr,** create it by selecting the **New Project** item in the File menu and click the **Save** button in the New Project box that opens to create **Untitled1.jpr.** Now select the **Save As** menu item in JBuilder's File menu, opening a dialog box titled **Save Untitled1.jpr As**. Save this project file as **Hello.jpr** in a folder named Hello. The default location for such folders in JBuilder is the JBuilder\myprojects folder, so this project will go in JBuilder\myprojects\Hello. Note that case counts in Java—as far as JBuilder is concerned, hello.java is not the same as Hello.java.

Writing Java Code

Now we have our new project file, Hello.jpr. The next step is to write some Java code. We'll let the JBuilder Applet Wizard write the starting code for us, so we won't need the default (and empty) files that are already in the Hello project, Applet1.html and Applet1.java.

To remove those files, simply select them one by one with the mouse and select **Remove from Project** in the JBuilder File menu. This leaves us with an empty project, named Hello, as shown in Figure 2.2.

Chapter 2

Figure 2.2 Our Hello project starts off empty.

Now we'll use the Applet Wizard to add files to our new project. To do that, select the **Applet Wizard** item in the JBuilder Wizards menu, opening the Applet Wizard as shown in Figure 2.3.

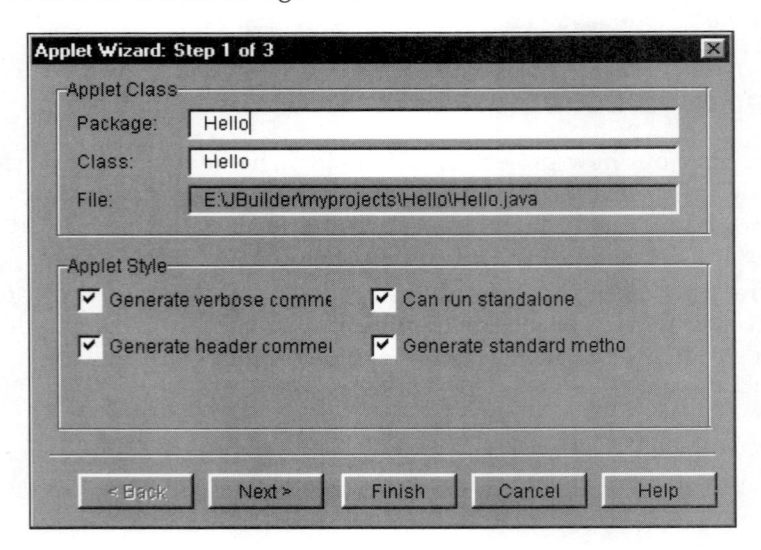

Figure 2.3 The Applet Wizard, Step 1.

Naming the Class and Package in the Applet Wizard

The Applet Wizard will guide us through the steps of creating an applet. In Step 1, we name the package we are creating. A Java *package* is a collection of Java pre-written code; we'll see a great deal more about packages soon. In this case, however, we'll only have one name, Hello, so place that name in both the Applet Wizard Package and Class boxes, as shown in Figure 2.3, and click the **Next** button.

Clicking the **Next** button brings us to Step 2 of the Applet Wizard, as shown in Figure 2.4. As you can see there, the Applet Wizard is asking for the names and values of parameters we want to pass from our Web page to the applet, and since we don't have any parameters this time, we click **Next** to go on to the last step of the Applet Wizard, as shown in Figure 2.5.

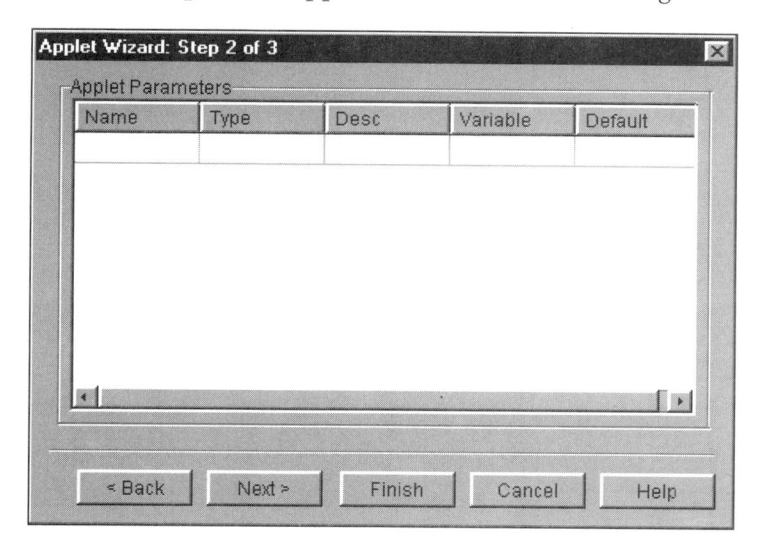

Figure 2.4. The Applet Wizard, Step 2

Creating the Project Files

In Figure 2.5, Applet Wizard asks if it should create a sample Web page for our apple. Accept the default settings, which means that the Applet Wizard will create a .html page for us, and click **Finish** now.

Chapter 2

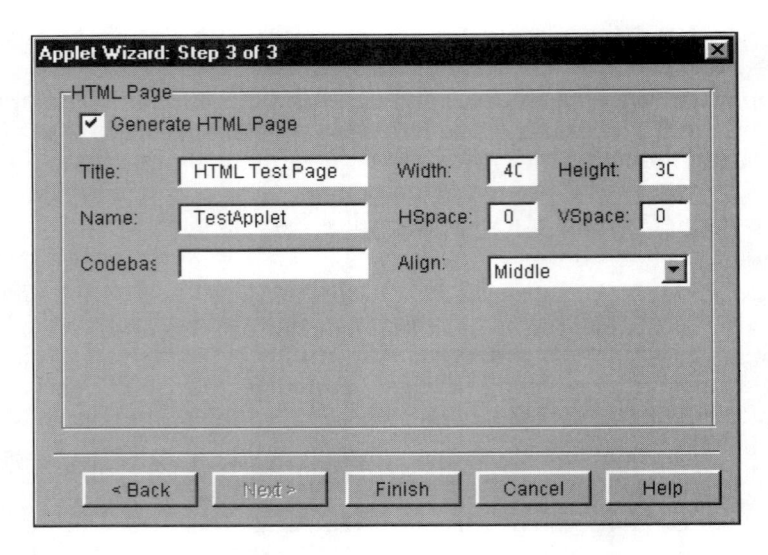

Figure 2.5 The Applet Wizard, Step 3.

This creates the files Hello.java and Hello.html for us. Double-click the hello.java file's entry in the Project window now, opening that file as shown in Figure 2.6.

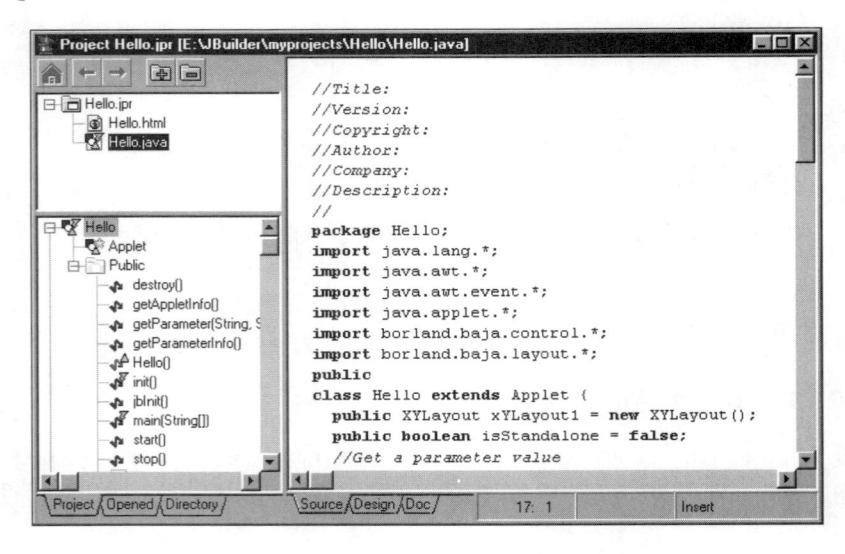

Figure 2.6 Editing Hello.java in the Project window.

At this point, we have all we need for a working applet, although it doesn't do anything—if you were to click **Run** in the JBuilder Run menu, JBuilder would compile the applet into the bytecode file Hello.class and display that applet in a Web page. But the Web page would be blank, because we haven't done anything yet.

Let's make the applet display our *Welcome to JBuilder!* message now. Then we'll run it to make sure that it works. Finally, we'll dissect this first example to see what makes it tick.

Displaying Text in Java

When a Java applet appears on the screen, a special function named `paint()` is called. The code in this function is responsible for displaying the applet's graphics (including text) on the screen.

To draw our text message on the screen, then, we have to place some new Java code in the paint() function. Let's see how this works now.

Select the Override Methods item in the JBuilder Wizards menu now (we'll see what overriding a method means in a moment). This opens the Override Inherited Methods box, as shown in Figure 2.7.

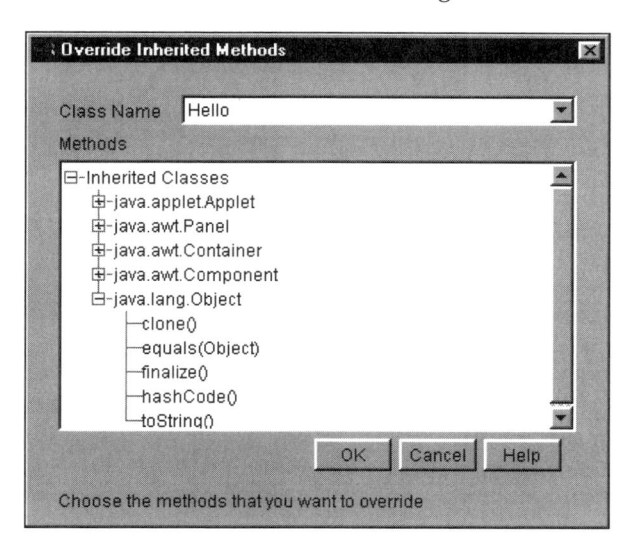

Figure 2.7 Overriding the paint( ) method.

Chapter 2

Each of the entries in Figure 2.7 represents a Java package, a pre-written collection of Java code. Here, we'll find the functions to which we can add Java code. Click the small + sign in font of the package that holds the `paint()` function now: java.awt.Component (AWT stands for Abstract Windowing Toolkit). This opens a list of the possible functions in this package that we can write code for, overriding the default version of those functions. Now find the entry that reads paint(Graphics), highlight it with the mouse, and click the **OK** button in the Override Inherited Methods box to close it.

When you close the Override Inherited Methods box, JBuilder adds a new function to Hello.java, `paint()`:

```
public void paint(Graphics g) {

  //TODO: override this java.awt.Component method;
  super.paint( g );

}
```

This function is where we can display our message, and we do that with the drawString() function this way—add this code now to the paint() function by simply typing it in in the Project window:

```
public void paint(Graphics g) {

  g.drawString("Welcome to JBuilder!", 10, 20);   <—

  super.paint( g );
}
```

Testing the New Applet

That's all we have to do! Now we're ready to see the applet at work. Select the **Run** item in the JBuilder Run menu, as shown in Figure 2.8. Our first applet works—we're creating applets with JBuilder!

JBuilder: Running Our First Programs

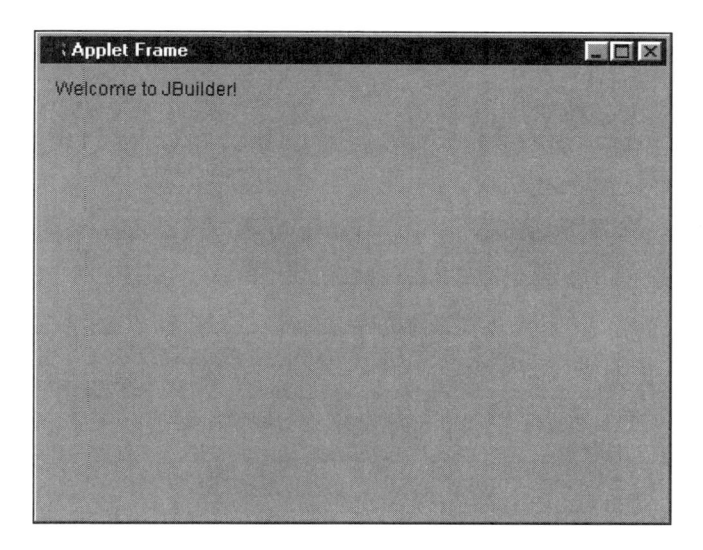

Figure 2.8 Our first applet at work.

When you compile the applet, JBuilder takes the code file Hello.java in JBuilder\myprojects\Hello and compiles it into Hello.class (we'll see why it has the extension .class in a moment), and places that new bytecode file in JBuilder\myclasses\Hello. This file is the applet itself, and it's this .class file that you upload to your ISP. Note, by the way, that if someone else wants to run your JBuilder-created applets, they'll have to have the .class files that come with JBuilder (in the JBuilder\classes folder) installed on their own system.

The next step is to dissect the code that JBuilder wrote for us so we'll know what's going on. That code, Hello.java, appears in Listing 2.1, and the HTML Web page that JBuilder created for the applet, Hello.html, appears in Listing 2.2.

Listing 2.1 Hello.java

```
//Title:
//Version:
//Copyright:
//Author:
//Company:
//Description:
//
```

Chapter 2

```java
package Hello;
import java.lang.*;
import java.awt.*;
import java.awt.event.*;
import java.applet.*;
import borland.jbcl.control.*;
import borland.jbcl.layout.*;

public
class Hello extends Applet {

  public XYLayout xYLayout1 = new XYLayout();
  public boolean isStandalone = false;

  //Get a parameter value
  public String getParameter(String key, String def) {

    return isStandalone ? System.getProperty(key, def) :
       (getParameter(key) != null ? getParameter(key) : def);

  }

  //Construct the applet
  public Hello() {

  }

  //Initialize the applet
  public void init() {

    try { jbInit(); } catch(Exception e) { e.printStackTrace(); };

  }

  //Component initialization
  public void jbInit() throws Exception{

    xYLayout1.setWidth(400);
    xYLayout1.setHeight(300);
```

JBuilder: Running Our First Programs

```java
    this.setLayout(xYLayout1);

}

//Start the applet
public void start() {

}

//Stop the applet
public void stop() {

}

//Destroy the applet
public void destroy() {

}

//Get Applet information
public String getAppletInfo() {

  return "Applet Information";
}

//Get parameter info
public String[][] getParameterInfo() {

  return null;

}
//Main method
static public void main(String[] args) {

  Hello applet = new Hello();
  applet.isStandalone = true;
  DecoratedFrame frame = new DecoratedFrame();
  frame.setTitle("Applet Frame");
  frame.add(applet, BorderLayout.CENTER);
```

Chapter 2

```
    applet.init();
    applet.start();
    frame.pack();
    Dimension d = Toolkit.getDefaultToolkit().getScreenSize();
    frame.setLocation((d.width - frame.getSize().width) / 2, (d.height
- frame.getSize().height) / 2);
    frame.setVisible(true);

  }

  public void paint(Graphics g) {

    g.drawString("Welcome to JBuilder!", 10, 20);

    super.paint( g);
  }
}
```

Listing 2.2 Hello.html

```
<HTML>
<TITLE>
HTML Test Page
</TITLE>
<BODY>
Hello.Hello will appear below in a Java enabled browser.
<APPLET
   CODEBASE = ""
   CODE     = "Hello.Hello.class"
   NAME     = "TestApplet"
   WIDTH    = 400
   HEIGHT   = 300
   HSPACE   = 0
   VSPACE   = 0
   ALIGN    = Middle
>
</APPLET>
</BODY>
</HTML>
```

JBuilder: Running Our First Programs

We've seen Hello.java at work. Now let's take it apart to actually *see* what makes it work.

At the beginning of Hello.java, we import the Java packages we'll need. A Java package is a collection of Java classes that are pre-written for you. What are classes? We'll see in a minute. As we've seen, the `paint()` function is part of the java.awt.Component package, and we include all of the java.awt packages with a line like this:

```
package Hello;
import java.lang.*;
import java.awt.*;                <--
import java.awt.event.*;
        .
        .
        .
```

Besides the Java packages themselves, we import the jbcl packages. These special added packages are a part of JBuilder, and we'll be working with the jbcl packages throughout this book:

```
package Hello;
import java.lang.*;
import java.awt.*;
import java.awt.event.*;
import java.applet.*;
import borland.jbcl.control.*;    <--
import borland.jbcl.layout.*;     <--
        .
        .
        .
```

Next, we define the class for our applet, naming this class Hello:

```
public
class Hello extends Applet {      <--
        .
        .
        .
```

Chapter 2

Now we're entering the area of object-oriented programming (OOP)—objects and classes. There has been a great deal of hype surrounding object oriented programming, so let's take a moment to cut through all that and get our concepts straight. After all, OOP is supposed to be a help to us, not a hindrance. So, just what *is* an object?

What Is a Java Object?

An object is really just a programming construct that wraps code and data together to form a single, self-sufficient programming entity. What does that mean? It means that using objects, you don't have to worry about all the internal details of, say, screen handling—you could just use, for example, a graphics object like this: GraphicsObject.drawLine (x1, y1, x2, y2) to draw a line on the screen from (x1, y1) to (x2, y2). In this case, all the details of raster scanning and memory buffers' internal data and I/O addresses are taken care of by the functions internal to the graphics object for us.

To see why this is useful, consider a refrigerator. You don't want to be responsible for regulating refrigerant flow, handling the thermostats and working the compressor yourself: you just want a refrigerator. There is a lot going on inside the refrigerator—internal functions interacting with internal data—that we never see. And because we never see those details, the refrigerator is a much more useful object to us.

That's what an object is: a programming construct that contains both internal data and functions—some of which are purely internal. There might be dozens of internal functions in a refrigerator, but we never see them because they are internal to the refrigerator. In a programming language, that means that the object can have internal data and functions that are never seen by the rest of the program, and that divides the program up into discrete and more easily-managed units.

That's an overview of objects. The next question is: what's a class?

What Is a Java Class?

A class is to an object as a cookie mold is to a cookie. The class defines the type of object we want, and when we declare an item of that type, that's the object.

If we were to declare an integer variable like this:

```
int myInt;
```

JBuilder: Running Our First Programs

then the type of our variable is int, and the variable itself is myInt. In the same way, if we set up a class named, say, `myClass`, then we could declare an object of that class named `myObject` this way:

```
myClass myObject;
```

That's the idea behind classes and objects—a class is like a variable type, except that it can contain functions and data, and an object is like a variable of that type. It turns out that Sun has already created a great number of pre-defined classes for us in Java, and most of what we do will be based on these classes. For example, this line in Hello.java:

```
    import java.applet.*;
        .
        .
        .
```

indicates that we want to get the applet classes from the Java libraries. In particular, this import statment imports java.applet.Applet, which is the base class of all applets.

This class allows us to create applet objects with all kinds of functionality built in already, such as drawing the applet's background in the Web page—with the `paint()` function—and handling starting and stopping of applets with the `start()` and `stop()` functions. In fact, functions built into a class (like `paint()`, `start()`, and `stop()`) are given a special name: *methods*.

Another pre-written Java class is the Graphics class, which we've already seen briefly. This class has many built-in methods, such as `drawLine()` and `drawRect()`. When we want to work with graphics in a Java applet, we'll create an object of the Graphics class, and then call the methods in it to draw lines or rectangles in our applet. And another pre-written Java class is the Math class, which contains math methods like `min()` to find the minimum of two integers, and `max()` to find the maximum of two integers.

In our Hello.java file, we're declaring our new class Hello, and *extending* the Applet class with this new class:

```
public
class Hello extends Applet {          <--
        .
        .
        .
```

Chapter 2

Extending a class like this means our new class will *inherit* the base class's methods and data.

What Is Java Inheritance?

Extending a class means that you are deriving a new class from a base class. In this case, we are deriving the Hello class from the Java Applet class. This means that the Hello class will have all the power of the Applet class built in already. Note also the keyword `public` above—this means that our new class is public, and other parts of the program have access to it. We'll see more about the public keyword in a moment.

When you derive a new class from a base class, that new class inherits all the methods of the base class, as well as being able to add methods of its own. That's what we mean by Java inheritance—a derived class can make use of its base class methods and data. We'll see what a powerful technique this is when we start writing code ourselves.

Next, the Applet Wizard has added some variables that it will use internally—here, it sets up a new XYLayout object named `xYLayout1`. The XYLayout class is very helpful, and lets us position items like buttons and check boxes in our applets as we like—we'll see more about that later too:

```
public
class Hello extends Applet {
  public XYLayout xYLayout1 = new XYLayout();        <--
       .
       .
       .
```

This is where you declare your data items that you want all methods in the class to have access to: outside all method declarations, and at the beginning of the class' definition. Data items that are members of a class are called *data members*, and data members that are accessible to all methods in a class are called *global data members*.

In addition, the Applet Wizard has set up a flag, `isStandalone`, which indicates whether this program can be run as a standalone application. That flag is false here, because Hello is meant to be run as an applet:

```
public
class Hello extends Applet {
```

JBuilder: Running Our First Programs

```
  public XYLayout xYLayout1 = new XYLayout();
  public boolean isStandalone = false;          <--
        .
        .
        .
}
```

Next, the Applet Wizard has written the method `getParameter()`:

```
public
class Hello extends Applet {
  public XYLayout xYLayout1 = new XYLayout();
  public boolean isStandalone = false;

  //Get a parameter value
  public String getParameter(String key, String def) {          <--

    return isStandalone ? System.getProperty(key, def) :          <--
      (getParameter(key) != null ? getParameter(key) : def);      <--

  }
        .
        .
        .
```

This method gets the parameters that we instructed the Applet Wizard to place in our Web page (there are no parameters in our Hello applet, however, so nothing is going on here). This makes those parameters available to us in code, as we'll see in this book.

The next item is the Hello class's constructor:

```
public
class Hello extends Applet {
  public XYLayout xYLayout1 = new XYLayout();
  public boolean isStandalone = false;

  //Get a parameter value
  public String getParameter(String key, String def) {
    return isStandalone ? System.getProperty(key, def) :
```

Chapter 2

```
            (getParameter(key) != null ? getParameter(key) : def);
    }

    //Construct the applet
    public Hello() {            <—

    }
          .
          .
          .
```

This is a very important method, and we'll look into just what constructors do now.

What Is a Java Constructor?

When you want to initialize data in a class, you can put that initialization code in the class constructor. This method has the same name as the class, and does not return anything. If you have data to initialize—recall that the data items that are part of a class are named data members—you can initialize them in the class's constructor. For example, if we had a variable that should hold the value 1, we can initialize it in the applet's constructor:

```
int should_be_one;

public Hello() {
    should_be_1 = 1;    <—
}
```

However, it is usually better to put initialization code in an applet's `init()` method, and we'll see why next.

Using the init( ) Method to Intialize Data

The `init()` method comes right after the constructor:

```
public
class Hello extends Applet {
```

JBuilder: Running Our First Programs

```
    public XYLayout xYLayout1 = new XYLayout();
    public boolean isStandalone = false;

    //Get a parameter value
    public String getParameter(String key, String def) {

      return isStandalone ? System.getProperty(key, def) :
        (getParameter(key) != null ? getParameter(key) : def);

    }

    //Construct the applet
    public Hello() {

    }

    //Initialize the applet
    public void init() {                <--

      try { jbInit(); } catch(Exception e) { e.printStackTrace(); };

    }
      .
      .
      .
}
```

This is where the initialization code for an applet usually goes, because when the applet's constructor is called, the applet has not been fully created yet. That means that we can't work with the various items in the applet like buttons and check boxes in the constructor—we have to place such code in the special `init()` method. For that reason, we'll usually place applet intialization code in the `init()` method throughout this book.

The Applet Wizard has also added a new method, `jbInit()`, to initialize the arrangement, or layout of the items in our applet, and this method is called in the `init()` method:

```
public
class Hello extends Applet {
```

Chapter 2

```
    public XYLayout xYLayout1 = new XYLayout();
    public boolean isStandalone = false;

    //Get a parameter value
    public String getParameter(String key, String def) {

      return isStandalone ? System.getProperty(key, def) :
        (getParameter(key) != null ? getParameter(key) : def);

    }

    //Construct the applet
    public Hello() {

    }

    //Initialize the applet
    public void init() {

      try { jbInit(); } catch(Exception e) { e.printStackTrace(); };   <—

    }

    //Component initialization
    public void jbInit() throws Exception{      <—

      xYLayout1.setWidth(400);                  <—
      xYLayout1.setHeight(300);                 <—
      this.setLayout(xYLayout1);                <—

    }
        .
        .
        .
```

We'll see how the applet's layout works starting in the next chapter.

Starting and Stopping the Applet

At this point in the code, we'll add the `start( )` and `stop( )` methods to applets later in the book. As we'll see when we work with graphics animation, and as you might guess, these methods are called when the applet is started and when it's stopped. We'll place code in these methods later on to start graphics animation:

```
public
class Hello extends Applet {
  public XYLayout xYLayout1 = new XYLayout();
  public boolean isStandalone = false;
  //Get a parameter value
  public String getParameter(String key, String def) {
    return isStandalone ? System.getProperty(key, def) :
      (getParameter(key) != null ? getParameter(key) : def);
  }
  //Construct the applet
  public Hello() {
  }
  //Initialize the applet
  public void init() {
    try { jbInit(); } catch(Exception e) { e.printStackTrace(); };
  }
  //Component initialization
  public void jbInit() throws Exception{
    xYLayout1.setWidth(400);
    xYLayout1.setHeight(300);
    this.setLayout(xYLayout1);
  }
  //Start the applet              <—
  public void start() {           <—
  }
  //Stop the applet               <—
  public void stop() {            <—
  }
```

Chapter 2

Now that we've seen all about getting an applet started, let's see about destroying it.

Destroying the Applet

The next method in the Hello.java file is Destroy(). This method is called when the applet is terminated and we will be able to perform cleanup here, deallocating resources that we've used:

```
public
class Hello extends Applet {

  public XYLayout xYLayout1 = new XYLayout();
  public boolean isStandalone = false;

  //Get a parameter value
  public String getParameter(String key, String def) {

    return isStandalone ? System.getProperty(key, def) :
      (getParameter(key) != null ? getParameter(key) : def);

  }

  //Construct the applet
  public Hello() {

  }

  //Initialize the applet
  public void init() {

    try { jbInit(); } catch(Exception e) { e.printStackTrace(); };

  }

  //Component initialization
  public void jbInit() throws Exception{

    xYLayout1.setWidth(400);
    xYLayout1.setHeight(300);
```

JBuilder: Running Our First Programs

```
    this.setLayout(xYLayout1);

}

//Start the applet
public void start() {

}

//Stop the applet
public void stop() {

}

//Destroy the applet
public void destroy() {         <—
}                               <—
```

Now we've seen the basics of how an applet works. There are two more methods, however, that the Applet Wizard includes—`getAppletInfo()` and `getParameterInfo()`. `getAppletInfo()` returns a descriptive string about the applet to the Web browser it's running in, and `getParameterInfo()` gets information about the parameters in the applet's Web page:

```
public
class Hello extends Applet {

  public XYLayout xYLayout1 = new XYLayout();
  public boolean isStandalone = false;

  //Get a parameter value
  public String getParameter(String key, String def) {

    return isStandalone ? System.getProperty(key, def) :
      (getParameter(key) != null ? getParameter(key) : def);

  }
    .
    .
    .
```

Chapter 2

```java
//Destroy the applet
public void destroy() {

}

//Get Applet information
public String getAppletInfo() {

  return "Applet Information";

}

//Get parameter info
public String[][] getParameterInfo() {

  return null;

}

//Main method
static public void main(String[] args) {

  Hello applet = new Hello();
  applet.isStandalone = true;
  DecoratedFrame frame = new DecoratedFrame();
  frame.setTitle("Applet Frame");
  frame.add(applet, BorderLayout.CENTER);
  applet.init();
  applet.start();
  frame.pack();
  Dimension d = Toolkit.getDefaultToolkit().getScreenSize();
  frame.setLocation((d.width - frame.getSize().width) / 2, (d.height
- frame.getSize().height) / 2);
  frame.setVisible(true);

}

public void paint(Graphics g) {

  g.drawString("Welcome to JBuilder!", 10, 20);
```

```
    super.paint( g );
  }
}
```

The next-to-last method is the `main()` method, and we'll turn to that now.

The main( ) Method

If you click the box marked **Can run standalone** in Step 1 of the Applet Wizard, the Applet Wizard will add a `main( )` method to your applet. When you run a Java program as a stand-alone application (you do that at the DOS prompt in Windows like this: c:\>java app.class), the `main()` method holds the code that is executed first. Adding a `main()` method to an applet does no harm—an applet never executes the code there:

```
public
class Hello extends Applet {

  public XYLayout xYLayout1 = new XYLayout();
  public boolean isStandalone = false;

  //Get a parameter value
  public String getParameter(String key, String def) {

    return isStandalone ? System.getProperty(key, def) :
      (getParameter(key) != null ? getParameter(key) : def);

  }
      .
      .
      .

  //Destroy the applet
  public void destroy() {

  }

  //Get Applet information
  public String getAppletInfo() {
```

```
    return "Applet Information";

}

//Get parameter info
public String[][] getParameterInfo() {

    return null;

}
//Main method
static public void main(String[] args) {                <—

    Hello applet = new Hello();
    applet.isStandalone = true;
    DecoratedFrame frame = new DecoratedFrame();
    frame.setTitle("Applet Frame");
    frame.add(applet, BorderLayout.CENTER);
    applet.init();
    applet.start();
    frame.pack();
    Dimension d = Toolkit.getDefaultToolkit().getScreenSize();
    frame.setLocation((d.width - frame.getSize().width) / 2, (d.height
- frame.getSize().height) / 2);
    frame.setVisible(true);

  }
}
```

The very last method in the Hello.java file is the `paint()` method, which we've added ourselves.

The paint( ) Method

In the `paint()` method, the program passes us an object of the Graphics class, and we use the `drawString()` method of that object to draw the string *Welcome to JBuilder!*:

```
public
class Hello extends Applet {
```

JBuilder: Running Our First Programs

```java
  public XYLayout xYLayout1 = new XYLayout();
  public boolean isStandalone = false;

  //Get a parameter value
  public String getParameter(String key, String def) {

    return isStandalone ? System.getProperty(key, def) :
      (getParameter(key) != null ? getParameter(key) : def);

  }
        .
        .
        .
  //Destroy the applet
  public void destroy() {

  }

  //Get Applet information
  public String getAppletInfo() {
    return "Applet Information";
  }
  //Get parameter info
  public String[][] getParameterInfo() {
    return null;
  }
  //Main method
  static public void main(String[] args) {
    Hello applet = new Hello();
    applet.isStandalone = true;
    DecoratedFrame frame = new DecoratedFrame();
    frame.setTitle("Applet Frame");
    frame.add(applet, BorderLayout.CENTER);
    applet.init();
    applet.start();
    frame.pack();
    Dimension d = Toolkit.getDefaultToolkit().getScreenSize();
    frame.setLocation((d.width - frame.getSize().width) / 2, (d.height
- frame.getSize().height) / 2);
```

Chapter 2

```
    frame.setVisible(true);

}

public void paint(Graphics g) {

    g.drawString("Welcome to JBuilder!", 10, 20);    <—

    super.paint( g);

}
}
```

In the call to `drawString()`, we pass three parameters—the string to display, and the two coordinates at which to display that string. These coordinates correspond to the lower-left corner of the text string on the screen, and we place that corner of the string at the location (10, 20) in our applet (all such measurements are in pixels), where the upper-left corner of the applet is (0, 0). X increases to the right, and Y increases downwards.

Notice also the call to `super.paint(g)` in the above code. The keyword `super` refers to a class's superclass, which is another way of saying the class it's derived from, its base class. In this case, we pass the Graphics object, g, that we were passed in this method back to the base class's `paint()` method so that the rest of the applet can be drawn in addition to our string of text.

Now we've gotten an introduction to how an applet works, but there's still a great deal that's not explained. How do we add controls to our applet like text fields? And how do we work with such controls in code? We'll look into those questions next.

Using Java Text Fields

The first type of control that we'll place in a Java applet is the Java text field control. This control lets the user enter text into our applets, or we can place text in the text field ourselves. A text field appears as a simple rectangular box in our applet:

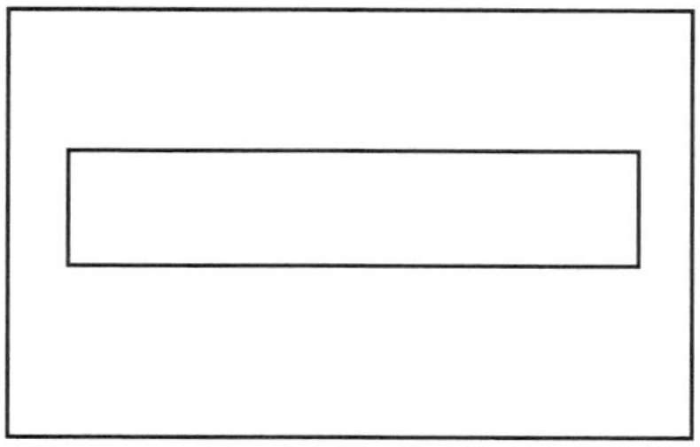

JBuilder: Running Our First Programs

[text field image]

When the user clicks the text field, a blinking caret, called the *insertion point*, appears, and the user can type text starting at the caret's location:

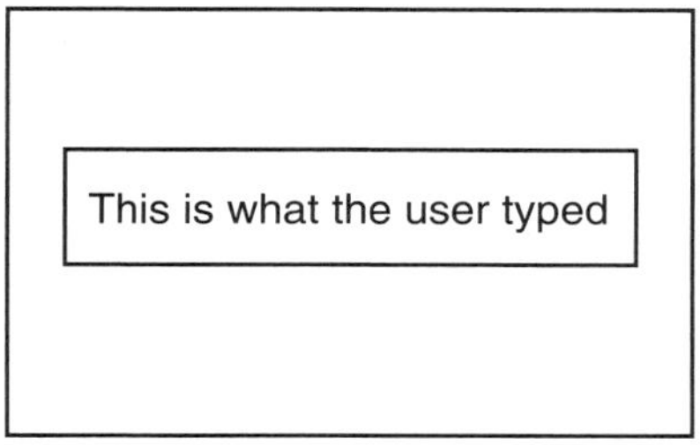

[text field showing "This is what the user typed"]

We can read the text with the java TextField class's `getText()` method, and set the text in a text field with the `setText()` method (actually, these are methods of the `TextField` class's base class, `TextComponent`, but the `TextField` class inherits them).

In our new example, which we can name textfields, we'll see how to place a text field in an applet and display our *Welcome to JBuilder!* message in the text field:

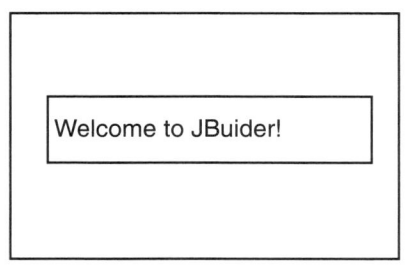

[text field showing "Welcome to JBuider!"]

Let's start this new applet now.

Chapter 2

Creating the textfields Applet

Create a new project in JBuilder now, saving the project file as **textfields.jpr**, and giving **textfields** as both the package and class name to the Applet Wizard. This creates the textfields project and the files **textfields.java** and **textfields.html**.

Now we can add a new text field to our applet.

Using the JBuilder Designer

To add a new text field to our applet, simply open the file **textfields.java** in the JBuilder editor and click the **Design** tab at the bottom of the editor window. Alternatively, you can right click the code in that file, as shown in Figure 2.9.

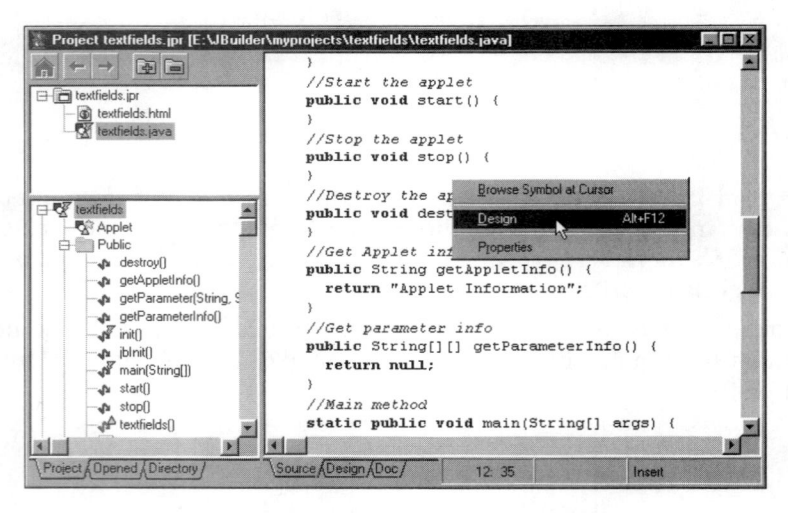

Figure 2.9 Designing the textfields applet.

You can see three items in the pop-up menu in Figure 2.9—Browse Symbol at Cursor, which looks up the word you have the mouse cursor on; Design, which opens the JBuilder designer; and Properties, which sets properties for the JBuilder environment. Click the **Design** item now. This opens the JBuilder designer, as shown in Figure 2.10.

JBuilder: Running Our First Programs

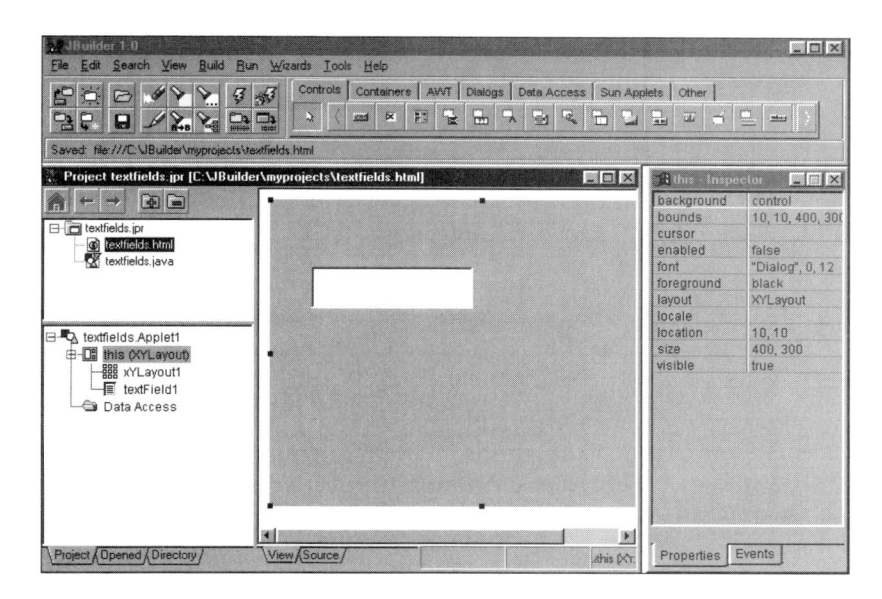

[Figure showing JBuilder 1.0 IDE with project textfields.jpr open, displaying the designer view with a text field, and the Inspector panel showing properties like background, bounds (10, 10, 400, 300), cursor, enabled (false), font ("Dialog", 0, 12), foreground (black), layout (XYLayout), locale, location (10, 10), size (400, 300), visible (true).]

Figure 2.10 The JBuilder Designer.

At right in Figure 2.10, we're able to see how our applet will look when it's running. Right now, the applet is simply blank, but we'll add a new text field to the applet now.

Adding Controls to an Applet

To add a new control like a text field to an applet under design, you move the mouse cursor up to the button bar near the top of Figure 2.10 with tabs **Controls**, **Containers**, **AWT**, and so on. The **AWT** tab corresponds to the standard Java controls like buttons and text fields, so click that tab now. The **Controls** tab corresponds to the jbcl controls that come with JBuilder, and so on—we'll see more about these tabs in chapters to come.

Right now, click the text field button in the component palette after clicking the **AWT** tab. Then, just draw a new text field in the applet, as shown in Figure 2.10. That's it—now we've added a text field to our applet.

JBuilder has already added the new text field to our applet; it has done so by declaring a new object of the TextField class named textField1 in our applet this way:

Chapter 2

```
package textfields;
import java.lang.*;
import java.awt.*;
import java.awt.event.*;
import java.applet.*;
import borland.jbcl.control.*;
import borland.jbcl.layout.*;

public
class textfields extends Applet {
  public XYLayout xYLayout1 = new XYLayout();
  public boolean isStandalone = false;
  TextField textField1 = new TextField();          <—
      .
      .
      .
}
```

The constructors and methods of the Java TextField class appear in Table 2.1. Those methods marked DEPRECATED are Java 1.0 methods that have become obsolete in Java 1.1, and should not be used.

Table 2.1 TextField Constructors and Methods

`TextField()`	Constructs a new TextField.
`TextField(int)`	Deprecated: Replaced by `TextField(String, int)`.
`TextField(String)`	Constructs a new TextField initialized with the given text.
`TextField(String, int)`	Constructs a new TextField initialized with the given text and columns.
`addActionListener ActionListener)`	Adds the given action listener to recieve action events from this textfield.`ActionListener)`
`addNotify()`	Creates the TextField's peer.
`echoCharIsSet()`	Returns true if TextField has a character set for echoing.
`getColumns()`	Returns the number of columns in this TextField.
`getEchoChar()`	Returns the character to be used for echoing.

JBuilder: Running Our First Programs

getMinimumSize()	Returns the minimum dimensions needed for this TextField.
getMinimumSize(int)	Returns the minimum dimensions needed for TextField with the given number of columns.
getPreferredSize()	Returns preferred size needed for this TextField.
getPreferredSize(int)	Returns the preferred size needed for this TextField with the given number of columns.
minimumSize()	Deprecated: Replaced by getMinimumSize().
minimumSize(int)	Deprecated: Replaced by getMinimumSize(int).
paramString()	Returns the String of parameters for this TextField.
preferredSize()	Deprecated: Replaced by getPreferredSize().
preferredSize(int)	Deprecated: Replaced by getPreferredSize(int).
processActionEvent ActionEvent)	Processes action events occurring on this textfield by dispatching them to any registered ActionListener objects.
processEvent(AWTEvent)	Processes events on this textfield.
removeActionListener (ActionListener)	Removes the given action listener so that it no longer receives action events from this textfield.
setColumns(int)	Sets the number of columns in this TextField.
setEchoChar(char)	Sets the echo character for this TextField.
setEchoCharacter(char)	Deprecated: Replaced by setEchoChar(char).

You may wonder how we can call the same function, TextField(), with a different number of parameters (i.e., none, one or two) as shown in Table 2.1. This is possible because of *function overloading*, which is possible in both C++ and in Java. To overload a function, you simply define it a number of times with a different parameter list each time like this:

```
int CalculateDaysFromToday(int Day){
            .
            .
            .
      }
      int CalculateDaysFromToday(int Day, int Month){
```

```
            .
            .
            .
      }
      int CalculateDaysFromToday(int Day, int Month, int Year){
            .
            .
            .
      }
```

How will the compiler know which one of these to use? It will determine that by the way you call the function. In the above case, the Java compiler will use the first function definition if you call the function as: `CalculateDaysFromToday(25);` and the third function definition if you call it this way: `CalculateDaysFromToday(25, 12, 1997);`.

In addition, JBuilder handles the placement of the new text field in the applet in the `jbInit()` method this way:

```
//Component initialization
  public void jbInit() throws Exception{

    xYLayout1.setWidth(400);
    xYLayout1.setHeight(300);
    this.setLayout(xYLayout1);
    this.add(textField1, new XYConstraints(38, 46, 156, 39));   <–

  }
```

Now we can run the applet, and type text directly into the text field, as shown in Figure 2.11. Now we're using controls in Java!

JBuilder: Running Our First Programs

Figure 2.11 Our textfields applet at work.

Intializing Text in a Text Field

Besides relying on the user to set the text in a text field, we can do so ourselves, using the TextField class's `setText()` method. We do that by adding this line to the `init()` method:

```
//Initialize the applet
  public void init() {

    textField1.setText("Welcome to JBuilder!");              <-

    try { jbInit(); } catch(Exception e) { e.printStackTrace(); };

  }
```

That's all it took—all we had to do was to call the textField1 object's `setText()` method, and the text we've placed in the text field will appear on the screen, as shown in Figure 2.12.

Chapter 2

Figure 2.12 Our textfields applet with pre-set text.

The textfields applet is a success. The code for this applet appears in Listing 2.3.

Listing 2.3 textfields.java

```
//Title:
//Version:
//Copyright:
//Author:
//Company:
//Description:
//

package textfields;
import java.lang.*;
import java.awt.*;
import java.awt.event.*;
import java.applet.*;
import borland.jbcl.control.*;
import borland.jbcl.layout.*;

public
```

```java
class textfields extends Applet {
  public XYLayout xYLayout1 = new XYLayout();
  public boolean isStandalone = false;
  TextField textField1 = new TextField();

  //Get a parameter value
  public String getParameter(String key, String def) {
    return isStandalone ? System.getProperty(key, def) :
      (getParameter(key) != null ? getParameter(key) : def);
  }

  //Construct the applet
  public textfields() {
  }

  //Initialize the applet
  public void init() {
    textField1.setText("Welcome to JBuilder!");
    try { jbInit(); } catch(Exception e) { e.printStackTrace(); };
  }
  //Component initialization
  public void jbInit() throws Exception{
    xYLayout1.setWidth(400);
    xYLayout1.setHeight(300);
    this.setLayout(xYLayout1);
    this.add(textField1, new XYConstraints(38, 46, 156, 39));
  }

  //Start the applet
  public void start() {
  }

  //Stop the applet
  public void stop() {
  }

  //Destroy the applet
  public void destroy() {
  }
```

Chapter 2

```
//Get Applet information
public String getAppletInfo() {
  return "Applet Information";
}

//Get parameter info
public String[][] getParameterInfo() {
  return null;
}

//Main method
static public void main(String[] args) {
  textfields applet = new textfields();
  applet.isStandalone = true;
  DecoratedFrame frame = new DecoratedFrame();
  frame.setTitle("Applet Frame");
  frame.add(applet, BorderLayout.CENTER);
  applet.init();
  applet.start();
  frame.pack();
  Dimension d = Toolkit.getDefaultToolkit().getScreenSize();
  frame.setLocation((d.width - frame.getSize().width) / 2, (d.height - frame.getSize().height) / 2);
  frame.setVisible(true);
  }
}
```

Now we've seen how to work with text fields. There is another type of control that is similar to text fields and is in fact superior in some respects—text areas—and we'll look into those controls next.

Handling Text Areas

A text field is fine if you have a small amount of text, but not if you have a lot. If you have a lot of text, you should use a text area.

A text area can display a multiline string of text, even including scroll bars:

JBuilder: Running Our First Programs

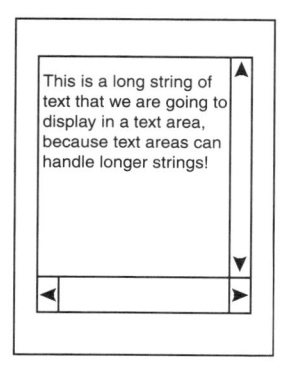

```
┌─────────────────────────┐
│  ┌───────────────────┐  │
│  │This is a long string of▲│  │
│  │text that we are going to│  │
│  │display in a text area,│  │
│  │because text areas can│  │
│  │handle longer strings!│  │
│  │                   │  │
│  │                  ▼│  │
│  │◄                 ►│  │
│  └───────────────────┘  │
└─────────────────────────┘
```

Let's see how to add text areas to our applets now.

Creating the textareas Applet

Create a new applet with the Applet Wizard now, naming this new applet **textareas**. Then open the textarea.java file and right-click it. Now select **Design** in the pop-up menu to open the JBuilder designer.

Now we can simply click the text area tool in the component palette—that tool is the third from the left in the AWT tab. If you don't know what tool a particular tool button stands for, just rest the mouse over that tool and a small window called a *tool tip* will appear, telling you what control or component the tool is for. Then we draw our new text area in the applet, as shown in Figure 2.13.

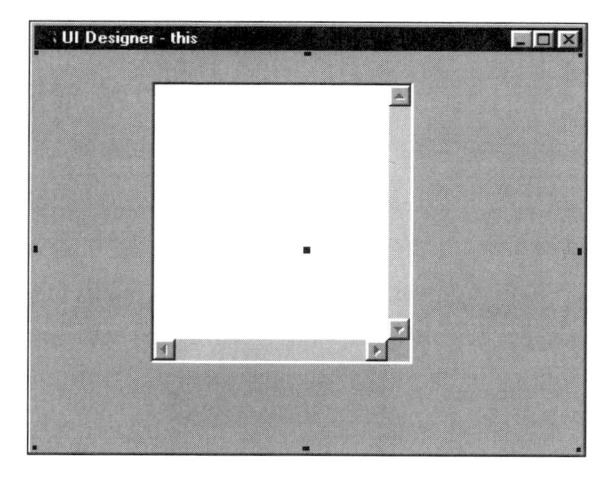

Figure 2.13 We design our new text area.

Chapter 2

As before, JBuilder has added code to our program to declare the new control:

```
public
class textareas extends Applet {
  public XYLayout xYLayout1 = new XYLayout();
  public boolean isStandalone = false;
  TextArea textArea1 = new TextArea();                <--
  //Construct the applet
  public textareas() {
  }
      .
      .
      .
}
```

The TextArea class's constructors and methods appear in Table 2.2.

Table 2.2 TextArea Constructors and Methods

`TextArea()`	Constructs a new TextArea.
`TextArea(int, int)`	Deprecated: Replaced by `TextArea(String, int, int)`.
`TextArea(String)`	Constructs a new TextArea with the given text displayed.
`TextArea (String, int, int)`	Constructs a new TextArea with the given text and number of rows and columns.
`TextArea (String, int, int, int)`	Constructs a new TextArea with the given text and number of rows, columns, and scrollbar visibility.
`addNotify()`	Creates the TextArea's peer.
`append(String)`	Appends the given text to the end.
`appendText(String)`	Deprecated: Replaced by `append(String)`.
`getColumns()`	Returns the number of columns in the TextArea.
`getMinimumSize()`	Returns the minimum size dimensions of the TextArea.
`getMinimumSize(int, int)`	Returns the given minimum size dimensions of the TextArea.

JBuilder: Running Our First Programs

`getPreferredSize()`	Returns the preferred size dimensions of the TextArea. `getPreferredSize` Returns the given row and column dimensions of the `(int, int)` TextArea.
`getRows()`	Returns the number of rows in the TextArea.
`getScrollbarVisibility()`	Returns the enumerated value describing which scrollbars the text area has.
`insert(String, int)`	Inserts the given text at the given position.
`insertText(String, int)`	Deprecated: Replaced by `insert(String, int)`.
`minimumSize()`	Deprecated: Replaced by `getMinimumSize()`.
`minimumSize(int, int)`	Deprecated: Replaced by `getMinimumSize (int, int)`.
`paramString()`	Returns the String of parameters for this TextArea.
`preferredSize()`	Deprecated: Replaced by `getPreferredSize()`.
`preferredSize(int, int)`	Deprecated: Replaced by `getPreferredSize (int, int)`.
`replaceRange (String, int, int)`	Replaces text from the indicated start to end position with the new text given.
`replaceText (String, int, int)`	Deprecated: Replaced by `replaceRange(String, int, int)`.
`setColumns(int)`	Sets the number of columns for this TextArea.
`setRows(int)`	Sets the number of rows for this TextArea.

JBuilder has also added code to place the new control in the layout of the applet:

```
//Component initialization
public void jbInit() throws Exception{

  xYLayout1.setWidth(400);
  xYLayout1.setHeight(300);
  this.setLayout(xYLayout1);
  this.add(textArea1, new XYConstraints(86, 23, 191, 211));    <—

}
```

Chapter 2

Now all we have to do is to place the text we want in the text area. We do that with the TextArea `insertText()` method (note that text areas do not have a `setText()` method as text fields do) in the `init()` method:

```
public void init() {

    textArea1.insertText("This is a long string of \ntext that we are
going to \ndisplay in a text area, \nbecause text areas can \nhandle
longer strings!", 0);          <—

    try { jbInit(); } catch(Exception e) { e.printStackTrace(); };

}
```

Note also that we used the text string \n at intervals in the string we placed into the text area—this "\n" string represents a carriage return, and indicates that we should move to the beginning of the next line (the \n code is patterned after the C and C++ newline code).

Now we can run the program, as shown in Figure 2.14. As you can see in that figure, our text area appears with the text we want in it.

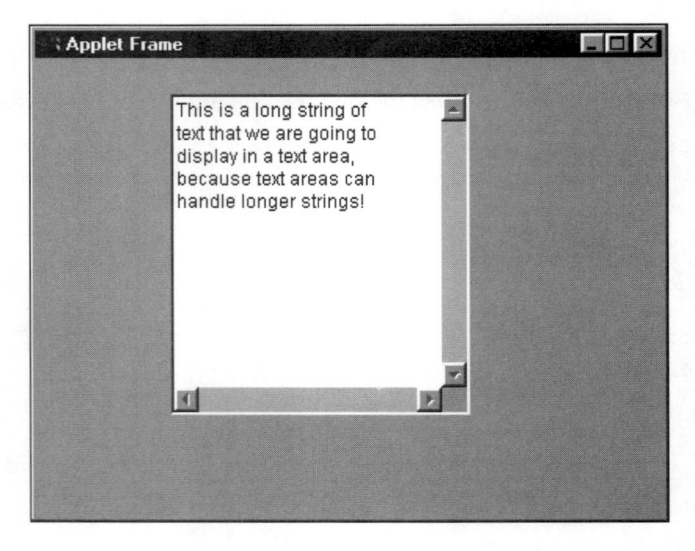

Figure 2.14 Our textareas applet with pre-set text.

JBuilder: Running Our First Programs

Our text area applet is a success—now we're working with text areas! The listing for this applet appears in Listing 2.4.

Listing 2.4 textareas.java

```java
//Title:
//Version:
//Copyright:
//Author:
//Company:
//Description:
//
package textareas;
import java.lang.*;
import java.awt.*;
import java.awt.event.*;
import java.applet.*;
import borland.jbcl.control.*;
import borland.jbcl.layout.*;

public
class textareas extends Applet {

  public XYLayout xYLayout1 = new XYLayout();
  public boolean isStandalone = false;
  TextArea textArea1 = new TextArea();

  //Construct the applet
  public textareas() {

  }

  //Initialize the applet
  public void init() {

    textArea1.insertText("This is a long string of \ntext that we are going to \ndisplay in a text area, \nbecause text areas can \nhandle longer strings!", 0);
```

Chapter 2

```
    try { jbInit(); } catch(Exception e) { e.printStackTrace(); };

}

//Component initialization
public void jbInit() throws Exception{

  xYLayout1.setWidth(400);
  xYLayout1.setHeight(300);
  this.setLayout(xYLayout1);
  this.add(textArea1, new XYConstraints(86, 23, 191, 211));

}

//Start the applet
public void start() {

}

//Stop the applet
public void stop() {

}

//Destroy the applet
public void destroy() {

}

//Get Applet information
public String getAppletInfo() {

  return "Applet Information";

}

//Get parameter info
public String[][] getParameterInfo() {
```

JBuilder: Running Our First Programs

```
    return null;

}

//Main method
static public void main(String[] args) {

    textareas applet = new textareas();
    applet.isStandalone = true;
    DecoratedFrame frame = new DecoratedFrame();
    frame.setTitle("Applet Frame");
    frame.add(applet, BorderLayout.CENTER);
    applet.init();
    applet.start();
    frame.pack();
    Dimension d = Toolkit.getDefaultToolkit().getScreenSize();
    frame.setLocation((d.width - frame.getSize().width) / 2, (d.height
- frame.getSize().height) / 2);
    frame.setVisible(true);

}


}
```

That's it for this chapter. Here, we've seen how to use JBuilder to create applets, and we've taken those applets apart piece by piece to see what they do and how they do it. We've also seen how to display text in an applet by overriding the `paint()` method. Next, we turned to placing controls into applets as we placed a text field in an applet and let it display some text for us. Finally, we saw how the use text areas to display larger amounts of text for us. All in all, we've gotten a good start in JBuilder programming in this chapter.

In Chapter 3, we'll start making our applets really do something. In particular, we'll start working with buttons, button bars, and more.

CHAPTER 3

Buttons and Text Fields

In this chapter, we are going to make our Java programs actually do something. In Chapter 2, we saw how to add controls to our programs when we added a text field. Now we're going to improve on that and add buttons as well.

If you've used Windows, you've seen buttons—they are those controls you can press with the mouse to perform some action or set some option. When you click them, they appear to be pressed momentarily and then spring back up. We're going to see how to add buttons to our programs in this chapter. We'll also learn how to use the new type of buttons that come with JBuilder in the jbcl package. These buttons offer more functionality than simple Java buttons do, and we'll see how to display an image in a button using jbcl buttons.

In addition, we'll see that JBuilder provides us with a way of grouping buttons together with *bevel panels* and *button bars*. We'll see how to make full use of both those techniques in this chapter.

There's a lot coming up in this chapter, so let's get started.

Our First Button Example

In our first button example, we will add a new button to an applet:

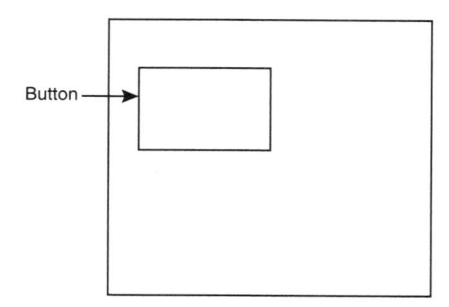

Chapter 3

An unlabeled button isn't much good, however, so we'll give this button the label Click Me:

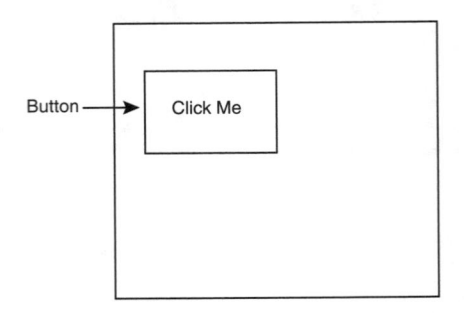

[Diagram: Applet window containing a button labeled "Click Me", with "Button" label pointing to it]

Next, we can add a text field to our applet:

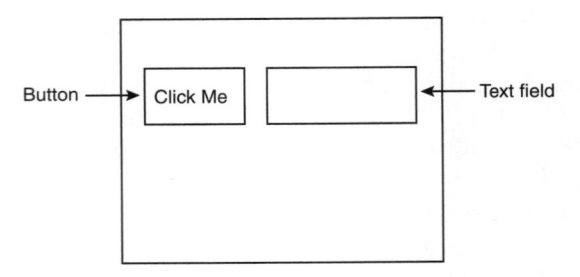

[Diagram: Applet window containing "Click Me" button and a text field, with labels "Button" and "Text field" pointing to them]

When the user clicks the button, we can display a message in the text field: *You clicked the button.*:

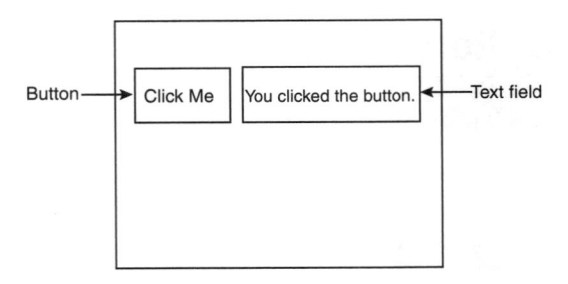

[Diagram: Applet window containing "Click Me" button and a text field displaying "You clicked the button.", with labels "Button" and "Text field" pointing to them]

Let's put this to work now. Start JBuilder, and create a new applet named button, giving it the package and class names "button" in lowercase (remember that case counts in Java). Now open **button.java**, right-click it, and open the JBuilder Designer.

We're ready to add our button to the applet. To do so, click the **AWT** tab in the component gallery, and click the button tool (it is the fourth from the left in the gallery and displays a button with the label *OK*).

Now draw the button in the applet with the mouse, as shown in Figure 3.1.

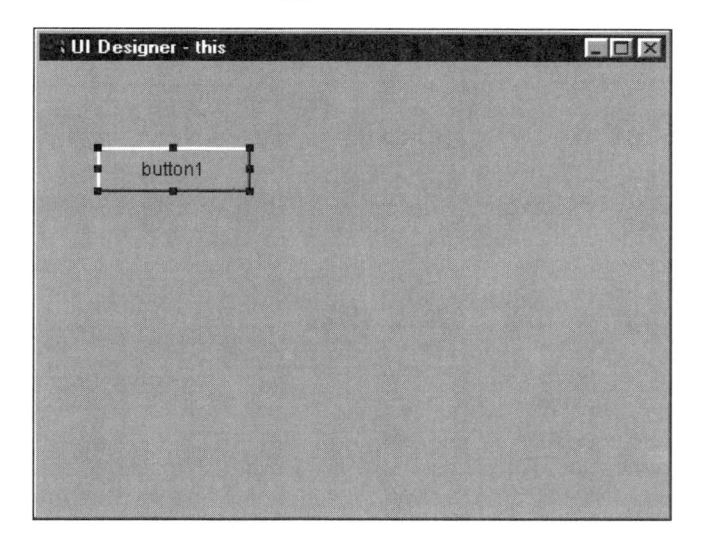

Figure 3.1 We create a new button.

Setting a Control's Properties

At present, our new button is labeled Button1, as you can see in Figure 3.1, but we can change that to Click Me. To do so, move over to the JBuilder Inspector window, shown in Figure 3.2. The Inspector lets us change various aspects of a control, called the control's *properties*, and set up methods in our program to handle a control's events. An *event* occurs as a result of some action on the user's part. For example, clicking our new button is an event, and using the Inspector, we'll be able to connect a new method to the program that will be automatically called when the user clicks our button.

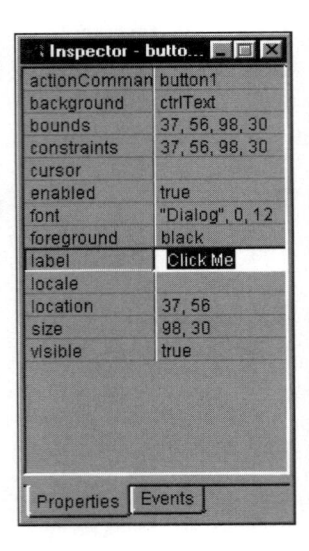

Figure 3.2 Changing a button's label.

To set the button's label to Click Me, find the label property in the Inspector and click the text field next to that property, as shown in Figure 3.2. This opens that text field for editing, and we type in the new label we want for the button.

The next step is to connect button clicks to our code.

Handling a Control's Events

When the user clicks the button, we can have the program call a specific method. Then we can place the code we need to display the *You clicked the button.* message in the text field in that new method. Let's set up this new method now.

Click the **Events** tab at the bottom of the Inspector now to see the possible events that the button can handle. You see quite a range of events, from componentHidden to mouseReleased. We can add event handlers for all these action. In this case, click the text field next to the top entry in the Inspector, actionPerformed, and then press **Enter**. This automatically creates a new method for the button, button1_actionPerformed(), and the name of this new method appears in the Inspector, as shown in Figure 3.3. As we'll see, simply clicking this entry has caused JBuilder to add code to our program.

Buttons and Text Fields

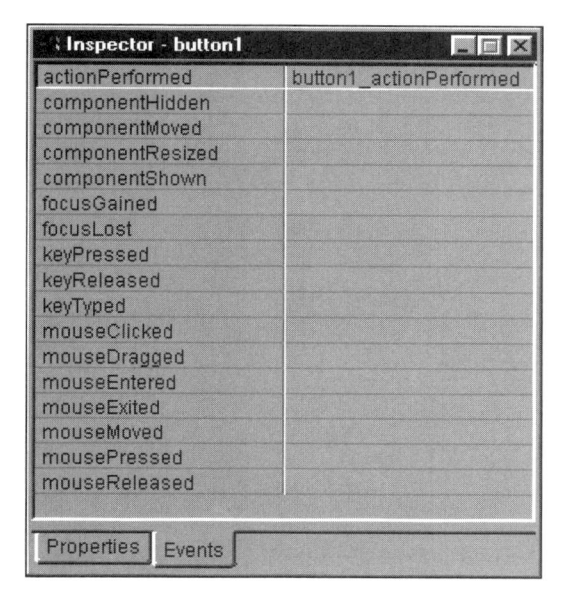

Figure 3.3 Setting up an event handler.

All that remains to complete the design of our applet is to add the text field, so we do that now, as shown in Figure 3.4 (click the text field tool in the component gallery and draw the new text field). Note that you can already see the button's new caption—Click Me—in the Designer.

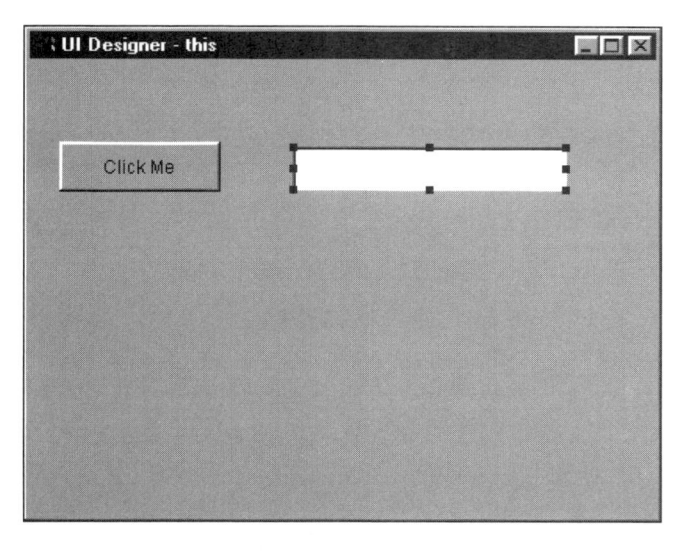

Figure 3.4 Drawing a new text field.

Chapter 3

Using Controls in Code

Now let's take a look at what JBuilder has done for us in code. Move back to the Project window and take a look at button.java, the source code for our applet. Notice at the very top of that program, JBuilder has added a new object of the Java `Button` class named `button1` to our code:

```
package button;
import java.lang.*;
import java.awt.*;
import java.awt.event.*;
import java.applet.*;
import borland.jbcl.control.*;
import borland.jbcl.layout.*;

public
class button extends Applet {

  public XYLayout xYLayout1 = new XYLayout();
  public boolean isStandalone = false;
  Button button1 = new Button();                    <—
  TextField textField1 = new TextField();
    .
    .
    .
```

The `Button` class supports buttons in Java, and its constructors and methods appear in Table 3.1.

Table 3.1 The Button Constructors and Methods

`Button()`	Constructs a `Button` with no label.
`Button(String)`	Constructs a `Button` with the given label.
`addActionListener(ActionListener)`	Adds the given action listener to receive action events from this button.
`addNotify()`	Creates the peer of the button.
`getActionCommand()`	Returns the command name of the action event fired by this button.

Buttons and Text Fields

`getLabel()`	Gets the label of the button.
`paramString()`	Returns the parameter `String` of this button.
`processActionEvent` `ActionEvent)`	Processes action events occurring on this button by dispatching them to `ActionListener` objects.
`processEvent(AWTEvent)`	Processes events on this button.
`removeActionListener` `(ActionListener)`	Removes the given action listener so it no longer receives action events from this button.
`setActionCommand` `(String)`	Sets the command name of the action event fired by this button.
`setLabel(String)`	Sets the button's label to the given label.

In addition, JBuilder has installed the new button in its `jbInit()` method:

```
        //Component initialization
        public void jbInit() throws Exception{

          xYLayout1.setWidth(400);
          xYLayout1.setHeight(300);
->        button1.setLabel("Click Me");
->        button1.addActionListener(new button_button1_ActionAdapter(this));
          this.setLayout(xYLayout1);
->        this.add(button1, new XYConstraints(37, 56, 98, 30));
          this.add(textField1, new XYConstraints(168, 57, 175, 29));

        }
```

Let's take a look at what's happening here. First, JBuilder sets the label of the new button to the label we chose, Click Me, using the Button class's `setLabel()` method:

```
        //Component initialization
        public void jbInit() throws Exception{

          xYLayout1.setWidth(400);
          xYLayout1.setHeight(300);
          button1.setLabel("Click Me");        <-
```

Chapter 3

```
    .
    .
}
```

Next, JBuilder calls the Button class's `addActionListener()` method:

```
//Component initialization
public void jbInit() throws Exception{

  xYLayout1.setWidth(400);
  xYLayout1.setHeight(300);
  button1.setLabel("Click Me");
-> button1.addActionListener(new button_button1_ActionAdapter(this));
    .
    .
    .
}
```

As we'll see in a moment, this is what does the actual work of connecting the button to our code. Finally, JBuilder adds the new controls to the applet with the `add()` method (unless the controls are added to the applet, which really adds the controls to the applet's `XYLayout` object, they will not appear when you run the applet):

```
//Component initialization
public void jbInit() throws Exception{

  xYLayout1.setWidth(400);
  xYLayout1.setHeight(300);
  button1.setLabel("Click Me");
  button1.addActionListener(new button_button1_ActionAdapter(this));
  this.setLayout(xYLayout1);
-> this.add(button1, new XYConstraints(37, 56, 98, 30));
-> this.add(textField1, new XYConstraints(168, 57, 175, 29));

}
```

Now what was that about the `addActionListener()` method? It is used to connect a control to an applet in Java 1.1, which is our next topic.

Action Listeners

If you've programmed in Java 1.0, you should be familiar with the `action()` method, which is called when the user performs some action or moves the mouse. Java 1.1 is different, however; it uses *action listeners* to handle control events such as button clicks.

What happens is this: the button control is connected to an action listener object with the `addActionListener()` method. When the user clicks the button, it sends a message to its action listener object. This message is then handled in the action listener object by a method called `actionPerformed()`.

Let's see how this looks in our program. In the `jbInit()` method, JBuilder connects a new action listener object to `button1` with `addActionListener()` this way, using the Java `new` operator to create a new object of the `button_button1_ActionAdapter` class:

```
        //Component initialization
        public void jbInit() throws Exception{

          xYLayout1.setWidth(400);
          xYLayout1.setHeight(300);
          button1.setLabel("Click Me");
->        button1.addActionListener(new button_button1_ActionAdapter(this));
          this.setLayout(xYLayout1);
          this.add(button1, new XYConstraints(37, 56, 98, 30));
          this.add(textField1, new XYConstraints(168, 57, 175, 29));

        }
```

This class, `button_button1_ActionAdapter`, has been specially written for us by JBuilder:

```
        class button_button1_ActionAdapter implements ActionListener {

          button adaptee;

          button_button1_ActionAdapter(button adaptee) {
            this.adaptee = adaptee;
          }
```

Chapter 3

```
public void actionPerformed(java.awt.event.ActionEvent e) {
  adaptee.button1_actionPerformed(e);
}

}
```

We'll take this new class apart line by line now to understand what's going on here (note that this class is not declared public, which means it's private and available only to other classes in the button.java file). In the first line, we declare the new class and add the keywords `implements ActionListener`:

```
class button_button1_ActionAdapter implements ActionListener {
    .
    .
    .
```

The keyword `implements` is much like the keyword `extends`. We've already seen that applets extend the `Applet` class:

```
public
class button extends Applet {
    .
    .
    .
```

Java Interfaces

We want the `button_button1_ActionAdapter` class to be an action listener object, but Java does not support multiple inheritance, which means you cannot use more than one class as a base class in any derived class. To get around this, Java defines many classes as *interfaces*.

An interface works much like a base class, but it's specially designed to get around the Java no-multiple-inheritance rule, which means that you can "inherit" as many interfaces as you like. In this case, we add the `JavaActionListener` interface to the `button_button1_ActionAdapter` class this way:

```
class button_button1_ActionAdapter implements ActionListener {
    .
    .
    .
```

Buttons and Text Fields

Next, JBuilder gives this new class a class constructor:

```
class button_button1_ActionAdapter implements ActionListener {

    button_button1_ActionAdapter(button adaptee) {       <--


    }                                                     <--


}
```

The purpose of this constructor is really just to get a reference to our main applet object, which is an object of the class we've named button (not Button, which is the Java Button class). We called the button_button1_ActionAdapter class's constructor with a this keyword in the amin applet object:

```
    //Component initialization
    public void jbInit() throws Exception{

      xYLayout1.setWidth(400);
      xYLayout1.setHeight(300);
      button1.setLabel("Click Me");
->    button1.addActionListener(new button_button1_ActionAdapter(this));
      this.setLayout(xYLayout1);
      this.add(button1, new XYConstraints(37, 56, 98, 30));
      this.add(textField1, new XYConstraints(168, 57, 175, 29));

    }
```

In Java, the this keyword refers to the current object, so we are passing a reference to the main applet object to the button_button1_ActionAdapter constructor. This way, the button_button1_ActionAdapter class will know which object to send messages to when the user clicks the button.

In the button_button1_ActionAdapter class's constructor, then, we save the reference to the main applet object as a new object named adaptee:

```
class button_button1_ActionAdapter implements ActionListener {
```

Chapter 3

```
->      button adaptee;

        button_button1_ActionAdapter(button adaptee) {
->        this.adaptee = adaptee;
        }

      }
```

Because we made the new `button_button1_ActionAdapter` object the button's action listener object, this object will receive messages from the button when it's clicked, and by default, those messages will go to a method called `actionPerformed()` in the `button_button1_ActionAdapter` class:

```
class button_button1_ActionAdapter implements ActionListener {

  button adaptee;

  button_button1_ActionAdapter(button adaptee) {
    this.adaptee = adaptee;
  }

  public void actionPerformed(java.awt.event.ActionEvent e) {   <-

  }                                                              <-

}
```

Here, this method is passed an object of the Java `ActionEvent` class, and we'll soon see what that object contains. In the `actionPerformed()` method, then, we can simply call a new method that JBuilder has added to our main applet's class named `button1_actionPerformed()`:

```
class button_button1_ActionAdapter implements ActionListener {

  button adaptee;

  button_button1_ActionAdapter(button adaptee) {
    this.adaptee = adaptee;
  }
```

Buttons and Text Fields

```
    public void actionPerformed(java.awt.event.ActionEvent e) {
      adaptee.button1_actionPerformed(e);                    <—
    }

  }
```

In this way, the `button_button1_ActionAdapter` class sends the button click message back to us in the main applet class, because the method it calls, `button1_actionPerformed()`, is a method in the main applet's class:

```
    public
    class button extends Applet {

      public XYLayout xYLayout1 = new XYLayout();
      public boolean isStandalone = false;
      Button button1 = new Button();
      TextField textField1 = new TextField();
               .
               .
               .
—>    void button1_actionPerformed(java.awt.event.ActionEvent e) {

—>    }
```

Here, finally, is where we can put the code to handle button clicks, in the `button1_actionPerformed()` method of the applet class. We want to display the message *You clicked the button*. Here's how:

```
    public
    class button extends Applet {

      public XYLayout xYLayout1 = new XYLayout();
      public boolean isStandalone = false;
      Button button1 = new Button();
      TextField textField1 = new TextField();
               .
               .
               .
      void button1_actionPerformed(java.awt.event.ActionEvent e) {
```

Chapter 3

```
        textField1.setText("You clicked the button.");        <−

    }
```

And by adding that one line of code, we've made our program work. Run it now, as shown in Figure 3.5, and click the button—when you do, you'll see our message displayed in the text field. Our button program is a success.

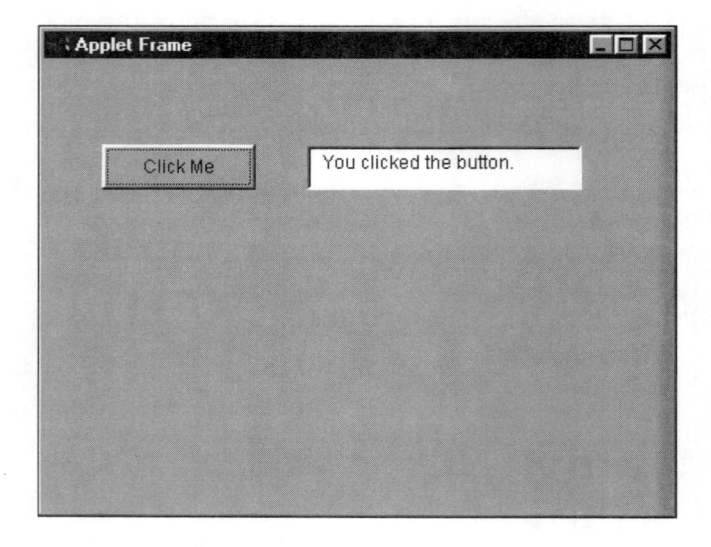

Figure 3.5 Drawing a new text field.

The listing for this program appears in Listing 3.1.

Listing 3.1 button.java

```
//Title:
//Version:
//Copyright:
//Author:
//Company:
//Description:
//

package button;
```

Buttons and Text Fields

```java
import java.lang.*;
import java.awt.*;
import java.awt.event.*;
import java.applet.*;
import borland.jbcl.control.*;
import borland.jbcl.layout.*;

public
class button extends Applet {

  public XYLayout xYLayout1 = new XYLayout();
  public boolean isStandalone = false;
  Button button1 = new Button();
  TextField textField1 = new TextField();

  //Construct the applet
  public button() {

  }

  //Initialize the applet
  public void init() {

    try { jbInit(); } catch(Exception e) { e.printStackTrace(); };

  }

  //Component initialization
  public void jbInit() throws Exception{

    xYLayout1.setWidth(400);
    xYLayout1.setHeight(300);
    button1.setLabel("Click Me");
    button1.addActionListener(new button_button1_ActionAdapter(this));
    this.setLayout(xYLayout1);
    this.add(button1, new XYConstraints(37, 56, 98, 30));
    this.add(textField1, new XYConstraints(168, 57, 175, 29));

  }
```

Chapter 3

```java
//Start the applet
public void start() {

}

//Stop the applet
public void stop() {

}

//Destroy the applet
public void destroy() {

}

//Get Applet information
public String getAppletInfo() {

  return "Applet Information";

}

//Get parameter info
public String[][] getParameterInfo() {

  return null;

}

//Main method
static public void main(String[] args) {

  button applet = new button();
  applet.isStandalone = true;
  DecoratedFrame frame = new DecoratedFrame();
  frame.setTitle("Applet Frame");
  frame.add(applet, BorderLayout.CENTER);
  applet.init();
  applet.start();
  frame.pack();
```

Buttons and Text Fields

```
        Dimension d = Toolkit.getDefaultToolkit().getScreenSize();
        frame.setLocation((d.width - frame.getSize().width) / 2,
(d.height - frame.getSize().height) / 2);
        frame.setVisible(true);

  }

  void button1_actionPerformed(java.awt.event.ActionEvent e) {

    textField1.setText("You clicked the button.");

  }

}

class button_button1_ActionAdapter implements ActionListener {

  button adaptee;

  button_button1_ActionAdapter(button adaptee) {
    this.adaptee = adaptee;
  }

  public void actionPerformed(java.awt.event.ActionEvent e) {
    adaptee.button1_actionPerformed(e);
  }

}
```

Now we've seen how to add a button. We just connect the `button1_actionPerformed()` method to the button and add the code we want to that method. If there are more buttons in a program, JBuilder will add new methods, like `button2_actionPerformed()` and `button3_actionPerformed()`, and so on, one such method per button.

We might observe in passing that you can actually make the main applet class into an action listener, and therefore place the `actionPerformed()` method directly in the main applet class instead of in a new class like `button_button1_ActionAdapter`. That makes the code much smaller, but Borland has elected to create a new class for each control for which you want an action listener. This is a good idea for programs with lots of controls, because instead of handling all those controls in one `actionPerformed()`

Chapter 3

method, your program will divide event handling into separate—and thus more manageable—methods such as `button1_actionPerformed()` and `button2_actionPerformed()`.

Now that we've seen how to use standard Java buttons, let's take a look at Borland's jbcl buttons, which offers something that Java buttons don't.

Using jbcl Buttons

In addition to the standard Java buttons, we can also use the jbcl buttons that come with JBuilder. Doing so will allow us to display an image in a button. Let's see how this works. The image we will display in a button is **image.gif**, which appears in Figure 3.6.

Figure 3.6 The image.gif file.

Start a new applet named jbButtons. Next, open the JBuilder Designer and click the **Controls** tab in the components gallery. Find the jbcl ButtonControl tool—it's the first tool on the left in the gallery—and draw a new button of that type and a standard text field in the applet, as shown in Figure 3.7.

This adds a new `ButtonControl` to our program, `buttonControl1`:

```
public
class jbButtons extends Applet {
  public XYLayout xYLayout1 = new XYLayout();
  public boolean isStandalone = false;
  ButtonControl buttonControl1 = new ButtonControl();     <-
  TextField textField1 = new TextField();
     .
     .
     .
```

Buttons and Text Fields

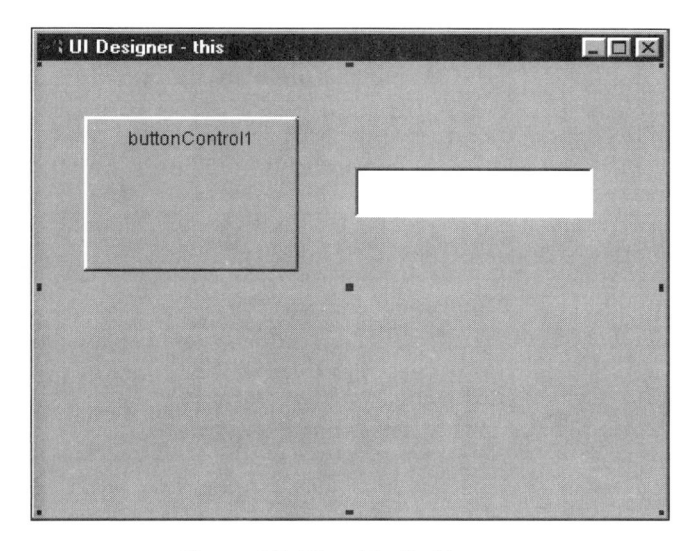

Figure 3.7 We add a jbcl button.

The ButtonControl constructors and methods appear in Table 3.2.

Table 3.2 The ButtonControl Constructors and Methods

ButtonControl()	Creates a button with default properties.
ButtonControl(Image image)	Creates a button. The given image is displayed on the button's surface.
ButtonControl(String path)	Creates a button. The image at the given location is displayed on the button's surface.
ButtonControl(URL url)	Creates a button. The image at the given URL is displayed on the button's surface.
getImage()	Gets the image's name
setImage(Image image)	Sets the image
setImage(URL url)	Specifies the location of the image to be displayed on the button.
setImage(String)	Sets the image to the name given.
getImageFirst()	Gets the imageFirst property
setImageFirst(boolean first)	Sets the imageFirst property
getLabel()	Gets the label.

Chapter 3

`setLabel(String l)`	Sets the label.
`getOrientation()`	Gets button's orientation
`setOrientation(int o)`	Sets button's orientation.
`void setImage(String path)`	Sets the image to the path and name given.

Now set the button's image property to image.gif, as shown in Figure 3.8.

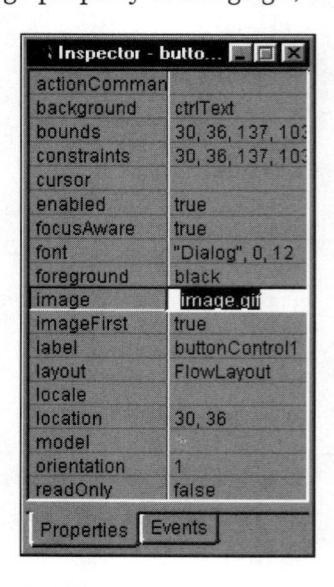

Figure 3.8 Add an image to a jbcl button.

Now click the new button's `actionPerformed` event, adding the method `buttonControl1_actionPerformed()` to the applet:

```
void
buttonControl1_actionPerformed(java.awt.event.ActionEvent e) {

}
```

Here, we'll display the same message as in the previous example in the text field:

```
void
buttonControl1_actionPerformed(java.awt.event.ActionEvent e) {
```

Buttons and Text Fields

```
        textField1.setText("You clicked the button.");    <-

    }
```

Now run the program. As you can see there, we've added a new button to our program, and we display the image, **image.gif**, in that button. Click the button now to see our message, as shown in Figure 3.9.

Figure 3.9 We add an image to a jbcl button.

Our new ButtonControl program works as expected. The complete code for this program appears in Listing 3.2.

Listing 3.2 jbButtons.java

```
        //Title:
        //Version:
        //Copyright:
        //Author:
        //Company:
        //Description:
        //

        package jbButtons;
        import java.lang.*;
        import java.awt.*;
        import java.awt.event.*;
        import java.applet.*;
        import borland.jbcl.control.*;
        import borland.jbcl.layout.*;
```

Chapter 3

```java
public
class jbButtons extends Applet {

  public XYLayout xYLayout1 = new XYLayout();
  public boolean isStandalone = false;
  ButtonControl buttonControl1 = new ButtonControl();
  TextField textField1 = new TextField();

  //Get a parameter value
  public String getParameter(String key, String def) {
    return isStandalone ? System.getProperty(key, def) :
      (getParameter(key) != null ? getParameter(key) : def);

  }

  //Construct the applet
  public jbButtons() {

  }

  //Initialize the applet
  public void init() {
    try { jbInit(); }catch(Exception e) { e.printStackTrace(); };

  }

  //Component initialization
  public void jbInit() throws Exception{
    xYLayout1.setWidth(400);
    xYLayout1.setHeight(300);
    buttonControl1.setLabel("buttonControl1");
    buttonControl1.setOrientation(1);
    buttonControl1.setImageName("image.gif");
    buttonControl1.addActionListener(new jbButtons_buttonControl1_ActionAdapter(this));
    this.setLayout(xYLayout1);
    this.add(buttonControl1, new XYConstraints(30, 36, 137, 103));
    this.add(textField1, new XYConstraints(203, 70, 152, 33));

  }
```

Buttons and Text Fields

```
//Start the applet
public void start() {

}

//Stop the applet
public void stop() {

}

//Destroy the applet
public void destroy() {

}

//Get Applet information
public String getAppletInfo() {
  return "Applet Information";

}

//Get parameter info
public String[][] getParameterInfo() {
  return null;

}

//Main method
static public void main(String[] args) {
  jbButtons applet = new jbButtons();
  applet.isStandalone = true;
  DecoratedFrame frame = new DecoratedFrame();
  frame.setTitle("Applet Frame");
  frame.add(applet, BorderLayout.CENTER);
  applet.init();
  applet.start();
  frame.pack();
  Dimension d = Toolkit.getDefaultToolkit().getScreenSize();
```

Chapter 3

```
        frame.setLocation((d.width - frame.getSize().width) / 2, (d.height -
frame.getSize().height) / 2);
        frame.setVisible(true);

    }

    void
    buttonControl1_actionPerformed(java.awt.event.ActionEvent e) {
        textField1.setText("You clicked the button.");

    }

}

class jbButtons_buttonControl1_ActionAdapter implements ActionListener{

    jbButtons adaptee;

    jbButtons_buttonControl1_ActionAdapter(jbButtons adaptee) {
        this.adaptee = adaptee;

    }

    public void actionPerformed(java.awt.event.ActionEvent e) {
        adaptee.buttonControl1_actionPerformed(e);

    }

}
```

Using Bevel Panels

JBuilder provides several ways to manage multiple controls in an applet, and we'll see how to use one such technique, *bevel panels*, now. In this case, we'll be able to add a bevel panel to an applet this way:

Buttons and Text Fields

Next, we'll add three buttons to the bevel panel, and let that panel arrange the buttons for us:

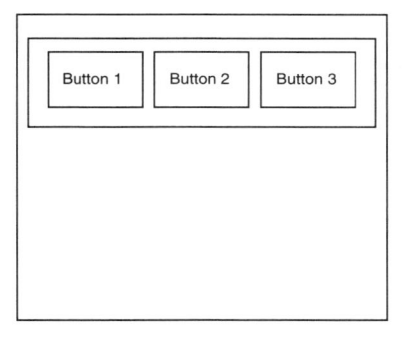

Finally, we'll add a text field to the applet:

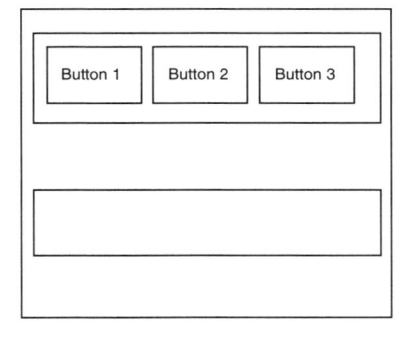

When the user clicks a particular button, we'll report which one it was.

Chapter 3

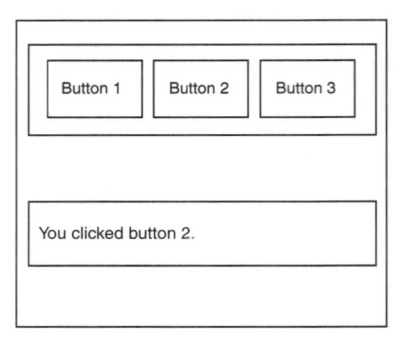

[Figure: applet showing Button 1, Button 2, Button 3 and a text field reading "You clicked button 2."]

Let's see this at work now. Create a new applet named `fPanel` now, and open it in the JBuilder Designer. Next, find the bevel panel tool in the component gallery. Click the **Containers** tab; the bevel-panel tool is the first tool on the left. Now draw a bevel panel in the applet, as shown in Figure 3.10.

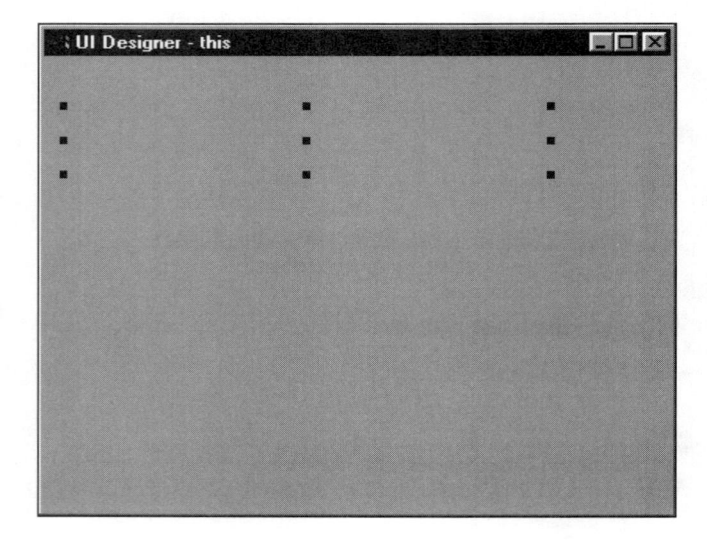

Figure 3.10 We add a bevel panel to an applet.

This bevel panel is the same color as the applet itself, but we can change that to make it stand out. We do that by clicking the panel's background property in the Inspector, and clicking the button with the three dots that appears in the text field next to the property name. This opens the background dialog box, as shown in Figure 3.11.

Buttons and Text Fields

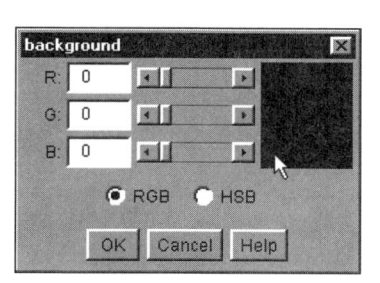

Figure 3.11 The background dialog box.

Here, we can set the red, green, and blue settings for the background color for our bevel panel. To make the panel stand out, we'll make it black, so set all three color settings to 0, as shown in Figure 3.11.

Selecting a New Layout

We will let the bevel panel arrange our buttons automatically. To do that, we set the panel's layout property to `FlowLayout`, as shown in Figure 3.12. This property indicates how controls in the bevel panel will be arranged.

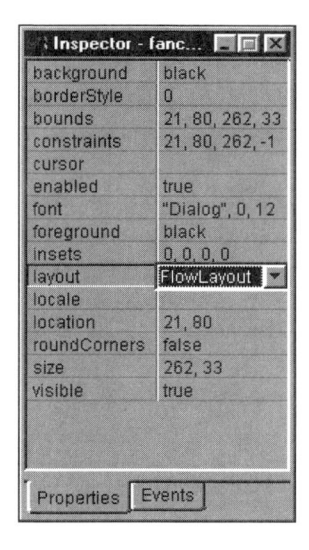

Figure 3.12 Setting a panel's layout property to FlowLayout.

Chapter 3

Usually in JBuilder, we use XYLayout, which means that controls stay where you place them. The flow layout, on the other hand (which is actually the default Java layout) moves the controls and arranges them rather like words on a page—when there are too many controls on a line, they "wrap" to the next line.

Now that we've set the bevel panel's layout to FlowLayout, add three new buttons to the panel by drawing them directly in the panel. The bevel panel will now shape and arrange them as shown in Figure 3.13.

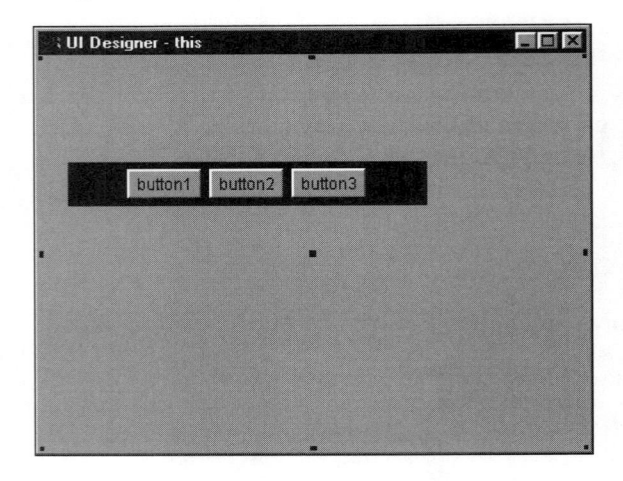

Figure 3.13 Arranging buttons in a bevel panel.

Next, add a text field, which JBuilder will name textField1, and go to the code in the project window. JBuilder has added the bevel panel to our new applet:

```
public
class fPanel extends Applet {
    public XYLayout xYLayout1 = new XYLayout();
    public boolean isStandalone = false;
    BevelPanel bevelPanel1 = new BevelPanel();
    Button button1 = new Button();
    Button button2 = new Button();
    Button button3 = new Button();
    FlowLayout flowLayout1 = new FlowLayout();    <-
    TextField textField1 = new TextField();
         .
         .
         .
```

Buttons and Text Fields

In addition, it's set the layout in the bevel panel to the `FlowLayout` layout in `jbInit()`:

```
//Component initialization
public void jbInit() throws Exception{

  xYLayout1.setWidth(400);
  xYLayout1.setHeight(300);
  bevelPanel1.setBackground(Color.black);
  bevelPanel1.setLayout(flowLayout1);          <-
    .
    .
    .
```

Then it sets up an action listener for each of the three buttons:

```
    //Component initialization
    public void jbInit() throws Exception{

      xYLayout1.setWidth(400);
      xYLayout1.setHeight(300);
      bevelPanel1.setBackground(Color.black);
      bevelPanel1.setLayout(flowLayout1);
      button1.setLabel("button1");
->    button1.addActionListener(new fPanel_button1_ActionAdapter(this));
      button2.setLabel("button2");
->    button2.addActionListener(new fPanel_button2_ActionAdapter(this));
      button3.setLabel("button3");
->    button3.addActionListener(new fPanel_button3_ActionAdapter(this));
        .
        .
        .
```

Next, it adds those three buttons to the bevel panel's layout with the `add()` method, which adds a component like a button to a layout:

```
//Component initialization
public void jbInit() throws Exception{
```

Chapter 3

```
xYLayout1.setWidth(400);
xYLayout1.setHeight(300);
bevelPanel1.setBackground(Color.black);
bevelPanel1.setLayout(flowLayout1);
button1.setLabel("button1");
button1.addActionListener(new fPanel_button1_ActionAdapter(this));
button2.setLabel("button2");
button2.addActionListener(new fPanel_button2_ActionAdapter(this));
button3.setLabel("button3");
button3.addActionListener(new fPanel_button3_ActionAdapter(this));
this.setLayout(xYLayout1);
this.add(bevelPanel1, new XYConstraints(31, 45, 238, 35));
bevelPanel1.add(button1, null);         <—
bevelPanel1.add(button2, null);         <—
bevelPanel1.add(button3, null);         <—
this.add(textField1, new XYConstraints(35, 113, 231, 31));

}
```

Since we've added action listeners for each of the buttons, we have a method for each button click in the main applet class:

```
void button1_actionPerformed(java.awt.event.ActionEvent e) {

}


void button2_actionPerformed(java.awt.event.ActionEvent e) {

}


void button3_actionPerformed(java.awt.event.ActionEvent e) {

}
```

Buttons and Text Fields

In each case, we simply indicate which button was clicked in the text field as follows:

```
void button1_actionPerformed(java.awt.event.ActionEvent e) {

    textField1.setText("You clicked button 1.");    <—


}


void button2_actionPerformed(java.awt.event.ActionEvent e) {

    textField1.setText("You clicked button 2.");    <—


}


void button3_actionPerformed(java.awt.event.ActionEvent e) {

    textField1.setText("You clicked button 3.");    <—


}
```

Now run the program. As you can see in Figure 3.14, our bevel panel holds and arranges the buttons just as it should, and those buttons work just as they should. Our program is a success.

Chapter 3

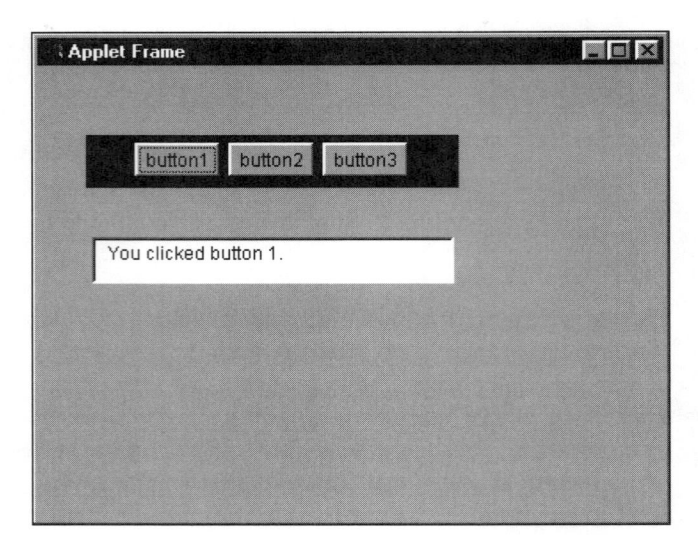

Figure 3.14 Our bevel panel at work.

We might also note, now that we're using a bevel panel, which is a *container* (an object that contains other objects) that the Tree window, shown in Figure 3.15, which appears in the Designer, is useful for keeping track of the various components in containers and what layouts they are using. In Figure 3.15, we can see that the main applet uses the XYLayout, but that the bevel panel uses the FlowLayout.

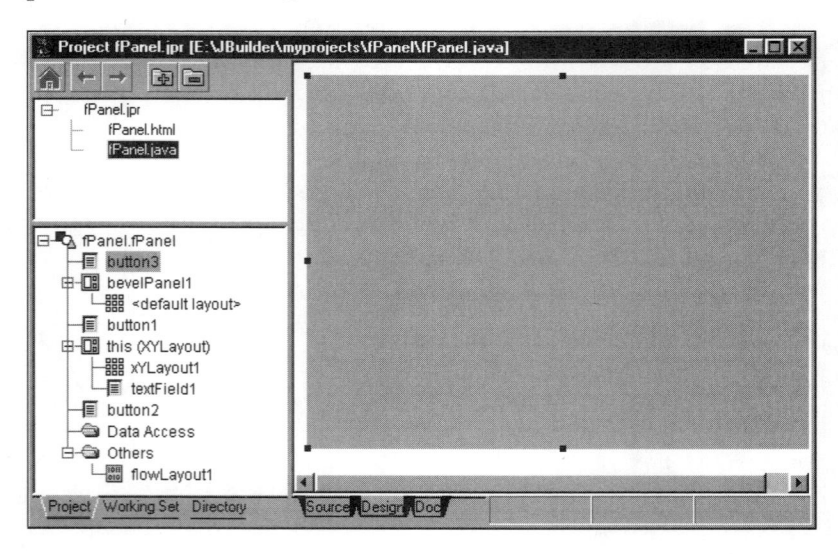

Figure 3.15 The Tree window.

Buttons and Text Fields

The complete code for this program appears in Listing 3.3.

Listing 3.3 fPanel.java

```java
//Title:
//Version:
//Copyright:
//Author:
//Company:
//Description:
//

package fPanel;
import java.lang.*;
import java.awt.*;
import java.awt.event.*;
import java.applet.*;
import borland.jbcl.control.*;
import borland.jbcl.layout.*;

public
class fPanel extends Applet {
  public XYLayout xYLayout1 = new XYLayout();
  public boolean isStandalone = false;
  BevelPanel bevelPanel1 = new BevelPanel();
  Button button1 = new Button();
  Button button2 = new Button();
  Button button3 = new Button();
  FlowLayout flowLayout1 = new FlowLayout();
  TextField textField1 = new TextField();

  //Construct the applet
  public fPanel() {

  }

  //Initialize the applet
  public void init() {
```

```
    try { jbInit(); } catch(Exception e) { e.printStackTrace(); };

}

//Component initialization
public void jbInit() throws Exception{

  xYLayout1.setWidth(400);
  xYLayout1.setHeight(300);
  bevelPanel1.setBackground(Color.black);
  bevelPanel1.setLayout(flowLayout1);
  button1.setLabel("button1");
  button1.addActionListener(new fPanel_button1_ActionAdapter(this));
  button2.setLabel("button2");
  button2.addActionListener(new fPanel_button2_ActionAdapter(this));
  button3.setLabel("button3");
  button3.addActionListener(new fPanel_button3_ActionAdapter(this));
  this.setLayout(xYLayout1);
  this.add(bevelPanel1, new XYConstraints(31, 45, 238, 35));
  bevelPanel1.add(button1, null);
  bevelPanel1.add(button2, null);
  bevelPanel1.add(button3, null);
  this.add(textField1, new XYConstraints(35, 113, 231, 31));

}

//Start the applet
public void start() {

}

//Stop the applet
public void stop() {

}

//Destroy the applet
public void destroy() {

}
```

Buttons and Text Fields

```
//Get Applet information
public String getAppletInfo() {

  return "Applet Information";

}

//Get parameter info
public String[][] getParameterInfo() {

  return null;

}

//Main method
static public void main(String[] args) {
  fPanel applet = new fPanel();
  applet.isStandalone = true;
  DecoratedFrame frame = new DecoratedFrame();
  frame.setTitle("Applet Frame");
  frame.add(applet, BorderLayout.CENTER);
  applet.init();
  applet.start();
  frame.pack();
  Dimension d = Toolkit.getDefaultToolkit().getScreenSize();
  frame.setLocation((d.width - frame.getSize().width) / 2,
(d.height - frame.getSize().height) / 2);
  frame.setVisible(true);

}

void button1_actionPerformed(java.awt.event.ActionEvent e) {

  textField1.setText("You clicked button 1.");

}

void button2_actionPerformed(java.awt.event.ActionEvent e) {

  textField1.setText("You clicked button 2.");
```

```java
  }

  void button3_actionPerformed(java.awt.event.ActionEvent e) {

    textField1.setText("You clicked button 3.");

  }
}

class fPanel_button1_ActionAdapter implements ActionListener {

  fPanel adaptee;

  fPanel_button1_ActionAdapter(fPanel adaptee) {

    this.adaptee = adaptee;

  }

  public void actionPerformed(java.awt.event.ActionEvent e) {

    adaptee.button1_actionPerformed(e);

  }

}

class fPanel_button2_ActionAdapter implements ActionListener {

  fPanel adaptee;

  fPanel_button2_ActionAdapter(fPanel adaptee) {

    this.adaptee = adaptee;

  }

  public void actionPerformed(java.awt.event.ActionEvent e) {

    adaptee.button2_actionPerformed(e);

  }

}
```

```
class fPanel_button3_ActionAdapter implements ActionListener {

  fPanel adaptee;

  fPanel_button3_ActionAdapter(fPanel adaptee) {

    this.adaptee = adaptee;

  }

  public void actionPerformed(java.awt.event.ActionEvent e) {

    adaptee.button3_actionPerformed(e);

  }

}
```

Now we've seen how to display buttons in a container class like the bevel panel, but there is another such container designed especially for buttons in JBuilder, and we'll take a look at it next.

Working with Button Bars

Much like bevel panels, button bars let you arrange controls in them, but button bars are specially designed to work with buttons.

In the next example, we'll place three buttons in a button bar:

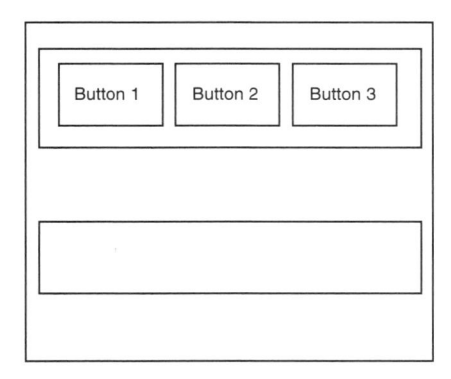

When the user clicks a button, we'll report which one was clicked:

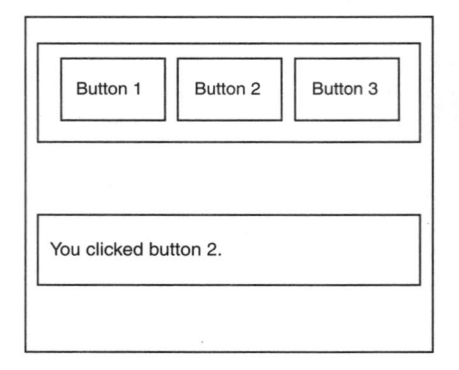

```
┌─────────────────────────────────────────┐
│  ┌────────┐  ┌────────┐  ┌────────┐    │
│  │Button 1│  │Button 2│  │Button 3│    │
│  └────────┘  └────────┘  └────────┘    │
│                                         │
│  ┌───────────────────────────────────┐ │
│  │ You clicked button 2.             │ │
│  └───────────────────────────────────┘ │
│                                         │
└─────────────────────────────────────────┘
```

Let's put this to work. Create a new applet with the name **bBar** (for button bar) and open the Designer. In the component gallery, find the button bar tool (second from the left in the Controls tab) and draw a new button bar in the applet.

The new button bar has no buttons in it. To add some, click the button bar's `labels` property in the Inspector window, and click the button with three dots that appears in the text field next to this property, opening the labels dialog box, as shown in Figure 3.16.

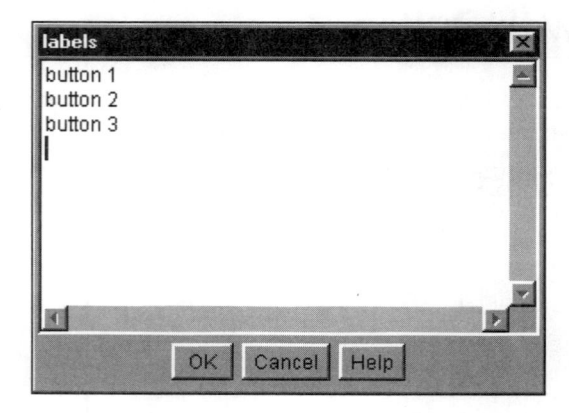

Figure 3.16 Adding buttons to a button bar.

Buttons and Text Fields

Creating Buttons in a Button Bar

To create three new buttons, we simply type in their labels, as shown in Figure 3.16, and then click the **OK** button. This adds three new buttons to the button bar as we see in the Designer, as shown in Figure 3.17. Also, add a text field to the applet, as shown in Figure 3.17.

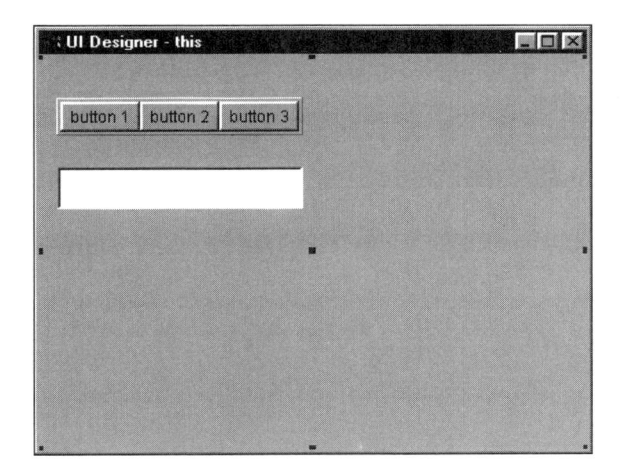

Figure 3.17 Three new buttons in the button bar.

Now we go back to the Project window to edit the code.

Handling Button-Bar Buttons in Code

We find that JBuilder has added our new button bar, buttonBar1, to the layout this way:

```
        //Component initialization
        public void jbInit() throws Exception{

          xYLayout1.setWidth(400);
          xYLayout1.setHeight(300);
  ->      buttonBar1.setLabels(new String[] { "button 1", "button 2", "button 3",
});
  ->      buttonBar1.addActionListener(new bBar_buttonBar1_ActionAdapter(this));
          this.setLayout(xYLayout1);
  ->      this.add(buttonBar1, new XYConstraints(13, 32, -1, -1));
```

Chapter 3

```
            this.add(textField1, new XYConstraints(14, 85, 141, 32));

      }
```

However, we see no mention of the individual buttons themselves. In fact, there is only an `actionPerformed` method for the button bar itself:

```
            void buttonBar1_actionPerformed(java.awt.event.ActionEvent e) {



            }
```

The reason for this is that we can determine which of the three buttons by checking the `actionCommand` data member of the `ActionEvent` object named `e` that's passed to us in this method. The `actionCommand` data member is a private data member of the `ActionEvent` class (i.e., it's defined with the `private` keyword, which means that only classes derived from `ActionEvent` have access to it), but we can still get that data member by calling the public `getActionCommand()` method. The `actionCommand` member holds the label of the button that was pressed, so we can start by checking to see if that label is *button 1*:

```
            void buttonBar1_actionPerformed(java.awt.event.ActionEvent e) {

                  if(e.getActionCommand() == "button 1"){



                  }


            }
```

If `button 1` was indeed pressed, we can notify the user of that fact with a message in the text field:

```
            void buttonBar1_actionPerformed(java.awt.event.ActionEvent e) {

                  if(e.getActionCommand() == "button 1"){

                        textField1.setText("You clicked button 1.");     <—
```

```
        }
          .
          .
          .
    }
```

We do the same for button 2 and button 3:

```
        void buttonBar1_actionPerformed(java.awt.event.ActionEvent e) {

            if(e.getActionCommand() == "button 1"){

                textField1.setText("You clicked button 1.");

            }

            if(e.getActionCommand() == "button 2"){

                textField1.setText("You clicked button 2.");

            }

            if(e.getActionCommand() == "button 3"){

                textField1.setText("You clicked button 3.");

            }

        }
```

Chapter 3

Now the applet is ready; run it now. As you can see in Figure 3.18, the button bar appears with three buttons in it. When you click one, the program reports which button was clicked. Our program is a success.

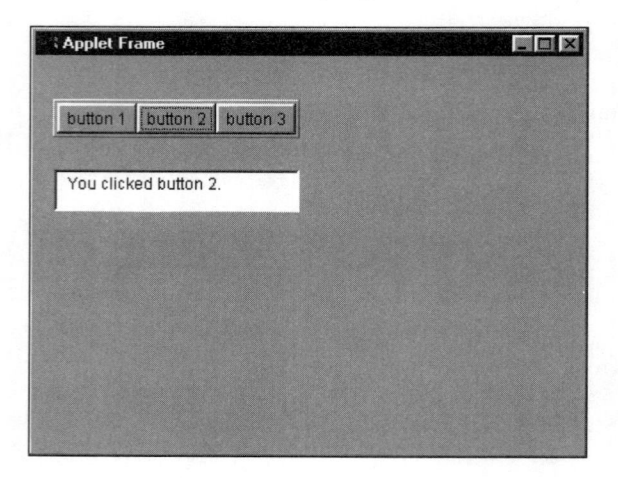

Figure 3.18 Our button bar example at work.

The complete code for this program appears in Listing 3.4.

Listing 3.4 bBar.java

```
//Title:
//Version:
//Copyright:
//Author:
//Company:
//Description:
//

package bBar;
import java.lang.*;
import java.awt.*;
import java.awt.event.*;
import java.applet.*;
import borland.jbcl.control.*;
import borland.jbcl.layout.*;
```

Buttons and Text Fields

```java
public
class bBar extends Applet {

   public XYLayout xYLayout1 = new XYLayout();
   public boolean isStandalone = false;
   ButtonBar buttonBar1 = new ButtonBar();
   TextField textField1 = new TextField();

   //Construct the applet
   public bBar() {

   }

   //Initialize the applet
   public void init() {

      try { jbInit(); } catch(Exception e) { e.printStackTrace(); };

   }

   //Component initialization
   public void jbInit() throws Exception{

      xYLayout1.setWidth(400);
      xYLayout1.setHeight(300);
      buttonBar1.setLabels(new String[] { "button 1", "button 2", "button 3", });
      buttonBar1.addActionListener(new bBar_buttonBar1_ActionAdapter(this));
      this.setLayout(xYLayout1);
      this.add(buttonBar1, new XYConstraints(13, 32, -1, -1));
      this.add(textField1, new XYConstraints(14, 85, 141, 32));

   }

   //Start the applet
   public void start() {

   }
```

Chapter 3

```java
//Stop the applet
public void stop() {

}

//Destroy the applet
public void destroy() {

}

//Get Applet information
public String getAppletInfo() {

    return "Applet Information";

}

//Get parameter info
public String[][] getParameterInfo() {

    return null;

}

//Main method
static public void main(String[] args) {

    bBar applet = new bBar();
    applet.isStandalone = true;
    DecoratedFrame frame = new DecoratedFrame();
    frame.setTitle("Applet Frame");
    frame.add(applet, BorderLayout.CENTER);
    applet.init();
    applet.start();
    frame.pack();
    Dimension d = Toolkit.getDefaultToolkit().getScreenSize();
    frame.setLocation((d.width - frame.getSize().width) / 2,
(d.height - frame.getSize().height) / 2);
    frame.setVisible(true);
```

```java
    }

    void buttonBar1_actionPerformed(java.awt.event.ActionEvent e) {

        if(e.getActionCommand() == "button 1"){

            textField1.setText("You clicked button 1.");

        }

        if(e.getActionCommand() == "button 2"){

            textField1.setText("You clicked button 2.");

        }

        if(e.getActionCommand() == "button 3"){

            textField1.setText("You clicked button 3.");

        }

    }

}

class bBar_buttonBar1_ActionAdapter implements ActionListener{

    bBar adaptee;

    bBar_buttonBar1_ActionAdapter(bBar adaptee) {

        this.adaptee = adaptee;

    }

    public void actionPerformed(java.awt.event.ActionEvent e) {

        adaptee.buttonBar1_actionPerformed(e);

    }

}
```

Chapter 3

We've come far in this chapter. We've seen how to add buttons to programs, how to use the Designer to set control properties, how to connect a button to code using the Inspector, how to use images in buttons, how to use bevel panels to arrange buttons, and now how to use button bars. We've gained a lot of JBuilder power.

In Chapter 4, we'll turn to new controls: check boxes, radio buttons, and more.

CHAPTER 4

Check Boxes and Radio Buttons

In this chapter, we're going to take a look at two new controls: check boxes and radio controls. These common controls will add a lot of power to our programs.

Check boxes are those small boxes that display a check mark when clicked, toggling on and off as the user clicks them. You can use as many check boxes as you like in a program, and click as many as you like—unlike radio buttons, check boxes are not specifically coordinated, so they operate independently. This means that some, all, or none of the check boxes in your program may be checked at a particular time.

Radio buttons are those circular controls that display a dot inside them when clicked. Unlike check boxes, radio buttons are supposed to work in groups, presenting the ability to make an exclusive choice. When you click one radio button, the others in the group lose their dots, and the one you clicked gains one. In this way, radio buttons allow the user to select only one option.

Both radio buttons and check boxes have their place and their purpose. Radio buttons present the user with options, only one of which may be chosen at a time; check boxes present the user with options, as many or as few at a time may be chosen. We'll see how to put check boxes and radio buttons together in this chapter, using their different specialties in a way that makes a program more effective. We'll also see how to make that program a Java application, not an applet.

There's a lot to cover, so let's start at once with check boxes.

Chapter 4

Using Check Boxes

In our first example, we'll display four check boxes in an applet:

```
Click a check box:
[ ] checkbox1
[ ] checkbox2
[ ] checkbox3
[ ] checkbox4
```

When the user clicks one, we'll indicate which check box they've clicked:

```
Click a check box:
[ ] checkbox1
[+] checkbox2      You clicked check box 2
[ ] checkbox3
[ ] checkbox4
```

Let's start this applet now; create it with the Applet Wizard and name it **checks**. Now select the check box tool—the fifth tool from the left when you click the AWT tab—and draw four check boxes in the applet, as shown in Figure 4.1.

In addition, we can add a prompt to our applet, encouraging the user to click a check box. To do that, use the label tool (first tool on the left in the AWT tab) to create a new label and set its text property to: *Click a check box:*.

Finally, add a text field to the applet, also shown in Figure 4.1.

Checkboxes and Radio Buttons

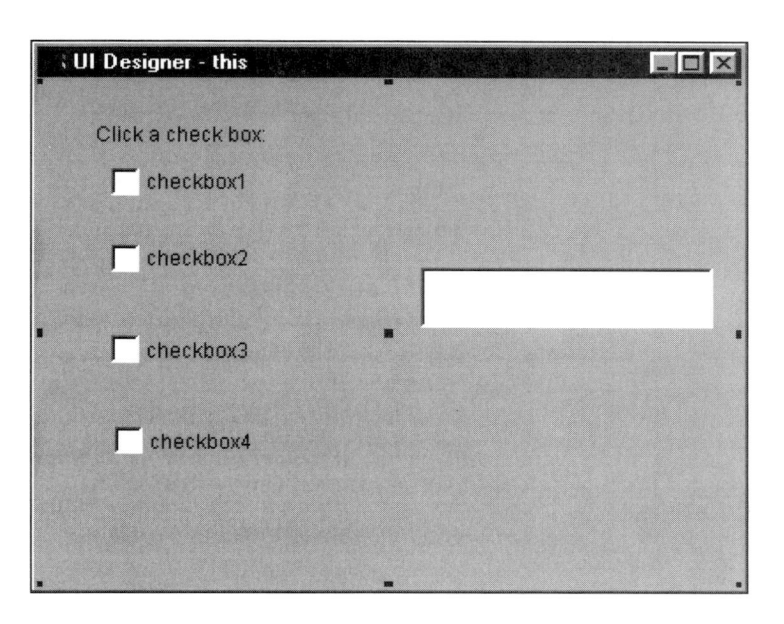

Figure 4.1 Designing the checks applet.

Connecting Check Boxes to Code

We've added our new check boxes to the applet:

```
public
class checks extends Applet {

    public XYLayout xYLayout1 = new XYLayout();
    public boolean isStandalone = false;
    Checkbox checkbox1 = new Checkbox();        <—
    Checkbox checkbox2 = new Checkbox();        <—
    Checkbox checkbox3 = new Checkbox();        <—
    Checkbox checkbox4 = new Checkbox();        <—
    TextField textField1 = new TextField();
    Label label1 = new Label();
        .
        .
        .
```

Chapter 4

The `Checkbox` class's constructors and methods appear in Table 4.1.

Table 4.1 The Checkbox Constructors and Methods

`Checkbox()`	Constructs a `Checkbox` with an empty label.
`Checkbox(String)`	Constructs a `Checkbox` with the given label.
`Checkbox(String, boolean)`	Constructs a `Checkbox` with the given label.
`Checkbox(String, boolean, CheckboxGroup)`	Constructs a `Checkbox` with the given label, set to the given state, and in the given check box group.
`Checkbox(String, CheckboxGroup, boolean)`	DEPRECATED: Replaced by `Checkbox(String, boolean, CheckboxGroup)`.
`addItemListener(ItemListener)`	Adds the given item listener to receive item events from this check box.
`addNotify()`	Creates the peer of the `Checkbox`.
`getCheckboxGroup()`	Returns the check box group.
`getLabel()`	Gets the label of the check box.
`getSelectedObjects()`	Returns the an array containing the check box label.
`getState()`	Returns the boolean state of the `Checkbox`.
`paramString()`	Returns the parameter String of this check box.
`processEvent(AWTEvent)`	Processes events on this check box.
`processItemEvent(ItemEvent)`	Processes item events occurring on this check box.
`removeItemListener(ItemListener)`	Removes the given item listener.
`setCheckboxGroup(CheckboxGroup)`	Sets the `CheckboxGroup` to the given group.
`setLabel(String)`	Sets check box's label to be the given string.
`setState(boolean)`	Sets the `Checkbox` to the specified boolean state.

The next step is to connect the check boxes to code. We do that by adding code to their `itemStateChanged` event. (Check boxes don't have an `actionPerformed` event.) Using the Inspector, add an event handler method to the `itemStateChanged` event for all three check boxes:

Checkboxes and Radio Buttons

```
void checkbox1_itemStateChanged(java.awt.event.ItemEvent e){

}

void checkbox2_itemStateChanged(java.awt.event.ItemEvent e){

}

void checkbox3_itemStateChanged(java.awt.event.ItemEvent e){

}

void checkbox4_itemStateChanged(java.awt.event.ItemEvent e) {

}
```

Now we display a message in the text field, indicating which check box the user has checked:

```
void checkbox1_itemStateChanged(java.awt.event.ItemEvent e){

  textField1.setText("You clicked check box 1.");   <—

}


void checkbox2_itemStateChanged(java.awt.event.ItemEvent e){

  textField1.setText("You clicked check box 2.");   <—
```

Chapter 4

```
  }


  void checkbox3_itemStateChanged(java.awt.event.ItemEvent e){

    textField1.setText("You clicked check box 3.");   <--

  }


  void checkbox4_itemStateChanged(java.awt.event.ItemEvent e) {

    textField1.setText("You clicked check box 4.");   <--

  }
```

That's all it takes. Run our checks applet now. Next, click a check box. When you do, the program reports which check box you clicked, as shown in Figure 4.2. The checks program is working as we designed it.

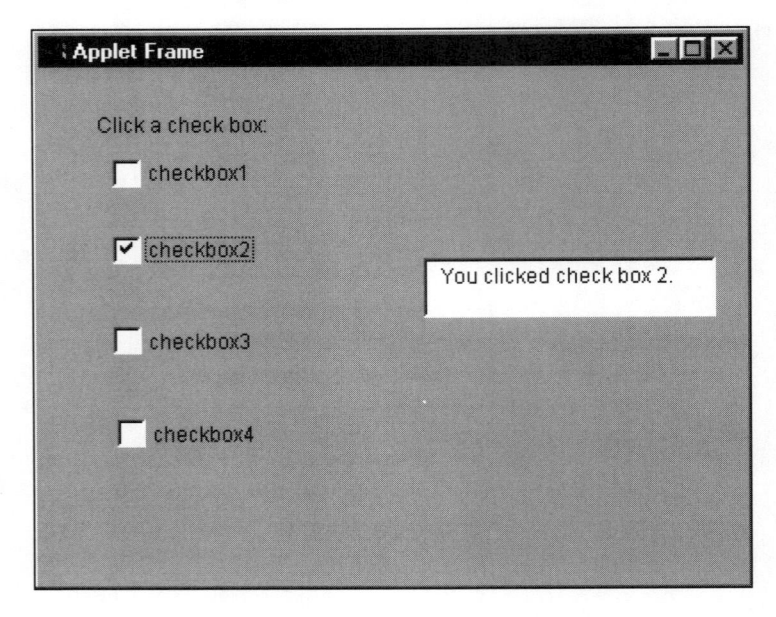

Figure 4.2 Our checks applet at work.

Checkboxes and Radio Buttons

The code for this example appears in Listing 4.1.

Listing 4.1 checks.java

```java
//Title:
//Version:
//Copyright:
//Author:
//Company:
//Description:
//

package checks;
import java.lang.*;
import java.awt.*;
import java.awt.event.*;
import java.applet.*;
import borland.jbcl.control.*;
import borland.jbcl.layout.*;

public
class checks extends Applet {

  public XYLayout xYLayout1 = new XYLayout();
  public boolean isStandalone = false;
  Checkbox checkbox1 = new Checkbox();
  Checkbox checkbox2 = new Checkbox();
  Checkbox checkbox3 = new Checkbox();
  Checkbox checkbox4 = new Checkbox();
  TextField textField1 = new TextField();
  Label label1 = new Label();

  //Construct the applet
  public checks() {

  }

  //Initialize the applet
  public void init() {

    try { jbInit(); } catch(Exception e) { e.printStackTrace(); };
```

Chapter 4

```
  }

//Component initialization
public void jbInit() throws Exception{

  xYLayout1.setWidth(400);
  xYLayout1.setHeight(300);
  checkbox1.setLabel("checkbox1");
  checkbox1.addItemListener(new checks_checkbox1_ItemAdapter(this));
  checkbox2.setLabel("checkbox2");
  checkbox2.addItemListener(new checks_checkbox2_ItemAdapter(this));
  checkbox3.setLabel("checkbox3");
  checkbox3.addItemListener(new checks_checkbox3_ItemAdapter(this));
  checkbox4.setLabel("checkbox4");
  label1.setText("Click a check box:");
  checkbox4.addItemListener(new checks_checkbox4_ItemAdapter(this));
  this.setLayout(xYLayout1);
  this.add(checkbox1, new XYConstraints(42, 46, 121, 30));
  this.add(checkbox2, new XYConstraints(42, 88, 123, 36));
  this.add(checkbox3, new XYConstraints(42, 139, 123, 41));
  this.add(checkbox4, new XYConstraints(44, 195, 124, 37));
  this.add(textField1, new XYConstraints(218, 111, 166, 35));
  this.add(label1, new XYConstraints(33, 24, 154, 18));

}

//Start the applet
public void start() {

}

//Stop the applet
public void stop() {

}

//Destroy the applet
public void destroy() {

}
```

Checkboxes and Radio Buttons

```java
//Get Applet information
public String getAppletInfo() {

   return "Applet Information";

}

//Get parameter info
public String[][] getParameterInfo() {

   return null;

}

//Main method
static public void main(String[] args) {

   checks applet = new checks();
   applet.isStandalone = true;
   DecoratedFrame frame = new DecoratedFrame();
   frame.setTitle("Applet Frame");
   frame.add(applet, BorderLayout.CENTER);
   applet.init();
   applet.start();
   frame.pack();
   Dimension d = Toolkit.getDefaultToolkit().getScreenSize();
   frame.setLocation((d.width - frame.getSize().width) / 2,
(d.height - frame.getSize().height) / 2);
   frame.setVisible(true);

}

 void checkbox1_itemStateChanged(java.awt.event.ItemEvent e){

    textField1.setText("You clicked check box 1.");

 }

 void checkbox2_itemStateChanged(java.awt.event.ItemEvent e){

    textField1.setText("You clicked check box 2.");
```

```
    }

    void checkbox3_itemStateChanged(java.awt.event.ItemEvent e){
      textField1.setText("You clicked check box 3.");
    }

    void checkbox4_itemStateChanged(java.awt.event.ItemEvent e) {
      textField1.setText("You clicked check box 4.");
    }
}

class checks_checkbox1_ItemAdapter implements ItemListener {
    checks adaptee;
    checks_checkbox1_ItemAdapter(checks adaptee) {
      this.adaptee = adaptee;
    }
    public void itemStateChanged(java.awt.event.ItemEvent e) {
      adaptee.checkbox1_itemStateChanged(e);
    }
}

class checks_checkbox2_ItemAdapter implements ItemListener {
    checks adaptee;
    checks_checkbox2_ItemAdapter(checks adaptee) {
      this.adaptee = adaptee;
    }
    public void itemStateChanged(java.awt.event.ItemEvent e) {
```

```
      adaptee.checkbox2_itemStateChanged(e);

    }

  }

  class checks_checkbox3_ItemAdapter implements ItemListener {

    checks adaptee;

    checks_checkbox3_ItemAdapter(checks adaptee) {

      this.adaptee = adaptee;

    }

    public void itemStateChanged(java.awt.event.ItemEvent e) {

      adaptee.checkbox3_itemStateChanged(e);

    }

  }

  class checks_checkbox4_ItemAdapter implements ItemListener {

    checks adaptee;

    checks_checkbox4_ItemAdapter(checks adaptee) {

      this.adaptee = adaptee;

    }

    public void itemStateChanged(java.awt.event.ItemEvent e) {

      adaptee.checkbox4_itemStateChanged(e);

    }

  }
```

Now that we've seen how to work with check boxes, let's turn to radio buttons.

Chapter 4

Handling Radio Buttons

In our radio button example, we'll see how to display four radio buttons. Such buttons usually operate as a group, so we'll enclose them in a group box this way:

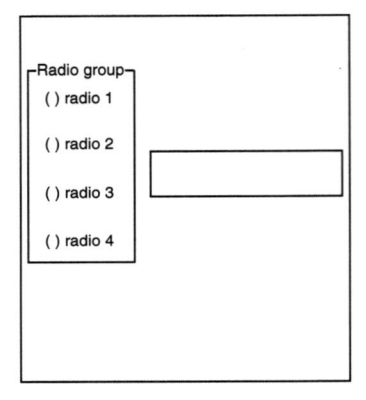

```
┌─Radio group─┐
│  ( ) radio 1 │
│              │
│  ( ) radio 2 │         ┌──────────┐
│              │         │          │
│  ( ) radio 3 │         └──────────┘
│              │
│  ( ) radio 4 │
└──────────────┘
```

When the user clicks a radio button, we can report which radio button was clicked in a text field:

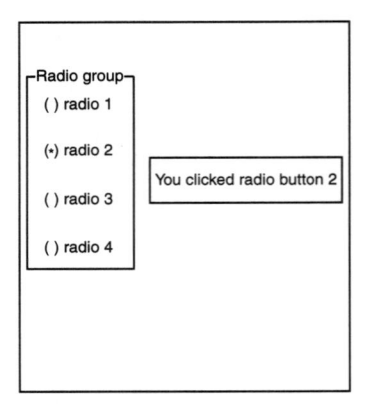

```
┌─Radio group─┐
│  ( ) radio 1 │
│              │
│  (•) radio 2 │         ┌──────────────────────────┐
│              │         │ You clicked radio button 2│
│  ( ) radio 3 │         └──────────────────────────┘
│              │
│  ( ) radio 4 │
└──────────────┘
```

Let's see this at work now. Create a new applet named **radios**, and open this applet in the Designer. Next we'll add the four radio buttons we'll need—we find there's no radio button tool for us to use. The reason is that radio buttons are actually modified check boxes. To turn check boxes into radio buttons, we have to connect them to a check box group.

Using Check Box Groups

We start the process of creating radio buttons by creating a new check box group; add this code to radios.java now:

```
public
class radios extends Applet {

    public XYLayout xYLayout1 = new XYLayout();
    public boolean isStandalone = false;
    CheckboxGroup checkboxgroup1 = new CheckboxGroup();   <-
        .
        .
        .
```

Now turn to the JBuilder designer and add a Group Box. You'll find the group box tool by clicking the **Containers** tab in JBuilder; it's the second tool from the left. Next, draw a new group box in the applet and set its label property to *Radio group*, as shown in Figure 4.3. The group box appears as a box with a title.

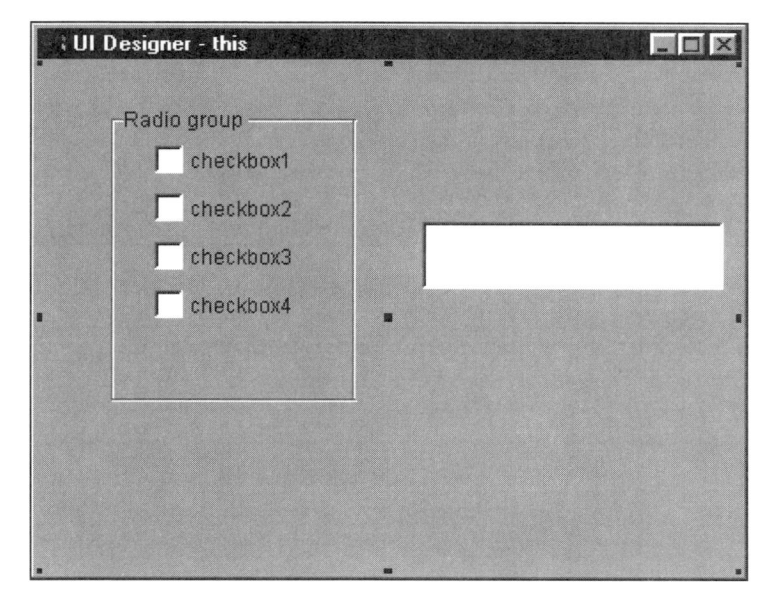

Figure 4.3 Designing the radios applet.

Chapter 4

Now add four check boxes to the group box by drawing them in the group box, as shown in Figure 4.3. The group box has its own layout, so it arranges the check boxes as shown. Also add a text field, (see Figure 4.3); we'll use this text field to report the user's actions.

Next, we will turn the check boxes into radio buttons. To do that, simply set each check box's checkboxGroup property to checkboxgroup1. This turns the check boxes into radio buttons. This is how we group radio buttons together in code—by making them part of the same check box group. Now change the label of each radio button to radio 1, radio 2, and so on, as shown in Figure 4.4.

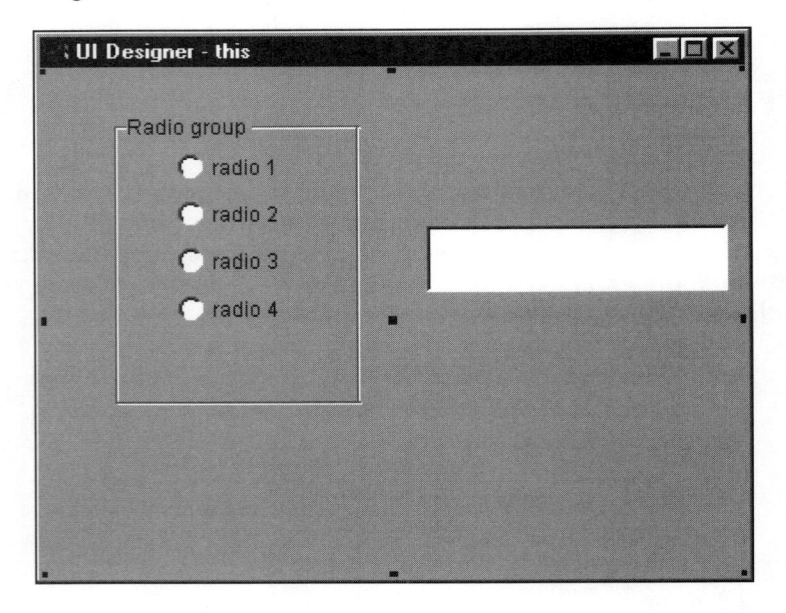

Figure 4.4 Creating radio buttons.

Finally, connect an event handler to each radio button's itemStateChanged event, like this:

```
void checkbox1_itemStateChanged(java.awt.event.ItemEvent e) {


}



void checkbox2_itemStateChanged(java.awt.event.ItemEvent e) {
```

Checkboxes and Radio Buttons

```
        }


    void checkbox3_itemStateChanged(java.awt.event.ItemEvent e) {


        }


    void checkbox4_itemStateChanged(java.awt.event.ItemEvent e) {


        }
```

Finally, we just report which item was clicked this way:

```
    void checkbox1_itemStateChanged(java.awt.event.ItemEvent e) {

        textField1.setText("You clicked radio button 1.");      <--

        }


    void checkbox2_itemStateChanged(java.awt.event.ItemEvent e) {

        textField1.setText("You clicked radio button 2.");      <--

        }


    void checkbox3_itemStateChanged(java.awt.event.ItemEvent e) {

        textField1.setText("You clicked radio button 3.");      <--
```

Chapter 4

```
    }

    void checkbox4_itemStateChanged(java.awt.event.ItemEvent e) {

        textField1.setText("You clicked radio button 4.");    <—

    }
```

The program is complete. Run it now. When you click a radio button, the program reports which one you chose, as shown in Figure 4.5. When you click another radio button, the first one is deselected and the new radio button is selected. The radios applet is a success.

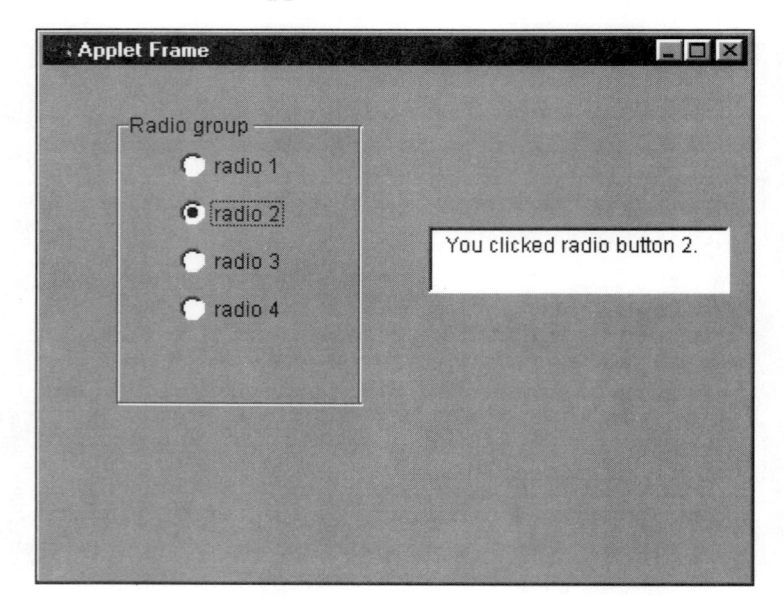

Figure 4.5 Our radios applet at work.

The code for this applet appears in Listing 4.2.

Checkboxes and Radio Buttons

Listing 4.2 radios.java

```java
//Title:
//Version:
//Copyright:
//Author:
//Company:
//Description:
//

package radios;
import java.lang.*;
import java.awt.*;
import java.awt.event.*;
import java.applet.*;
import borland.jbcl.control.*;
import borland.jbcl.layout.*;

public
class radios extends Applet {

  public XYLayout xYLayout1 = new XYLayout();
  public boolean isStandalone = false;
  CheckboxGroup checkboxgroup1 = new CheckboxGroup();
  Checkbox checkbox1 = new Checkbox("radio 1", checkboxgroup1, false);
  Checkbox checkbox2 = new Checkbox("radio 2", checkboxgroup1, false);
  Checkbox checkbox3 = new Checkbox("radio 3", checkboxgroup1, false);
  Checkbox checkbox4 = new Checkbox("radio 4", checkboxgroup1, false);
  GroupBox groupBox1 = new GroupBox();
  TextField textField1 = new TextField();

  //Construct the applet
  public radios() {
```

Chapter 4

```java
}

//Initialize the applet
public void init() {

  try { jbInit(); } catch(Exception e) { e.printStackTrace(); };

}

//Component initialization
public void jbInit() throws Exception{

  xYLayout1.setWidth(400);
  xYLayout1.setHeight(300);
  checkbox4.addItemListener(new radios_checkbox4_ItemAdapter(this));
  checkbox3.addItemListener(new radios_checkbox3_ItemAdapter(this));
  checkbox2.addItemListener(new radios_checkbox2_ItemAdapter(this));
  checkbox1.addItemListener(new radios_checkbox1_ItemAdapter(this));
  //checkbox1.setLabel("checkbox1");
  groupBox1.setLabel("Radio group ");
  //checkbox4.setLabel("checkbox3");
  //checkbox2.setLabel("checkbox2");
  this.setLayout(xYLayout1);
  this.add(groupBox1, new XYConstraints(35, 27, 152, 178));
  groupBox1.add(checkbox1, null);
  groupBox1.add(checkbox2, null);
  groupBox1.add(checkbox3, null);
  groupBox1.add(checkbox4, null);
  this.add(textField1, new XYConstraints(219, 94, 171, 39));

}

//Start the applet
public void start() {

}

//Stop the applet
public void stop() {
```

Checkboxes and Radio Buttons

```java
    }

    //Destroy the applet
    public void destroy() {

    }

    //Get Applet information
    public String getAppletInfo() {

        return "Applet Information";

    }

    //Get parameter info
    public String[][] getParameterInfo() {

        return null;

    }

    //Main method
    static public void main(String[] args) {

        radios applet = new radios();
        applet.isStandalone = true;
        DecoratedFrame frame = new DecoratedFrame();
        frame.setTitle("Applet Frame");
        frame.add(applet, BorderLayout.CENTER);
        applet.init();
        applet.start();
        frame.pack();
        Dimension d = Toolkit.getDefaultToolkit().getScreenSize();
        frame.setLocation((d.width - frame.getSize().width) / 2,
(d.height - frame.getSize().height) / 2);
        frame.setVisible(true);

    }
```

Chapter 4

```java
void checkbox1_itemStateChanged(java.awt.event.ItemEvent e) {

  textField1.setText("You clicked radio button 1.");

}

void checkbox2_itemStateChanged(java.awt.event.ItemEvent e) {

  textField1.setText("You clicked radio button 2.");

}

void checkbox3_itemStateChanged(java.awt.event.ItemEvent e) {

  textField1.setText("You clicked radio button 3.");

}

void checkbox4_itemStateChanged(java.awt.event.ItemEvent e) {

    textField1.setText("You clicked radio button 4.");

  }

}

class radios_checkbox1_ItemAdapter implements ItemListener {

  radios adaptee;

  radios_checkbox1_ItemAdapter(radios adaptee) {

    this.adaptee = adaptee;

  }

  public void itemStateChanged(java.awt.event.ItemEvent e) {

    adaptee.checkbox1_itemStateChanged(e);

  }

}
```

Checkboxes and Radio Buttons

```java
class radios_checkbox2_ItemAdapter implements ItemListener {

  radios adaptee;

  radios_checkbox2_ItemAdapter(radios adaptee) {

    this.adaptee = adaptee;

  }

  public void itemStateChanged(java.awt.event.ItemEvent e) {

    adaptee.checkbox2_itemStateChanged(e);

  }

}

class radios_checkbox3_ItemAdapter implements ItemListener {

  radios adaptee;

  radios_checkbox3_ItemAdapter(radios adaptee) {

    this.adaptee = adaptee;

  }

  public void itemStateChanged(java.awt.event.ItemEvent e) {

    adaptee.checkbox3_itemStateChanged(e);

  }

}

class radios_checkbox4_ItemAdapter implements ItemListener {

  radios adaptee;

  radios_checkbox4_ItemAdapter(radios adaptee) {

    this.adaptee = adaptee;
```

Chapter 4

```
    }

    public void itemStateChanged(java.awt.event.ItemEvent e) {

      adaptee.checkbox4_itemStateChanged(e);

    }

 }
```

We've gotten a good introduction to both radio buttons and check boxes. It's time to see how they work together.

Putting Check Boxes and Radio Buttons Together

In the next example, we will put radio buttons and check boxes together in one program. In this case, we'll set up an applet that allows the user to select various package tours:

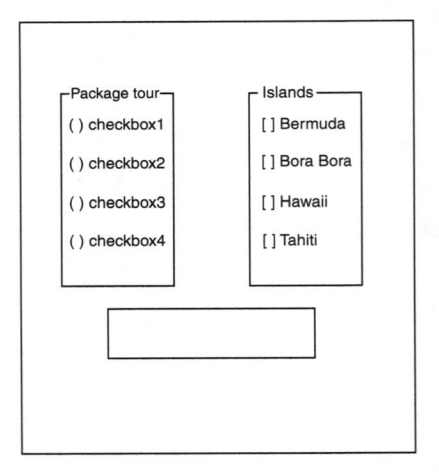

```
┌─────────────────────────────────────────────┐
│  ┌─Package tour─┐   ┌─ Islands ──┐          │
│  │              │   │            │          │
│  │ ( ) checkbox1│   │ [ ] Bermuda│          │
│  │              │   │            │          │
│  │ ( ) checkbox2│   │ [ ] Bora Bora          │
│  │              │   │            │          │
│  │ ( ) checkbox3│   │ [ ] Hawaii │          │
│  │              │   │            │          │
│  │ ( ) checkbox4│   │ [ ] Tahiti │          │
│  └──────────────┘   └────────────┘          │
│                                             │
│         ┌─────────────────────┐             │
│         │                     │             │
│         └─────────────────────┘             │
└─────────────────────────────────────────────┘
```

When the user clicks a radio button, we'll indicate which islands are visited in the tour by setting check marks in check boxes, and we'll indicate the tour package's price in a text field:

Checkboxes and Radio Buttons

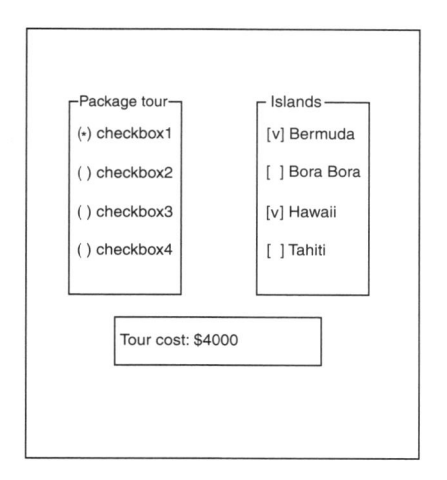

```
┌─Package tour─┐  ┌─Islands────┐
│ (•) checkbox1│  │ [v] Bermuda│
│ ( ) checkbox2│  │ [ ] Bora Bora│
│ ( ) checkbox3│  │ [v] Hawaii │
│ ( ) checkbox4│  │ [ ] Tahiti │
└──────────────┘  └────────────┘

   ┌─────────────────┐
   │ Tour cost: $4000│
   └─────────────────┘
```

When the user clicks another radio button, we'll display the new tour's islands and price:

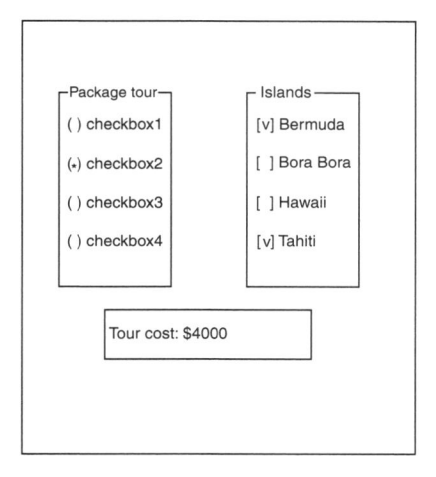

```
┌─Package tour─┐  ┌─Islands────┐
│ ( ) checkbox1│  │ [v] Bermuda│
│ (•) checkbox2│  │ [ ] Bora Bora│
│ ( ) checkbox3│  │ [ ] Hawaii │
│ ( ) checkbox4│  │ [v] Tahiti │
└──────────────┘  └────────────┘

   ┌─────────────────┐
   │ Tour cost: $4000│
   └─────────────────┘
```

Let's see this at work—create a new applet now named **retailer**, and add two group boxes: Tour package and Islands, as shown in Figure 4.6.

Chapter 4

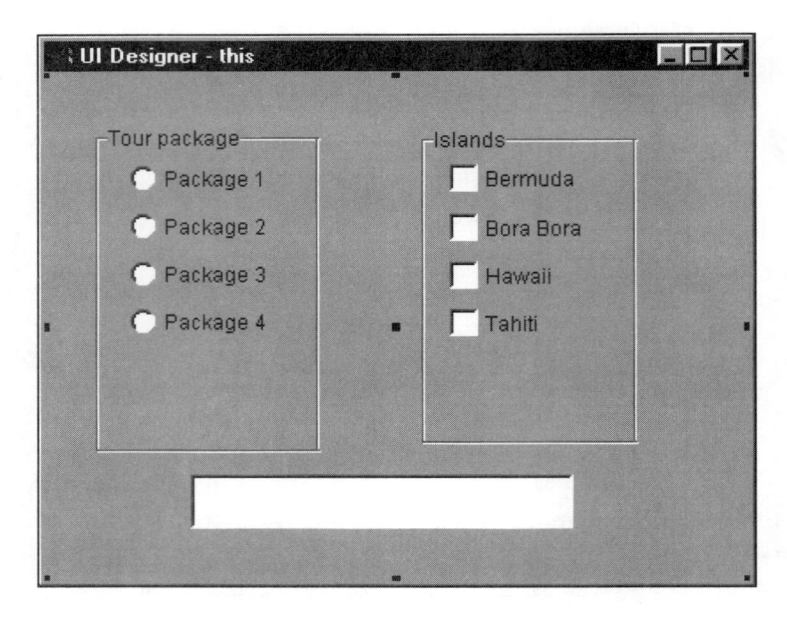

Figure 4.6 Designing the retailer program.

In addition, we add the four radio buttons and the four check boxes we'll need to the program. Add a new check box group to the program for the radio buttons:

```
public
class retailer extends Applet {
    public XYLayout xYLayout1 = new XYLayout();
    public boolean isStandalone = false;
    CheckboxGroup checkboxgroup1 = new CheckboxGroup(); <—
        .
        .
        .
```

Now create the new buttons, labeling them as shown in Figure 4.6. Also, add a text field, also shown in Figure 4.6.

This creates the following code in the applet, setting up our new controls:

```
public
class retailer extends Applet {
```

Checkboxes and Radio Buttons

```
  public XYLayout xYLayout1 = new XYLayout();
  public boolean isStandalone = false;
  CheckboxGroup checkboxgroup1 = new CheckboxGroup();
  GroupBox groupBox1 = new GroupBox();
  GroupBox groupBox2 = new GroupBox();
  Checkbox checkbox1 = new Checkbox("Package 1",
checkboxgroup1, false);
  Checkbox checkbox2 = new Checkbox("Package 2",
checkboxgroup1, false);
  Checkbox checkbox3 = new Checkbox("Package 3",
checkboxgroup1, false);
  Checkbox checkbox4 = new Checkbox("Package 4",
checkboxgroup1, false);
  Checkbox checkbox5 = new Checkbox();
  Checkbox checkbox6 = new Checkbox();
  Checkbox checkbox7 = new Checkbox();
  Checkbox checkbox8 = new Checkbox();
  TextField textField1 = new TextField();
  XYLayout xYLayout2 = new XYLayout();
    .
    .
    .
```

Next, add an `itemStateChanged` event handler to each radio button, like this example using radio button 1:

```
  void checkbox1_itemStateChanged(java.awt.event.ItemEvent e) {


  }
```

In this case, we want to set the checks in the check boxes to match the islands we visit on this tour (for tour package 1, that's the first and third islands, Bermuda and Hawaii). We do that with the check box's `setState()` method, passing a value of `true` to set the check mark and `false` to clear the check box:

```
  void checkbox1_itemStateChanged(java.awt.event.ItemEvent e) {

    checkbox5.setState(true);           <—
```

Chapter 4

```
    checkbox6.setState(false);      <—
    checkbox7.setState(true);       <—
    checkbox8.setState(false);      <—
        .
        .
        .
}
```

In addition, we place the tour cost in the text field:

```
void checkbox1_itemStateChanged(java.awt.event.ItemEvent e) {

    checkbox5.setState(true);
    checkbox6.setState(false);
    checkbox7.setState(true);
    checkbox8.setState(false);
    textField1.setText("Tour cost: $4000");     <—

}
```

Now we're done with the first radio button, and we can add similar code for the other radio buttons, setting the check boxes as appropriate:

```
void checkbox2_itemStateChanged(java.awt.event.ItemEvent e) {

    checkbox5.setState(false);
    checkbox6.setState(true);
    checkbox7.setState(false);
    checkbox8.setState(true);
    textField1.setText("Tour cost: $4000");

}

void checkbox3_itemStateChanged(java.awt.event.ItemEvent e) {

    checkbox5.setState(true);
    checkbox6.setState(false);
    checkbox7.setState(true);
```

```
        checkbox8.setState(true);
        textField1.setText("Tour cost: $6000");

    }

    void checkbox4_itemStateChanged(java.awt.event.ItemEvent e) {

        checkbox5.setState(true);
        checkbox6.setState(true);
        checkbox7.setState(true);
        checkbox8.setState(true);
        textField1.setText("Tour cost: $8000");

    }
```

Run the applet now. When you click a radio button, the program sets the corresponding check boxes, as shown in Figure 4.7. Our retailer program is successful—we're using both check boxes and radio buttons!

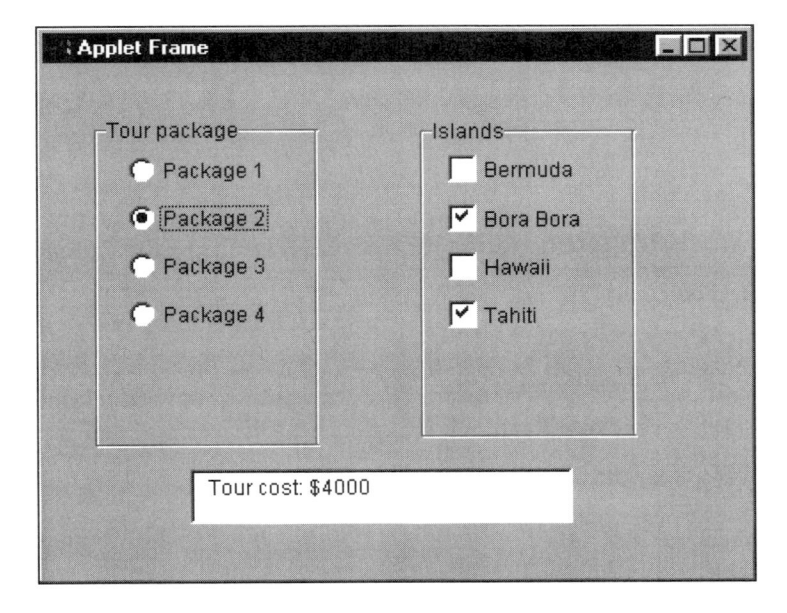

Figure 4.7 Our retailer program at work.

The listing for this program appears in Listing 4.3.

Chapter 4

Listing 4.3 retailer.java

```java
//Title:
//Version:
//Copyright:
//Author:
//Company:
//Description:
//

package retailer;
import java.lang.*;
import java.awt.*;
import java.awt.event.*;
import java.applet.*;
import borland.jbcl.control.*;
import borland.jbcl.layout.*;

public
class retailer extends Applet {
  public XYLayout xYLayout1 = new XYLayout();
  public boolean isStandalone = false;
  CheckboxGroup checkboxgroup1 = new CheckboxGroup();
  GroupBox groupBox1 = new GroupBox();
  GroupBox groupBox2 = new GroupBox();
  Checkbox checkbox1 = new Checkbox("Package 1",
checkboxgroup1, false);
  Checkbox checkbox2 = new Checkbox("Package 2",
checkboxgroup1, false);
  Checkbox checkbox3 = new Checkbox("Package 3",
checkboxgroup1, false);
  Checkbox checkbox4 = new Checkbox("Package 4",
checkboxgroup1, false);
  Checkbox checkbox5 = new Checkbox();
  Checkbox checkbox6 = new Checkbox();
  Checkbox checkbox7 = new Checkbox();
  Checkbox checkbox8 = new Checkbox();
  TextField textField1 = new TextField();
```

Checkboxes and Radio Buttons

```java
    XYLayout xYLayout2 = new XYLayout();

    //Construct the applet
    public retailer() {

    }

    //Initialize the applet
    public void init() {

      try { jbInit(); } catch(Exception e) { e.printStackTrace(); };

    }

    //Component initialization
    public void jbInit() throws Exception{

      xYLayout1.setWidth(400);
      xYLayout1.setHeight(300);
      groupBox1.setLabel("Tour package");
      groupBox2.setLayout(xYLayout2);
      groupBox2.setLabel("Islands");
      checkbox1.setLabel("Package 1");
      checkbox1.addItemListener(new
retailer_checkbox1_ItemAdapter(this));
      checkbox2.setLabel("Package 2");
      checkbox2.addItemListener(new
retailer_checkbox2_ItemAdapter(this));
      checkbox3.setLabel("Package 3");
      checkbox3.addItemListener(new
retailer_checkbox3_ItemAdapter(this));
      checkbox4.setLabel("Package 4");
      checkbox4.addItemListener(new
retailer_checkbox4_ItemAdapter(this));
      checkbox5.setLabel("Bermuda");
      checkbox6.setLabel("Bora Bora");
      checkbox7.setLabel("Hawaii");
      checkbox8.setLabel("Tahiti");
      this.setLayout(xYLayout1);
```

```java
        this.add(groupBox1, new XYConstraints(22, 31, 140, 199));
        groupBox1.add(checkbox1, null);
        groupBox1.add(checkbox2, null);
        groupBox1.add(checkbox3, null);
        groupBox1.add(checkbox4, null);
        this.add(groupBox2, new XYConstraints(207, 32, 135, 193));
        groupBox2.add(checkbox6, new XYConstraints(8, 33, -1, -1));
        groupBox2.add(checkbox7, new XYConstraints(8, 61, -1, -1));
        groupBox2.add(checkbox8, new XYConstraints(8, 89, -1, -1));
        groupBox2.add(checkbox5, new XYConstraints(8, 4, -1, -1));
        this.add(textField1, new XYConstraints(83, 237, 217, 32));

    }

    //Start the applet
    public void start() {

    }

    //Stop the applet
    public void stop() {

    }

    //Destroy the applet
    public void destroy() {

    }

    //Get Applet information
    public String getAppletInfo() {

        return "Applet Information";

    }

    //Get parameter info
    public String[][] getParameterInfo() {
```

Checkboxes and Radio Buttons

```java
      return null;

  }

  //Main method
  static public void main(String[] args) {
    retailer applet = new retailer();
    applet.isStandalone = true;
    DecoratedFrame frame = new DecoratedFrame();
    frame.setTitle("Applet Frame");
    frame.add(applet, BorderLayout.CENTER);
    applet.init();
    applet.start();
    frame.pack();
    Dimension d = Toolkit.getDefaultToolkit().getScreenSize();
    frame.setLocation((d.width - frame.getSize().width) / 2,
(d.height - frame.getSize().height) / 2);
    frame.setVisible(true);
  }

  void checkbox1_itemStateChanged(java.awt.event.ItemEvent e) {

    checkbox5.setState(true);
    checkbox6.setState(false);
    checkbox7.setState(true);
    checkbox8.setState(false);
    textField1.setText("Tour cost: $4000");

  }

  void checkbox2_itemStateChanged(java.awt.event.ItemEvent e) {

    checkbox5.setState(false);
    checkbox6.setState(true);
    checkbox7.setState(false);
    checkbox8.setState(true);
    textField1.setText("Tour cost: $4000");

  }
```

Chapter 4

```java
void checkbox3_itemStateChanged(java.awt.event.ItemEvent e) {

  checkbox5.setState(true);
  checkbox6.setState(false);
  checkbox7.setState(true);
  checkbox8.setState(true);
  textField1.setText("Tour cost: $6000");

}

void checkbox4_itemStateChanged(java.awt.event.ItemEvent e) {

  checkbox5.setState(true);
  checkbox6.setState(true);
  checkbox7.setState(true);
  checkbox8.setState(true);
  textField1.setText("Tour cost: $8000");

}

}

class retailer_checkbox1_ItemAdapter implements ItemListener {

  retailer adaptee;

  retailer_checkbox1_ItemAdapter(retailer adaptee) {

    this.adaptee = adaptee;

  }

  public void itemStateChanged(java.awt.event.ItemEvent e) {

    adaptee.checkbox1_itemStateChanged(e);

  }

}

class retailer_checkbox2_ItemAdapter implements ItemListener {
```

Checkboxes and Radio Buttons

```java
  retailer adaptee;

  retailer_checkbox2_ItemAdapter(retailer adaptee) {

    this.adaptee = adaptee;

  }

  public void itemStateChanged(java.awt.event.ItemEvent e) {

    adaptee.checkbox2_itemStateChanged(e);

  }

}

class retailer_checkbox3_ItemAdapter implements ItemListener {

  retailer adaptee;

  retailer_checkbox3_ItemAdapter(retailer adaptee) {

    this.adaptee = adaptee;

  }

  public void itemStateChanged(java.awt.event.ItemEvent e) {

    adaptee.checkbox3_itemStateChanged(e);

  }

}

class retailer_checkbox4_ItemAdapter implements ItemListener {

  retailer adaptee;

  retailer_checkbox4_ItemAdapter(retailer adaptee) {

    this.adaptee = adaptee;

  }
```

Chapter 4

```
public void itemStateChanged(java.awt.event.ItemEvent e) {

  adaptee.checkbox4_itemStateChanged(e);

}

}
```

Next, we'll elaborate the retailer program into a new version called retailer2 to give us more skills. This new program will be the same as retailer, except that it will be a standalone application instead of an applet. In addition, we will allow the user to click the check boxes as they like so that we can see how to read check box's state in addition to just setting that state.

Retailer2

This next program will be a stand-alone application, not an applet, so click the **Application Wizard** item in the JBuilder Wizard menu now. This opens the Application Wizard, as shown in Figure 4.8. Place the text **retailer2** in the Package and Class boxes in the Application Wizard. Then click the **Finish** button to create the new application.

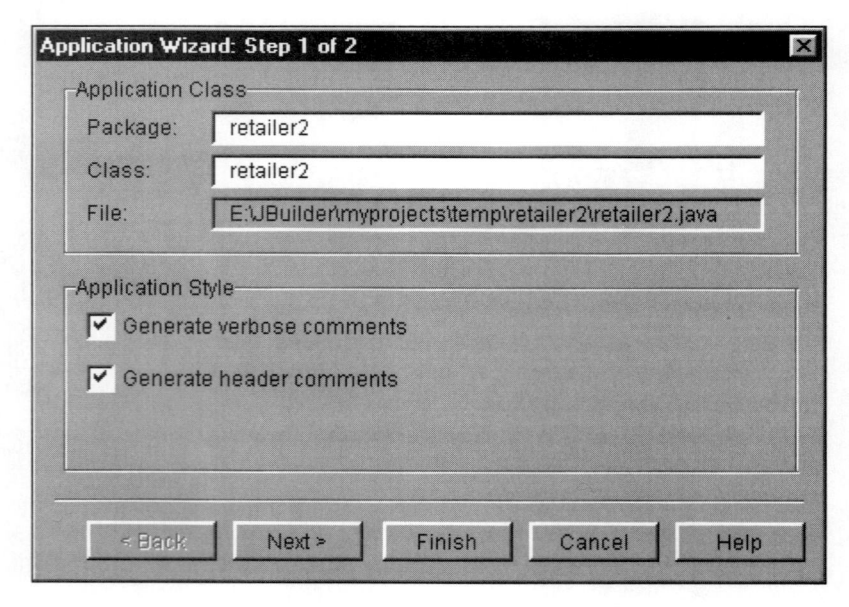

Figure 4.8 Designing the retailer2 application.

Checkboxes and Radio Buttons

We've created two new files, **retailer2.java** and **Frame1.java**. Frame1.java holds the definition of our new application's window, and we'll see how windows work later in this book. The code in retailer2.java is run first when the application starts, and its main job is to place a window of the Frame1 class on the screen:

```
//Title:
//Version:
//Copyright:
//Author:
//Company:
//Description:
//

package retailer2;
import java.lang.*;

public
class retailer2 {
  //Construct the application
  public retailer2() {

    Frame1 frame = new Frame1();          <--
    frame.setVisible(true);               <--

  }

  //Main method
  static public void main(String[] args) {

    new retailer2();

  }

}
```

The real action in our new application takes place in the Frame1 object, which is the window for our application. The Application Wizard has already placed code in the Frame1 class' `jbInit()` method to set up a menu, tool bar, and status bar in our application:

Chapter 4

```java
public void jbInit() throws Exception{

    this.setLayout(borderLayout1);
    this.setTitle("Frame Title");

    //Add menu bar
    menuFile.setLabel("File");
    menuFileExit.setLabel("Exit");
    menuFileExit.addActionListener(new
Frame1_menuFileExit_ActionAdapter(this));
    menuFile.add(menuFileExit);
    menuHelp.setLabel("Help");
    menuHelpAbout.setLabel("About");
    menuHelpAbout.addActionListener(new
Frame1_menuHelpAbout_ActionAdapter(this));
    menuHelp.add(menuHelpAbout);
    menuBar1.add(menuFile);
    menuBar1.add(menuHelp);
    this.setMenuBar(menuBar1);

    //Add tool bar
    buttonBar.setButtonType(ButtonBar.IMAGE_ONLY);
    buttonBar.setLabels(new String[] {"Open", "Close", "Help"});
    buttonBar.setImageDirectory("borland/jbcl/control/images");
    buttonBar.setImageNames(new String[] {"openfile.gif",
"closefile.gif", "help.gif"});
    this.add(buttonBar, BorderLayout.NORTH);

    //Add status bar
    statusBar.setText("");
    groupBox1.setLabel("Package tour");
    groupBox2.setLayout(xYLayout2);
    groupBox2.setLabel("Islands");
    checkbox1.setLabel("Package 1");
    checkbox1.addItemListener(new
Frame1_checkbox1_ItemAdapter(this));
    checkbox2.setLabel("Package 2");
    checkbox2.addItemListener(new
Frame1_checkbox2_ItemAdapter(this));
    checkbox3.setLabel("Package 3");
```

Checkboxes and Radio Buttons

```
    checkbox3.addItemListener(new
Frame1_checkbox3_ItemAdapter(this));
    checkbox4.setLabel("Package 4");
    checkbox4.addItemListener(new
Frame1_checkbox4_ItemAdapter(this));
    checkbox5.setLabel("Bermuda");
    checkbox5.addItemListener(new
Frame1_checkbox5_ItemAdapter(this));
    checkbox6.setLabel("Bora Bora");
    checkbox6.addItemListener(new
Frame1_checkbox6_ItemAdapter(this));
    checkbox7.setLabel("Hawaii");
    checkbox7.addItemListener(new
Frame1_checkbox7_ItemAdapter(this));
    checkbox8.setLabel("Tahiti");
    checkbox8.addItemListener(new
Frame1_checkbox8_ItemAdapter(this));
    this.add(statusBar, BorderLayout.SOUTH);

    //Add center panel
    panel1.setLayout(xYLayout1);
    xYLayout1.setWidth(400);
    xYLayout1.setHeight(300);
    this.add(panel1, BorderLayout.CENTER);
    panel1.add(groupBox1, new XYConstraints(22, 25, 137,
202));
    groupBox1.add(checkbox1, null);
    groupBox1.add(checkbox2, null);
    groupBox1.add(checkbox3, null);
    groupBox1.add(checkbox4, null);
    panel1.add(groupBox2, new XYConstraints(200, 27, 131,
198));
    groupBox2.add(checkbox5, new XYConstraints(4, 6, -1, -1));
    groupBox2.add(checkbox6, new XYConstraints(6, 34, -1, -1));
    groupBox2.add(checkbox7, new XYConstraints(6, 61, -1, -1));
    groupBox2.add(checkbox8, new XYConstraints(6, 89, -1, -1));
    panel1.add(textField1, new XYConstraints(103, 237, 184,
42));
    this.pack();
```

Chapter 4

```
    //Center the window
    Dimension dimScreen =
Toolkit.getDefaultToolkit().getScreenSize();
    Dimension dimFrame = this.getPreferredSize();
    if(dimFrame.height > dimScreen.height) dimFrame.height =
dimScreen.height;
    if(dimFrame.width > dimScreen.width) dimFrame.width =
dimScreen.width;
    this.setBounds( (dimScreen.width - dimFrame.width) / 2,
(dimScreen.height - dimFrame.height) / 2, dimFrame.width,
dimFrame.height);
  }
```

When we run our application, we'll see our new menu system, tool bar, and status bar, ready to use.

Customizing the retailer2 Application

Let's customize the retailer2 application now. Find Frame1.java in the JBuilder Project window, and open that file in the JBuilder Designer. Next, add the controls and containers that we used in the retailer applet: two group boxes, four radio buttons (we will add the check box group checkboxgroup1 for the radio buttons, just as we did before), four check boxes, and a text field.

Next, connect an `itemStateChanged` method to each of the four radio buttons, just as in the retailer applet. In retailer2, we will improve on retailer by allowing the user to click the check boxes as well as the radio buttons, so add `itemStateChanged` handlers to the check boxes as well as the radio buttons.

We'll have to set up some way of setting the price in the text field to match the check boxes the user checked. To do that, we'll simply add $2000 for each check box clicked. Since we'll set the price each time the user clicks a check box or radio button, we should set up a new method we can call easily to set the price depending on which check boxes have been checked. We'll call that method `setPrice()`—add this code to Frame1.java now:

```
    void setPrice(){
         .
         .
         .
    }
```

Checkboxes and Radio Buttons

Next, we have to check the check boxes, starting with the top check box (checkbox5). If that check box is checked, which we check with the `getCheck()` method, we add $2000 to the running total price. This is stored in the integer named `price`:

```
void setPrice(){
    int price = 0;                    <-

    if(checkbox5.getState()){         <-
        price += 2000;                <-
    }
    .
    .
    .
```

Then we examine the other check boxes as well, adding $2000 to the total price for every check box that's checked:

```
void setPrice(){
    int price = 0;

    if(checkbox5.getState()){
        price += 2000;
    }

    if(checkbox6.getState()){         <-
        price += 2000;
    }

    if(checkbox7.getState()){         <-
        price += 2000;
    }

    if(checkbox8.getState()){         <-
        price += 2000;
    }
    .
    .
```

Chapter 4

```
        }

    }
```

Finally, we place the new price in the text field. We can convert the value in the integer price to a string with the Java String method valueOf():

```
    void setPrice(){
        String outString = "Your price: $ ";    <-
        int price = 0;

        if(checkbox5.getState()){
          price += 2000;
        }

        if(checkbox6.getState()){
          price += 2000;
        }

        if(checkbox7.getState()){
          price += 2000;
        }

        if(checkbox8.getState()){
          price += 2000;
        }

        textField1.setText(outString + String.valueOf(price));    <-
    }
}
```

That completes the setPrice() method. Now when the user clicks radio button 1, we set the check boxes to match and call setPrice() to place the total price in the text field:

```
    void checkbox1_itemStateChanged(java.awt.event.ItemEvent e) {

        checkbox5.setState(true);            <-
```

```
checkbox6.setState(false);     <--
checkbox7.setState(true);      <--
checkbox8.setState(false);     <--
setPrice();                    <--
}
```

And we do the same for the other radio buttons as well:

```
void checkbox2_itemStateChanged(java.awt.event.ItemEvent e) {

    checkbox5.setState(false);
    checkbox6.setState(true);
    checkbox7.setState(false);
    checkbox8.setState(true);
    setPrice();

}

void checkbox3_itemStateChanged(java.awt.event.ItemEvent e) {

    checkbox5.setState(true);
    checkbox6.setState(true);
    checkbox7.setState(false);
    checkbox8.setState(true);
    setPrice();

}

void checkbox4_itemStateChanged(java.awt.event.ItemEvent e) {

    checkbox5.setState(true);
    checkbox6.setState(true);
    checkbox7.setState(true);
    checkbox8.setState(true);
    setPrice();

}
```

Chapter 4

We also want to let the user click individual check boxes, customizing each tour package as they like, so we add a call to the `setPrice()` method each time the user clicks a check box:

```
void checkbox5_itemStateChanged(java.awt.event.ItemEvent e) {

  setPrice();    <—
}

void checkbox6_itemStateChanged(java.awt.event.ItemEvent e) {

  setPrice();    <—

}

void checkbox7_itemStateChanged(java.awt.event.ItemEvent e) {

  setPrice();    <—

}

void checkbox8_itemStateChanged(java.awt.event.ItemEvent e) {

  setPrice();    <—

}
```

Now run the application. You can see the new application resources like a menu and tool bar in Figure 4.9 (and we'll see how to work with such resources later in this book). When you click a radio button, the corresponding check boxes are selected and the tour's price appears. When you click a check box, the corresponding island is added to the tour package, and the displayed price is updated to reflect it. The retailer2 application is a success.

Checkboxes and Radio Buttons

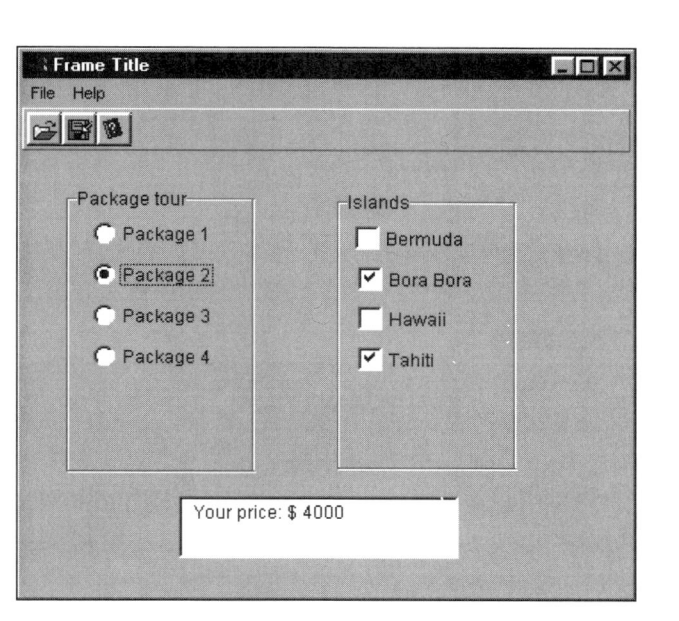

Figure 4.9 Running the retailer2 application.

The code for this application appears in Listings 4.4. and 4.5.

Listing 4.4 Frame1.java

```
//Title:
//Version:
//Copyright:
//Author:
//Company:
//Description:
//

package retailer2;
import java.awt.*;
import java.awt.event.*;
import java.lang.*;
import borland.jbcl.control.*;
import borland.jbcl.layout.*;

public
```

Chapter 4

```java
class Frame1 extends DecoratedFrame {

  public BorderLayout borderLayout1 = new BorderLayout();
  public Panel panel1 = new Panel();
  public XYLayout xYLayout1 = new XYLayout();
  public MenuBar menuBar1 = new MenuBar();
  public Menu menuFile = new Menu();
  public MenuItem menuFileExit = new MenuItem();
  public Menu menuHelp = new Menu();
  public MenuItem menuHelpAbout = new MenuItem();
  public ButtonBar buttonBar = new ButtonBar();
  public Label statusBar = new Label();
  CheckboxGroup checkboxgroup1 = new CheckboxGroup();
  GroupBox groupBox1 = new GroupBox();
  GroupBox groupBox2 = new GroupBox();
  Checkbox checkbox1 = new Checkbox("Package 1", checkboxgroup1, false);
  Checkbox checkbox2 = new Checkbox("Package 2", checkboxgroup1, false);
  Checkbox checkbox3 = new Checkbox("Package 3", checkboxgroup1, false);
  Checkbox checkbox4 = new Checkbox("Package 4", checkboxgroup1, false);
  Checkbox checkbox5 = new Checkbox();
  Checkbox checkbox6 = new Checkbox();
  Checkbox checkbox7 = new Checkbox();
  Checkbox checkbox8 = new Checkbox();
  TextField textField1 = new TextField();
  XYLayout xYLayout2 = new XYLayout();

  //Construct the frame
  public Frame1() {

    try { jbInit(); } catch(Exception e) { e.printStackTrace(); };

  }

  //Component initialization
  public void jbInit() throws Exception{
```

Checkboxes and Radio Buttons

```
    this.setLayout(borderLayout1);
    this.setTitle("Frame Title");

    //Add menu bar
    menuFile.setLabel("File");
    menuFileExit.setLabel("Exit");
    menuFileExit.addActionListener(new
Frame1_menuFileExit_ActionAdapter(this));
    menuFile.add(menuFileExit);
    menuHelp.setLabel("Help");
    menuHelpAbout.setLabel("About");
    menuHelpAbout.addActionListener(new
Frame1_menuHelpAbout_ActionAdapter(this));
    menuHelp.add(menuHelpAbout);
    menuBar1.add(menuFile);
    menuBar1.add(menuHelp);
    this.setMenuBar(menuBar1);
    //Add tool bar
    buttonBar.setButtonType(ButtonBar.IMAGE_ONLY);
    buttonBar.setLabels(new String[] {"Open", "Close",
"Help"});
    buttonBar.setImageDirectory("borland/jbcl/control/images");
    buttonBar.setImageNames(new String[] {"openfile.gif",
"closefile.gif", "help.gif"});
    this.add(buttonBar, BorderLayout.NORTH);
    //Add status bar
    statusBar.setText("");
    groupBox1.setLabel("Package tour");
    groupBox2.setLayout(xYLayout2);
    groupBox2.setLabel("Islands");
    checkbox1.setLabel("Package 1");
    checkbox1.addItemListener(new
Frame1_checkbox1_ItemAdapter(this));
    checkbox2.setLabel("Package 2");
    checkbox2.addItemListener(new
Frame1_checkbox2_ItemAdapter(this));
    checkbox3.setLabel("Package 3");
    checkbox3.addItemListener(new
Frame1_checkbox3_ItemAdapter(this));
```

Chapter 4

```
        checkbox4.setLabel("Package 4");
        checkbox4.addItemListener(new
Frame1_checkbox4_ItemAdapter(this));
        checkbox5.setLabel("Bermuda");
        checkbox5.addItemListener(new
Frame1_checkbox5_ItemAdapter(this));
        checkbox6.setLabel("Bora Bora");
        checkbox6.addItemListener(new
Frame1_checkbox6_ItemAdapter(this));
        checkbox7.setLabel("Hawaii");
        checkbox7.addItemListener(new
Frame1_checkbox7_ItemAdapter(this));
        checkbox8.setLabel("Tahiti");
        checkbox8.addItemListener(new
Frame1_checkbox8_ItemAdapter(this));
    this.add(statusBar, BorderLayout.SOUTH);
    //Add center panel
    panel1.setLayout(xYLayout1);
    xYLayout1.setWidth(400);
    xYLayout1.setHeight(300);
    this.add(panel1, BorderLayout.CENTER);
    panel1.add(groupBox1, new XYConstraints(22, 25, 137,
202));
    groupBox1.add(checkbox1, null);
    groupBox1.add(checkbox2, null);
    groupBox1.add(checkbox3, null);
    groupBox1.add(checkbox4, null);
    panel1.add(groupBox2, new XYConstraints(200, 27, 131,
198));
    groupBox2.add(checkbox5, new XYConstraints(4, 6, -1, -1));
    groupBox2.add(checkbox6, new XYConstraints(6, 34, -1, -
1));
    groupBox2.add(checkbox7, new XYConstraints(6, 61, -1, -
1));
    groupBox2.add(checkbox8, new XYConstraints(6, 89, -1, -
1));
    panel1.add(textField1, new XYConstraints(103, 237, 184,
42));
    this.pack();
```

Checkboxes and Radio Buttons

```
    //Center the window
    Dimension dimScreen =
Toolkit.getDefaultToolkit().getScreenSize();
    Dimension dimFrame = this.getPreferredSize();
    if(dimFrame.height > dimScreen.height) dimFrame.height =
dimScreen.height;
    if(dimFrame.width > dimScreen.width) dimFrame.width =
dimScreen.width;
    this.setBounds( (dimScreen.width - dimFrame.width) / 2,
(dimScreen.height - dimFrame.height) / 2, dimFrame.width,
dimFrame.height);
  }

  //File | Exit action performed
  public void fileExit_actionPerformed(ActionEvent e) {

    System.exit(0);

  }

  //Help | About action performed
  public void helpAbout_actionPerformed(ActionEvent e) {

  }

  void checkbox1_itemStateChanged(java.awt.event.ItemEvent e) {

    checkbox5.setState(true);
    checkbox6.setState(false);
    checkbox7.setState(true);
    checkbox8.setState(false);
    setPrice();

  }

  void checkbox2_itemStateChanged(java.awt.event.ItemEvent e) {

    checkbox5.setState(false);
    checkbox6.setState(true);
```

Chapter 4

```java
        checkbox7.setState(false);
        checkbox8.setState(true);
        setPrice();

    }

    void checkbox3_itemStateChanged(java.awt.event.ItemEvent e) {

        checkbox5.setState(true);
        checkbox6.setState(true);
        checkbox7.setState(false);
        checkbox8.setState(true);
        setPrice();

    }

    void checkbox4_itemStateChanged(java.awt.event.ItemEvent e) {

        checkbox5.setState(true);
        checkbox6.setState(true);
        checkbox7.setState(true);
        checkbox8.setState(true);
        setPrice();

    }

    void checkbox5_itemStateChanged(java.awt.event.ItemEvent e) {

        setPrice();
    }

    void checkbox6_itemStateChanged(java.awt.event.ItemEvent e) {

        setPrice();

    }

    void checkbox7_itemStateChanged(java.awt.event.ItemEvent e) {
```

Checkboxes and Radio Buttons

```java
    setPrice();

  }

  void checkbox8_itemStateChanged(java.awt.event.ItemEvent e) {

    setPrice();

  }

  void setPrice(){
      String outString = "Your price: $ ";
      int price = 0;

      if(checkbox5.getState()){
        price += 2000;
      }

      if(checkbox6.getState()){
        price += 2000;
      }

      if(checkbox7.getState()){
        price += 2000;
      }

      if(checkbox8.getState()){
        price += 2000;
      }

      textField1.setText(outString + String.valueOf(price));
  }
}

class Frame1_menuFileExit_ActionAdapter implements
ActionListener {
  Frame1 adaptee;
  Frame1_menuFileExit_ActionAdapter(Frame1 adaptee) {
    this.adaptee = adaptee;
```

```
    }
    public void actionPerformed(ActionEvent e) {
      adaptee.fileExit_actionPerformed(e);
    }
  }

  class Frame1_menuHelpAbout_ActionAdapter implements
  ActionListener {
    Frame1 adaptee;
    Frame1_menuHelpAbout_ActionAdapter(Frame1 adaptee) {
      this.adaptee = adaptee;
    }
    public void actionPerformed(ActionEvent e) {
      adaptee.helpAbout_actionPerformed(e);
    }
  }

  class Frame1_checkbox1_ItemAdapter implements ItemListener {
    Frame1 adaptee;
    Frame1_checkbox1_ItemAdapter(Frame1 adaptee) {
      this.adaptee = adaptee;
    }
    public void itemStateChanged(java.awt.event.ItemEvent e) {
      adaptee.checkbox1_itemStateChanged(e);
    }
  }

  class Frame1_checkbox2_ItemAdapter implements ItemListener {
    Frame1 adaptee;
    Frame1_checkbox2_ItemAdapter(Frame1 adaptee) {
      this.adaptee = adaptee;
    }
    public void itemStateChanged(java.awt.event.ItemEvent e) {
      adaptee.checkbox2_itemStateChanged(e);
    }
  }

  class Frame1_checkbox3_ItemAdapter implements ItemListener {
```

```java
    Frame1 adaptee;
    Frame1_checkbox3_ItemAdapter(Frame1 adaptee) {
      this.adaptee = adaptee;
    }
    public void itemStateChanged(java.awt.event.ItemEvent e) {
      adaptee.checkbox3_itemStateChanged(e);
    }
}

class Frame1_checkbox4_ItemAdapter implements ItemListener {
    Frame1 adaptee;
    Frame1_checkbox4_ItemAdapter(Frame1 adaptee) {
      this.adaptee = adaptee;
    }
    public void itemStateChanged(java.awt.event.ItemEvent e) {
      adaptee.checkbox4_itemStateChanged(e);
    }
}

class Frame1_checkbox5_ItemAdapter implements ItemListener{
    Frame1 adaptee;
    Frame1_checkbox5_ItemAdapter(Frame1 adaptee) {
      this.adaptee = adaptee;
    }
    public void itemStateChanged(java.awt.event.ItemEvent e) {
      adaptee.checkbox5_itemStateChanged(e);
    }
}

class Frame1_checkbox6_ItemAdapter implements ItemListener{
    Frame1 adaptee;
    Frame1_checkbox6_ItemAdapter(Frame1 adaptee) {
      this.adaptee = adaptee;
    }
    public void itemStateChanged(java.awt.event.ItemEvent e) {
      adaptee.checkbox6_itemStateChanged(e);
    }
}
```

Chapter 4

```java
class Frame1_checkbox7_ItemAdapter implements ItemListener{
  Frame1 adaptee;
  Frame1_checkbox7_ItemAdapter(Frame1 adaptee) {
    this.adaptee = adaptee;
  }
  public void itemStateChanged(java.awt.event.ItemEvent e) {
    adaptee.checkbox7_itemStateChanged(e);
  }
}

class Frame1_checkbox8_ItemAdapter implements ItemListener{
  Frame1 adaptee;
  Frame1_checkbox8_ItemAdapter(Frame1 adaptee) {
    this.adaptee = adaptee;
  }
  public void itemStateChanged(java.awt.event.ItemEvent e) {
    adaptee.checkbox8_itemStateChanged(e);
  }
}
```

Listing 4.5 retailer2.java

```java
//Title:
//Version:
//Copyright:
//Author:
//Company:
//Description:
//

package retailer2;
import java.lang.*;

public
class retailer2 {
  //Construct the application
  public retailer2() {
```

Checkboxes and Radio Buttons

```
    Frame1 frame = new Frame1();
    frame.setVisible(true);

  }

  //Main method
  static public void main(String[] args) {

    new retailer2();

  }

}
```

We've seen a good deal about radio buttons and check boxes in this chapter. We've seen how to use check boxes and radio buttons by themselves—and then we saw how to use them together. We've also seen how to create and use Java applications in JBuilder. In Chapter 5, we'll continue our exploration of JBuilder controls like popup menus, list boxes, choice controls, and more.

CHAPTER 5

Lists, Choices, Popups, and Scroll Bars

In this chapter, we're going to explore several new controls that will give us a great deal more power. We'll see how to integrate these controls into our programs and put them to use for us.

We'll start off by taking a look at list boxes, called *lists* or *scrolling lists* in Java. These controls present the user with a vertical list of items that they can select. When they make a choice, we'll report which item they've chosen.

Another new control is the choice control. This control is like a combo box in Windows; it presents the user with a dropdown list of choices. When they make a selection, we'll display that item in a text field.

In addition, we'll see how to create and use popup menus in this chapter. These controls are just like real menus, but they're not attached to a menu bar. In particular, we'll see how to display a popup menu when the user clicks the right mouse button, and how to determine which selection they've made.

Finally, we'll take a look at scroll bars. Everyone's familiar with scroll bars—those controls with the little box, called a *thumb*, that slides up and down (or left and right) in response to the user's mouse movements. We'll see how to put scroll bars around the edges of an applet in this chapter. With all this going on, then, let's get started at once.

Chapter 5

Using Lists

Our first example in this chapter will use a list control to display a list of options to the user:

```
Double-click a list item...
    Item 1    |^|
    Item 2    |v|

    [                    ]
```

When the user double-clicks the list, we will display which item they've chosen in a text field this way:

```
Double-click a list item...
    Item 1    |^|
    Item 2    |v|

    [ Item 2              ]
```

Create this new applet named **lists** now, and open it in the JBuilder Designer. Next, add a new list control, using the list tool (sixth control from the left when you click the AWT tab) as well as a text field and a prompt label reading: *Double-click a list item....*

This adds a new list control, `list1`, of class `List` to our program. The List class' constructors and methods appear in Table 5.1.

Lists, Choices, Popups, and Scroll Bars

Table 5.1 The List Class' Constructors and Methods

`List()`	Creates a new scrolling list
`List(int)`	Creates a new scrolling list initialized with the given number of visible lines
`List(int, boolean)`	Creates a new scrolling list initialized with the given number of visible lines and a boolean stating whether multiple selections are allowed or not.
`add(String)`	Adds the given item to the end of scrolling list.
`add(String, int)`	Adds the given item to the scrolling list at the given position.
`addActionListener(ActionListener)`	Adds the given action listener.
`addItem(String)`	DEPRECATED: Replaced by `add(String)`.
`addItem(String, int)`	DEPRECATED: Replaced by `add(String, int)`.
`addItemListener(ItemListener)`	Adds the given item listener.
`addNotify()`	Creates the peer for the list.
`allowsMultipleSelections()`	DEPRECATED: Replaced by `isMultipleMode()`.
`clear()`	DEPRECATED: Replaced by `removeAll()`.
`countItems()`	DEPRECATED: Replaced by `getItemCount()`.
`delItem(int)`	DEPRECATED: Replaced by `remove(String)`.
`delItems(int, int)`	DEPRECATED: Not for public use in the future.
`deselect(int)`	Deselects the item at the given index.
`getItem(int)`	Gets the item associated with the given index.
`getItemCount()`	Gets the number of items in the list.
`getItems()`	Gets the items in the list.
`getMinimumSize()`	Gets the minimum dimensions for the list.
`getMinimumSize(int)`	Gets the minimum dimensions for the given number of rows.
`getPreferredSize()`	Gets the preferred dimensions needed for the list.
`getPreferredSize(int)`	Gets the preferred dimensions needed for the given number of rows.
`getRows()`	Gets the number of visible lines in this list.
`getSelectedIndex()`	Get the selected item's index in the list.

(continued)

Chapter 5

Table 5.1 The List Class' Constructors and Methods *(continued)*

`getSelectedIndexes()`	Gets the selected indexes on the list.
`getSelectedItem()`	Gets the selected item in the list.
`getSelectedItems()`	Gets the selected items in an array.
`getSelectedObjects()`	Gets the selected items in an Object array.
`getVisibleIndex()`	Gets the index of the item that was last made visible.
`isIndexSelected(int)`	True if the item at the given index has been selected.
`isMultipleMode()`	True if this list allows multiple selections.
`isSelected(int)`	DEPRECATED: Replaced by `isIndexSelected(int)`.
`makeVisible(int)`	Forces the item at the index to be visible.
`minimumSize()`	DEPRECATED: Replaced by `getMinimumSize()`.
`minimumSize(int)`	DEPRECATED: Replaced by `etMinimumSize(int)`.
`paramString()`	Gets the parameter `String` of this list.
`preferredSize()`	DEPRECATED: Replaced by `getPreferredSize()`.
`preferredSize(int)`	DEPRECATED: Replaced `getPreferredSize(int)`.
`processActionEvent(ActionEvent)`	Processes action events.
`processEvent(AWTEvent)`	Processes events in this list.
`processItemEvent(ItemEvent)`	Processes item events.
`remove(int)`	Removes an item from the list.
`remove(String)`	Remove the first occurrence of item.
`removeActionListener(ActionListener)`	Removes given action listener.
`removeAll()`	Removes all items from the list.
`removeItemListener(ItemListener)`	Removes given item listener.
`removeNotify()`	Removes peer for this list.
`replaceItem(String, int)`	Replaces item at the given index.
`select(int)`	Selects the item at the given index.
`setMultipleMode(boolean)`	Sets if list should allow multiple selections.
`setMultipleSelections(boolean)`	DEPRECATED: Replaced by `getMultipleMode(boolean)`.

Filling a List Control with Items

To place items in a list, we'll use the List `addItem()` method. In particular, we can place three new items in the list: "Item 1", "Item 2", and "Item 3" in the `init()` method:

```
public void init() {

    list1.addItem("Item 1");              <--
    list1.addItem("Item 2");              <--
    list1.addItem("Item 3");              <--

    try { jbInit(); } catch(Exception e) { e.printStackTrace(); };

}
```

We've loaded our list with items. (When a list has too many items to display at once, it automatically adds scroll bars, becoming a scrolling list.) The next step is to determine which item the user selects by double-clicking it.

Getting the User's Selection

Use the JBuilder Inspector now to connect a method to the list's `actionPerformed` event:

```
void list1_actionPerformed(java.awt.event.ActionEvent e) {

    textField1.setText(e.getActionCommand());

}
```

This is the method that will be called when the user double-clicks the list. Here, we'll place the item the user selected into the text field—but which item is that? It turns out that we can get the text of the item the user double-clicked by calling the `getActionCommand()` method of the `ActionEvent` object passed to us:

Chapter 5

```
void list1_actionPerformed(java.awt.event.ActionEvent e) {

    textField1.setText(e.getActionCommand());      <—


}
```

Run the applet now, then double-click an item in the list. When you do, the program reports which item you've selected, as shown in Figure 5.1. Our lists program is a success.

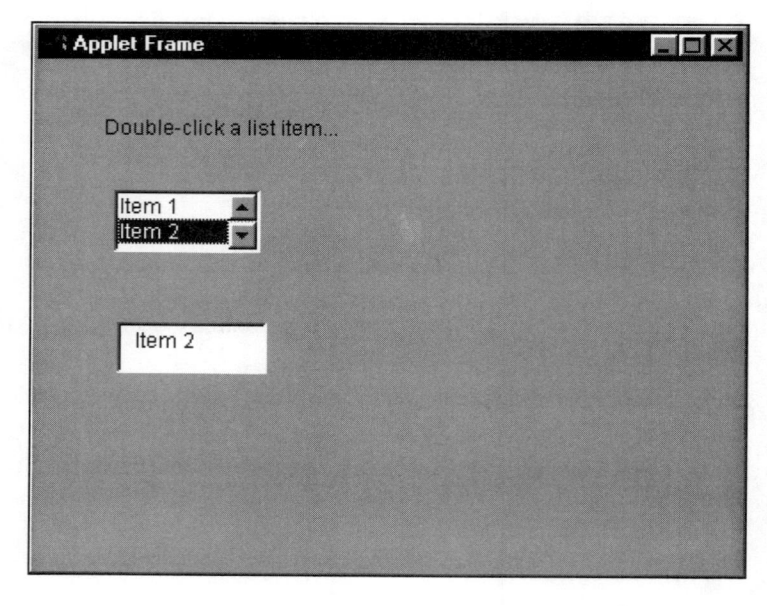

Figure 5.1 Our lists program at work.

The code for this applet appears in Listing 5.1.

Listing 5.1 lists.java

```
//Title:
//Version:
//Copyright:
//Author:
//Company:
```

Lists, Choices, Popups, and Scroll Bars

```java
//Description:
//

package lists;
import java.lang.*;
import java.awt.*;
import java.awt.event.*;
import java.applet.*;
import borland.jbcl.control.*;
import borland.jbcl.layout.*;

public
class lists extends Applet {

  public XYLayout xYLayout1 = new XYLayout();
  public boolean isStandalone = false;
  List list1 = new List();
  TextField textField1 = new TextField();
  Label label1 = new Label();

  //Construct the applet
  public lists() {

  }

  //Initialize the applet
  public void init() {

    list1.addItem("Item 1");
    list1.addItem("Item 2");
    list1.addItem("Item 3");

    try { jbInit(); } catch(Exception e) { e.printStackTrace(); };

  }

  //Component initialization
  public void jbInit() throws Exception{
```

Chapter 5

```
        xYLayout1.setWidth(400);
        xYLayout1.setHeight(300);
        label1.setText("Double-click a list item...");
        list1.addActionListener(new
lists_list1_ActionAdapter(this));
        this.setLayout(xYLayout1);
        this.add(list1, new XYConstraints(44, 77, 83, 37));
        this.add(textField1, new XYConstraints(46, 155, 85, 30));
        this.add(label1, new XYConstraints(38, 30, 132, 20));

    }

    //Start the applet
    public void start() {

    }

    //Stop the applet
    public void stop() {

    }

    //Destroy the applet
    public void destroy() {

    }

    //Get Applet information
    public String getAppletInfo() {

        return "Applet Information";

    }

    //Get parameter info
    public String[][] getParameterInfo() {

        return null;

    }
```

Lists, Choices, Popups, and Scroll Bars

```java
//Main method
static public void main(String[] args) {

  lists applet = new lists();
  applet.isStandalone = true;
  DecoratedFrame frame = new DecoratedFrame();
  frame.setTitle("Applet Frame");
  frame.add(applet, BorderLayout.CENTER);
  applet.init();
  applet.start();
  frame.pack();
  Dimension d = Toolkit.getDefaultToolkit().getScreenSize();
  frame.setLocation((d.width - frame.getSize().width) / 2,
(d.height - frame.getSize().height) / 2);
  frame.setVisible(true);

}

  void list1_actionPerformed(java.awt.event.ActionEvent e) {

    textField1.setText(e.getActionCommand());

  }

}

class lists_list1_ActionAdapter implements ActionListener{

  lists adaptee;

  lists_list1_ActionAdapter(lists adaptee) {

    this.adaptee = adaptee;

  }

  public void actionPerformed(java.awt.event.ActionEvent e) {

    adaptee.list1_actionPerformed(e);

  }

}
```

Chapter 5

Now we've seen lists in action—it's time to turn to the next control, choice controls.

Using Choice Controls

Our choice control displays a text field along with a small button showing a downward arrow:

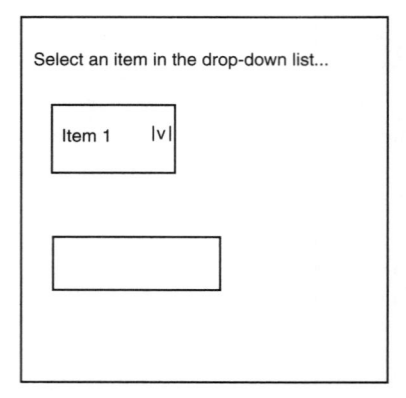

When the user clicks the arrow button, a list of selections opens:

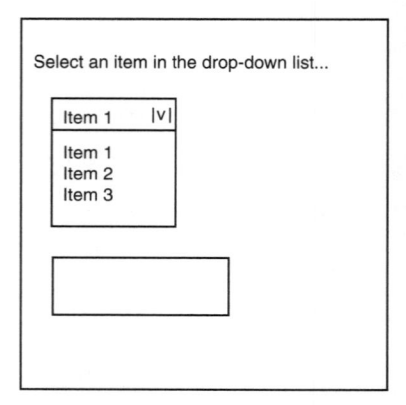

When the user makes a selection from this list, we can display which item they've chose in a text field this way:

Lists, Choices, Popups, and Scroll Bars

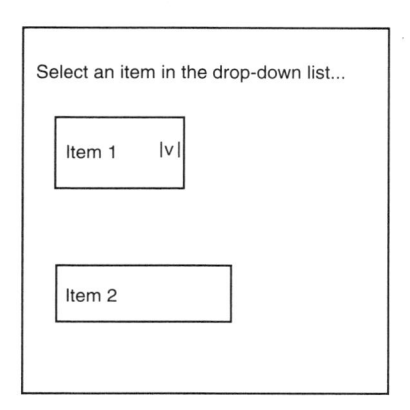

```
┌─────────────────────────────┐
│  Select an item in the drop-down list...  │
│    ┌──────────────┐         │
│    │ Item 1   |v| │         │
│    └──────────────┘         │
│                             │
│                             │
│    ┌──────────────┐         │
│    │ Item 2       │         │
│    └──────────────┘         │
└─────────────────────────────┘
```

Let's put this new applet together now. Create this applet and call it **choices**. Next, open the applet in the Designer and add a new choice control (the seventh control from the left when you click the AWT tab). This adds a new choice control, `choice1`, of class `Choice` to our program. The Choice class' constructors and methods appear in Table 5.2.

Table 5.2 The Choice Class' Constructors and Methods

`Choice()`	Constructs a new Choice.
`add(String)`	Adds an item to this Choice.
`addItem(String)`	DEPRECATED: Replaced by `add(String)`.
`addItemListener(ItemListener)`	Adds the given item listener.
`addNotify()`	Creates the Choice's peer.
`countItems()`	DEPRECATED: Replaced by `getItemCount()`.
`getItem(int)`	Gets the `String` at the given index.
`getItemCount()`	Gets the number of items in this Choice.
`getSelectedIndex()`	Gets the index of the currently selected item.
`getSelectedItem()`	Gets a `String` representation of the current choice.
`getSelectedObjects()`	Gets an array containing the selected item.
`insert(String, int)`	Inserts the item into this choice at the given position.
`paramString()`	Gets the parameter `String` of this Choice.

(continued)

Chapter 5

Table 5.2 The Choice Class' Constructors and Methods (continued)

processEvent(AWTEvent)	Processes events on this Choice.
processItemEvent (ItemEvent)	Processes item events in this Choice.
remove(int)	Removes an item from the choice menu.
remove(String)	Remove first occurrence of item.
removeAll()	Removes all items from the choice menu.
removeItemListener (ItemListener)	Removes given item listener.
select(int)	Selects the item with the given postion.
select(String)	Selects the item matching the given String.

Filling a Choice Control with Items

Just as we did with the list control in our previous example, we use the choice control's `addItem()` method to add three new items to the choice control:

```
public void init() {

    choice1.addItem("Item 1");
    choice1.addItem("Item 2");
    choice1.addItem("Item 3");

    try { jbInit(); } catch(Exception e) { e.printStackTrace(); };

}
```

This adds those items to the choice control. The next step is to determine which of those items the user selects.

Getting the User's Selection

The choice control has an `itemStateChanged` event, not an `actionPerformed` event, so connect a new method to the `itemStateChanged` event now:

Lists, Choices, Popups, and Scroll Bars

```
void choice1_itemStateChanged(java.awt.event.ItemEvent e) {

}
```

This method is called when the user makes a choice from the drop-down list in the choice control, and we want to report the user's choice in the text field. But what item did the user choose? We can determine that with the Choice class' `getSelectedItem()` method, and we get a reference to the choice control itself with the `getItemSelectable()` method. Putting those two methods together, we can get the selected item this way, placing its text in the text field:

```
void choice1_itemStateChanged(java.awt.event.ItemEvent e) {

    textField1.setText(((Choice)e.getItemSelectable()).getSelectedItem());

}
```

Run the applet now, and select an item in the choice control's drop-down list. When you do, the applet displays the choice you've made, as shown in Figure 5.2. Now we're using choice controls!

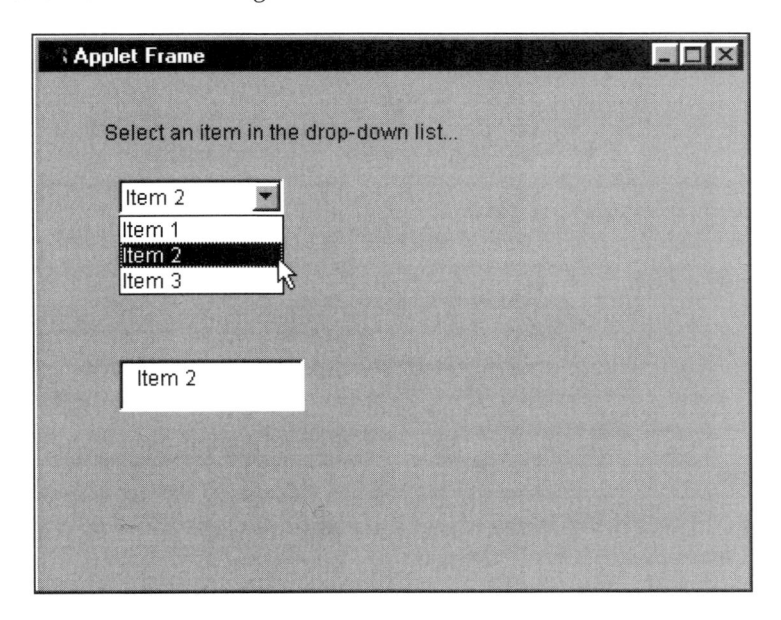

Figure 5.2 Using a choice control.

Chapter 5

The code for this applet appears in Listing 5.2.

Listing 5.2 choices.java

```java
//Title:
//Version:
//Copyright:
//Author:
//Company:
//Description:
//

package choices;
import java.lang.*;
import java.awt.*;
import java.awt.event.*;
import java.applet.*;
import borland.jbcl.control.*;
import borland.jbcl.layout.*;

public
class choices extends Applet {

  public XYLayout xYLayout1 = new XYLayout();
  public boolean isStandalone = false;
  Choice choice1 = new Choice();
  TextField textField1 = new TextField();
  Label label1 = new Label();

  //Construct the applet
  public choices() {

  }

  //Initialize the applet
  public void init() {

    choice1.addItem("Item 1");
```

Lists, Choices, Popups, and Scroll Bars

```
        choice1.addItem("Item 2");
        choice1.addItem("Item 3");

        try { jbInit(); } catch(Exception e) { e.printStackTrace(); };

    }

    //Component initialization
    public void jbInit() throws Exception{

        xYLayout1.setWidth(400);
        xYLayout1.setHeight(300);
        label1.setText("Select an item in the drop-down list...");
        choice1.addItemListener(new
choices_choice1_ItemAdapter(this));
        this.setLayout(xYLayout1);
        this.add(choice1, new XYConstraints(45, 47, 94, 99));
        this.add(textField1, new XYConstraints(45, 168, 105, 30));
        this.add(label1, new XYConstraints(37, 23, 233, 24));

    }

    //Start the applet
    public void start() {

    }

    //Stop the applet
    public void stop() {

    }

    //Destroy the applet
    public void destroy() {

    }

    //Get Applet information
    public String getAppletInfo() {
```

Chapter 5

```
    return "Applet Information";

}

//Get parameter info
public String[][] getParameterInfo() {

    return null;

}

//Main method
static public void main(String[] args) {

    choices applet = new choices();
    applet.isStandalone = true;
    DecoratedFrame frame = new DecoratedFrame();
    frame.setTitle("Applet Frame");
    frame.add(applet, BorderLayout.CENTER);
    applet.init();
    applet.start();
    frame.pack();
    Dimension d = Toolkit.getDefaultToolkit().getScreenSize();
    frame.setLocation((d.width - frame.getSize().width) / 2,
(d.height - frame.getSize().height) / 2);
    frame.setVisible(true);

}

  void choice1_itemStateChanged(java.awt.event.ItemEvent e) {

    textField1.setText(((Choice)e.getItemSelectable()).getSelectedItem());

  }

}

class choices_choice1_ItemAdapter implements ItemListener{

  choices adaptee;
```

Lists, Choices, Popups, and Scroll Bars

```
choices_choice1_ItemAdapter(choices adaptee) {

  this.adaptee = adaptee;

}

public void itemStateChanged(java.awt.event.ItemEvent e) {

  adaptee.choice1_itemStateChanged(e);

}

}
```

We've examined both lists and choices. The next control we'll take a look at is a very popular one: the popup menu control.

Using Popup Menus

In this next example, we'll display an applet with the prompt "Right-click the mouse...":

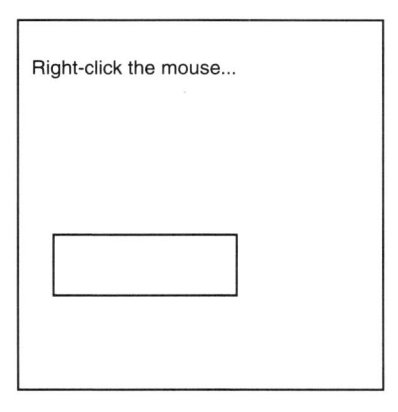

When the user does right-click the mouse, we'll show a new popup menu at the mouse location:

Chapter 5

```
┌─────────────────────────────┐
│ Right-click the mouse...    │
│                             │
│                  ┌────────┐ │
│                  │ Item 1 │ │
│                  │ Item 2 │ │
│                  │ Item 3 │ │
│                  └────────┘ │
│                             │
│   ┌──────────────┐          │
│   │              │          │
│   └──────────────┘          │
│                             │
└─────────────────────────────┘
```

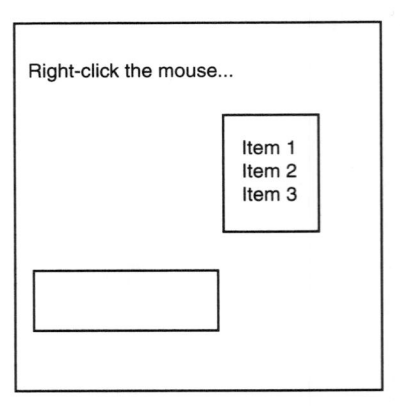

When the user clicks one of the items in the popup menu, we'll hide that menu and display the item they've selected:

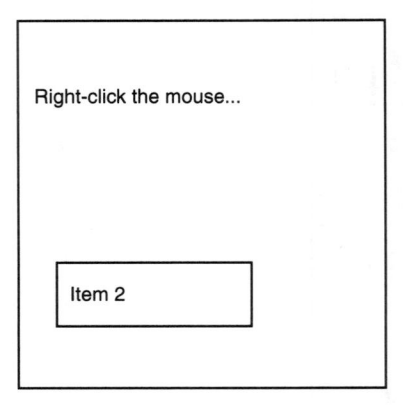

```
┌─────────────────────────────┐
│ Right-click the mouse...    │
│                             │
│                             │
│                             │
│                             │
│   ┌──────────────┐          │
│   │ Item 2       │          │
│   └──────────────┘          │
│                             │
└─────────────────────────────┘
```

Let's write this applet now. Create this applet with the Applet Wizard, calling it **popups**. Now open this applet in the Designer and find the popup menu tool (eleventh tool from the left when you click the AWT tab).

Placing Items in a Popup Menu

Instead of drawing a new popup menu in the applet, just click the popup menu tool, and then click the **popups.popups** item at the very top of the Tree window (the middle window in the Designer display). A new popup menu object, popupMenu1, will appear in the Tree window—this is how we add non-visible objects to an applet. We now have a new popup menu, popupMenu1, of the PopupMenu class in our applet. The PopupMenu class's Constructors and Methods appear in Table 5.3.

Lists, Choices, Popups, and Scroll Bars

Table 5.3 The PopupMenu Class's Constructors and Methods

`PopupMenu()`	Creates a new popup menu.
`PopupMenu(String)`	Creates a new popup menu with the specified name.
`addNotify()`	Creates the popup menu's peer.
`show(Component, int, int)`	Shows the popup menu at the x, y position.

Now double-click the **popupMenu1** entry in the Tree window, opening the JBuilder menu designer, as shown in Figure 5.3.

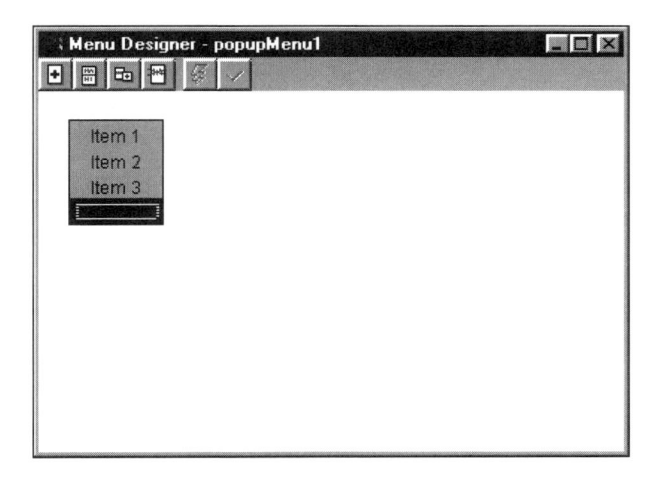

Figure 5.3 Using the menu editor on a popup menu.

We'll see how to use the menu designer in more depth in Chapter 6. For now, just type the names of the items—**"Item 1"**, **"Item 2"**, and **"Item 3"**—pressing the **Enter** key after each name. This adds all three items to the new popup menu, as seen in Figure 5.3.

Each item in the popup menu has its own `actionPerformed` event. To connect an event handler to that event, select each item in turn in the menu designer by clicking it with the mouse, and add an event handler to its `actionPerformed` event in the JBuilder Inspector. Now close the menu designer.

Now we've designed our new popup menu. The next step is to display that menu when the user right-clicks the mouse.

Chapter 5

Displaying the Popup Menu

To determine when the user right-clicks the mouse, we will override the `mouseDown` event. This event occurs when the user presses a mouse button. To override this event, click the **Override Methods** item in the JBuilder Wizards menu now.

This opens the Override Inherited Methods box. Make sure the popups item is selected in the Class Name box, and click the **+** sign next to the java.awt.Component entry in the Methods box. Now find the `mouseDown()` method, highlight it with the mouse, and click **OK** to close the Override Inherited Methods box.

This adds the `mouseDown()` event handler to our code:

```
public boolean mouseDown(Event evt, int x, int y) {

    //TODO: override this java.awt.Component method;

    return super.mouseDown( evt,  x,  y);

}
```

Now that the mouse has gone down, our first task is to determine if the button the user pressed was the right mouse button. To check that, we examine the modifiers variable in the Event object passed to us. If this variable holds the value 4, the user pressed the right mouse button (this variable would hold 0 if the user clicked the left mouse button):

```
public boolean mouseDown(Event evt, int x, int y) {

    if(evt.modifiers == 4){          <--

    }


    return super.mouseDown( evt,  x,  y);

}
```

Lists, Choices, Popups, and Scroll Bars

Since the user has right-clicked the mouse, we will show the popup menu. We place that menu at the same location the user clicked the mouse, which is passed to us in `mouseDown()` in the x and y parameters. This means we can pass those parameters to the popup menu's `show()` method, along with a `this` keyword to indicate that the applet is the popup menu's parent:

```
public boolean mouseDown(Event evt, int x, int y) {

    if(evt.modifiers == 4){

        popupMenu1.show(this, x, y);            <—

    }

    return super.mouseDown( evt,  x,   y);

}
```

Now the popup menu appears. The user makes a selection by clicking an item, and the menu disappears. Next, we'll turn to the menu items' `actionPerformed` handlers to indicate which item the user clicked.

Getting the User's Selection

We've already added an `actionPerformed` handler for each menu item to our applet:

```
void menuItem1_actionPerformed(java.awt.event.ActionEvent e) {

}


void menuItem2_actionPerformed(java.awt.event.ActionEvent e) {

}
```

Chapter 5

```
void menuItem3_actionPerformed(java.awt.event.ActionEvent e) {

}
```

These methods are called when the corresponding menu item is selected, so we indicate which item was selected by placing a message in the text field as follows:

```
void menuItem1_actionPerformed(java.awt.event.ActionEvent e) {

    textField1.setText("You chose item 1.");      <--

}


void menuItem2_actionPerformed(java.awt.event.ActionEvent e) {

    textField1.setText("You chose item 2.");      <--

}


void menuItem3_actionPerformed(java.awt.event.ActionEvent e) {

    textField1.setText("You chose item 3.");      <--

}
```

Run the applet now, and right-click the applet. This brings up the popup menu, as shown in Figure 5.4.

Now make a selection in the popup menu by clicking it with the mouse. The menu disappears and the item you've selected appears in the text field, as shown in Figure 5.5. Now we're using popup menus!

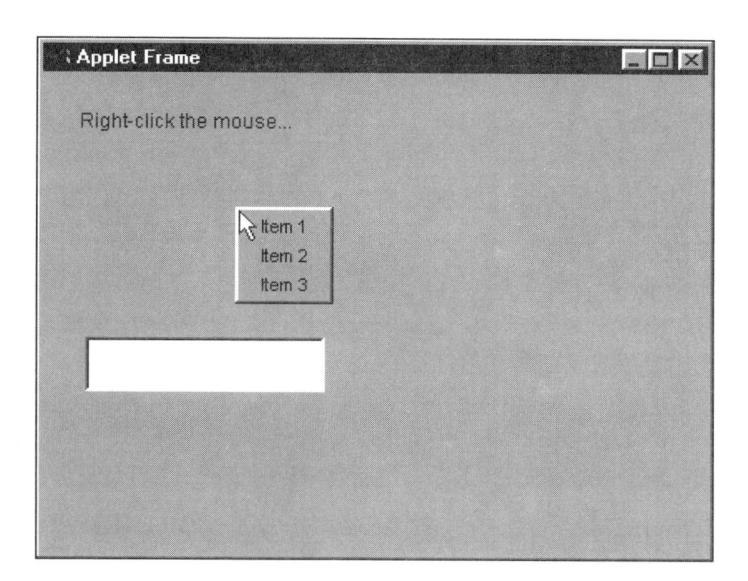

Figure 5.4 Using popup menus.

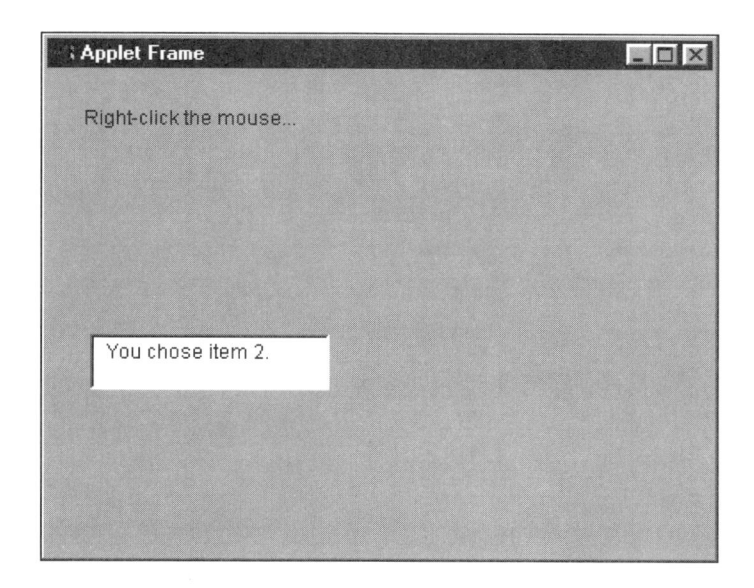

Figure 5.5 Using popup menus.

The listing for this applet appears in Listing 5.3.

Chapter 5

Listing 5.3 popups.java

```java
//Title:
//Version:
//Copyright:
//Author:
//Company:
//Description:
//

package popups;
import java.lang.*;
import java.awt.*;
import java.awt.event.*;
import java.applet.*;
import borland.jbcl.control.*;
import borland.jbcl.layout.*;

public
class popups extends Applet {

  public XYLayout xYLayout1 = new XYLayout();
  public boolean isStandalone = false;
  PopupMenu popupMenu1 = new PopupMenu();
  MenuItem menuItem1 = new MenuItem();
  MenuItem menuItem2 = new MenuItem();
  MenuItem menuItem3 = new MenuItem();
  TextField textField1 = new TextField();
  Label label1 = new Label();

  //Construct the applet
  public popups() {

  }

  //Initialize the applet
  public void init() {

    try { jbInit(); } catch(Exception e) { e.printStackTrace(); };
```

Lists, Choices, Popups, and Scroll Bars

```
    }

    //Component initialization
    public void jbInit() throws Exception{

       xYLayout1.setWidth(400);
       xYLayout1.setHeight(300);
       menuItem1.setLabel("Item 1");
       menuItem1.addActionListener(new
popups_menuItem1_ActionAdapter(this));
       menuItem2.setLabel("Item 2");
       menuItem2.addActionListener(new
popups_menuItem2_ActionAdapter(this));
       menuItem3.setLabel("Item 3");
       label1.setText("Right-click the mouse...");
       menuItem3.addActionListener(new
popups_menuItem3_ActionAdapter(this));
       this.setLayout(xYLayout1);
       popupMenu1.add(menuItem1);
       popupMenu1.add(menuItem2);
       popupMenu1.add(menuItem3);
       this.add(popupMenu1);
       this.add(textField1, new XYConstraints(26, 164, 144, 34));
       this.add(label1, new XYConstraints(22, 20, 182, 19));

    }

    //Start the applet
    public void start() {

    }

    //Stop the applet
    public void stop() {

    }

    //Destroy the applet
    public void destroy() {
```

Chapter 5

```java
    }

    //Get Applet information
    public String getAppletInfo() {

        return "Applet Information";

    }

    //Get parameter info
    public String[][] getParameterInfo() {

        return null;

    }

    //Main method
    static public void main(String[] args) {

        popups applet = new popups();
        applet.isStandalone = true;
        DecoratedFrame frame = new DecoratedFrame();
        frame.setTitle("Applet Frame");
        frame.add(applet, BorderLayout.CENTER);
        applet.init();
        applet.start();
        frame.pack();
        Dimension d = Toolkit.getDefaultToolkit().getScreenSize();
        frame.setLocation((d.width - frame.getSize().width) / 2,
 (d.height - frame.getSize().height) / 2);
        frame.setVisible(true);

    }

    void menuItem1_actionPerformed(java.awt.event.ActionEvent e) {

        textField1.setText("You chose item 1.");

    }
```

```
void menuItem2_actionPerformed(java.awt.event.ActionEvent e) {

  textField1.setText("You chose item 2.");

}

void menuItem3_actionPerformed(java.awt.event.ActionEvent e) {

  textField1.setText("You chose item 3.");

}

public boolean mouseDown(Event evt, int x, int y) {

  //TODO: override this java.awt.Component method;

  if(evt.modifiers == 4){

    popupMenu1.show(this, x, y);

  }

  return super.mouseDown( evt,   x,   y);

 }

}

class popups_menuItem1_ActionAdapter implements ActionListener

{

  popups adaptee;

  popups_menuItem1_ActionAdapter(popups adaptee) {

    this.adaptee = adaptee;

  }

  public void actionPerformed(java.awt.event.ActionEvent e) {

    adaptee.menuItem1_actionPerformed(e);
```

      }

    }

    class popups_menuItem2_ActionAdapter implements ActionListener
    {
      popups adaptee;

      popups_menuItem2_ActionAdapter(popups adaptee) {
        this.adaptee = adaptee;
      }

      public void actionPerformed(java.awt.event.ActionEvent e) {
        adaptee.menuItem2_actionPerformed(e);
      }
    }

    class popups_menuItem3_ActionAdapter implements ActionListener
    {
      popups adaptee;

      popups_menuItem3_ActionAdapter(popups adaptee) {
        this.adaptee = adaptee;
      }

      public void actionPerformed(java.awt.event.ActionEvent e) {
        adaptee.menuItem3_actionPerformed(e);
      }
    }

Lists, Choices, Popups, and Scroll Bars

We've explored lists, choices, and popup menus. The next topic we'll examine is how to use scroll bars.

Scroll Bars

In our next example, we'll set up an applet with four scroll bars around the edges and a button labeled *Click Me*:

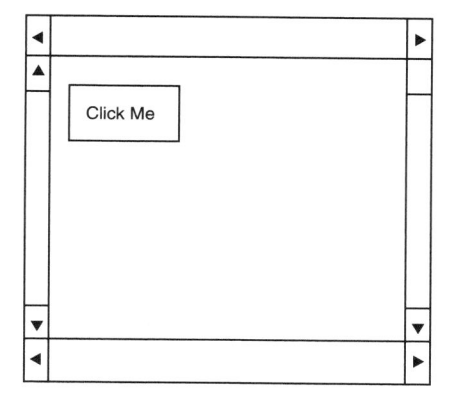

When the user moves the scroll bars by moving the scroll bar thumbs, we'll move the button to match:

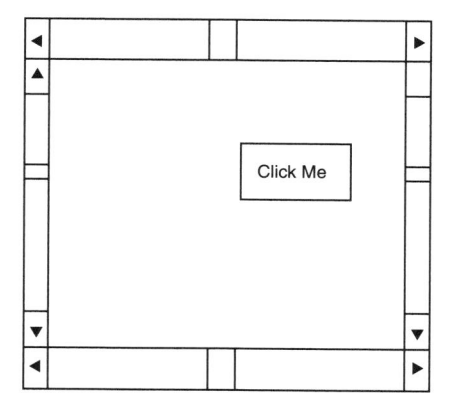

We'll use a panel in which to place our button control so we can scroll it. Create the new applet, which we'll call **panels**, now. Open the applet in the Designer.

Chapter 5

Using Panels

Now add four new scroll bars to the applet (the scroll bar tool is the ninth tool from the left when you click the AWT tab) as shown in Figure 5.6. Also add a new panel to the applet (the panel tool is the eighth tool from the left when you click the AWT tab in JBuilder).

Panel controls can contain other controls. In this case, add a new button to the panel, and give that button the caption **Click Me** (the panel control is invisible itself, but we show it as selected with sizing handles in Figure 5.6).

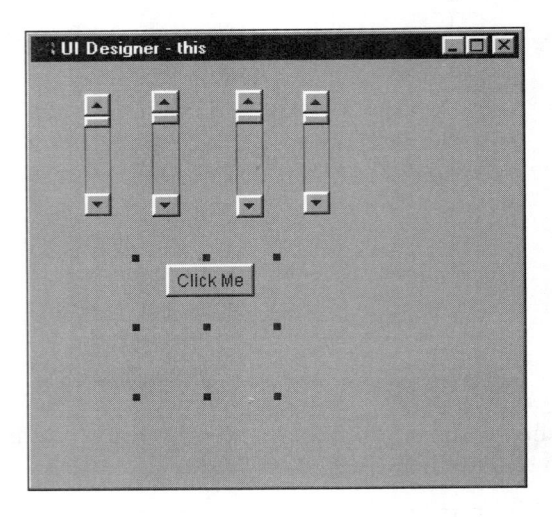

Figure 5.6 Adding four scroll bars.

Now change the orientation property of two of the scroll bars from 1 to 0. This makes them horizontal scroll bars, as shown in Figure 5.7.

Using the Border Layout

Finally, change the applet's layout property from Default to BorderLayout. This is the layout that we'll use to place the scroll bars around the border of the applet. In this layout, there are five items: four around the border (the scroll bars here) and one in the middle (the panel with the button in it). Arrange the controls until they appear as shown in Figure 5.8.

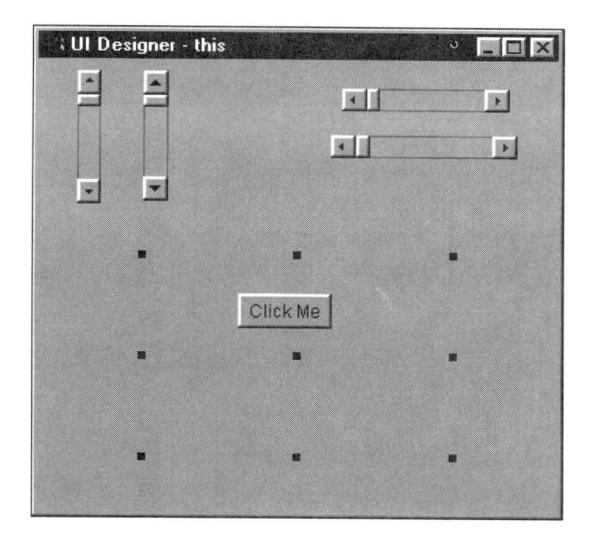

Figure 5.7 Making two scroll bars horizontal.

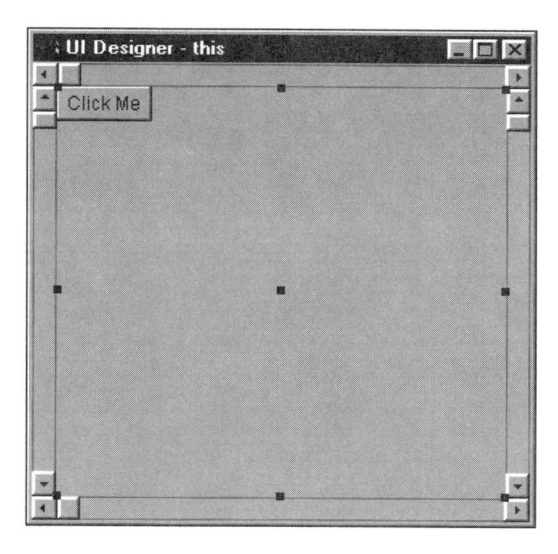

Figure 5.8 Setting up a border layout.

This adds our new scroll bars to the applet, setting up the scroll bars in a border layout. This layout adds controls in compass orientations: NORTH, EAST, SOUTH, and WEST; the panel is placed in the center, so it gets the keyword CENTER:

Chapter 5

```
public void jbInit() throws Exception{

    this.setLayout(borderLayout1);
    scrollbar1.setOrientation(0);
    scrollbar1.addAdjustmentListener(new
panels_scrollbar1_AdjustmentAdapter(this));
    scrollbar2.addAdjustmentListener(new
panels_scrollbar2_AdjustmentAdapter(this));
    scrollbar3.setOrientation(0);
    scrollbar3.addAdjustmentListener(new
panels_scrollbar3_AdjustmentAdapter(this));
    scrollbar4.addAdjustmentListener(new
panels_scrollbar4_AdjustmentAdapter(this));
    button1.setLabel("Click Me");
    button1.addActionListener(new
panels_button1_ActionAdapter(this));
    scrollbar1.setMinimum(0);
    scrollbar1.setMaximum(200);
    scrollbar2.setMinimum(0);
    scrollbar2.setMaximum(200);
    scrollbar3.setMinimum(0);
    scrollbar3.setMaximum(200);
    scrollbar4.setMinimum(0);
    scrollbar4.setMaximum(200);
    panel2.setLayout(xYLayout1);
    this.add(scrollbar2, BorderLayout.WEST);      <—
    this.add(scrollbar1, BorderLayout.SOUTH);     <—
    this.add(scrollbar3, BorderLayout.NORTH);     <—
    this.add(scrollbar4, BorderLayout.EAST);      <—
    this.add(panel2, BorderLayout.CENTER);        <—
    panel2.add(button1, new XYConstraints(-1, -1, -1, -1));
    panel2.add(panel1, new XYConstraints(70, 11, -1, -1));
    button1.setLocation(0, 0);

}
```

The Scrollbar class's constructors and methods appear in Table 5.4.

Lists, Choices, Popups, and Scroll Bars

Table 5.4 The Scrollbar Class's Constructors and Methods

Scrollbar()	Constructs a new vertical Scrollbar.
Scrollbar(int)	Constructs a Scrollbar with given orientation.
Scrollbar (int, int, int, int, int)	Constructs a new Scrollbar with given orientation, value, page size, and minimum and maximum values.
addAdjustmentListener (AdjustmentListener)	Adds the given adjustment listener.
addNotify()	Creates the Scrollbar's peer.
getBlockIncrement()	Gets the block increment for this scrollbar.
getLineIncrement()	DEPRECATED: Replaced by getUnitIncrement().
getMaximum()	Gets the maximum value of this Scrollbar.
getMinimum()	Gets the minimum value of this Scrollbar.
getOrientation()	Gets the orientation for this Scrollbar.
getPageIncrement()	DEPRECATED: Replaced by getBlockIncrement().
getUnitIncrement()	Gets the unit increment for this scrollbar.
getValue()	Gets the current value of this Scrollbar.
getVisible()	DEPRECATED: Replaced by getVisibleAmount().
getVisibleAmount()	Gets the visible amount of this Scrollbar.
paramString()	Gets the String parameters for this Scrollbar.
processAdjustmentEvent (AdjustmentEvent)	Processes adjustment events.
processEvent(AWTEvent)	Processes events on scrollbar.
removeAdjustmentListener (AdjustmentListener)	Removes adjustment listener.
setBlockIncrement(int)	Sets block increment for scrollbar.
setLineIncrement(int)	DEPRECATED: Replaced by setUnitIncrement(int).
setMaximum(int)	Sets maximum value for this Scrollbar.
setMinimum(int)	Sets minimum value for this Scrollbar.

(continued)

Chapter 5

Table 5.4 The Scrollbar Class's Constructors and Methods (continued)

setOrientation(int)	Sets orientation for this Scrollbar.
setPageIncrement(int)	DEPRECATED: Replaced by setBlockIncrement().
setUnitIncrement(int)	Sets the unit increment for this scrollbar.
setValue(int)	Sets value of Scrollbar.
setValues(int, int, int, int)	Sets values for Scrollbar.
setVisibleAmount(int)	Sets the visible amount of Scrollbar

The next task is to handle the user's scroll bar actions.

Determining User Actions

Scroll bars use the `adjustmentValueChanged` event, so add a new `adjustmentValueChanged` method to each scroll bar in the Inspector:

```
void scrollbar1_adjustmentValueChanged(java.awt.event.AdjustmentEvent e) {

}


void scrollbar2_adjustmentValueChanged(java.awt.event.AdjustmentEvent e) {

}


void scrollbar3_adjustmentValueChanged(java.awt.event.AdjustmentEvent e) {

}


void scrollbar4_adjustmentValueChanged(java.awt.event.AdjustmentEvent e) {

}
```

Lists, Choices, Popups, and Scroll Bars

When the user moves a scroll bar, these are the methods that will be called, and we want to move the button to match. We do that with the button's `setLocation()` method, getting the new setting of the scroll bars from the `getValue()` method of the AdjustmentEvent object passed to us:

```
        void scrollbar1_adjustmentValueChanged(java.awt.event.AdjustmentEvent e) {

->          button1.setLocation(button1.getLocation().x, e.getValue());


        }


        void scrollbar2_adjustmentValueChanged(java.awt.event.AdjustmentEvent e) {

->          button1.setLocation(button1.getLocation().x, e.getValue());


        }


        void scrollbar3_adjustmentValueChanged(java.awt.event.AdjustmentEvent e) {

->          button1.setLocation(e.getValue(), button1.getLocation().y);


        }


        void scrollbar4_adjustmentValueChanged(java.awt.event.AdjustmentEvent e) {

->          button1.setLocation(button1.getLocation().x, e.getValue());


        }
```

Chapter 5

Note that when the user scrolls one scroll bar, we should move the scroll bar opposite to it to match (because we have two vertical scroll bars and two horizontal ones, and both sets should stay coordinated). We can do that with the scroll bar `setValue()` method:

```
void scrollbar1_adjustmentValueChanged(java.awt.event.AdjustmentEvent e) {

    button1.setLocation(button1.getLocation().x, e.getValue());

->  scrollbar3.setValue(e.getValue());

}

void scrollbar2_adjustmentValueChanged(java.awt.event.AdjustmentEvent e) {

    button1.setLocation(button1.getLocation().x, e.getValue());

->  scrollbar4.setValue(e.getValue());

}

void scrollbar3_adjustmentValueChanged(java.awt.event.AdjustmentEvent e) {

    button1.setLocation(e.getValue(), button1.getLocation().y);

->  scrollbar1.setValue(e.getValue());

}

void scrollbar4_adjustmentValueChanged(java.awt.event.AdjustmentEvent e) {
```

```
        button1.setLocation(button1.getLocation().x, e.getValue());


->      scrollbar2.setValue(e.getValue());


    }
```

Finally, we can even let the button do something—we can change the button's caption from *Click Me* to *Clicked!* when the user clicks it. We can reach the button itself in the `actionPerformed` method with the ActionEvent `getSource()` method, and we set the button's label with its `setLabel()` method:

```
void button1_actionPerformed(java.awt.event.ActionEvent e) {

    ((Button)e.getSource()).setLabel("Clicked!");


}
```

Now run the applet. When you move the scroll bars, the button moves to match, as shown in Figure 5.9. Our panels applet is a success—now we're using scroll bars!

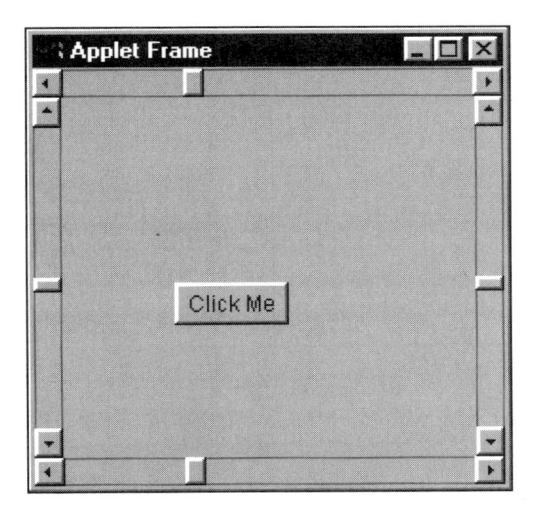

Figure 5.9 Our panels applet lets the user use scroll bars.

The listing for this applet appears in Listing 5.4.

Chapter 5

Listing 5.4 panels.java

```java
//Title:
//Version:
//Copyright:
//Author:
//Company:
//Description:
//

package panels;
import java.lang.*;
import java.awt.*;
import java.awt.event.*;
import java.applet.*;
import borland.jbcl.control.*;
import borland.jbcl.layout.*;

public
class panels extends Applet {

  public boolean isStandalone = false;
  Panel panel1 = new Panel();
  Scrollbar scrollbar1 = new Scrollbar();
  Scrollbar scrollbar2 = new Scrollbar();
  Scrollbar scrollbar3 = new Scrollbar();
  Scrollbar scrollbar4 = new Scrollbar();
  Panel panel2 = new Panel();
  Button button1 = new Button();
  BorderLayout borderLayout1 = new BorderLayout();
  XYLayout xYLayout1 = new XYLayout();

  //Construct the applet
  public panels() {

  }

  //Initialize the applet
```

Lists, Choices, Popups, and Scroll Bars

```java
public void init() {

  try { jbInit(); } catch(Exception e) { e.printStackTrace(); };

}

//Component initialization
public void jbInit() throws Exception{

  this.setLayout(borderLayout1);
  scrollbar1.setOrientation(0);
  scrollbar1.addAdjustmentListener(new
panels_scrollbar1_AdjustmentAdapter(this));
  scrollbar2.addAdjustmentListener(new
panels_scrollbar2_AdjustmentAdapter(this));
  scrollbar3.setOrientation(0);
  scrollbar3.addAdjustmentListener(new
panels_scrollbar3_AdjustmentAdapter(this));
  scrollbar4.addAdjustmentListener(new
panels_scrollbar4_AdjustmentAdapter(this));
  button1.setLabel("Click Me");
  button1.addActionListener(new
panels_button1_ActionAdapter(this));
  scrollbar1.setMinimum(0);
  scrollbar1.setMaximum(200);
  scrollbar2.setMinimum(0);
  scrollbar2.setMaximum(200);
  scrollbar3.setMinimum(0);
  scrollbar3.setMaximum(200);
  scrollbar4.setMinimum(0);
  scrollbar4.setMaximum(200);
  panel2.setLayout(xYLayout1);
  this.add(scrollbar2, BorderLayout.WEST);
  this.add(scrollbar1, BorderLayout.SOUTH);
  this.add(scrollbar3, BorderLayout.NORTH);
  this.add(scrollbar4, BorderLayout.EAST);
  this.add(panel2, BorderLayout.CENTER);
  panel2.add(button1, new XYConstraints(-1, -1, -1, -1));
  panel2.add(panel1, new XYConstraints(70, 11, -1, -1));
```

Chapter 5

```java
    button1.setLocation(0, 0);

}

//Start the applet
public void start() {

}

//Stop the applet
public void stop() {

}

//Destroy the applet
public void destroy() {

}

//Get Applet information
public String getAppletInfo() {

   return "Applet Information";

}

//Get parameter info
public String[][] getParameterInfo() {

   return null;

}

//Main method
static public void main(String[] args) {

   panels applet = new panels();
   applet.isStandalone = true;
   DecoratedFrame frame = new DecoratedFrame();
```

Lists, Choices, Popups, and Scroll Bars

```java
        frame.setTitle("Applet Frame");
        frame.add(applet, BorderLayout.CENTER);
        applet.init();
        applet.start();
        frame.pack();
        Dimension d = Toolkit.getDefaultToolkit().getScreenSize();
        frame.setLocation((d.width - frame.getSize().width) / 2,
    (d.height - frame.getSize().height) / 2);
        frame.setVisible(true);

    }

    void scrollbar1_adjustmentValueChanged(java.awt.event.AdjustmentEvent e)
{

        button1.setLocation(e.getValue(), button1.getLocation().y);

        scrollbar3.setValue(e.getValue());

    }

    void scrollbar2_adjustmentValueChanged(java.awt.event.AdjustmentEvent e)
{

        button1.setLocation(button1.getLocation().x, e.getValue());

        scrollbar4.setValue(e.getValue());

    }

    void scrollbar3_adjustmentValueChanged(java.awt.event.AdjustmentEvent e)
{

        button1.setLocation(e.getValue(), button1.getLocation().y);

        scrollbar1.setValue(e.getValue());

    }

    void scrollbar4_adjustmentValueChanged(java.awt.event.AdjustmentEvent e)
{

        button1.setLocation(button1.getLocation().x, e.getValue());
```

Chapter 5

```java
        scrollbar2.setValue(e.getValue());
    }
    void button1_actionPerformed(java.awt.event.ActionEvent e) {
        ((Button)e.getSource()).setLabel("Clicked!");
    }
}
class panels_scrollbar4_AdjustmentAdapter implements AdjustmentListener {
    panels adaptee;
    panels_scrollbar4_AdjustmentAdapter(panels adaptee) {
        this.adaptee = adaptee;
    }
    public void adjustmentValueChanged(java.awt.event.AdjustmentEvent e) {
        adaptee.scrollbar4_adjustmentValueChanged(e);
    }
}
class panels_scrollbar3_AdjustmentAdapter implements AdjustmentListener {
    panels adaptee;
    panels_scrollbar3_AdjustmentAdapter(panels adaptee) {
        this.adaptee = adaptee;
    }
```

```java
    public void
adjustmentValueChanged(java.awt.event.AdjustmentEvent e) {
    adaptee.scrollbar3_adjustmentValueChanged(e);
  }
}
class panels_scrollbar2_AdjustmentAdapter implements
AdjustmentListener {
  panels adaptee;
  panels_scrollbar2_AdjustmentAdapter(panels adaptee) {
    this.adaptee = adaptee;
  }
  public void
adjustmentValueChanged(java.awt.event.AdjustmentEvent e) {
    adaptee.scrollbar2_adjustmentValueChanged(e);
  }
}
class panels_scrollbar1_AdjustmentAdapter implements
AdjustmentListener {
  panels adaptee;
  panels_scrollbar1_AdjustmentAdapter(panels adaptee) {
    this.adaptee = adaptee;
  }
```

Chapter 5

```
    public void
adjustmentValueChanged(java.awt.event.AdjustmentEvent e) {
    adaptee.scrollbar1_adjustmentValueChanged(e);
  }
}
class panels_button1_ActionAdapter implements ActionListener{
  panels adaptee;
  panels_button1_ActionAdapter(panels adaptee) {
    this.adaptee = adaptee;
  }
  public void actionPerformed(java.awt.event.ActionEvent e) {
    adaptee.button1_actionPerformed(e);
  }
}
```

That's it for this chapter. We've seen list controls, choice controls, popup menus, and now scroll bars arranged in a border layout. These new controls add even more power to our JBuilder arsenal.

We'll continue our JBuilder guided tour in Chapter 6, when we take a look at some very popular topics: windows, menus, and dialog boxes.

CHAPTER 6

Windows, Menus, and Dialog Boxes

In this chapter, we're going to dig into some extraordinarily powerful JBuilder techniques. These new techniques will lift our programs from the commonplace towards the professional.

Here, we'll see how to create, show, and hide frame windows (they are called frame windows because they have a frame which the user can usually resize, minimize or maximize). You can display new frame windows from either applets or applications in Java, and we'll see how to do just that.

Next, we'll see how to attach a menu system to such windows—you need a window to attach a menu to, because you can't use a menu in a standard applet as it stands. We'll see how to determine when the user has selected a menu item, how to place check marks in front of such items as well as gray them out, and even support submenus.

Finally, we'll see how to work with dialog boxes in Java and JBuilder. These are special frame windows used to get input from the user, and they usually have at least two buttons: OK and Cancel.

Let's start at once with frame windows.

Creating Frame Windows

In our new frame window example, we'll display an applet with two buttons: Show window and Hide window:

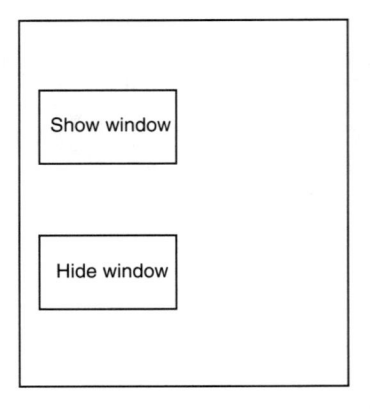

When the user clicks the **Show** window button, we display a new frame window with the message *Welcome to windows!* and a button marked Close:

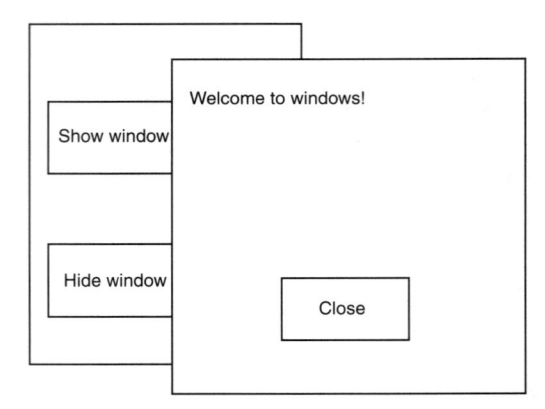

When the user clicks the **Close** button, the frame window closes:

Let's start this new applet, named windows, now. Create it using the Applet Wizard and add two new buttons to the applet, Show window and Hide window.

Windows, Menus, and Dialog Boxes

We'll need our new frame window. That window will be a new object of the JBuilder DecoratedFrame class, so let's create it now.

Creating a New Frame Window

The new class JBuilder will create for us, Frame1, is the class we'll use for our frame window, and JBuilder will place the code for this class in a new file, **Frame1.java**.

To create this new class, select the Object Gallery item in the JBuilder Tools menu, opening the Object Gallery as shown in Figure 6.1.

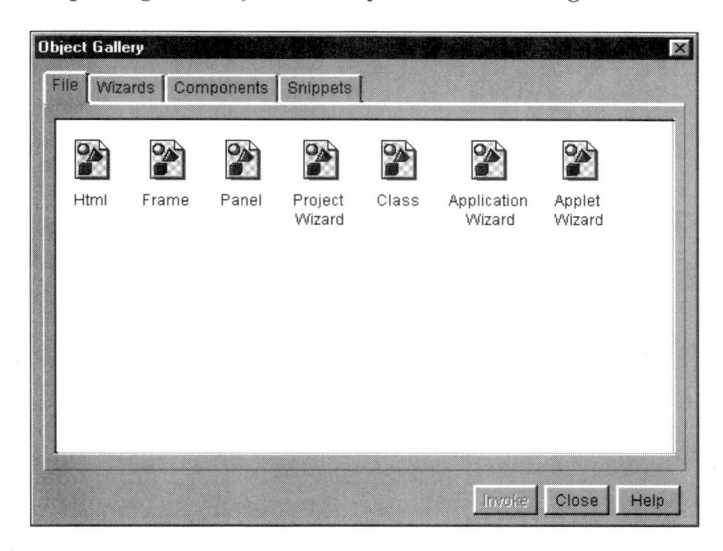

FIGURE 6.1 THE OBJECT GALLERY

The Object Gallery holds the types of items we can add to our JBuilder programs. Here, we are interested in adding a new frame window, so double-click the **Frame** entry in the Object Gallery now. This adds a new frame window class, Frame1, to our applet. This class is of the JBuilder DecoratedFrame class, which is based on the Java Window class. We'll use the Java Window methods `show()` and `hide()` to show and hide our windows in this chapter; the Window class' constructors and methods appear in Table 6.1.

Chapter 6

TABLE 6.1 THE JAVA WINDOW CLASS'S CONSTRUCTORS AND METHODS

`Window(Frame)`	Constructs a new window.
`addNotify()`	Creates the window's peer.
`dispose()`	Disposes of the window.
`getFocusOwner()`	Returns the child component which has the focus.
`getLocale()`	Gets the locale for the window.
`getToolkit()`	Returns the toolkit of this frame.
`getWarningString()`	Gets the warning string for this window.
`pack()`	Packs the components of the window.
`postEvent(Event)`	DEPRECATED: replace by `processEvent`.
`show()`	Shows the window.
`toBack()`	Places window at bottom of stacking order.
`toFront()`	Places window at top of stacking order.

This new class, Frame1, extends the JBuilder DecoratedFrame class (from Frame1.java):

```
public
class Frame1 extends DecoratedFrame {
    .
    .
    .
```

Just as in our applet, the new frame window supports a layout—the XYLayout is the default—and has a constructor (but not an `init()` method) which calls the usual `jbinit()` method:

```
public
class Frame1 extends DecoratedFrame {

    XYLayout xYLayout1 = new XYLayout();

    public Frame1() {
        try {
            jbInit();
```

Windows, Menus, and Dialog Boxes

```
    }
    catch (Exception e) {
      e.printStackTrace();
    };
  }

  void jbInit() throws Exception{

    xYLayout1.setWidth(500);
    xYLayout1.setHeight(300);
    this.setLayout(xYLayout1);

  }
```

Adding Controls to a Window

The inclusion of the `jbinit()` method here shows that we can use the JBuilder Designer with this new frame window, so find the Frame1.java entry in the Project window now and double-click it. This opens that window in the Designer, as shown in Figure 6.2.

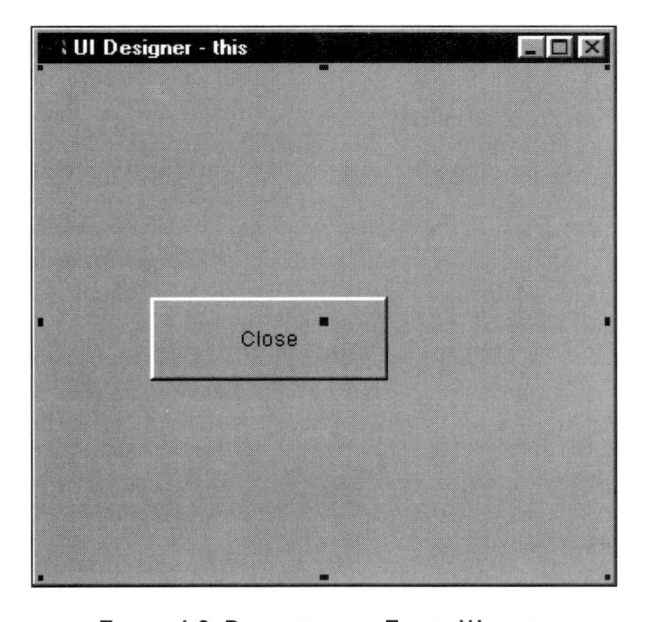

FIGURE 6.2 DESIGNING OUR FRAME WINDOW.

Chapter 6

We can add a new button now to our frame window just as we have our other programs—we draw that button in our frame window, as shown in Figure 6.2. Next, click the button's `actionPerformed` event in the JBuilder Inspector to add a new event handler for the button click event in the Frame1 class:

```
void button1_actionPerformed(java.awt.event.ActionEvent e) {


}
```

Now we place the code here that will hide the window again—the Window method `hide()`:

```
void button1_actionPerformed(java.awt.event.ActionEvent e) {

    hide();          <—


}
```

Besides adding controls to a window, we can override window methods as well.

Overriding Window Methods

Using the Override Methods item in the Wizards menu as we have before, override the `paint()` method:

```
public void paint(Graphics g) {

    //TODO: override this java.awt.Component method;


    super.paint( g );


}
```

Windows, Menus, and Dialog Boxes

Here, we'll place the string *Welcome to windows!* in the window when it is painted:

```
public void paint(Graphics g) {

    g.drawString("Welcome to windows!", 10, 50);
    super.paint( g);

}
```

Now our window class, Frame1, is complete. It's time to create an object of that class and use it to show the frame window on the screen.

Displaying and Hiding a Window

Open the applet class file, **windows.java**, in the Project window now. To use the new frame window class, we need an object of that class, so we create a new object named `frame` of the Frame1 class now in our applet class windows:

```
package windows;
import java.lang.*;
import java.awt.*;
import java.awt.event.*;
import java.applet.*;
import borland.jbcl.control.*;
import borland.jbcl.layout.*;

public
class windows extends Applet {

  public XYLayout xYLayout1 = new XYLayout();
  public boolean isStandalone = false;
  Button button1 = new Button();
  Button button2 = new Button();
  Frame1 frame = new Frame1();                    <--
       .
       .
       .
```

Chapter 6

Now we're free to use the new Frame1 object, frame. We'll start by placing that window on the screen when the user clicks the **Show window** button.

We've already added the Show window and Hide window buttons to our applet; connect an `actionPerformed` event handler to each button now. In the `button1_actionPerformed()` method (corresponding to the Show window button), we first resize the frame window as we want it, using its `resize()` method:

```
void button1_actionPerformed(java.awt.event.ActionEvent e) {

    frame.resize(300, 300);     <—
    .
    .
    .
}
```

Next, we show the window using its `show()` method:

```
void button1_actionPerformed(java.awt.event.ActionEvent e) {

    frame.resize(300, 300);
    frame.show();                <—

}
```

That's it—the window appears on the screen. To hide it when the user clicks the **Hide window** button, as use the frame object's `hide()` window:

```
void button2_actionPerformed(java.awt.event.ActionEvent e) {

    frame.hide();                <—


}
```

Our program is complete. Run it now, as shown in Figure 6.3. When you click the **Show window** button, the new frame window appears.

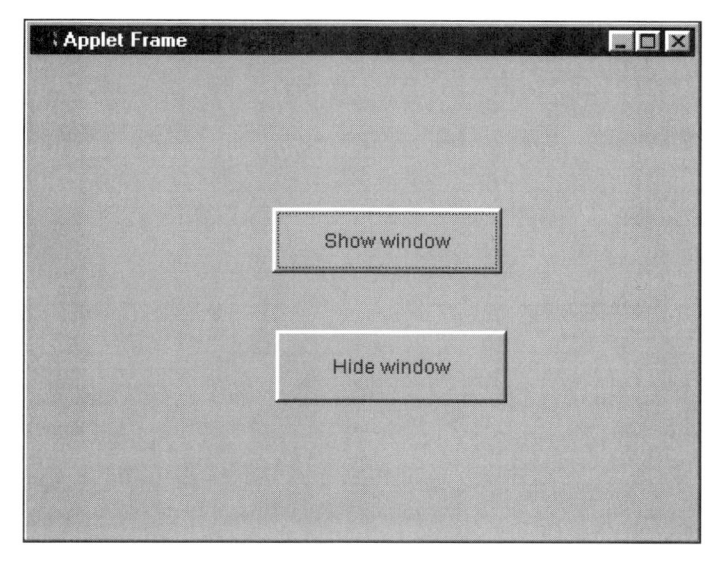

FIGURE 6.3 OUR WINDOWS APPLET.

You can see our message in Figure 6.4 — the program is a success. To dismiss the window from the screen, click the **Close** button.

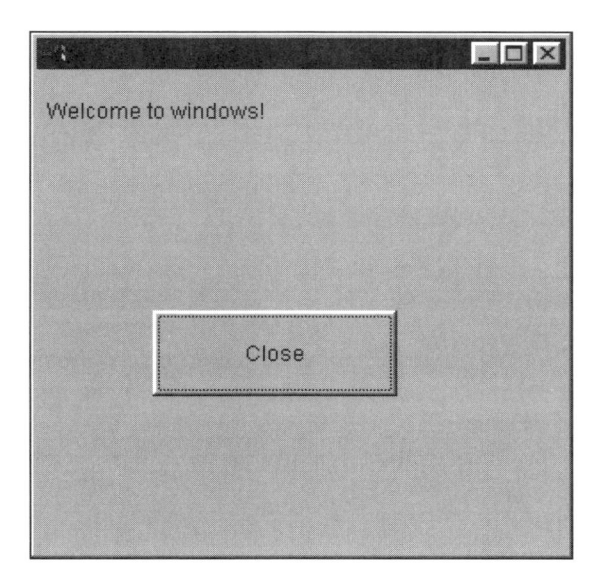

FIGURE 6.4 OUR FIRST FRAME WINDOW.

Chapter 6

The code for this program appears in Listing 6.1 (windows.java) and Listing 6.2 (Frame1.java).

LISTING 6.1 WINDOWS.JAVA

```java
//Title:
//Version:
//Copyright:
//Author:
//Company:
//Description:
//

package windows;
import java.lang.*;
import java.awt.*;
import java.awt.event.*;
import java.applet.*;
import borland.jbcl.control.*;
import borland.jbcl.layout.*;

public
class windows extends Applet {

  public XYLayout xYLayout1 = new XYLayout();
  public boolean isStandalone = false;
  Button button1 = new Button();
  Button button2 = new Button();
  Frame1 frame = new Frame1();

  //Construct the applet
  public windows() {

  }

  //Initialize the applet
  public void init() {
```

Windows, Menus, and Dialog Boxes

```java
        try { jbInit(); } catch(Exception e) { e.printStackTrace(); };

    }

    //Component initialization
    public void jbInit() throws Exception{

        xYLayout1.setWidth(400);
        xYLayout1.setHeight(300);
        button1.setLabel("Show window");
        button1.addActionListener(new
windows_button1_ActionAdapter(this));
        button2.setLabel("Hide window");
        button2.addActionListener(new
windows_button2_ActionAdapter(this));
        this.setLayout(xYLayout1);
        this.add(button1, new XYConstraints(146, 94, 138, 41));
        this.add(button2, new XYConstraints(148, 171, 139, 45));
    }

    //Start the applet
    public void start() {

    }

    //Stop the applet
    public void stop() {

    }

    //Destroy the applet
    public void destroy() {

    }

    //Get Applet information
    public String getAppletInfo() {
```

Chapter 6

```
        return "Applet Information";

    }

    //Get parameter info
    public String[][] getParameterInfo() {

        return null;

    }

    //Main method
    static public void main(String[] args) {

        windows applet = new windows();
        applet.isStandalone = true;
        DecoratedFrame frame = new DecoratedFrame();
        frame.setTitle("Applet Frame");
        frame.add(applet, BorderLayout.CENTER);
        applet.init();
        applet.start();
        frame.pack();
        Dimension d = Toolkit.getDefaultToolkit().getScreenSize();
        frame.setLocation((d.width - frame.getSize().width) / 2,
    (d.height - frame.getSize().height) / 2);
        frame.setVisible(true);

    }

    void button1_actionPerformed(java.awt.event.ActionEvent e) {

        frame.resize(300, 300);
        frame.show();

    }

    void button2_actionPerformed(java.awt.event.ActionEvent e) {
```

```java
      frame.hide();
   }
}
class windows_button1_ActionAdapter implements ActionListener{
   windows adaptee;
   windows_button1_ActionAdapter(windows adaptee) {
      this.adaptee = adaptee;
   }
   public void actionPerformed(java.awt.event.ActionEvent e) {
      adaptee.button1_actionPerformed(e);
   }
}
class windows_button2_ActionAdapter implements ActionListener{
   windows adaptee;
   windows_button2_ActionAdapter(windows adaptee) {
      this.adaptee = adaptee;
   }
   public void actionPerformed(java.awt.event.ActionEvent e) {
      adaptee.button2_actionPerformed(e);
   }
}
```

Chapter 6

LISTING 6.2 FRAME1.JAVA

```java
//Title:
//Version:
//Copyright:
//Author:
//Company:
//Description:
//

package windows;

import java.awt.*;
import java.awt.event.*;
import borland.jbcl.layout.*;
import borland.jbcl.control.*;

public
class Frame1 extends DecoratedFrame {

  XYLayout xYLayout1 = new XYLayout();
  Button button1 = new Button();
  public Frame1() {
    try {
      jbInit();
    }
    catch (Exception e) {
      e.printStackTrace();
    };
  }

  void jbInit() throws Exception{

    xYLayout1.setWidth(500);
    xYLayout1.setHeight(300);
    button1.setLabel("Close");
    button1.addActionListener(new
Frame1_button1_ActionAdapter(this));
    this.setLayout(xYLayout1);
```

```
      this.add(button1, new XYConstraints(64, 135, 135, 49));
   }

   public void paint(Graphics g) {

      //TODO: override this java.awt.Component method;
      g.drawString("Welcome to windows!", 10, 50);
      super.paint( g);

   }
   void button1_actionPerformed(java.awt.event.ActionEvent e) {

      hide();

   }

}

class Frame1_button1_ActionAdapter implements ActionListener{

   Frame1 adaptee;

   Frame1_button1_ActionAdapter(Frame1 adaptee) {

      this.adaptee = adaptee;

   }

   public void actionPerformed(java.awt.event.ActionEvent e) {

      adaptee.button1_actionPerformed(e);

   }

}
```

Now that we've seen how to use frame windows, let's see how to use a special resource you can use with windows in Java: menus.

Chapter 6

Using Menus

In our next example, we'll see how to use menus. We'll need a frame window to support menus, so we will create an applet with a Show window and Hide window button as before:

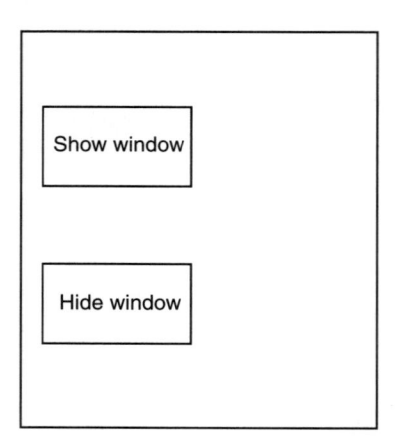

When the user clicks the **Show window** button, we'll display a new window with a File menu, a prompt inviting the user to use the File menu, and a text field:

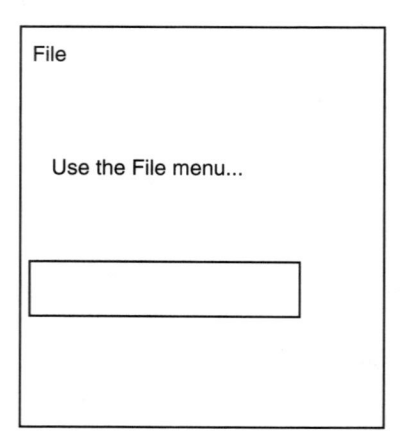

The user can then open the File menu to reveal one item in it, Hello:

Windows, Menus, and Dialog Boxes

```
File
┌─────┐
│Hello│
└─────┘
   Use the File menu...


┌──────────────────┐
│                  │
└──────────────────┘
```

When they select that menu item, we'll display a message reporting their action in the text field:

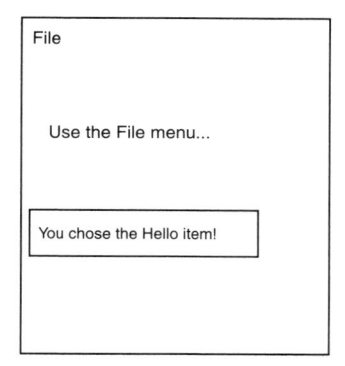

```
File


   Use the File menu...



┌──────────────────────────┐
│ You chose the Hello item!│
└──────────────────────────┘
```

Create this new applet, which we'll name menus, now. Add two buttons, Show window and Hide window, to the applet. We'll need a new frame window in this applet as well, so add a new frame window using the Object Gallery now, and open that new frame window, Frame1, in the Designer. Add a new text field in which to display the user's actions in to the frame window now. Our next step is to add a new menu bar to the frame window.

Adding a Menu Bar

To add a new menu bar to the Frame1 class now open in the Designer, find the MenuBar tool in JBuilder (the tenth tool from the left when you click the AWT tab) and click it. To add this menu bar to the window, just click the Frame1 in the Designer adding the new menu bar —it's not visible yet, but you can see menuBar1 in the tree of controls at left in Figure 6.5.

Chapter 6

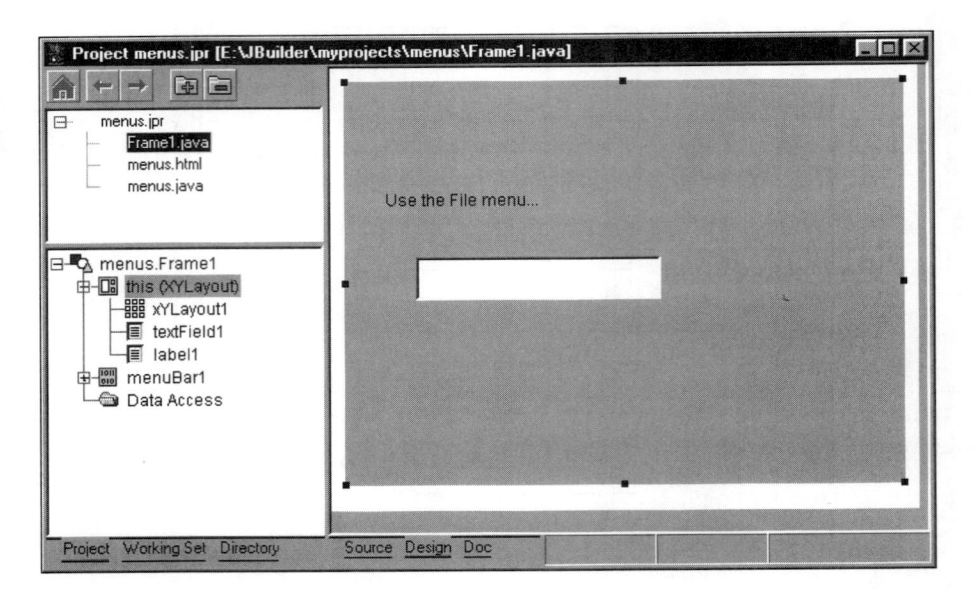

FIGURE 6.5 ADDING A NEW MENU BAR.

Double-click the **menuBar1** entry in the Tree window now, opening the Menu Designer, as shown in Figure 6.6.

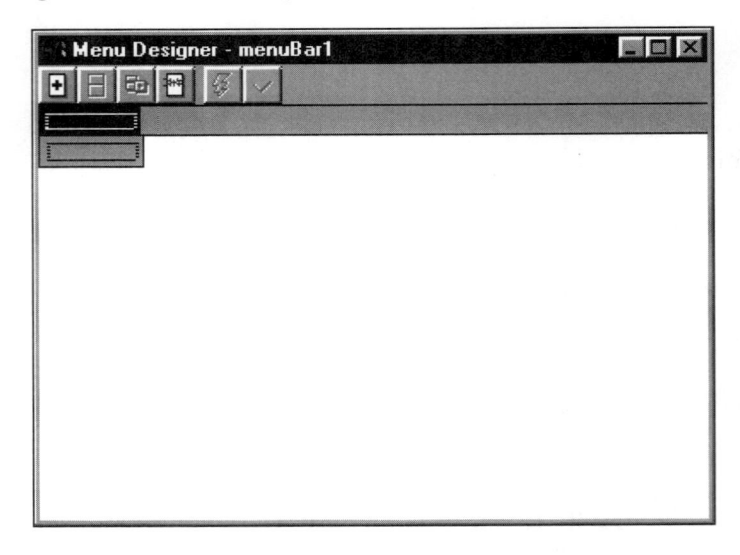

FIGURE 6.6 THE MENU DESIGNER.

Windows, Menus, and Dialog Boxes

This tool lets us design our menu system. Start by clicking the first menu (now showing a blank box) and typing **File**, creating a new File menu, as shown in Figure 6.7.

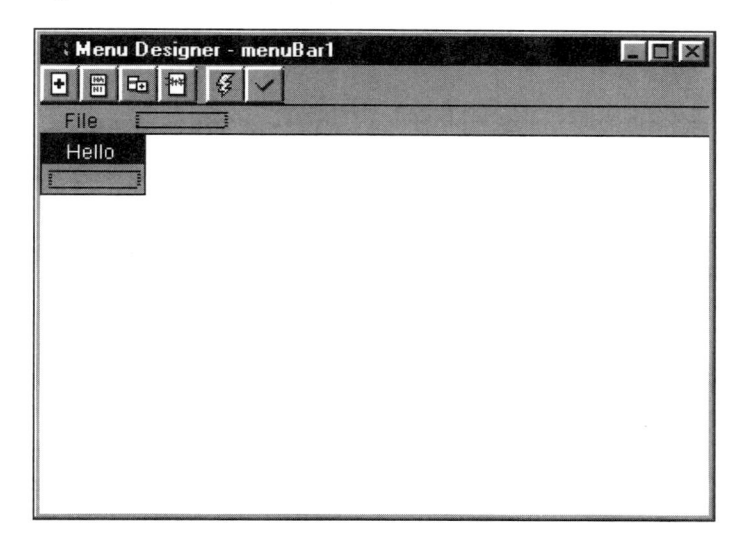

FIGURE 6.7 ADDING A FILE MENU.

Now press **Enter**, moving us down to the first line in the new File menu. Type the new entry, Hello, there, as shown in Figure 6.7. This adds our new menu and its new menu item.

To connect an event handler to the new menu item, just select it in the Menu Designer and move to the Inspector window, adding an actionPerformed handler, as we have for any other control. Now close the Menu Designer.

The above steps have added a new menu bar and menu item to our Frame1 class — notice the program uses the Window class's `setMenuBar()` method to add our new menu bar to the window:

```
    public
    class Frame1 extends DecoratedFrame {

        XYLayout xYLayout1 = new XYLayout();
        MenuBar menuBar1 = new MenuBar();            <--
        Menu menu1 = new Menu();                     <--
        MenuItem menuItem1 = new MenuItem();         <--
```

Chapter 6

```
    TextField textField1 = new TextField();
    Label label1 = new Label();
    public Frame1() {
      try {
        jbInit();
      }
      catch (Exception e) {
        e.printStackTrace();
      };
    }

    void jbInit() throws Exception{
      this.setMenuBar(menuBar1);              <—
      xYLayout1.setWidth(500);
      xYLayout1.setHeight(300);
      menu1.setLabel("File");                 <—
      menuItem1.setLabel("Hello");            <—
      label1.setText("Use the File menu...");
      menuItem1.addActionListener(new
   Frame1_menuItem1_ActionAdapter(this));    <—
      this.setLayout(xYLayout1);
      menuBar1.add(menu1);                    <—
      menu1.add(menuItem1);                   <—
      this.add(textField1, new XYConstraints(51, 130, 175, 32));
      this.add(label1, new XYConstraints(29, 76, -1, -1));

    }
```

The Menubar class' constructors and methods appear in Table 6.2, and the Menu class' constructors and methods appear in Table 6.3.

TABLE 6.2 THE MENUBAR CLASS'S CONSTRUCTORS AND METHODS

MenuBar()	Creates a new menu bar.
add(Menu)	Adds the given menu to the menu bar.
addNotify()	Creates the menu bar's peer.
countMenus()	DEPRECATED: Replaced by getMenuCount().
deleteShortcut (MenuShortcut)	Delete the given MenuShortcut.

(continued)

Windows, Menus, and Dialog Boxes

TABLE 6.2 (CONTINUED)

getHelpMenu()	Gets the help menu on the menu bar.
getMenu(int)	Gets the given menu.
getMenuCount()	Counts the number of menus on the menu bar.
getShortcutMenuItem(MenuShortcut)	Return the MenuItem associated with a MenuShortcut
remove(int)	Removes the menu located at the given index
remove(MenuComponent)	Removes the given menu from the menu bar.
removeNotify()	Removes the menu bar's peer.
setHelpMenu(Menu)	Sets the help menu to the given menu on the menu bar.
shortcuts()	Get an Enumeration of all MenuShortcuts this MenuBar manages.

TABLE 6.3 THE MENU CLASS'S CONSTRUCTORS AND METHODS

Menu()	Constructs a new menu with an empty label.
Menu(String)	Constructs a new menu with the given label.
Menu(String, boolean)	Constructs a new menu with the given label.
add(MenuItem)	Adds the given item to this menu.
add(String)	Adds an item with with the given label.
addNotify()	Creates the menu's peer.
addSeparator()	Adds a separator line.
countItems()	DEPRECATED: Replaced by getItemCount().
getItem(int)	Returns the item located at the given index of this menu.
getItemCount()	Returns the number of elements in this menu.
insert(MenuItem, int)	Inserts the MenuItem to this menu at the given position.
insert(String, int)	Inserts item in menu at the given position.
insertSeparator(int)	Inserts a separator at the given position
isTearOff()	Returns true if this is a tear-off menu.
paramString()	Returns the String parameter of the menu.

(continued)

Chapter 6

Table 6.3 (continued)

`remove(int)`	Deletes the item from this menu at the given index.
`remove(MenuComponent)`	Deletes the given item from this menu.
`removeAll()`	Deletes all items from this menu.
`removeNotify()`	Removes the menu's peer.

We've connected an `actionPerformed` method to the Hello menu item:

```
void menuItem1_actionPerformed(java.awt.event.ActionEvent e) {


}
```

And we can report to the user that they've selected that item by placing a message in the text field this way:

```
void menuItem1_actionPerformed(java.awt.event.ActionEvent e) {


    textField1.setText("You chose the Hello item!");     <—



}
```

Finally, we add a new object, `frame`, of the Frame1 class to the menus main class:

```
package menus;
import java.lang.*;
import java.awt.*;
import java.awt.event.*;
import java.applet.*;
import borland.jbcl.control.*;
import borland.jbcl.layout.*;

public
class menus extends Applet {

  public XYLayout xYLayout1 = new XYLayout();
  public boolean isStandalone = false;
  Button button1 = new Button();
```

Windows, Menus, and Dialog Boxes

```
Button button2 = new Button();
Frame1 frame = new Frame1();      <—
      .
      .
      .
```

And we show and hide the window as before, making the Show window and Hide window buttons active:

```
void button1_actionPerformed(java.awt.event.ActionEvent e) {

    frame.resize(300, 300);       <—
    frame.show();                 <—

}

void button2_actionPerformed(java.awt.event.ActionEvent e) {

    frame.hide();                 <—

}
```

Run the applet now and open the File menu, as shown in Figure 6.8.

FIGURE 6.8 OUR NEW FILE MENU.

Chapter 6

Next, select the **Hello** item in the File menu. When you do, our message appears as shown in Figure 6.9. The menus applet works as we want it to. Now we're using menus!

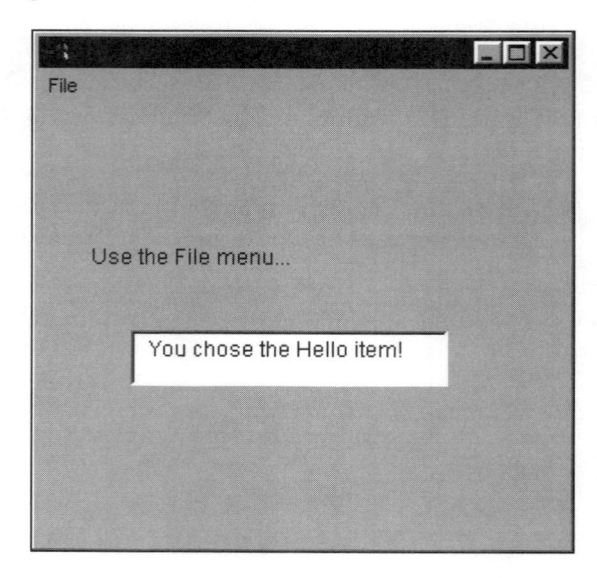

FIGURE 6.9 WE USE THE FILE MENU

The code for this applet appears in Listing 6.3, menus.java, and Listing 6.4, Frame1.java.

LISTING 6.3 MENUS.JAVA

```
//Title:
//Version:
//Copyright:
//Author:
//Company:
//Description:
//

package menus;
import java.lang.*;
import java.awt.*;
import java.awt.event.*;
import java.applet.*;
```

Windows, Menus, and Dialog Boxes

```java
import borland.jbcl.control.*;
import borland.jbcl.layout.*;

public
class menus extends Applet {

  public XYLayout xYLayout1 = new XYLayout();
  public boolean isStandalone = false;
  Button button1 = new Button();
  Button button2 = new Button();
  Frame1 frame = new Frame1();

  //Construct the applet
  public menus() {

  }

  //Initialize the applet
  public void init() {

    try { jbInit(); } catch(Exception e) { e.printStackTrace(); };

  }

  //Component initialization
  public void jbInit() throws Exception{

    xYLayout1.setWidth(400);
    xYLayout1.setHeight(300);
    button1.setLabel("Show window");
    button1.addActionListener(new
menus_button1_ActionAdapter(this));
    button2.setLabel("Hide window");
    button2.addActionListener(new
menus_button2_ActionAdapter(this));
    this.setLayout(xYLayout1);
    this.add(button1, new XYConstraints(88, 87, 119, 45));
    this.add(button2, new XYConstraints(89, 173, 121, 44));
  }
```

Chapter 6

```java
//Start the applet
public void start() {

}

//Stop the applet
public void stop() {

}

//Destroy the applet
public void destroy() {

}

//Get Applet information
public String getAppletInfo() {

   return "Applet Information";
}

//Get parameter info
public String[][] getParameterInfo() {

   return null;

}

//Main method
static public void main(String[] args) {

  menus applet = new menus();
  applet.isStandalone = true;
  DecoratedFrame frame = new DecoratedFrame();
  frame.setTitle("Applet Frame");
  frame.add(applet, BorderLayout.CENTER);
  applet.init();
  applet.start();
  frame.pack();
```

```java
    Dimension d = Toolkit.getDefaultToolkit().getScreenSize();
    frame.setLocation((d.width - frame.getSize().width) / 2,
(d.height - frame.getSize().height) / 2);
    frame.setVisible(true);
  }
  void button1_actionPerformed(java.awt.event.ActionEvent e) {
    frame.resize(300, 300);
    frame.show();
  }
  void button2_actionPerformed(java.awt.event.ActionEvent e) {
    frame.hide();
  }
}
class menus_button1_ActionAdapter implements ActionListener{
  menus adaptee;
  menus_button1_ActionAdapter(menus adaptee) {
    this.adaptee = adaptee;
  }
  public void actionPerformed(java.awt.event.ActionEvent e) {
    adaptee.button1_actionPerformed(e);
  }
}
class menus_button2_ActionAdapter implements ActionListener{
  menus adaptee;
  menus_button2_ActionAdapter(menus adaptee) {
    this.adaptee = adaptee;
  }
  public void actionPerformed(java.awt.event.ActionEvent e) {
    adaptee.button2_actionPerformed(e);
  }
}
```

LISTING 6.4 FRAME1.JAVA

```java
//Title:
//Version:
//Copyright:
//Author:
//Company:
```

Chapter 6

```java
//Description:
//

package menus;

import java.awt.*;
import java.awt.event.*;
import borland.jbcl.layout.*;
import borland.jbcl.control.*;

public
class Frame1 extends DecoratedFrame {

  XYLayout xYLayout1 = new XYLayout();
  MenuBar menuBar1 = new MenuBar();
  Menu menu1 = new Menu();
  MenuItem menuItem1 = new MenuItem();
  TextField textField1 = new TextField();
  Label label1 = new Label();
  public Frame1() {
    try {
      jbInit();
    }
    catch (Exception e) {
      e.printStackTrace();
    };
  }

  void jbInit() throws Exception{
    this.setMenuBar(menuBar1);
    xYLayout1.setWidth(500);
    xYLayout1.setHeight(300);
    menu1.setLabel("File");
    menuItem1.setLabel("Hello");
    label1.setText("Use the File menu...");
    menuItem1.addActionListener(new
Frame1_menuItem1_ActionAdapter(this));
    this.setLayout(xYLayout1);
    menuBar1.add(menu1);
```

Windows, Menus, and Dialog Boxes

```
      menu1.add(menuItem1);
      this.add(textField1, new XYConstraints(51, 130, 175, 32));
      this.add(label1, new XYConstraints(29, 76, -1, -1));
   }

   void menuItem1_actionPerformed(java.awt.event.ActionEvent e) {

      textField1.setText("You chose the Hello item!");

   }

}

class Frame1_menuItem1_ActionAdapter implements ActionListener
{

   Frame1 adaptee;

   Frame1_menuItem1_ActionAdapter(Frame1 adaptee) {

      this.adaptee = adaptee;

   }

   public void actionPerformed(java.awt.event.ActionEvent e) {

      adaptee.menuItem1_actionPerformed(e);

   }

}
```

We've gotten a good start in menus now — but there's more to come. Next, we'll go wild with menus, seeing what they can do.

Full Menus

In our next example, we'll build a more extensive menu system that includes an item that can display a check mark, an item that's grayed out, and an item that supports a submenu:

Chapter 6

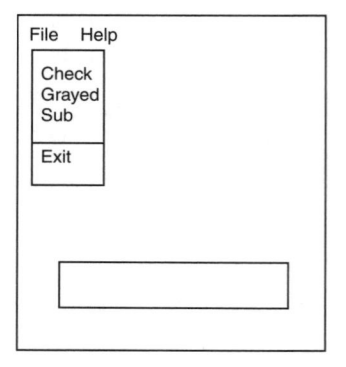

When the user clicks the **Check** menu, a check mark appears in front of that item, and we can report the user's action in the text field:

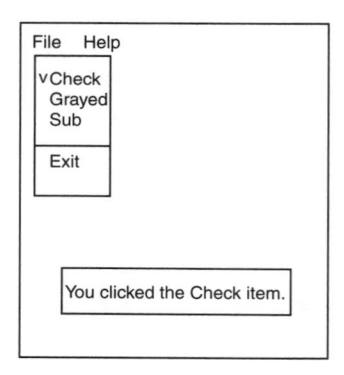

The Grayed item is grayed out, so the user can't select that item. In addition, when the user selects the **Sub** item, a submenu opens:

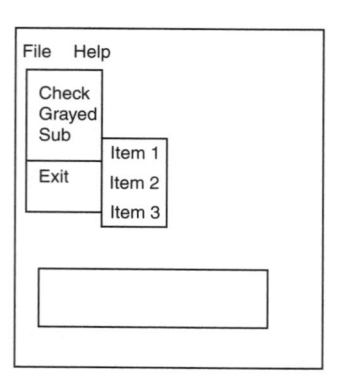

Windows, Menus, and Dialog Boxes

When the user selects an item in that submenu, we'll report which item they've selected:

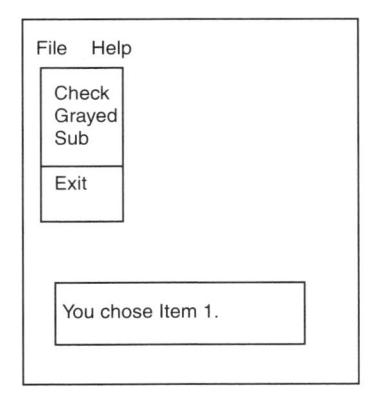

```
File  Help
      ┌─────────┐
      │ Check   │
      │ Grayed  │
      │ Sub     │
      ├─────────┤
      │ Exit    │
      └─────────┘

      ┌──────────────────┐
      │ You chose Item 1.│
      └──────────────────┘
```

Let's create this new program now. We'll make this an application (applications already have a File menu built in) so use the Application Wizard. Call this application fullmenus.

The fullmenus application already has a frame class, Frame1, built in, so open that now, and double-click the **menuBar1** item in the Tree window. Now, open the Menu Designer (as shown in Figure 6.10).

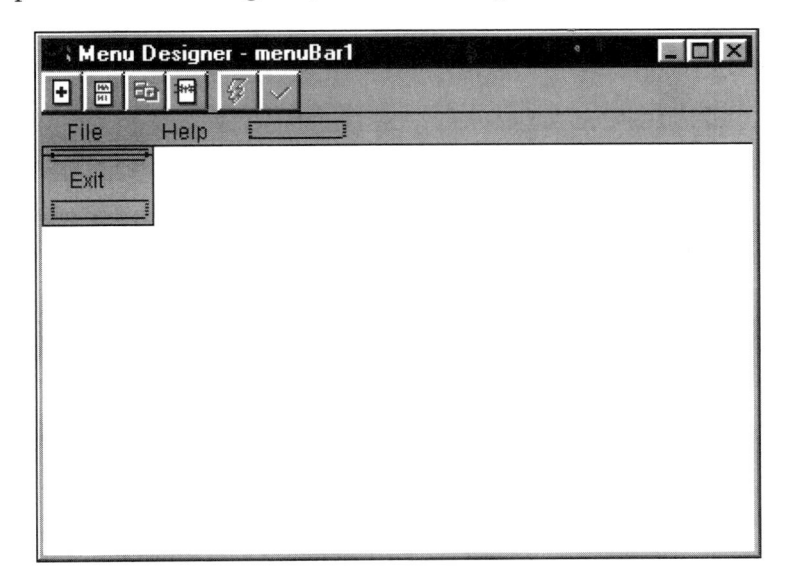

FIGURE 6.10 WE INSERT A MENU SEPARATOR

Adding Menu Separators

Open the File menu and select the **Exit** item already there. We will place a menu separator above this item, so click the **menu separator** button in the Menu Designer now (that button is the second from the left in the Menu Designer button bar). This inserts a new menu separator, as shown in Figure 6.10.

Next, we'll add an item the user can check.

Adding Check Menu Items

Now add a new menu item in the File menu by selecting the **menu separator** and pressing the button with a plus sign in the Menu Editor (the first button on the left in the Menu Designer button bar). Give this item the label **Check** by simply typing that label in.

Next, make this a check menu item by clicking the check button in the Menu Designer — the sixth button from the left. This adds a check mark in front of the check item, as shown in Figure 6.11.

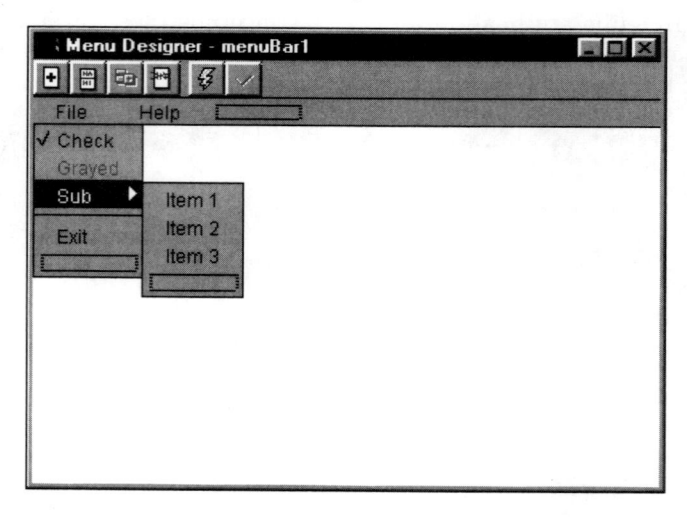

FIGURE 6.11 DESIGNING OUR NEW MENU SYSTEM

Adding Grayed Menu Items

Now add a new item, giving it the label **Grayed**. To make this item grayed out, select the **Active/Inactive** button in the Menu Designer (the fifth tool on the left), graying this new menu item out as shown in Figure 6.11.

Windows, Menus, and Dialog Boxes

Adding Submenu Items

Next, add a new menu item, **Sub**, and click the **submenu** button (the third button from the left in the Menu Designer button bar) to add a new submenu. That menu opens and we can add new items to that submenu, just as we have to the menu itself. We add three items: **Item 1**, **Item 2**, and **Item 3** to the sub menu, as shown in Figure 6.11.

Now, connect an `actionPerformed` event handler to each of the three submenu items using the JBuilder Inspector. We'll place code in those event handlers to inform the user which item they've selected:

```
void menuItem2_actionPerformed(java.awt.event.ActionEvent e) {


}


void menuItem3_actionPerformed(java.awt.event.ActionEvent e) {


}


void menuItem4_actionPerformed(java.awt.event.ActionEvent e) {


}
```

All we have to do is to place an appropriate message into the text field when the user clicks a menu item:

```
void menuItem2_actionPerformed(java.awt.event.ActionEvent e) {

  textField1.setText("You chose Item 1.");    <—
}

void menuItem3_actionPerformed(java.awt.event.ActionEvent e) {

  textField1.setText("You chose Item 2.");    <—

}

void menuItem4_actionPerformed(java.awt.event.ActionEvent e) {
```

Chapter 6

```
        textField1.setText("You chose Item 3.");     <—

    }
```

In addition, we can determine when the check menu item changes state (checked to unchecked, or unchecked to checked) by connecting an `itemStateChanged` event handler to that item in the Inspector:

```
    void
    checkboxMenuItem1_itemStateChanged(java.awt.event.ItemEvent e) {

    }
```

In this event handler, we display a message letting the user know they've changed the state of the check item:

```
    void
    checkboxMenuItem1_itemStateChanged(java.awt.event.ItemEvent e) {

        textField1.setText("You clicked the Check item.");   <—

    }
```

Run the program. You can see our menu system in Figure 6.12—select item 3 in the submenu now, as also shown in Figure 6.12.

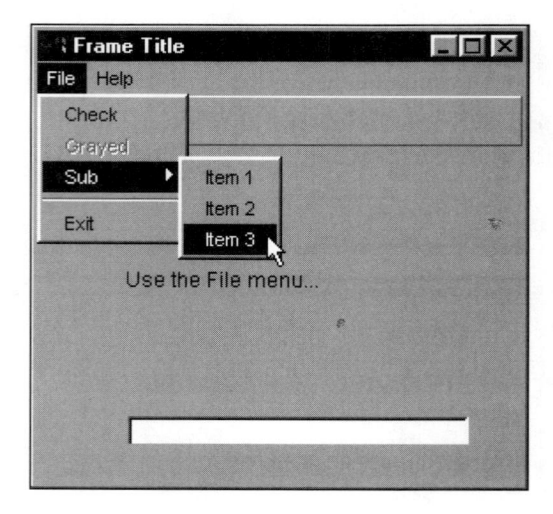

FIGURE 6.12 OUR NEW MENU SYSTEM

This displays the message informing us which item we've chosen, as shown in Figure 6.13.

FIGURE 6.13 WE SELECT A SUBMENU ITEM.

In addition, we can check the check menu item simply by selecting it — do that now, as shown in Figure 6.14.

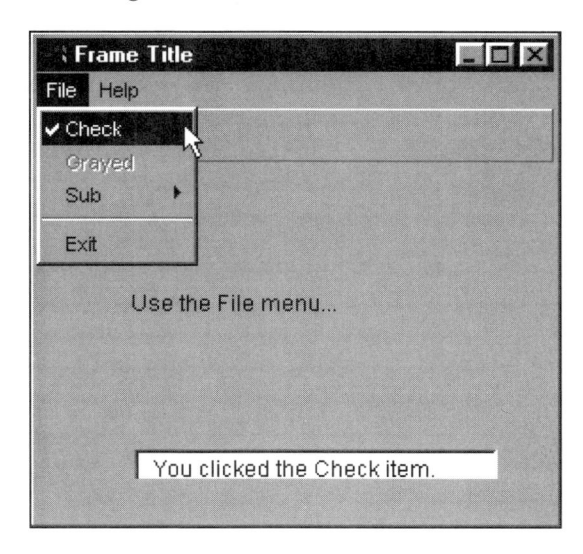

FIGURE 6.14 WE CHECK A MENU ITEM

Chapter 6

The menus application is a success; we're now using check menu items, grayed menu items, and submenus. The code for this application appears in Listing 6.5, fullmenus.java, and Listing 6.6, Frame1.java.

LISTING 6.5 FULLMENUS.JAVA

```java
//Title:
//Version:
//Copyright:
//Author:
//Company:
//Description:
//

package fullmenus;
import java.lang.*;

public
class fullmenus {

  //Construct the application
  public fullmenus() {
    Frame1 frame = new Frame1();
    frame.setVisible(true);
  }

  //Main method
  static public void main(String[] args) {

    new fullmenus();

  }

}
```

LISTING 6.6 FRAME1.JAVA

```java
//Title:
//Version:
//Copyright:
//Author:
```

Windows, Menus, and Dialog Boxes

```java
//Company:
//Description:
//

package fullmenus;
import java.awt.*;
import java.awt.event.*;
import java.lang.*;
import borland.jbcl.control.*;
import borland.jbcl.layout.*;

public
class Frame1 extends DecoratedFrame {

  public BorderLayout borderLayout1 = new BorderLayout();
  public Panel panel1 = new Panel();
  public MenuBar menuBar1 = new MenuBar();
  public Menu menuFile = new Menu();
  public MenuItem menuFileExit = new MenuItem();
  public Menu menuHelp = new Menu();
  public MenuItem menuHelpAbout = new MenuItem();
  public ButtonBar buttonBar = new ButtonBar();
  public Label statusBar = new Label();
  Menu menu1 = new Menu();
  MenuItem menuItem1 = new MenuItem();
  MenuItem menuItem2 = new MenuItem();
  MenuItem menuItem3 = new MenuItem();
  MenuItem menuItem4 = new MenuItem();
  CheckboxMenuItem checkboxMenuItem1 = new CheckboxMenuItem();
  TextField textField1 = new TextField();
  Label label1 = new Label();
  XYLayout xYLayout1 = new XYLayout();
  //Construct the frame
  public Frame1() {
    try { jbInit(); } catch(Exception e) {
e.printStackTrace(); };
  }
  //Component initialization
  public void jbInit() throws Exception{
    this.setLayout(borderLayout1);
```

Chapter 6

```java
    this.setTitle("Frame Title");
    //Add menu bar
    menuFile.setLabel("File");
    menuFileExit.setLabel("Exit");
    menuFileExit.addActionListener(new
Frame1_menuFileExit_ActionAdapter(this));
    menuFile.add(checkboxMenuItem1);
    menuFile.add(menuItem1);
    menuFile.add(menu1);
    menuFile.addSeparator();
    menuFile.add(menuFileExit);
    menuHelp.setLabel("Help");
    menuHelpAbout.setLabel("About");
    menuHelpAbout.addActionListener(new
Frame1_menuHelpAbout_ActionAdapter(this));
    menuHelp.add(menuHelpAbout);
    menuBar1.add(menuFile);
    menuBar1.add(menuHelp);
    this.setMenuBar(menuBar1);
    panel1.setLayout(xYLayout1);
    //Add tool bar
    buttonBar.setButtonType(ButtonBar.IMAGE_ONLY);
    buttonBar.setLabels(new String[] {"Open", "Close",
"Help"});
    buttonBar.setImageDirectory("borland/jbcl/control/images");
    buttonBar.setImageNames(new String[] {"openfile.gif",
"closefile.gif", "help.gif"});
    this.add(buttonBar, BorderLayout.NORTH);
    //Add status bar
    statusBar.setText("");
    menu1.setLabel("Sub");
    menuItem2.setLabel("Item 1");
    menuItem2.addActionListener(new
Frame1_menuItem2_ActionAdapter(this));
    menuItem3.setLabel("Item 2");
    menuItem3.addActionListener(new
Frame1_menuItem3_ActionAdapter(this));
    menuItem4.setLabel("Item 3");
```

Windows, Menus, and Dialog Boxes

```
    menuItem4.addActionListener(new
Frame1_menuItem4_ActionAdapter(this));
    checkboxMenuItem1.setLabel("Check");
    checkboxMenuItem1.addItemListener(new
Frame1_checkboxMenuItem1_ItemAdapter(this));
    menuItem1.setLabel("Grayed");
    menuItem1.setEnabled(false);
    label1.setText("Use the File menu...");
    checkboxMenuItem1.addActionListener(new
Frame1_checkboxMenuItem1_ActionAdapter(this));
    this.add(statusBar, BorderLayout.SOUTH);
    this.add(panel1, BorderLayout.CENTER);
    panel1.add(textField1, new XYConstraints(52, 158, 193,
35));
    panel1.add(label1, new XYConstraints(50, 62, 189, 31));
    //Add center panel
    menu1.add(menuItem2);
    menu1.add(menuItem3);
    menu1.add(menuItem4);
    this.pack();
    //Center the window
    Dimension dimScreen =
Toolkit.getDefaultToolkit().getScreenSize();
    Dimension dimFrame = this.getPreferredSize();
    if(dimFrame.height > dimScreen.height) dimFrame.height =
dimScreen.height;
    if(dimFrame.width > dimScreen.width) dimFrame.width =
dimScreen.width;
    this.setBounds( (dimScreen.width - dimFrame.width) / 2,
(dimScreen.height - dimFrame.height) / 2, dimFrame.width,
dimFrame.height);
  }
  //File | Exit action performed
  public void fileExit_actionPerformed(ActionEvent e) {
    System.exit(0);
  }
  //Help | About action performed
  public void helpAbout_actionPerformed(ActionEvent e) {
  }
```

Chapter 6

```java
    void checkboxMenuItem1_actionPerformed(java.awt.event.ActionEvent e) {

    }

    void menuItem2_actionPerformed(java.awt.event.ActionEvent e) {

        textField1.setText("You chose Item 1.");
    }

    void menuItem3_actionPerformed(java.awt.event.ActionEvent e) {

        textField1.setText("You chose Item 2.");

    }

    void menuItem4_actionPerformed(java.awt.event.ActionEvent e) {

        textField1.setText("You chose Item 3.");

    }

    void checkboxMenuItem1_itemStateChanged(java.awt.event.ItemEvent e) {

        textField1.setText("You clicked the Check item.");

    }
}

class Frame1_menuFileExit_ActionAdapter implements ActionListener{

    Frame1 adaptee;

    Frame1_menuFileExit_ActionAdapter(Frame1 adaptee) {

        this.adaptee = adaptee;

    }
```

```java
  public void actionPerformed(ActionEvent e) {

    adaptee.fileExit_actionPerformed(e);

  }

}

class Frame1_menuHelpAbout_ActionAdapter implements

ActionListener {

  Frame1 adaptee;

  Frame1_menuHelpAbout_ActionAdapter(Frame1 adaptee) {

    this.adaptee = adaptee;

  }

  public void actionPerformed(ActionEvent e) {

    adaptee.helpAbout_actionPerformed(e);

  }

}

class Frame1_checkboxMenuItem1_ActionAdapter implements

ActionListener{

  Frame1 adaptee;

  Frame1_checkboxMenuItem1_ActionAdapter(Frame1 adaptee) {

    this.adaptee = adaptee;

  }

  public void actionPerformed(java.awt.event.ActionEvent e) {

    adaptee.checkboxMenuItem1_actionPerformed(e);

  }
```

```java
}

class Frame1_menuItem2_ActionAdapter implements ActionListener
{
  Frame1 adaptee;

  Frame1_menuItem2_ActionAdapter(Frame1 adaptee) {
    this.adaptee = adaptee;
  }

  public void actionPerformed(java.awt.event.ActionEvent e) {
    adaptee.menuItem2_actionPerformed(e);
  }
}

class Frame1_menuItem3_ActionAdapter implements ActionListener
{
  Frame1 adaptee;

  Frame1_menuItem3_ActionAdapter(Frame1 adaptee) {
    this.adaptee = adaptee;
  }

  public void actionPerformed(java.awt.event.ActionEvent e) {
    adaptee.menuItem3_actionPerformed(e);
  }
}
```

```
class Frame1_menuItem4_ActionAdapter implements ActionListener
{
  Frame1 adaptee;
  Frame1_menuItem4_ActionAdapter(Frame1 adaptee) {
    this.adaptee = adaptee;
  }
  public void actionPerformed(java.awt.event.ActionEvent e) {
    adaptee.menuItem4_actionPerformed(e);
  }
}
class Frame1_checkboxMenuItem1_ItemAdapter implements
ItemListener{
  Frame1 adaptee;
  Frame1_checkboxMenuItem1_ItemAdapter(Frame1 adaptee) {
    this.adaptee = adaptee;
  }
  public void itemStateChanged(java.awt.event.ItemEvent e) {
    adaptee.checkboxMenuItem1_itemStateChanged(e);
  }
}
```

We've seen how to create menus in JBuilder — let's turn now to the last topic for this chapter: dialog boxes.

Chapter 6

Using Dialog Boxes

Next, we'll show how to create a dialog box. This dialog box will let the user type some text into a text field and if the user clicks the **OK** button in the dialog box, the dialog box will pass that text back to the main window to be displayed in a text field. In the main applet, we'll have two buttons, **Show dialog box** and **Hide dialog box**, and a text field:

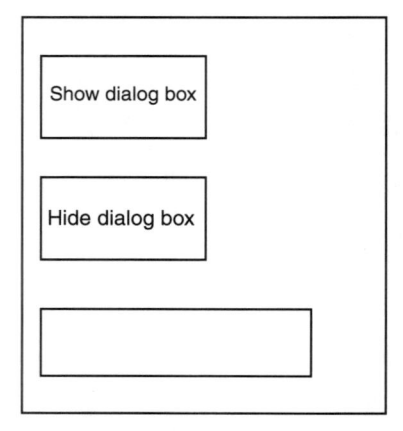

```
Show dialog box

Hide dialog box
```

When the user clicks the **Show dialog box** button, we place a dialog box on the screen, and the user can type some text into the dialog's text field:

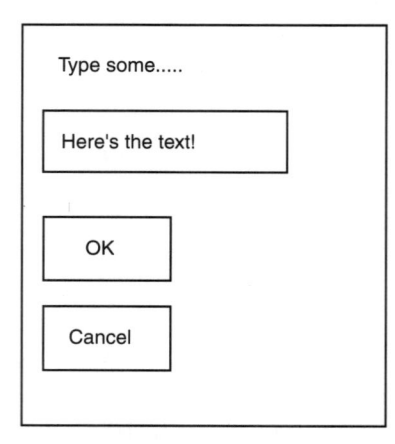

```
Type some.....

Here's the text!

OK

Cancel
```

Windows, Menus, and Dialog Boxes

If the user clicks **OK**, the dialog box closes and the text is displayed in the applet window's text field:

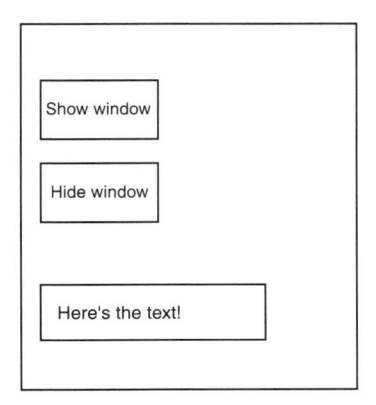

```
┌─────────────────────────────┐
│                             │
│      ┌─────────────┐        │
│      │ Show window │        │
│      └─────────────┘        │
│                             │
│      ┌─────────────┐        │
│      │ Hide window │        │
│      └─────────────┘        │
│                             │
│                             │
│     ┌────────────────┐      │
│     │ Here's the text!│     │
│     └────────────────┘      │
│                             │
└─────────────────────────────┘
```

Let's put this program to work. Create a new applet named dialogs now, and add a new frame window class, Frame1, to the project.

The frame window object needs to communicate with the applet object in order to pass the text the user typed back to the applet object. To make that easier, we can set up a new method in the Frame1 class now, which we'll call `display()`. This method works just like the frame window `show()` method, except it is also passed a reference to the main applet object, which is of class dialogs:

```
void display(dialogs d){


}
```

In this new method, we'll just save the reference to the applet object as the variable caller, and call the `show()` method ourselves to display the frame window:

```
void display(dialogs d){

    caller = d;          <—
    show();              <—

}
```

Chapter 6

We also set up the `caller` variable in the Frame1 class:

```
import java.awt.*;
import java.awt.event.*;
import borland.jbcl.layout.*;
import borland.jbcl.control.*;

public
class Frame1 extends DecoratedFrame {
  XYLayout xYLayout1 = new XYLayout();
  Button button1 = new Button();
  Button button2 = new Button();
  TextField textField1 = new TextField();
  dialogs caller;                              <--
  Label label1 = new Label();
    .
    .
    .
```

Now we create a new object of the Frame1 class in the applet class dialogs:

```
package dialogs;
import java.lang.*;
import java.awt.*;
import java.awt.event.*;
import java.applet.*;
import borland.jbcl.control.*;
import borland.jbcl.layout.*;

public
class dialogs extends Applet {

  public XYLayout xYLayout1 = new XYLayout();
  public boolean isStandalone = false;
  Button button1 = new Button();
  Button button2 = new Button();
  Frame1 frame = new Frame1();              <--
    .
    .
    .
```

In the `actionPerformed` event handler for the Show dialog box button, we can call the frame object's `display()` method:

```
void button1_actionPerformed(java.awt.event.ActionEvent e) {

    frame.resize(300, 300);


    frame.display(this);


}
```

This displays the new dialog box on the screen.

Sending Data from Dialog Box to Applets

When the user types some text in the dialog box's text field and clicks the **OK** button, we can pass the text they've typed back to the text field in the main applet object. Add the OK and Cancel buttons to the dialog box Frame1 now, and add the text field as well. When the user clicks the **OK** button, we will pass the text they've typed back to the main applet object this way:

```
void button1_actionPerformed(java.awt.event.ActionEvent e) {

    (caller.textField1).setText(textField1.getText());
        .
        .
        .
}
```

Finally, because the user has clicked the **OK** button, we hide the dialog box:

```
void button1_actionPerformed(java.awt.event.ActionEvent e) {

    (caller.textField1).setText(textField1.getText());
```

Chapter 6

```
        hide();    <—


    }
```

We also add code to the Cancel button so the dialog box disappears—without passing the text back to the applet object—when the user clicks this button:

```
    void button2_actionPerformed(java.awt.event.ActionEvent e) {

        hide();    <—


    }
```

The dialogs program is complete. Run it now, and click the **Show dialog box** button. Type some text into the dialog box, as shown in Figure 6.15.

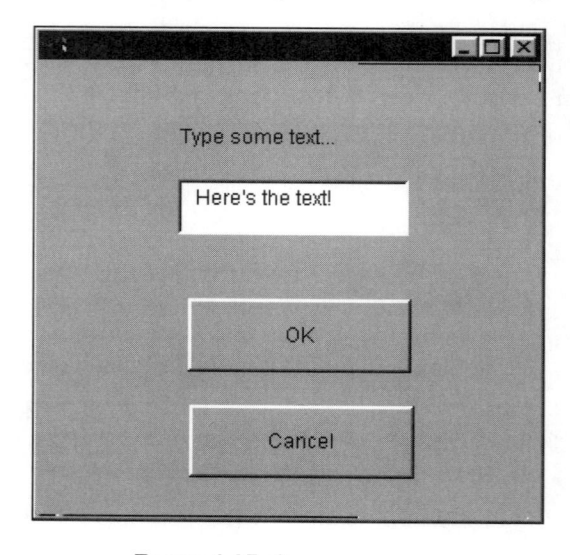

FIGURE 6.15 OUR DIALOG BOX.

Now click the **OK** button. The dialog box closes and the text appears in the main applet, as shown in Figure 6.16.

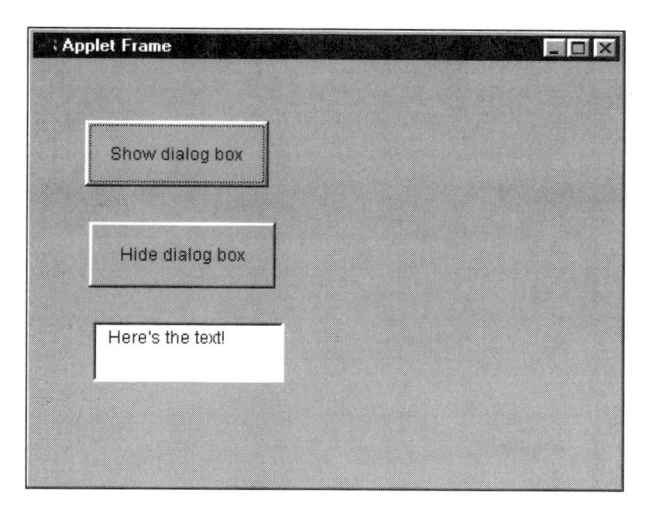

FIGURE 6.16 RETRIEVING TEXT FROM OUR DIALOG BOX.

The dialogs applet is a success. The code for this applet, dialogs.java, appears in Listing 6.7, and the code for Frame1.java appears in Listing 6.8.

LISTING 6.7 DIALOGS.JAVA

```
//Title:
//Version:
//Copyright:
//Author:
//Company:
//Description:
//

package dialogs;
import java.lang.*;
import java.awt.*;
import java.awt.event.*;
import java.applet.*;
import borland.jbcl.control.*;
import borland.jbcl.layout.*;
```

Chapter 6

```java
public
class dialogs extends Applet {

  public XYLayout xYLayout1 = new XYLayout();
  public boolean isStandalone = false;
  Button button1 = new Button();
  Button button2 = new Button();
  Frame1 frame = new Frame1();
  TextField textField1 = new TextField();
  //Construct the applet
  public dialogs() {
  }

  //Initialize the applet
  public void init() {

    try { jbInit(); } catch(Exception e) { e.printStackTrace(); };

  }

  //Component initialization
  public void jbInit() throws Exception{

    xYLayout1.setWidth(400);
    xYLayout1.setHeight(300);
    button1.setLabel("Show dialog box");
    button1.addActionListener(new
dialogs_button1_ActionAdapter(this));
    button2.setLabel("Hide dialog box");
    button2.addActionListener(new
dialogs_button2_ActionAdapter(this));
    this.setLayout(xYLayout1);
    this.add(button1, new XYConstraints(36, 43, 125, 47));
    this.add(button2, new XYConstraints(39, 115, 127, 46));
    this.add(textField1, new XYConstraints(42, 185, 130, 42));

  }

  //Start the applet
```

```
public void start() {

}

//Stop the applet
public void stop() {

}

//Destroy the applet
public void destroy() {

}

//Get Applet information
public String getAppletInfo() {

   return "Applet Information";

}

//Get parameter info
public String[][] getParameterInfo() {

   return null;

}

//Main method
static public void main(String[] args) {

   dialogs applet = new dialogs();
   applet.isStandalone = true;
   DecoratedFrame frame = new DecoratedFrame();
   frame.setTitle("Applet Frame");
   frame.add(applet, BorderLayout.CENTER);
   applet.init();
   applet.start();
   frame.pack();
```

Chapter 6

```java
        Dimension d = Toolkit.getDefaultToolkit().getScreenSize();
        frame.setLocation((d.width - frame.getSize().width) / 2,
(d.height - frame.getSize().height) / 2);
        frame.setVisible(true);

    }

    void button1_actionPerformed(java.awt.event.ActionEvent e) {

      frame.resize(300, 300);

      frame.display(this);

    }

    void button2_actionPerformed(java.awt.event.ActionEvent e) {

      frame.hide();

    }

}

class dialogs_button1_ActionAdapter implements ActionListener{

  dialogs adaptee;

  dialogs_button1_ActionAdapter(dialogs adaptee) {

    this.adaptee = adaptee;

  }

  public void actionPerformed(java.awt.event.ActionEvent e) {

    adaptee.button1_actionPerformed(e);

  }

}

class dialogs_button2_ActionAdapter implements ActionListener{

  dialogs adaptee;
```

Windows, Menus, and Dialog Boxes

```
    dialogs_button2_ActionAdapter(dialogs adaptee) {

      this.adaptee = adaptee;

    }

    public void actionPerformed(java.awt.event.ActionEvent e) {

      adaptee.button2_actionPerformed(e);

    }

  }
```

LISTING 6.8 FRAME1.JAVA

```
//Title:
//Version:
//Copyright:
//Author:
//Company:
//Description:
//

package dialogs;

import java.awt.*;
import java.awt.event.*;
import borland.jbcl.layout.*;
import borland.jbcl.control.*;

public
class Frame1 extends DecoratedFrame {
  XYLayout xYLayout1 = new XYLayout();
  Button button1 = new Button();
  Button button2 = new Button();
  TextField textField1 = new TextField();
  dialogs caller;
  Label label1 = new Label();
```

Chapter 6

```java
public Frame1() {
  try {
    jbInit();
  }
  catch (Exception e) {
    e.printStackTrace();
  };
}

void jbInit() throws Exception{

  xYLayout1.setWidth(500);
  xYLayout1.setHeight(300);
  button1.setLabel("OK");
  button1.addActionListener(new
Frame1_button1_ActionAdapter(this));
  button2.setLabel("Cancel");
  label1.setText("Type some text...");
  button2.addActionListener(new
Frame1_button2_ActionAdapter(this));
  this.setLayout(xYLayout1);
  this.add(button1, new XYConstraints(87, 142, 131, 44));
  this.add(button2, new XYConstraints(88, 206, 132, 44));
  this.add(textField1, new XYConstraints(81, 71, 135, 33));
  this.add(label1, new XYConstraints(82, 35, 139, 19));

}

void display(dialogs d){

  caller = d;
  show();

}

void button1_actionPerformed(java.awt.event.ActionEvent e) {

  (caller.textField1).setText(textField1.getText());

  hide();
```

```java
  }

  void button2_actionPerformed(java.awt.event.ActionEvent e) {

    hide();

  }

}

class Frame1_button1_ActionAdapter implements ActionListener{

  Frame1 adaptee;

  Frame1_button1_ActionAdapter(Frame1 adaptee) {

    this.adaptee = adaptee;

  }

  public void actionPerformed(java.awt.event.ActionEvent e) {

    adaptee.button1_actionPerformed(e);

  }

}

class Frame1_button2_ActionAdapter implements ActionListener{

  Frame1 adaptee;

  Frame1_button2_ActionAdapter(Frame1 adaptee) {

    this.adaptee = adaptee;

  }

  public void actionPerformed(java.awt.event.ActionEvent e) {

    adaptee.button2_actionPerformed(e);

  }

}
```

Chapter 6

That's it for our chapter on windows, menus, and dialog boxes. We've seen a great deal in this chapter, from how to display a new window to using menus with check items, grayed items, and submenus, and now dialog boxes. There's a lot of programming power in these techniques. Next, we'll turn to a very popular JBuilder topic: graphics.

CHAPTER 7

Graphics: Image Handling and Text

In this chapter, we're going to start taking a look at a very popular JBuilder topic: graphics. We'll see how to use images in JBuilder—how to load them in from disk and display them. Then we'll improve on that, displaying them in all different shapes, stretching our images as we like.

Next, we'll see how to use the JBuilder Image Control to automatically read in and display images for us. All we'll have to do is to set the image control's `imageName` property to a graphics file name, and the image control will display that graphics file for us at once.

Then we'll move on to handling and displaying text. You may be surprised to find text handling in a graphics chapter, but in a graphics environment like Web browsers and Java applications, all displayed items are graphics, even text. In fact, it's important to know how to handle text in a graphical environment, because text placement and alignment is often an issue.

We'll see two text-handling programs in this chapter. The first writer allows us to click a location in our window and type text at that location in a variety of fonts and with a variety of options. Next, we'll see how to display text in various locations in a window—justified in the center, right-justified, and left-justified as well.

Let's start now by seeing how the `Image` class works.

Chapter 7

Using the Image Class

Using the Java `Image` class, we'll be able to read in an image from disk and display it:

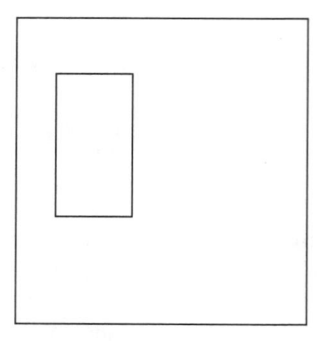

Let's see how this works—we'll use **image.gif**, shown in Figure 7.1.

Figure 7.1 image.gif.

Create a new applet named **imager** now. We'll create a new `Image` object named image in the imager applet this way:

```
package imager;
import java.lang.*;
import java.awt.*;
import java.awt.event.*;
import java.applet.*;
import borland.jbcl.control.*;
import borland.jbcl.layout.*;

public
class imager extends Applet {
  public XYLayout xYLayout1 = new XYLayout();
```

Graphics: Image Handling and Text

```
public boolean isStandalone = false;
Image image;                              <—
    .
    .
    .
```

The Java Image class' constructors and methods appear in Table 7.1.

Table 7.1 The Image Class's Constructors and Methods

`Image()`	Constructs a new Image object
`createScaledImage (int, int, int)`	Creates a scaled image.
`flush()`	Flushes all resources.
`getGraphics()`	Gets a graphics object to draw into this image.
`getHeight(ImageObserver)`	Gets the actual height of the image.
`getProperty (String, ImageObserver)`	Gets a property by name.
`getSource()`	Gets the object that produces the pixels for the image.
`getWidth(ImageObserver)`	Gets the actual width of the image.

Next, we can load the image.gif file into the image object with the Applet class's `getImage()` method. We need to indicate where that image file is to the `getImage()` method, and we'll use the `getCodebase()` method to do that. This method, `getCodebase()`, usually returns the location of the .class file for the applet:

```
public void init() {

  image = getImage(getCodeBase(), "image.gif");    <—

  try { jbInit(); } catch(Exception e) { e.printStackTrace(); };
}
```

In fact, one of the parameters in the sample Web page for this applet is CODEBASE:

Chapter 7

```
<HTML>
<TITLE>
HTML Test Page
</TITLE>
<BODY>
imager.imager will appear below in a Java enabled browser.
<APPLET
  CODEBASE = ""
  CODE     = "imager.imager.class"
  NAME     = "TestApplet"
  WIDTH    = 400
  HEIGHT   = 300
  HSPACE   = 0
  VSPACE   = 0
  ALIGN    = Middle
>
</APPLET>
</BODY>
</HTML>
```

In our case, we'll store the image.gif file in the folder **c:/jbuilder/myclasses/imager**, so we set the CODEBASE parameter to that value by editing the sample Web page's HTML:

```
<HTML>
<TITLE>
HTML Test Page
</TITLE>
<BODY>
imager.imager will appear below in a Java enabled browser.
<APPLET
  CODEBASE = "c:/jbuilder/myclasses/imager"      <—
  CODE     = "imager.imager.class"
  NAME     = "TestApplet"
  WIDTH    = 400
  HEIGHT   = 300
  HSPACE   = 0
  VSPACE   = 0
  ALIGN    = Middle
```

Graphics: Image Handling and Text

```
        >
    </APPLET>
    </BODY>
    </HTML>
```

Now override the `paint()` method, because that's where we'll draw our image:

```
public void paint(Graphics g) {

  //TODO: override this java.awt.Component method;


  super.paint( g);


}
```

To draw the image now in the object we've named image, we will use the Graphics class' `drawimage()` method. We just pass the following parameters: the x and y location of the upper left corner of the image as we want to place it in the applet, its width and height, and an `ImageObserver` object. This `ImageObserver` object oversees several aspects of reading in the image, and we'll use the applet object as our `ImageObserver` by passing a this keyword:

```
public void paint(Graphics g) {

  g.drawImage(image, 40, 40, 135, 91, this);    <-


  super.paint( g);


}
```

This draws the image in the applet. Run the applet now, as shown in Figure 7.2. There is an odd bug in JBuilder that sometimes occurs when you're testing a program that uses the `getCodeBase()` method which causes `getCodeBase()` to crash; if that happens to you, highlight the name of the .html file in the Project window and try again. You can see our image displayed in the applet—now we're displaying images!

Chapter 7

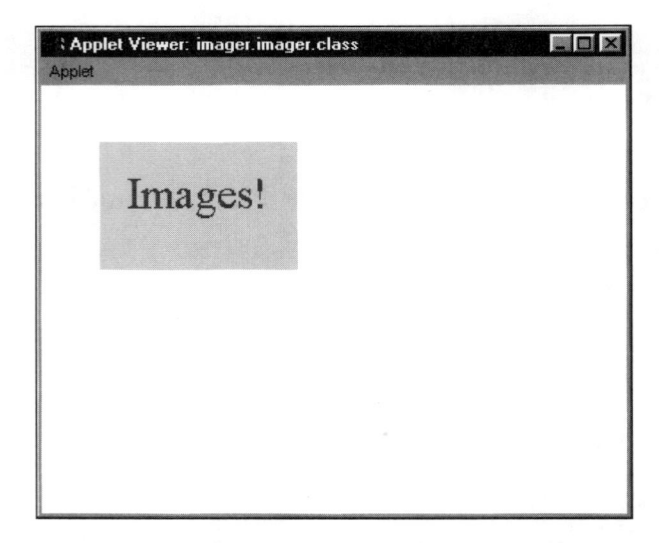

Figure 7.2 We display an image in an applet.

The code for this applet appears in Listing 7.1.

Listing 7.1 imager.java

```
//Title:
//Version:
//Copyright:
//Author:
//Company:
//Description:
//

package imager;
import java.lang.*;
import java.awt.*;
import java.awt.event.*;
import java.applet.*;
import borland.jbcl.control.*;
import borland.jbcl.layout.*;

public
```

Graphics: Image Handling and Text

```java
class imager extends Applet {
  public XYLayout xYLayout1 = new XYLayout();
  public boolean isStandalone = false;
  Image image;

  //Construct the applet
  public imager() {
  }
  //Initialize the applet
  public void init() {

    image = getImage(getCodeBase(), "image.gif");
    try { jbInit(); } catch(Exception e) { e.printStackTrace(); };
  }

  //Component initialization
  public void jbInit() throws Exception{
    xYLayout1.setWidth(400);
    xYLayout1.setHeight(300);
    this.setLayout(xYLayout1);
  }

  //Start the applet
  public void start() {

  }

  //Stop the applet
  public void stop() {

  }

  //Destroy the applet
  public void destroy() {

  }

  //Get Applet information
  public String getAppletInfo() {
```

Chapter 7

```java
        return "Applet Information";

    }

    //Get parameter info
    public String[][] getParameterInfo() {

        return null;

    }

    //Main method
    static public void main(String[] args) {

        imager applet = new imager();
        applet.isStandalone = true;
        DecoratedFrame frame = new DecoratedFrame();
        frame.setTitle("Applet Frame");
        frame.add(applet, BorderLayout.CENTER);
        applet.init();
        applet.start();
        frame.pack();
        Dimension d = Toolkit.getDefaultToolkit().getScreenSize();
        frame.setLocation((d.width - frame.getSize().width) / 2,
    (d.height - frame.getSize().height) / 2);
        frame.setVisible(true);
    }

    public void paint(Graphics g) {

        //TODO: override this java.awt.Component method;
        g.drawImage(image, 40, 40, 135, 91, this);
        super.paint( g);

    }

}
```

We've seen how to display an image. Now, let's see how to stretch it!

Graphics: Image Handling and Text

Scaling Images to Different Sizes

You might note that we passed the width and height of the image we wanted to draw to the `drawImage()` method. In fact, we can pass a new width and height for our image, and `drawImage` will scale it accordingly. We can even draw several versions of the same figure, scaled to different widths and heights:

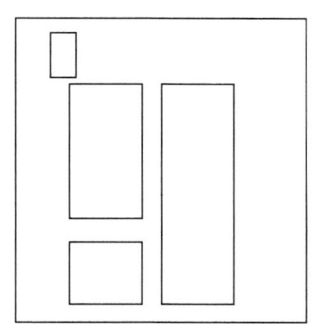

Let's give this a try. We start by creating a new applet named **scaler.** This applet will start by reading in the image.gif file and placing it into the `Image` object we've named `image`:

```
public
class scaler extends Applet {
  public XYLayout xYLayout1 = new XYLayout();
  public boolean isStandalone = false;
  Image image;                                        <—
    .
    .
    .
```

And we read the image in as we did the previous example:

```
public void init() {

    image = getImage(getCodeBase(), "image.gif");    <—
```

Chapter 7

```
        try { jbInit(); } catch(Exception e) { e.printStackTrace(); };

}
```

Scaling an Image

Now we can draw that image four times at different locations, and with different widths and heights to scale it by overriding the `paint()` method:

```
public void paint(Graphics g) {

    g.drawImage(image, 40, 70, 100, 180, this);      <—
    g.drawImage(image, 1, 1, 60, 60, this);          <—
    g.drawImage(image, 200, 10, 160, 280, this);     <—
    g.drawImage(image, 30, 270, 160, 50, this);      <—

    super.paint( g );
}
```

The result appears in Figure 7.3. You can see our image.gif image stretched several different ways. Our scaler program is a success. Now we're scaling bitmaps.

Figure 7.3 Scaling an image

Graphics: Image Handling and Text

The code for this applet appears in Listing 7.2.

Listing 7.2 scaler.java

```java
//Title:
//Version:
//Copyright:
//Author:
//Company:
//Description:
//

package scaler;
import java.lang.*;
import java.awt.*;
import java.awt.event.*;
import java.applet.*;
import borland.jbcl.control.*;
import borland.jbcl.layout.*;

public
class scaler extends Applet {
  public XYLayout xYLayout1 = new XYLayout();
  public boolean isStandalone = false;
  Image image;

  //Construct the applet
  public scaler() {

  }

  //Initialize the applet
  public void init() {

  image = getImage(getCodeBase(), "image.gif");

    try { jbInit(); } catch(Exception e) { e.printStackTrace(); };

  }
```

Chapter 7

```
//Component initialization
public void jbInit() throws Exception{

  xYLayout1.setWidth(400);
  xYLayout1.setHeight(300);
  this.setLayout(xYLayout1);

}

//Start the applet
public void start() {

}

//Stop the applet
public void stop() {

}

//Destroy the applet
public void destroy() {

}

//Get Applet information
public String getAppletInfo() {

  return "Applet Information";

}

//Get parameter info
public String[][] getParameterInfo() {

  return null;

}

//Main method
```

Graphics: Image Handling and Text

```
    static public void main(String[] args) {

      scaler applet = new scaler();
      applet.isStandalone = true;
      DecoratedFrame frame = new DecoratedFrame();
      frame.setTitle("Applet Frame");
      frame.add(applet, BorderLayout.CENTER);
      applet.init();
      applet.start();
      frame.pack();
      Dimension d = Toolkit.getDefaultToolkit().getScreenSize();
      frame.setLocation((d.width - frame.getSize().width) / 2,
    (d.height - frame.getSize().height) / 2);
      frame.setVisible(true);


    public void paint(Graphics g) {

      //TODO: override this java.awt.Component method;
      g.drawImage(image, 40, 70, 100, 180, this);
      g.drawImage(image, 1, 1, 60, 60, this);
      g.drawImage(image, 200, 10, 160, 280, this);
      g.drawImage(image, 30, 270, 160, 50, this);
      super.paint( g);

    }

  }
```

At this point, then, we've seen how to draw and display images directly with the `drawImage()` method. Next, we'll see how to use the JBuilder Image control to do the same thing for us.

Using the Image Control

In the next example, we'll see how to load an image into a JBuilder Image control; these are special controls designed to display an image:

Chapter 7

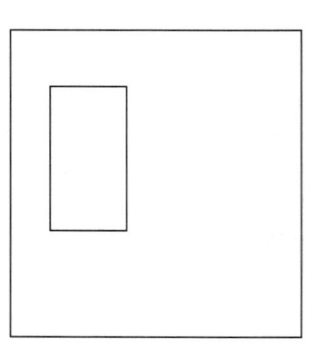

Create a new applet named imagecontrol now, and open it in the JBuilder Designer. We'll add a new Image control to the applet now. Use the Image control now (the sixth tool from the left when you click the **Controls** tab in Jbuilder) and draw a new Image control in the applet. This adds a new Image control object named `iamgeControl1` to the applet:

```
public
class imagecontrol extends Applet {

    public XYLayout xYLayout1 = new XYLayout();
    public boolean isStandalone = false;
    ImageControl imageControl1 = new ImageControl();      <--
         .
         .
         .
```

Copy the image.gif file over to the source code folder for the imagecontrol program (e.g., **c:\JBuilder\myprojects\imagecontrol**), and then set the Image control's `imageName` property to **image.gif**. This is the code that JBuilder adds to do that:

```
public void jbInit() throws Exception{
    xYLayout1.setWidth(400);
    xYLayout1.setHeight(300);
    imageControl1.setImageName("image.gif");      <--
    this.setLayout(xYLayout1);
    this.add(imageControl1, new XYConstraints(29, 31, 143, 108));
}
```

Graphics: Image Handling and Text

That's all we need—run the program now, as shown in Figure 7.4. As you can see, the Image control is doing its job—displaying an image.

Figure 7.4 Using the JBuilder Image control.

The code for this applet appears in Listing 7.3.

Listing 7.3 imagecontrol.java

```
//Title:
//Version:
//Copyright:
//Author:
//Company:
//Description:
//

package imagecontrol;
import java.lang.*;
import java.awt.*;
import java.awt.event.*;
import java.applet.*;
import borland.jbcl.control.*;
import borland.jbcl.layout.*;
```

Chapter 7

```java
public
class imagecontrol extends Applet {

  public XYLayout xYLayout1 = new XYLayout();
  public boolean isStandalone = false;
  ImageControl imageControl1 = new ImageControl();

  //Construct the applet
  public imagecontrol() {

  }

  //Initialize the applet
  public void init() {

    try { jbInit(); } catch(Exception e) { e.printStackTrace(); };

  }

  //Component initialization
  public void jbInit() throws Exception{

    xYLayout1.setWidth(400);
    xYLayout1.setHeight(300);
    imageControl1.setImageName("image.gif");
    this.setLayout(xYLayout1);
    this.add(imageControl1, new XYConstraints(29, 31, 143, 108));

  }

  //Start the applet
  public void start() {

  }

  //Stop the applet
  public void stop() {

  }
```

Graphics: Image Handling and Text

```
    //Destroy the applet
    public void destroy() {

    }

    //Get Applet information
    public String getAppletInfo() {

       return "Applet Information";

    }

    //Get parameter info
    public String[][] getParameterInfo() {

       return null;

    }

    //Main method
    static public void main(String[] args) {

       imagecontrol applet = new imagecontrol();
       applet.isStandalone = true;
       DecoratedFrame frame = new DecoratedFrame();
       frame.setTitle("Applet Frame");
       frame.add(applet, BorderLayout.CENTER);
       applet.init();
       applet.start();
       frame.pack();
       Dimension d = Toolkit.getDefaultToolkit().getScreenSize();
       frame.setLocation((d.width - frame.getSize().width) / 2,
(d.height - frame.getSize().height) / 2);
       frame.setVisible(true);

    }

}
```

We've gotten a good introduction to image handling in JBuilder. Our next step will be to start taking a look at text handling.

Chapter 7

The Writer Applet

In this next example, we'll create an applet that will let the user type at the keyboard, and we'll display what they type at a location in the applet they choose. They'll be able to choose the text options they want: Times Roman or Courier font; setting the font size to large; making the text bold, italic, or plain (meaning we reset all text options):

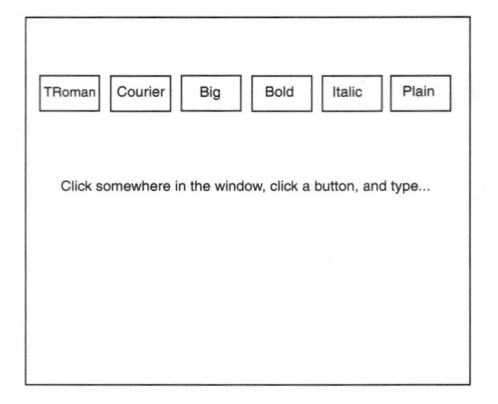

```
┌─────────────────────────────────────────────┐
│ [TRoman] [Courier] [Big] [Bold] [Italic] [Plain] │
│                                             │
│   Click somewhere in the window, click a button, and type... │
│                                             │
│                                             │
│                                             │
└─────────────────────────────────────────────┘
```

The user clicks a location in the applet, then clicks one or more buttons to make the text bold, italic, and so on, and then types their text. The text appears at the location they've clicked:

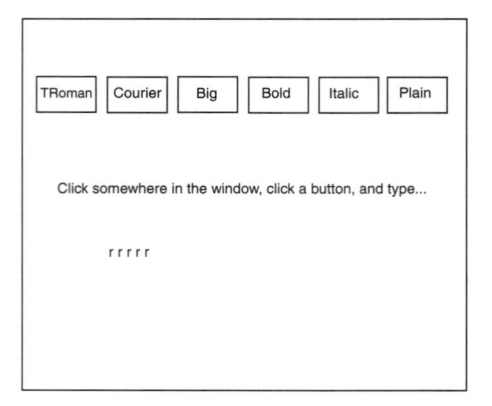

```
┌─────────────────────────────────────────────┐
│ [TRoman] [Courier] [Big] [Bold] [Italic] [Plain] │
│                                             │
│   Click somewhere in the window, click a button, and type... │
│                                             │
│          r r r r r                          │
│                                             │
└─────────────────────────────────────────────┘
```

Then they can click another location in the applet, click other font options, and type another string of text:

Graphics: Image Handling and Text

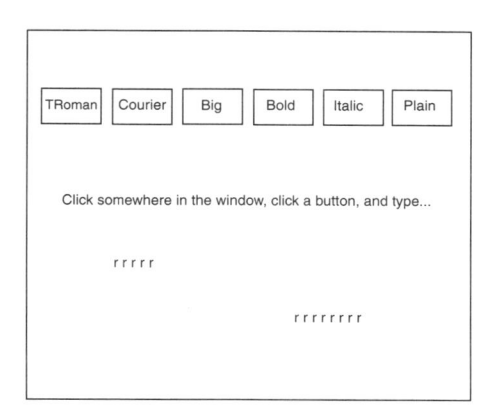

Let's see this at work now. Create the writer applet and open it in the Designer.

Setting the Writer Applet's Flags

We'll use six buttons in the writer applet: TRoman (to set the font to Times Roman), Courier, Big (to set the font size to a large size), Bold, Italic, and Plain. Add those buttons now, as shown in Figure 7.5. Also, add a label with the prompt: **Click somewhere in the window, click a button, and type...**, as also shown in Figure 7.5.

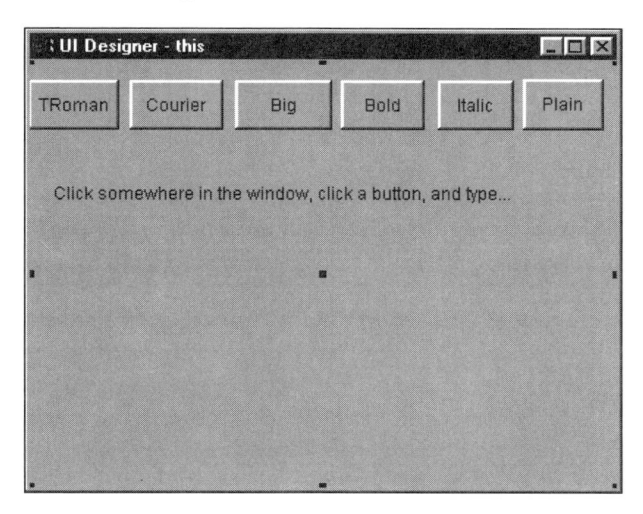

Figure 7.5 Adding writer's buttons.

Chapter 7

We will set up a Boolean flag, which can hold the values true or false, for each button. This records the new text option the user has set:

```
package writer;
import java.lang.*;
import java.awt.*;
import java.awt.event.*;
import java.applet.*;
import borland.jbcl.control.*;
import borland.jbcl.layout.*;

public
class writer extends Applet{

    public XYLayout xYLayout1 = new XYLayout();
    public boolean isStandalone = false;

    boolean bFont1Flag = false;                 <--
    boolean bFont2Flag = false;                 <--
    boolean bBigFlag = false;                   <--
    boolean bBoldFlag = false;                  <--
    boolean bItalicFlag = false;                <--
    boolean bPlainFlag = false;                 <--
        .
        .
        .
```

Now we have to set the boolean flags to match the user's button clicks. For example, we'll set the `bFont1Flag` to `true` when the user clicks the **TRoman** button. Since we can only have one font active at a time, when we set `bFont1Flag` to `true`, we'll set the flag for Courier font to `false`:

```
void button1_actionPerformed(java.awt.event.ActionEvent e) {

    bFont1Flag = true;              <--
    bFont2Flag = false;             <--

}
```

And when the user selects Courier, we set that flag `true` and set the Times Roman flag `false`:

```
void button2_actionPerformed(java.awt.event.ActionEvent e) {

    bFont2Flag = true;              <--
    bFont1Flag = false;             <--

}
```

Then we just set the Big, Bold, and Italic flags to `true` when clicked:

```
void button3_actionPerformed(java.awt.event.ActionEvent e) {

    bBigFlag = true;

}


void button4_actionPerformed(java.awt.event.ActionEvent e) {

    bBoldFlag = true;

}


void button5_actionPerformed(java.awt.event.ActionEvent e) {

    bItalicFlag = true;

}
```

When the user clicks the **Plain** button, we reset the flags back to plain text:

Chapter 7

```
void button6_actionPerformed(java.awt.event.ActionEvent e) {

    bPlainFlag = true;
    bFont2Flag = false;
    bBigFlag = false;
    bBoldFlag = false;
    bItalicFlag = false;
    bFont1Flag = false;

}
```

Now that we've handled button clicks, we will handle mouse actions.

Using the Mouse in Writer

When the user presses the mouse button, we want to record the location at which the click occurred so we can display the user's typed text there. To read mouse clicks, click the **mousePressed** event in the Inspector, adding a `mousePressed` event handler to our applet (we'll see more about mouse handling in the next Chapter 8):

```
void this_mousePressed(java.awt.event.MouseEvent e) {

}
```

Next, we record the location at which the mouse was clicked, and we get that with the `getX()` and `getY()` methods of the `MouseEvent` object passed to us. We record the (x, y) position of the mouse as `(StartX, StartY)`:

```
void this_mousePressed(java.awt.event.MouseEvent e) {

    StartX = e.getX();
    StartY = e.getY();




}
```

Graphics: Image Handling and Text

And we set aside space for those integers in the applet:

```
package writer;
import java.lang.*;
import java.awt.*;
import java.awt.event.*;
import java.applet.*;
import borland.jbcl.control.*;
import borland.jbcl.layout.*;

public
class writer extends Applet{

  public XYLayout xYLayout1 = new XYLayout();
  public boolean isStandalone = false;

  int StartX = 0;                       <--
  int StartY = 0;                       <--
  boolean bFont1Flag = false;
  boolean bFont2Flag = false;
  boolean bBigFlag = false;
  boolean bBoldFlag = false;
  boolean bItalicFlag = false;
  boolean bPlainFlag = false;
     .
     .
     .
```

In addition, we'll store the characters the user types in the string inString, and we set that string to the empty string when they click the mouse to start a new string:

```
        void this_mousePressed(java.awt.event.MouseEvent e) {

          StartX = e.getX();
          StartY = e.getY();
          inString = "";         <--

        }
```

Chapter 7

We also set aside space for the `inString` variable in the applet:

```
package writer;
import java.lang.*;
import java.awt.*;
import java.awt.event.*;
import java.applet.*;
import borland.jbcl.control.*;
import borland.jbcl.layout.*;

public
class writer extends Applet{

    public XYLayout xYLayout1 = new XYLayout();
    public boolean isStandalone = false;

    String inString = "";                    <--
    int StartX = 0;
    int StartY = 0;
    boolean bFont1Flag = false;
    boolean bFont2Flag = false;
    boolean bBigFlag = false;
    boolean bBoldFlag = false;
    boolean bItalicFlag = false;
    boolean bPlainFlag = false;
          .
          .
          .
```

We've recorded the position in which the mouse has gone down. Now we're ready to read key strokes.

Reading Keystrokes

When the user clicks a key, our applet gets a `keyPressed` event, so using the Inspector, add an event handler for that event now:

```
void this_keyPressed(java.awt.event.KeyEvent e) {

}
```

Graphics: Image Handling and Text

We can get the actual character the user typed with the `getKeyChar()` method, so we add that new character to the `inString` string:

```
void this_keyPressed(java.awt.event.KeyEvent e) {

    inString = inString + e.getKeyChar();       <--
    .
    .
    .

}
```

To draw the text in the applet, we'll add code to the `paint()` method, and to make sure the `paint()` method is called, we call `repaint()` in `this_keyPressed()`:

```
void this_keyPressed(java.awt.event.KeyEvent e) {

    inString = inString + e.getKeyChar();
    repaint();

}
```

There is one more issue to consider: when the user clicks a button, the button gets the focus (that is, becomes the keyboard target). When they type characters, our applet class won't get any `keyPressed` events, because the button has the focus. That means the applet should request the focus back after each time a button is pressed, and we can issue that request with the `requestFocus()` method:

```
void button1_actionPerformed(java.awt.event.ActionEvent e) {

    bFont1Flag = true;
    bFont2Flag = false;
    requestFocus();                              <--

}

void button2_actionPerformed(java.awt.event.ActionEvent e) {

    bFont2Flag = true;
    bFont1Flag = false;
```

Chapter 7

```
        requestFocus();                              <—

    }

    void button3_actionPerformed(java.awt.event.ActionEvent e) {

        bBigFlag = true;
        requestFocus();                              <—

    }

    void button4_actionPerformed(java.awt.event.ActionEvent e) {

        bBoldFlag = true;
        requestFocus();                              <—

    }

    void button5_actionPerformed(java.awt.event.ActionEvent e) {

        bItalicFlag = true;
        requestFocus();                              <—

    }

    void button6_actionPerformed(java.awt.event.ActionEvent e) {

        bPlainFlag = true;
        bFont2Flag = false;
        bBigFlag = false;
        bBoldFlag = false;
        bItalicFlag = false;
        bFont1Flag = false;

        requestFocus();                              <—

    }
```

Now we're ready to start displaying text.

Selecting a Font and Drawing Text

At this point, the user has indicated how they want the text they've typed displayed, and we know where to display that text. We're ready to display the text in the `inString` string now, and we'll do that in the `paint()` method.

We start by setting the default values for our font: Times Roman, 18 point text:

```
public void paint (Graphics g) {

    String fontName = "TimesRoman";     <--
    int fontType = Font.PLAIN;          <--
    int fontSize = 18;                  <--
        .
        .
        .
```

Next, we modify those options to match the way the user selected text options: according to the flags we've set when the user has clicked a button:

```
public void paint (Graphics g) {

    String fontName = "TimesRoman";
    int fontType = Font.PLAIN;
    int fontSize = 18;

    if(bFont1Flag){                     <--
        fontName = "TimesRoman";        <--
    }                                   <--

    if(bFont2Flag){                     <--
        fontName = "Courier";           <--
    }                                   <--

    if(bBigFlag){                       <--
        fontSize = 36;                  <--
    }                                   <--

    if(bBoldFlag){                      <--
```

Chapter 7

```
        fontType = Font.BOLD;           <—
    }                                    <—

    if(bItalicFlag){                     <—
        fontType = fontType | Font.ITALIC;  <—
    }                                    <—
        .
        .
        .
```

Now we're ready to create a new font object. After we create that new object, we can install it in the Graphics object passed to us in the `paint()` method. We create the new font object, `drawFont`, as follows:

```
public void paint (Graphics g) {

    String fontName = "TimesRoman";
    int fontType = Font.PLAIN;
    int fontSize = 18;
    Font drawFont;                       <—

    if(bFont1Flag){
        fontName = "TimesRoman";
    }

    if(bFont2Flag){
        fontName = "Courier";
    }

    if(bBigFlag){
        fontSize = 36;
    }

    if(bBoldFlag){
        fontType = Font.BOLD;
    }

    if(bItalicFlag){
        fontType = fontType | Font.ITALIC;
```

Graphics: Image Handling and Text

```
      }

      drawFont = new Font(fontName, fontType, fontSize);    <—
      .
      .
      .
```

The Font class' constructors and methods appear in Table 7.2.

Table 7.2 The Font Class's Constructors and Methods

`Font(String, int, int)`	Creates a new font with the given name, style and point size.
`decode(String)`	Gets the given font.
`equals(Object)`	Compares this object to the specifed object.
`getFamily()`	Gets the platform-specific family name of the font.
`getFont(String)`	Gets a font from the system properties list.
`getFont(String, Font)`	Gets the given font from the system properties list.
`getName()`	Gets the logical name of the font.
`getPeer()`	Gets the peer of the font.
`getSize()`	Gets the point size of the font.
`getStyle()`	Gets the style of the font.
`hashCode()`	Returns a hashcode for this font.
`isBold()`	Returns true if the font is bold.
`isItalic()`	Returns true if the font is italic.
`isPlain()`	Returns true if the font is plain.
`toString()`	Converts this object to a string representation.

Now our drawFont object holds the text options the user has selected, so we install that new object in the Graphics object `g` passed to us:

```
      public void paint (Graphics g) {

          String fontName = "TimesRoman";
```

Chapter 7

```
        int fontType = Font.PLAIN;
        int fontSize = 18;
        Font drawFont;

        if(bFont1Flag){
            fontName = "TimesRoman";
        }

        if(bFont2Flag){
            fontName = "Courier";
        }

        if(bBigFlag){
            fontSize = 36;
        }

        if(bBoldFlag){
            fontType = Font.BOLD;
        }

        if(bItalicFlag){
            fontType = fontType | Font.ITALIC;
        }

        drawFont = new Font(fontName, fontType, fontSize);

        g.setFont(drawFont);                              <--
            .
            .
            .
```

Now we're ready to display the text in `inString` using this new font. We do that with the `drawString()` method, starting the string at the location at which the user has clicked the mouse, `(StartX, StartY)`:

```
        public void paint (Graphics g) {
```

Graphics: Image Handling and Text

```
        String fontName = "TimesRoman";
        int fontType = Font.PLAIN;
        int fontSize = 18;
        Font drawFont;

        if(bFont1Flag){
            fontName = "TimesRoman";
        }

        if(bFont2Flag){
            fontName = "Courier";
        }

        if(bBigFlag){
            fontSize = 36;
        }

        if(bBoldFlag){
            fontType = Font.BOLD;
        }

        if(bItalicFlag){
            fontType = fontType | Font.ITALIC;
        }

        drawFont = new Font(fontName, fontType, fontSize);

        g.setFont(drawFont);
        g.drawString(inString, StartX, StartY);          <—

    }
```

There's one more trick we'll use here. Every time we call the `repaint()` method to redraw our window, the `update()` method is called first to blank the window. That means all previous strings the user has typed in other locations in our applet will be removed. To avoid that, we'll override the `update()` method and simply call the `paint()` method directly without blanking the applet's window:

Chapter 7

```
public void update(Graphics g){

    paint(g);


}
```

Now we run the applet. Click somewhere in the applet window, then click some font options, and type some text as shown in Figure 7.6—now we're using fonts!

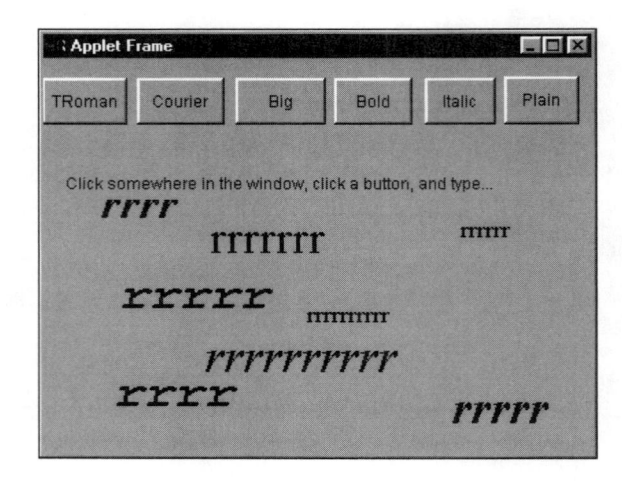

Figure 7.6 Our writer applet at work.

The code for this applet appears in Listing 7.4.

Listing 7.4 writer.java

```
//Title:
//Version:
//Copyright:
//Author:
//Company:
//Description:
//
```

Graphics: Image Handling and Text

```
package writer;
import java.lang.*;
import java.awt.*;
import java.awt.event.*;
import java.applet.*;
import borland.jbcl.control.*;
import borland.jbcl.layout.*;

public
class writer extends Applet{

  public XYLayout xYLayout1 = new XYLayout();
  public boolean isStandalone = false;

  String inString = "";
  int StartX = 0;
  int StartY = 0;
  boolean bFont1Flag = false;
  boolean bFont2Flag = false;
  boolean bBigFlag = false;
  boolean bBoldFlag = false;
  boolean bItalicFlag = false;
  boolean bPlainFlag = false;

  Button button1 = new Button();
  Button button2 = new Button();
  Button button3 = new Button();
  Button button4 = new Button();
  Button button5 = new Button();
  Button button6 = new Button();
  Label label1 = new Label();

  //Construct the applet
  public writer() {


  }

  //Initialize the applet
  public void init() {
```

Chapter 7

```java
        try { jbInit(); } catch(Exception e) { e.printStackTrace(); };

    }

    //Component initialization
    public void jbInit() throws Exception{

        this.addKeyListener(new writer_this_KeyAdapter(this));
        this.addMouseListener(new writer_this_MouseAdapter(this));
        xYLayout1.setWidth(400);
        xYLayout1.setHeight(300);
        button1.setLabel("TRoman");
        button1.addActionListener(new
writer_button1_ActionAdapter(this));
        button2.setLabel("Courier");
        button2.addActionListener(new
writer_button2_ActionAdapter(this));
        button3.setLabel("Big");
        button3.addActionListener(new
writer_button3_ActionAdapter(this));
        button4.setLabel("Bold");
        button4.addActionListener(new
writer_button4_ActionAdapter(this));
        button5.setLabel("Italic");
        button5.addActionListener(new
writer_button5_ActionAdapter(this));
        button6.setLabel("Plain");
        label1.setText("Click somewhere in the window, click a
button, and type...");
        button6.addActionListener(new
writer_button6_ActionAdapter(this));
        this.setLayout(xYLayout1);
        this.add(button1, new XYConstraints(-1, 14, 62, 35));
        this.add(button2, new XYConstraints(68, 14, 64, 35));
        this.add(button3, new XYConstraints(140, 14, 66, 35));
        this.add(button4, new XYConstraints(212, 14, 57, 35));
        this.add(button5, new XYConstraints(278, 14, 52, 35));
        this.add(button6, new XYConstraints(336, 13, 55, 36));
        this.add(label1, new XYConstraints(16, 81, 342, 25));
```

```
}

//Start the applet
public void start() {

}

//Stop the applet
public void stop() {

}

//Destroy the applet
public void destroy() {

}

//Get Applet information
public String getAppletInfo() {

    return "Applet Information";

}

//Get parameter info
public String[][] getParameterInfo() {

    return null;

}

//Main method
static public void main(String[] args) {

    writer applet = new writer();
    applet.isStandalone = true;
    DecoratedFrame frame = new DecoratedFrame();
    frame.setTitle("Applet Frame");
    frame.add(applet, BorderLayout.CENTER);
```

Chapter 7

```java
    applet.init();
    applet.start();
    frame.pack();
    Dimension d = Toolkit.getDefaultToolkit().getScreenSize();
    frame.setLocation((d.width - frame.getSize().width) / 2,
(d.height - frame.getSize().height) / 2);
    frame.setVisible(true);

}

void button1_actionPerformed(java.awt.event.ActionEvent e) {

    bFont1Flag = true;
    bFont2Flag = false;
    requestFocus();

}

void button2_actionPerformed(java.awt.event.ActionEvent e) {

    bFont2Flag = true;
    bFont1Flag = false;
    requestFocus();

}

void button3_actionPerformed(java.awt.event.ActionEvent e) {

    bBigFlag = true;
    requestFocus();
}

void button4_actionPerformed(java.awt.event.ActionEvent e) {

    bBoldFlag = true;
    requestFocus();

}
```

Graphics: Image Handling and Text

```java
void button5_actionPerformed(java.awt.event.ActionEvent e) {

    bItalicFlag = true;
    requestFocus();
}

void button6_actionPerformed(java.awt.event.ActionEvent e) {

    bPlainFlag = true;
    bFont2Flag = false;
    bBigFlag = false;
    bBoldFlag = false;
    bItalicFlag = false;
    bFont1Flag = false;

    requestFocus();

}

public void paint (Graphics g) {

    String fontName = "TimesRoman";
    int fontType = Font.PLAIN;
    int fontSize = 18;
    Font drawFont;

    if(bFont1Flag){
        fontName = "TimesRoman";
    }

    if(bFont2Flag){
        fontName = "Courier";
    }

    if(bBigFlag){
        fontSize = 36;
    }

    if(bBoldFlag){
```

Chapter 7

```java
            fontType = Font.BOLD;
        }

        if(bItalicFlag){
            fontType = fontType | Font.ITALIC;
        }

        drawFont = new Font(fontName, fontType, fontSize);
        g.setFont(drawFont);
        g.drawString(inString, StartX, StartY);

    }

    void this_keyPressed(java.awt.event.KeyEvent e) {

        inString = inString + e.getKeyChar();
        repaint();

    }

    void this_mousePressed(java.awt.event.MouseEvent e) {

        StartX = e.getX();
        StartY = e.getY();
        inString = "";

    }

    public void update(Graphics g){

        paint(g);

    }

}

class writer_button1_ActionAdapter implements ActionListener {

    writer adaptee;

    writer_button1_ActionAdapter(writer adaptee) {
```

```java
      this.adaptee = adaptee;
   }
   public void actionPerformed(java.awt.event.ActionEvent e) {
      adaptee.button1_actionPerformed(e);
   }
}
class writer_button2_ActionAdapter implements ActionListener{
   writer adaptee;
   writer_button2_ActionAdapter(writer adaptee) {
      this.adaptee = adaptee;
   }
   public void actionPerformed(java.awt.event.ActionEvent e) {
      adaptee.button2_actionPerformed(e);
   }
}
class writer_button3_ActionAdapter implements ActionListener{
   writer adaptee;
   writer_button3_ActionAdapter(writer adaptee) {
      this.adaptee = adaptee;
   }
   public void actionPerformed(java.awt.event.ActionEvent e) {
      adaptee.button3_actionPerformed(e);
```

Chapter 7

```java
      }

   }

class writer_button4_ActionAdapter implements ActionListener{

   writer adaptee;

   writer_button4_ActionAdapter(writer adaptee) {

      this.adaptee = adaptee;

   }

   public void actionPerformed(java.awt.event.ActionEvent e) {

      adaptee.button4_actionPerformed(e);

   }

}

class writer_button5_ActionAdapter implements ActionListener{

   writer adaptee;

   writer_button5_ActionAdapter(writer adaptee) {

      this.adaptee = adaptee;

   }

   public void actionPerformed(java.awt.event.ActionEvent e) {

      adaptee.button5_actionPerformed(e);

   }

}

class writer_button6_ActionAdapter implements ActionListener{

   writer adaptee;
```

```
    writer_button6_ActionAdapter(writer adaptee) {

      this.adaptee = adaptee;

    }

    public void actionPerformed(java.awt.event.ActionEvent e) {

      adaptee.button6_actionPerformed(e);

    }

}

class writer_this_KeyAdapter extends KeyAdapter {

    writer adaptee;

    writer_this_KeyAdapter(writer adaptee) {

      this.adaptee = adaptee;

    }

    public void keyPressed(java.awt.event.KeyEvent e) {

      adaptee.this_keyPressed(e);

    }

}

class writer_this_MouseAdapter extends MouseAdapter {

    writer adaptee;

    writer_this_MouseAdapter(writer adaptee) {

      this.adaptee = adaptee;

    }

    public void mousePressed(java.awt.event.MouseEvent e) {
```

Chapter 7

```
        adaptee.this_mousePressed(e);

    }

}
```

Our last topic in this chapter concerns how to place text in a window: text justification.

Justifying Text

In this last example for this chapter, we'll see how to place the text *Here is the text!* in three different locations in a window: at top left, in the center, and at bottom right:

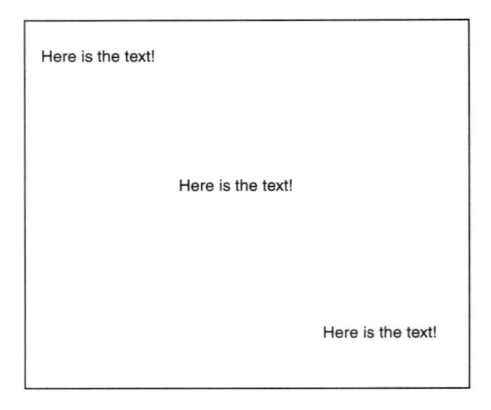

```
┌─────────────────────────────────┐
│ Here is the text!               │
│                                 │
│                                 │
│            Here is the text!    │
│                                 │
│                                 │
│                  Here is the text! │
└─────────────────────────────────┘
```

Let's see this new applet, named **justify,** in action. Create this applet now and override the `paint()` method:

```
public void paint (Graphics g) {

}
```

This is where we'll draw our justified text. We start by making the font in the Graphics object g passed to us a large font, which we call `justifyFont`:

```
public void paint (Graphics g) {
```

Graphics: Image Handling and Text

```
        justifyFont = new Font("TimesRoman", Font.PLAIN, 24);
        g.setFont(justifyFont);
            .
            .
            .
```

And we also declare this font object in the applet:

```
package justify;
import java.lang.*;
import java.awt.*;
import java.awt.event.*;
import java.applet.*;
import borland.jbcl.control.*;
import borland.jbcl.layout.*;
public
class justify extends Applet {
  public XYLayout xYLayout1 = new XYLayout();
  public boolean isStandalone = false;
  Font justifyFont;                          <--
     .
     .
     .
```

Now we're ready to start the process of displaying our text. Since we will justify this text, we need to know the dimensions of the string we want to display on the screen. To determine those dimensions, we will use a FontMetrics object we'll call justifyFontMetrics:

```
    public void paint (Graphics g) {

        justifyFont = new Font("TimesRoman", Font.PLAIN, 24);
        g.setFont(justifyFont);

        justifyFontMetrics = getFontMetrics(justifyFont);   <--
            .
            .
            .
```

Chapter 7

The FontMetrics class tells us a great deal about a particular font, such as the height of that font's characters. The FontMetrics class' constructors and methods appear in Table 7.3.

Table 7.3 The FontMetrics Class's Constructors and Methods

FontMetrics(Font)	Creates a new FontMetrics object.
bytesWidth (byte[], int, int)	Returns the total width for showing the given array of bytes.
charsWidth (char[], int, int)	Returns the total width for showing the given array of characters.
charWidth(char)	Returns the width of the given character.
charWidth(int)	Returns the width of the given character.
getAscent()	Gets the font ascent.
getDescent()	Gets the font descent.
getFont()	Gets the font.
getHeight()	Gets the standard height of a line of text.
getLeading()	Gets the standard leading, or line spacing, for the font.
getMaxAscent()	Gets the maximum ascent of all characters.
getMaxDescent()	Gets the maximum descent of all characters.
getWidths()	Gets the widths of the first 256 characters.
stringWidth(String)	Returns the total width for showing the given string.
toString()	Returns the string representation of this FontMetric's values.

We also declare our justifyFontMetrics object in the applet this way:

```
package justify;
import java.lang.*;
import java.awt.*;
import java.awt.event.*;
import java.applet.*;
import borland.jbcl.control.*;
import borland.jbcl.layout.*;
public
```

Graphics: Image Handling and Text

```
class justify extends Applet {
   public XYLayout xYLayout1 = new XYLayout();
   public boolean isStandalone = false;
   Font justifyFont;
   FontMetrics justifyFontMetrics;         <—
      .
      .
      .
```

The message we'll display is *Here is the text!*, and we can set up that string now, as an object named `msg`:

```
package justify;
import java.lang.*;
import java.awt.*;
import java.awt.event.*;
import java.applet.*;
import borland.jbcl.control.*;
import borland.jbcl.layout.*;
public
class justify extends Applet {
   public XYLayout xYLayout1 = new XYLayout();
   public boolean isStandalone = false;
   Font justifyFont;
   FontMetrics justifyFontMetrics;
   String msg = "Here is the text!";        <—
      .
      .
      .
```

Now we can display that string at upper left in the applet window. When you pass a location to the `drawString()` method, that method uses that location as the bottom left corner of the text when it places it on the screen. That means that to display our string at upper left in the applet window, we need to find out how tall the string is as displayed, and we can determine that with the `justifyFontMetrics` method `getHeight()`—this gives us the y location for our string:

```
public void paint (Graphics g) {
```

Chapter 7

```
justifyFont = new Font("TimesRoman", Font.PLAIN, 24);
g.setFont(justifyFont);

justifyFontMetrics = getFontMetrics(justifyFont);

XPos = 0;
YPos = justifyFontMetrics.getHeight();       <—
   .
   .
   .
```

Now we can display the text string at location (XPos, YPos) with `drawString()` this way:

```
public void paint (Graphics g) {

    justifyFont = new Font("TimesRoman", Font.PLAIN, 24);
    g.setFont(justifyFont);

    justifyFontMetrics = getFontMetrics(justifyFont);

    XPos = 0;
    YPos = justifyFontMetrics.getHeight();
    g.drawString(msg, XPos, YPos);                    <—
       .
       .
       .
```

We also add the integer `XPos` and `YPose` to the applet this way:

```
package justify;
import java.lang.*;
import java.awt.*;
import java.awt.event.*;
import java.applet.*;
import borland.jbcl.control.*;
import borland.jbcl.layout.*;
public
class justify extends Applet {
```

Graphics: Image Handling and Text

```
public XYLayout xYLayout1 = new XYLayout();
public boolean isStandalone = false;
Font justifyFont;
FontMetrics justifyFontMetrics;
String msg = "Here is the text!";
int XPos, YPos;                        <—
   .
   .
   .
```

Next, we can center the string in the applet. To do that, we'll need to know the width and height of the applet window. We can find those with the Component method `getSize()`. (The Applet class is derived from the Component class.) This method returns an object of the Dimension class, and we can use that object's width and height data members to find the width and height of the applet's window.

In addition, we'll need the the width of our string as it appears on the screen, and we can get that with the FontMetrics method `stringWidth()`:

```
          public void paint (Graphics g) {

            justifyFont = new Font("TimesRoman", Font.PLAIN, 24);
            g.setFont(justifyFont);

            justifyFontMetrics = getFontMetrics(justifyFont);

            XPos = 0;
            YPos = justifyFontMetrics.getHeight();
            g.drawString(msg, XPos, YPos);

  –>        XPos = (getSize()().width - justifyFontMetrics.stringWidth(msg)) / 2;
  –>        YPos = (getSize()().height + justifyFontMetrics.getHeight()) / 2;
  –>        g.drawString(msg, XPos, YPos);
               .
               .
               .

          }
```

Chapter 7

Finally, we'll place our string of text at the bottom of the applet, at lower right:

```
public void paint (Graphics g) {

    justifyFont = new Font("TimesRoman", Font.PLAIN, 24);
    g.setFont(justifyFont);

    justifyFontMetrics = getFontMetrics(justifyFont);

    XPos = 0;
    YPos = justifyFontMetrics.getHeight();
    g.drawString(msg, XPos, YPos);

    XPos = (getSize()().width - justifyFontMetrics.stringWidth(msg)) / 2;
    YPos = (getSize()().height + justifyFontMetrics.getHeight()) / 2;
    g.drawString(msg, XPos, YPos);

->    XPos = getSize()().width - justifyFontMetrics.stringWidth(msg);
->    YPos = getSize()().height; // - justifyFontMetrics.getHeight();
->    g.drawString(msg, XPos, YPos);
}
```

Now the applet is ready to go. Run it as shown in Figure 7.7. You can see our text appearing there, just as we have planned. The justify applet is a success.

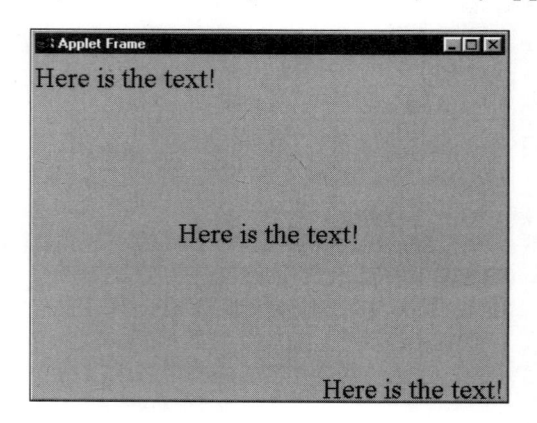

Figure 7.7 Our justify applet justifies text.

Graphics: Image Handling and Text

The listing for this applet appears in Listing 7.5.

Listing 7.5 justify.java

```java
//Title:
//Version:
//Copyright:
//Author:
//Company:
//Description:
//

package justify;
import java.lang.*;
import java.awt.*;
import java.awt.event.*;
import java.applet.*;
import borland.jbcl.control.*;
import borland.jbcl.layout.*;
public
class justify extends Applet {
  public XYLayout xYLayout1 = new XYLayout();
  public boolean isStandalone = false;
  Font justifyFont;
  FontMetrics justifyFontMetrics;
  String msg = "Here is the text!";
  int XPos, YPos;

  //Construct the applet
  public justify() {
  }
  //Initialize the applet
  public void init() {
     try { jbInit(); } catch(Exception e) {
e.printStackTrace(); };
  }
  //Component initialization
  public void jbInit() throws Exception{
    xYLayout1.setWidth(400);
```

Chapter 7

```
    xYLayout1.setHeight(300);
    this.setLayout(xYLayout1);
}
//Start the applet
public void start() {
}
//Stop the applet
public void stop() {
}
//Destroy the applet
public void destroy() {
}
//Get Applet information
public String getAppletInfo() {
    return "Applet Information";
}
//Get parameter info
public String[][] getParameterInfo() {
    return null;
}

public void paint (Graphics g) {
    justifyFont = new Font("TimesRoman", Font.PLAIN, 24);
    g.setFont(justifyFont);

    justifyFontMetrics = getFontMetrics(justifyFont);

    XPos = 0;
    YPos = justifyFontMetrics.getHeight();
    g.drawString(msg, XPos, YPos);

    XPos = (getSize()().width - justifyFontMetrics.stringWidth(msg)) / 2;
    YPos = (getSize()().height + justifyFontMetrics.getHeight()) / 2;
    g.drawString(msg, XPos, YPos);

    XPos = getSize()().width - justifyFontMetrics.stringWidth(msg);
    YPos = getSize()().height; // - justifyFontMetrics.getHeight();
    g.drawString(msg, XPos, YPos);
}
```

Graphics: Image Handling and Text

```
    //Main method
    static public void main(String[] args) {
      justify applet = new justify();
      applet.isStandalone = true;
      DecoratedFrame frame = new DecoratedFrame();
      frame.setTitle("Applet Frame");
      frame.add(applet, BorderLayout.CENTER);
      applet.init();
      applet.start();
      frame.pack();
      Dimension d = Toolkit.getDefaultToolkit().getScreenGetSize()();
      frame.setLocation((d.width - frame.getSize()().width) / 2,
  (d.height - frame.getSize()().height) / 2);
      frame.setVisible(true);
    }
  }
```

That's it for our start in graphics. We've come a long way in this chapter: we have examined image handling, loading images in from disk and displaying them, as well as stretching them. We've also seen how to use the Image control. Next, we turned to working with fonts, and we saw how to let the user display text, selecting various font options like bold and italic. Finally, we saw how to justify text in a window. That's quite a lot of power for one chapter.

On the other hand, we've just started our graphics work! In Chapter 8, we'll see how to draw circles, ellipses, lines, rectangles, and more.

CHAPTER 8

Graphics: A Mouse-Driven Paint Program

In this chapter, we're going to dig into more graphics topics. We got our start with graphics in Chapter 7, and now we'll continue our exploration.

We'll see how to draw rectangles, circles, ovals, lines, and more in this chapter. To do that, we'll construct a complete mouse-driven paint program. The user can select one of our drawing tools—one of six buttons in the applet—to draw, say, a line. They press the mouse button when the mouse cursor is at the location where they want to start the line, then drag the mouse to the other end of the line and release the mouse button. When the mouse button goes up, we draw the line connecting the two points they've indicated to our program.

To create this applet, we'll need to work a little more closely with the mouse. We've seen a little about the mouse already in this book, but we'll take a closer look in this chapter so we know how to handle all the mouse events needed in our painting program.

Let's start working with the mouse at once.

Handling the Mouse

In our first example for this chapter, we'll see how to work with the mouse. Our new program, **mouser,** will display a prompt to the user and a text field:

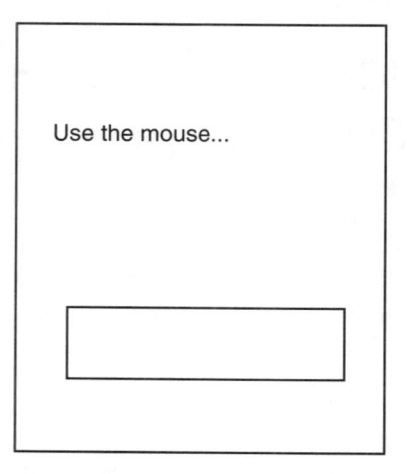

```
┌─────────────────────────┐
│                         │
│  Use the mouse...       │
│                         │
│                         │
│   ┌─────────────────┐   │
│   │                 │   │
│   └─────────────────┘   │
│                         │
└─────────────────────────┘
```

We'll make this program an application to point out some new programming issues. When the mouse cursor enters our program's area on the screen, we'll inform the user with a message:

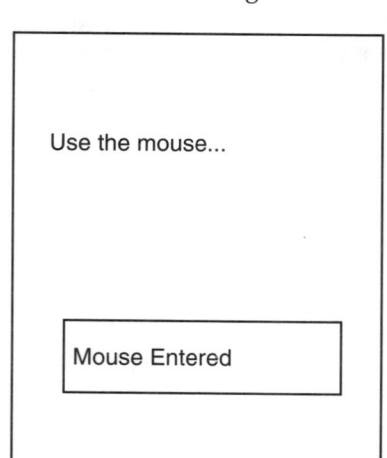

```
┌─────────────────────────┐
│                         │
│  Use the mouse...       │
│                         │
│                         │
│   ┌─────────────────┐   │
│   │ Mouse Entered   │   │
│   └─────────────────┘   │
│                         │
└─────────────────────────┘
```

When the user drags the mouse, we can indicate that as well:

```
┌─────────────────────────┐
│                         │
│  Use the mouse...       │
│                         │
│                         │
│       ┌───────────────┐ │
│       │ Mouse Dragged │ │
│       └───────────────┘ │
│                         │
└─────────────────────────┘
```

When the user presses the mouse button, we will report the location at which the button went down:

```
┌─────────────────────────┐
│                         │
│  Use the mouse...       │
│                         │
│                         │
│     ┌────────────────────┐
│     │ Mouse down at 45, 186 │
│     └────────────────────┘
│                         │
└─────────────────────────┘
```

Similarly, when the user releases the mouse button, we'll indicate the location where that button went up:

Chapter 8

```
┌─────────────────────────┐
│                         │
│  Use the mouse...       │
│                         │
│                         │
│                         │
│      ┌──────────────────┤
│      │ Mouse up at 201, 43 │
│      └──────────────────┤
│                         │
└─────────────────────────┘
```

Finally, when the user moves the mouse away from our program, we'll indicate that the mouse has exited:

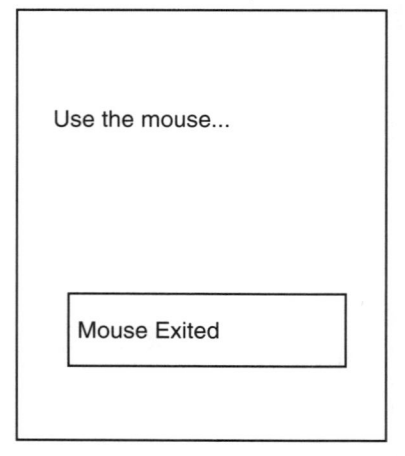

```
┌─────────────────────────┐
│                         │
│  Use the mouse...       │
│                         │
│                         │
│                         │
│      ┌──────────────┐   │
│      │ Mouse Exited │   │
│      └──────────────┘   │
│                         │
└─────────────────────────┘
```

Create this new program now. Make it an application named mouser, and open it in the Designer, as shown in Figure 8.1. We want to handle various mouse events in this application, but an important point to recognize is that the client area (the area of a window in which we draw—that is, the window excluding the menu bar, tool bar, and status bar) of a JBuilder application is covered with a panel object. This means it is really the panel object that we should add the mouse event handlers to, not the frame window itself.

Graphics: A Mouse-Driven Paint Program

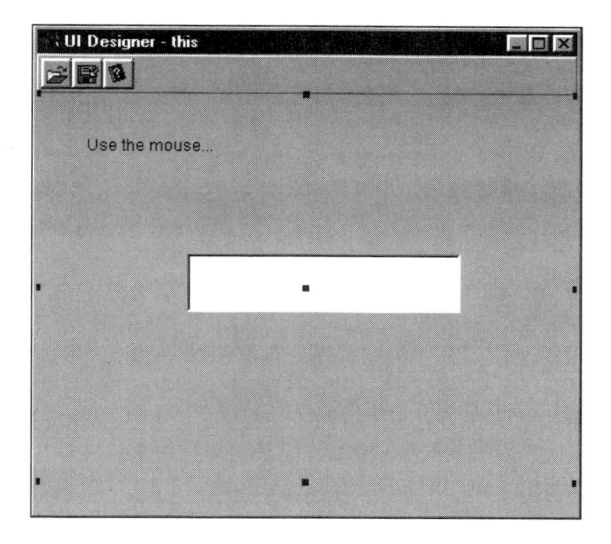

FIGURE 8.1 DESIGNING THE MOUSER APPLICATION.

Click the application's panel now by the black sizing handles, as shown in Figure 8.1. Next, move to the Inspector and click the following events: **mouseDragged**, **mouseEntered**, **mouseExited**, **mousePressed**, and **mouseReleased**. These are the events we'll use in this application.

Now we've added those mouse events to our application. JBuilder has added two new classes to our application—a class that implements the `MouseMotionListener` interface to handle the `mouseDragged` event and a class that implements the `MouseListener` class for all the other mouse events we're working with:

```
//Component initialization
public void jbInit() throws Exception{

    this.setLayout(borderLayout1);
    this.setTitle("Frame Title");
    //Add menu bar
    menuFile.setLabel("File");
    menuFileExit.setLabel("Exit");
    menuFileExit.addActionListener(new
Frame1_menuFileExit_ActionAdapter(this));
    menuFile.add(menuFileExit);
```

Chapter 8

```
        menuHelp.setLabel("Help");
        menuHelpAbout.setLabel("About");
        menuHelpAbout.addActionListener(new
Frame1_menuHelpAbout_ActionAdapter(this));
        menuHelp.add(menuHelpAbout);
        menuBar1.add(menuFile);
        menuBar1.add(menuHelp);
        this.setMenuBar(menuBar1);
        //Add tool bar
        buttonBar.setButtonType(ButtonBar.IMAGE_ONLY);
        buttonBar.setLabels(new String[] {"Open", "Close", "Help"});
        buttonBar.setImageDirectory("borland/jbcl/control/images");
        buttonBar.setImageNames(new String[] {"openfile.gif",
    "closefile.gif", "help.gif"});
        this.add(buttonBar, BorderLayout.NORTH);
        //Add status bar
        statusBar.setText("");
–>      panel1.addMouseListener(new Frame1_panel1_MouseAdapter(this));
–>      panel1.addMouseMotionListener(new Frame1_panel1_MouseMotionAdapter(this));
          .
          .
          .
```

In addition, add a text field to the application's panel (not the underlying frame window) so that we can report the user's mouse actions.

Let's start working with mouse events, beginning with the `mouseEntered` event.

The MouseEntered Event

When the mouse enters our program, a `mouseEntered` event occurs, and we intercept that event in the event handler we've set up:

```
        void panel1_mouseEntered(java.awt.event.MouseEvent e) {

        }
```

Graphics: A Mouse-Driven Paint Program

Note that this event handler is called when mouse enters the panel's surface in our program, not when it enters the frame window. In this way, we are responding to client area mouse events in this program, and letting the program handle the mouse events for the menu bar, tool bar and so on itself.

Here, we simply indicate to the user that the mouse has entered the client area with a message in the text field:

```
void panel1_mouseEntered(java.awt.event.MouseEvent e) {

    textField1.setText("Mouse Entered");           <—


}
```

The result appears in Figure 8.2—now we're using the mouseEnter mouse event.

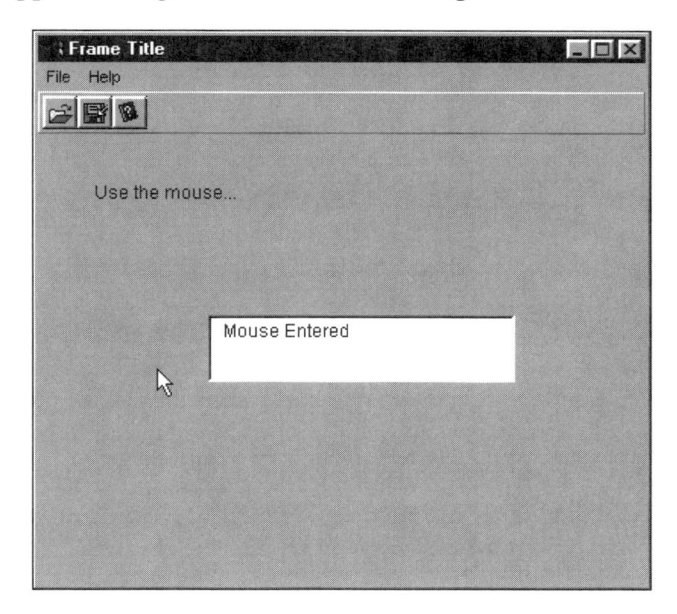

FIGURE 8.2 WE DISPLAY A MOUSEENTERED EVENT.

The next mouse event we'll take a look at is the mouseDragged event.

Chapter 8

The MouseDragged Event

When the user drags the mouse, our `panel1_mouseDragged()` method is called:

```
void panel1_mouseDragged(java.awt.event.MouseEvent e) {

}
```

In this case, we'll just place a *Mouse Dragged* message in the text field:

```
void panel1_mouseDragged(java.awt.event.MouseEvent e) {

    textField1.setText("Mouse Dragged");        <--

}
```

Now we've made use of the `mouseDragged` event, and we'll see it again soon in our painter program. Next, we turn to the `mousePressed` event.

The MousePressed Event

When the user presses the mouse button in our program's client area, our new `panel1_mousePressed()` method is called:

```
void panel1_mousePressed(java.awt.event.MouseEvent e) {

}
```

In this case, we are passed an object, e, of the MouseEvent class. To get the location at which the mouse button went down, we can call that object's `getX()` and `getY()` methods:

```
void panel1_mousePressed(java.awt.event.MouseEvent e) {

     textField1.setText("Mouse down at: " +
String.valueOf(e.getX()) + "," + String.valueOf(e.getY()));    <--

}
```

Graphics: A Mouse-Driven Paint Program

And that's it—now we're able to report the location at which the user pressed the mouse button, as shown in Figure 8.3.

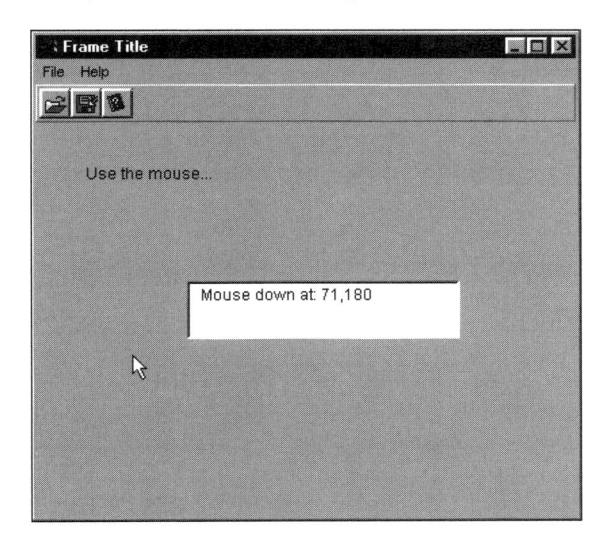

FIGURE 8.3 THE MOUSEDOWN EVENT.

When the user releases the mouse button, we get a `mouseReleased` event.

The MouseReleased Event

We are passed a MouseEvent object, e, in the `panel1_mouseReleased()` event:

```
void panel1_mouseReleased(java.awt.event.MouseEvent e) {


}
```

Just as in the `mousePressed` event handler, we can get the location at which the mouse button was released with the MouseEvent object's `getX()` and `getY()` methods:

```
void panel1_mouseReleased(java.awt.event.MouseEvent e) {

    textField1.setText("Mouse up at: " +
String.valueOf(e.getX()) + "," + String.valueOf(e.getY()));    <—

}
```

Chapter 8

In this way, we're able to indicate to the user when the mouse button goes up. We'll see this method in our painter program soon. The final mouse event we'll take a look at here is the `mouseExited` event.

The MouseExited Event

When the mouse leaves the panel's area in our program, our `panel1_mouseExited()` method is called:

```
void panel1_mouseExited(java.awt.event.MouseEvent e) {


}
```

Here, we just indicate to the user that the mouse has left our client area:

```
void panel1_mouseExited(java.awt.event.MouseEvent e) {

    textField1.setText("Mouse Exited");      <--


}
```

The result of this code appears in Figure 8.4.

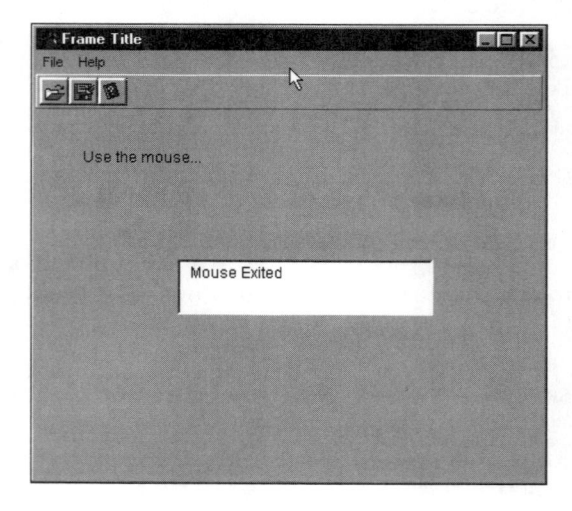

FIGURE 8.4 THE MOUSEEXITED EVENT.

Graphics: A Mouse-Driven Paint Program

That's it—now we've gotten a good introduction to working with mouse events. Let's turn to our painter program now. The code for the mouser program appears in Listing 8.1, mouser.java, and Listing 8.2, Frame1.java.

LISTING 8.1 MOUSER.JAVA

```java
//Title:
//Version:
//Copyright:
//Author:
//Company:
//Description:
//

package mouser;
import java.lang.*;

public
class mouser {

    //Construct the application
    public mouser() {

        Frame1 frame = new Frame1();
        frame.setVisible(true);

    }

    //Main method
    static public void main(String[] args) {

        new mouser();

    }

}
```

Chapter 8

LISTING 8.2 FRAME1.JAVA

```java
//Title:
//Version:
//Copyright:
//Author:
//Company:
//Description:
//

package mouser;
import java.awt.*;
import java.awt.event.*;
import java.lang.*;
import borland.jbcl.control.*;
import borland.jbcl.layout.*;

public
class Frame1 extends DecoratedFrame {
  public BorderLayout borderLayout1 = new BorderLayout();
  public XYLayout xYLayout1 = new XYLayout();
  public MenuBar menuBar1 = new MenuBar();
  public Menu menuFile = new Menu();
  public MenuItem menuFileExit = new MenuItem();
  public Menu menuHelp = new Menu();
  public MenuItem menuHelpAbout = new MenuItem();
  public ButtonBar buttonBar = new ButtonBar();
  public Label statusBar = new Label();
  TextField textField1 = new TextField();
  public Panel panel1 = new MousePanel(textField1);
  Label label1 = new Label();

  //Construct the frame
  public Frame1() {

    try { jbInit(); } catch(Exception e) { e.printStackTrace(); };

  }
```

Graphics: A Mouse-Driven Paint Program

```
//Component initialization
public void jbInit() throws Exception{

    this.setLayout(borderLayout1);
    this.setTitle("Frame Title");
    //Add menu bar
    menuFile.setLabel("File");
    menuFileExit.setLabel("Exit");
    menuFileExit.addActionListener(new
Frame1_menuFileExit_ActionAdapter(this));
    menuFile.add(menuFileExit);
    menuHelp.setLabel("Help");
    menuHelpAbout.setLabel("About");
    menuHelpAbout.addActionListener(new
Frame1_menuHelpAbout_ActionAdapter(this));
    menuHelp.add(menuHelpAbout);
    menuBar1.add(menuFile);
    menuBar1.add(menuHelp);
    this.setMenuBar(menuBar1);
    //Add tool bar
    buttonBar.setButtonType(ButtonBar.IMAGE_ONLY);
    buttonBar.setLabels(new String[] {"Open", "Close", "Help"});
    buttonBar.setImageDirectory("borland/jbcl/control/images");
    buttonBar.setImageNames(new String[] {"openfile.gif",
"closefile.gif", "help.gif"});
    this.add(buttonBar, BorderLayout.NORTH);
    //Add status bar
    statusBar.setText("");
    panel1.addMouseListener(new Frame1_panel1_MouseAdapter(this));
    panel1.addMouseMotionListener(new Frame1_panel1_MouseMotionAdapter(this));
    label1.setText("Use the mouse...");
    this.add(statusBar, BorderLayout.SOUTH);
    //Add center panel
    panel1.setLayout(xYLayout1);
    xYLayout1.setWidth(400);
    xYLayout1.setHeight(300);
    this.add(panel1, BorderLayout.CENTER);
    panel1.add(textField1, new XYConstraints(112, 123, 202,
45));
```

Chapter 8

```
    panel1.add(label1, new XYConstraints(37, 26, 164, 27));
    this.pack();
    //Center the window
    Dimension dimScreen =
Toolkit.getDefaultToolkit().getScreenSize();
    Dimension dimFrame = this.getPreferredSize();
    if(dimFrame.height > dimScreen.height) dimFrame.height =
dimScreen.height;
    if(dimFrame.width > dimScreen.width) dimFrame.width =
dimScreen.width;
    this.setBounds( (dimScreen.width - dimFrame.width) / 2,
(dimScreen.height - dimFrame.height) / 2, dimFrame.width,
dimFrame.height);

  }

  //File | Exit action performed
  public void fileExit_actionPerformed(ActionEvent e) {

    System.exit(0);

  }

  //Help | About action performed
  public void helpAbout_actionPerformed(ActionEvent e) {

  }

  void panel1_mouseDragged(java.awt.event.MouseEvent e) {

      textField1.setText("Mouse Dragged");

  }

  void panel1_mouseEntered(java.awt.event.MouseEvent e) {

      textField1.setText("Mouse Entered");

  }
```

```
  void panel1_mouseExited(java.awt.event.MouseEvent e) {

    textField1.setText("Mouse Exited");

  }

  void panel1_mousePressed(java.awt.event.MouseEvent e) {

    textField1.setText("Mouse down at: " +
String.valueOf(e.getX()) + "," + String.valueOf(e.getY()));

  }

  void panel1_mouseReleased(java.awt.event.MouseEvent e) {

    textField1.setText("Mouse up at: " +
String.valueOf(e.getX()) + "," + String.valueOf(e.getY()));

  }

}

class Frame1_menuFileExit_ActionAdapter implements

ActionListener {

  Frame1 adaptee;

  Frame1_menuFileExit_ActionAdapter(Frame1 adaptee) {

    this.adaptee = adaptee;

  }

  public void actionPerformed(ActionEvent e) {

    adaptee.fileExit_actionPerformed(e);
```

Chapter 8

```
    }

  }

class Frame1_menuHelpAbout_ActionAdapter implements

ActionListener {

  Frame1 adaptee;

  Frame1_menuHelpAbout_ActionAdapter(Frame1 adaptee) {

    this.adaptee = adaptee;

  }

  public void actionPerformed(ActionEvent e) {

    adaptee.helpAbout_actionPerformed(e);

  }

}

class MousePanel extends Panel{

  TextField textField1;

  MousePanel(TextField textfield){

    super();
    textField1 = textfield;

  }

}

class Frame1_panel1_MouseMotionAdapter extends

MouseMotionAdapter {
```

```
   Frame1 adaptee;

   Frame1_panel1_MouseMotionAdapter(Frame1 adaptee) {

      this.adaptee = adaptee;

   }

   public void mouseDragged(java.awt.event.MouseEvent e) {

      adaptee.panel1_mouseDragged(e);

   }

}

class Frame1_panel1_MouseAdapter extends MouseAdapter {

   Frame1 adaptee;

   Frame1_panel1_MouseAdapter(Frame1 adaptee) {

      this.adaptee = adaptee;

   }

   public void mouseEntered(java.awt.event.MouseEvent e) {

      adaptee.panel1_mouseEntered(e);

   }

   public void mouseExited(java.awt.event.MouseEvent e) {

      adaptee.panel1_mouseExited(e);

   }

   public void mousePressed(java.awt.event.MouseEvent e) {

      adaptee.panel1_mousePressed(e);

   }
```

Chapter 8

```
public void mouseReleased(java.awt.event.MouseEvent e) {
    adaptee.panel1_mouseReleased(e);
}
}
```

Now that we've seen some mouse event handling in action, we'll write the painter program to let the user draw graphics figures.

A Mouse-Driven Paint Program

Our painter applet will let us examine graphics handling in JBuilder; here's where we're going to draw lines, circles, rectangles, and even freehand objects with the mouse. This applet will present the user with six buttons, our drawing tools:

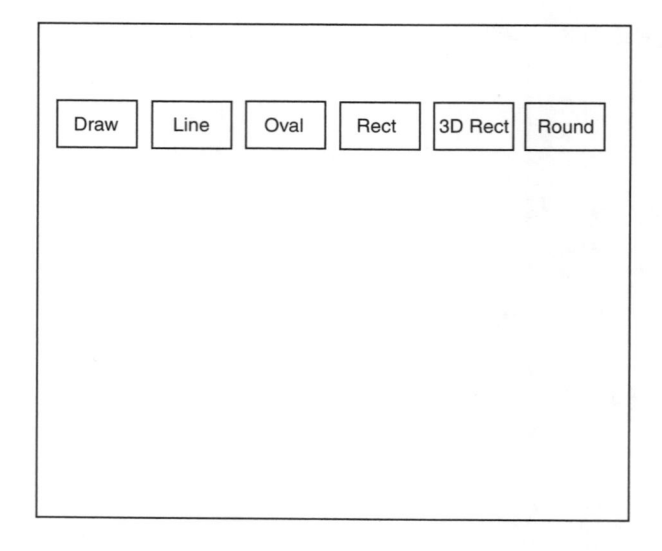

Let's say the user selects the line tool. After they click the **Line** button, they move to the drawing area and press the mouse button. This establishes one end of the line, the end we'll call the *Anchor point*:

Graphics: A Mouse-Driven Paint Program

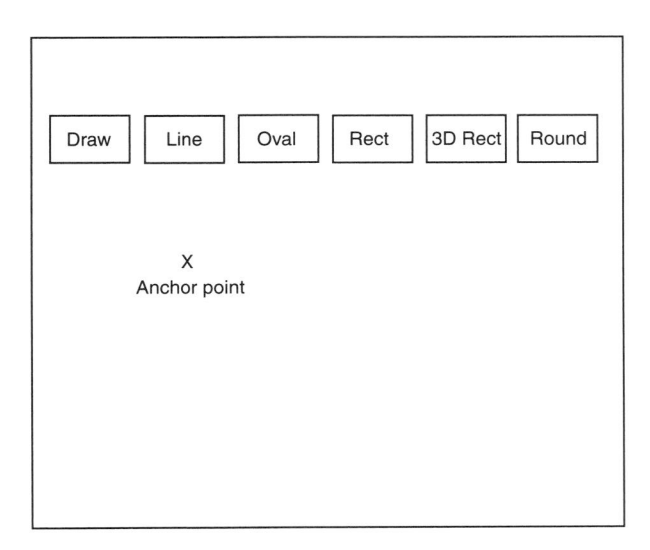

[Figure: Drawing window with toolbar buttons "Draw | Line | Oval | Rect | 3D Rect | Round" and an X marked "Anchor point"]

Then the user moves the mouse to the other end of the line they want to draw—the *Draw To* point:

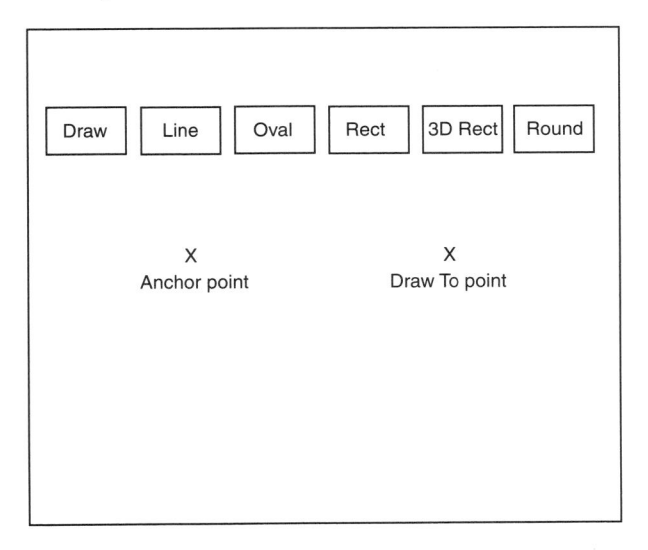

[Figure: Drawing window with toolbar buttons "Draw | Line | Oval | Rect | 3D Rect | Round" and two X marks labeled "Anchor point" and "Draw To point"]

When they release the mouse button, we have the two points we need to draw the line, and we do so:

Chapter 8

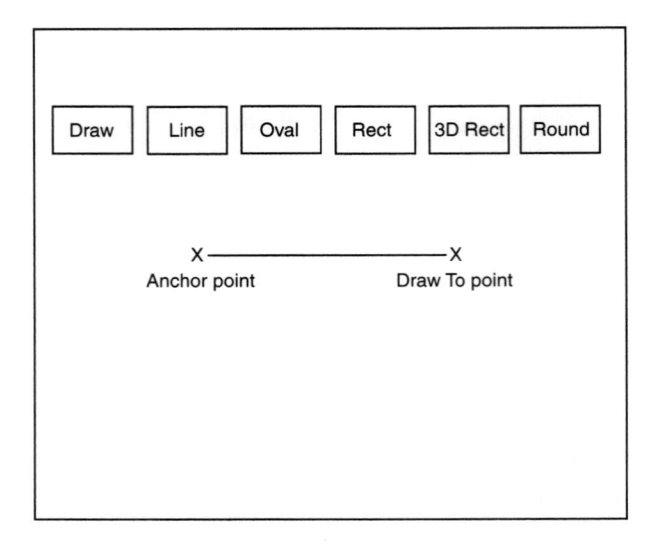

```
┌─────────────────────────────────────────────────┐
│                                                 │
│   ┌──────┐ ┌──────┐ ┌──────┐ ┌──────┐ ┌───────┐ │
│   │ Draw │ │ Line │ │ Oval │ │ Rect │ │3D Rect│ │ Round │
│   └──────┘ └──────┘ └──────┘ └──────┘ └───────┘ │
│                                                 │
│                                                 │
│         X─────────────────────X                 │
│       Anchor point         Draw To point        │
│                                                 │
│                                                 │
└─────────────────────────────────────────────────┘
```

That's how we'll draw lines. In fact, with the exception of drawing freehand objects, we'll only need two points (the Anchor point and the Draw To point) to define our graphics figures. For example, if the user wants to draw a rectangle, they click the **Rect** button and then click the mouse at one corner of the rectangle, the point we'll call the Anchor point:

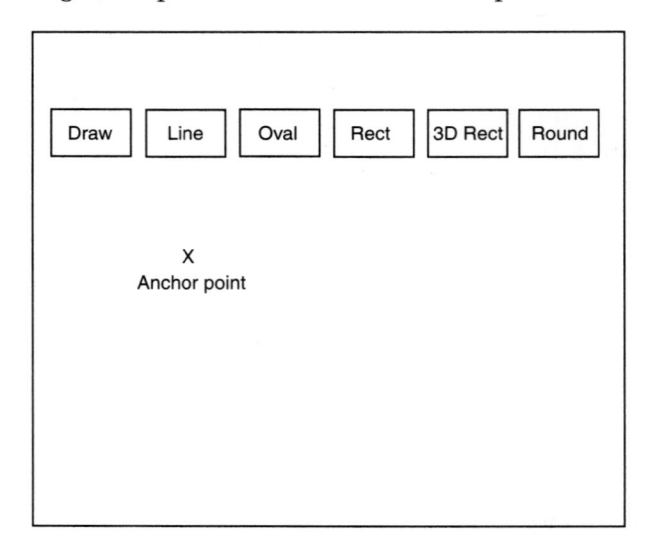

```
┌─────────────────────────────────────────────────┐
│                                                 │
│   ┌──────┐ ┌──────┐ ┌──────┐ ┌──────┐ ┌───────┐ ┌───────┐ │
│   │ Draw │ │ Line │ │ Oval │ │ Rect │ │3D Rect│ │ Round │ │
│   └──────┘ └──────┘ └──────┘ └──────┘ └───────┘ └───────┘ │
│                                                 │
│                    X                            │
│                Anchor point                     │
│                                                 │
└─────────────────────────────────────────────────┘
```

Then they move the mouse to the opposite corner of the rectangle and release the mouse button, establishing the Draw To point:

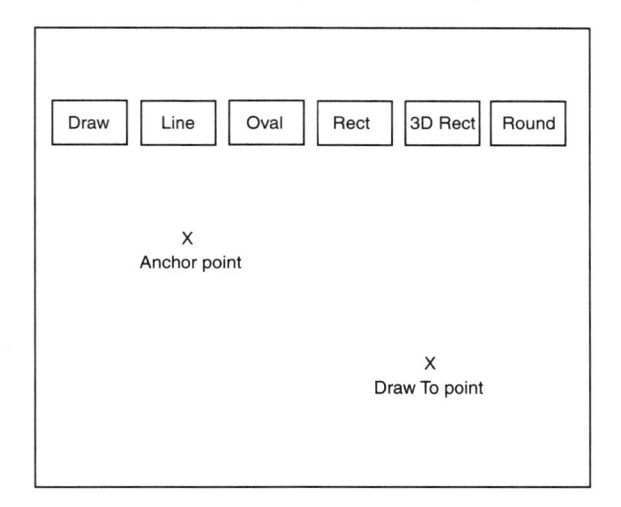

```
┌─────────────────────────────────────────────┐
│  ┌────┐ ┌────┐ ┌────┐ ┌────┐ ┌──────┐ ┌─────┐│
│  │Draw│ │Line│ │Oval│ │Rect│ │3D Rect│ │Round││
│  └────┘ └────┘ └────┘ └────┘ └──────┘ └─────┘│
│                                              │
│                    X                         │
│              Anchor point                    │
│                                              │
│                                              │
│                              X               │
│                         Draw To point        │
│                                              │
└─────────────────────────────────────────────┘
```

When the mouse button goes up, we'll draw the rectangle:

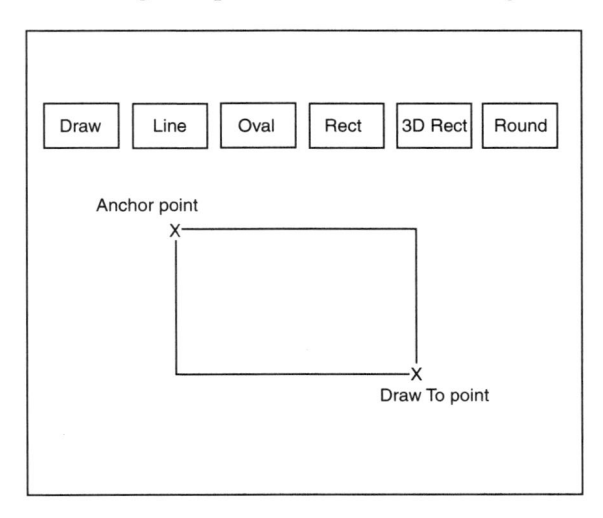

```
┌─────────────────────────────────────────────┐
│  ┌────┐ ┌────┐ ┌────┐ ┌────┐ ┌──────┐ ┌─────┐│
│  │Draw│ │Line│ │Oval│ │Rect│ │3D Rect│ │Round││
│  └────┘ └────┘ └────┘ └────┘ └──────┘ └─────┘│
│         Anchor point                         │
│         X────────────────────┐               │
│         │                    │               │
│         │                    │               │
│         │                    │               │
│         └────────────────────X               │
│                         Draw To point        │
└─────────────────────────────────────────────┘
```

When the user draws freehand objects with the mouse, on the other hand, there won't be any Anchor or Draw To points—just lines connecting the locations the mouse travels over:

Chapter 8

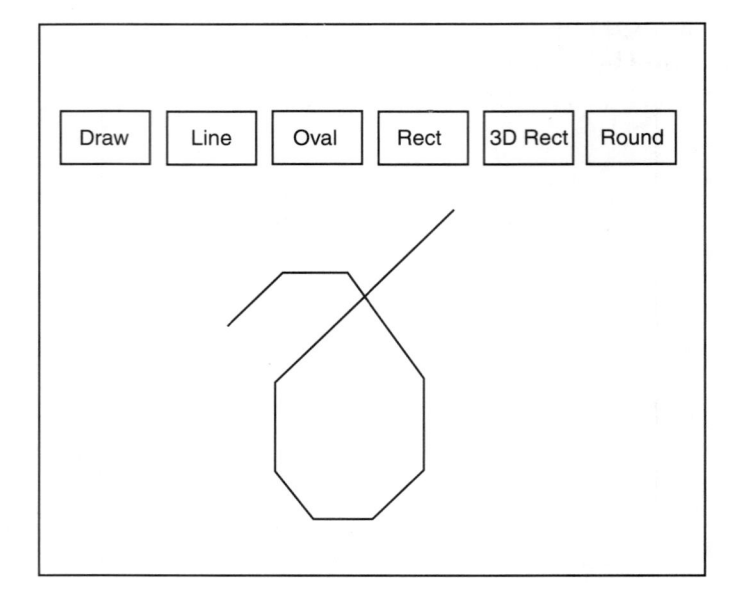

Now that we've gotten an overview, let's start putting our painter program together.

Designing the Painter Program's User Interface

The first step in using our painter applet is to choose a drawing tool, which means clicking a button like the Line button. To keep track of which figure we're supposed to be drawing, we'll set a Boolean flag to match each drawing tool. For example, when the user clicks the **Line** button, we'll set the flag `bLineFlag` to true, when they click the **Rect** button, we'll set the `bRectFlag` to true, and so on. In this way, we'll be able to divide the program up into the user interface part—dealing with the buttons and mouse clicks— and the drawing part of the program. The drawing part will only have to check the flags to see what it is supposed to be doing.

Create the new applet named painter now, and add the six buttons we'll need, as shown in Figure 8.5. In addition, add an `actionPerformed` event handler to each button in the JBuilder Inspector.

Graphics: A Mouse-Driven Paint Program

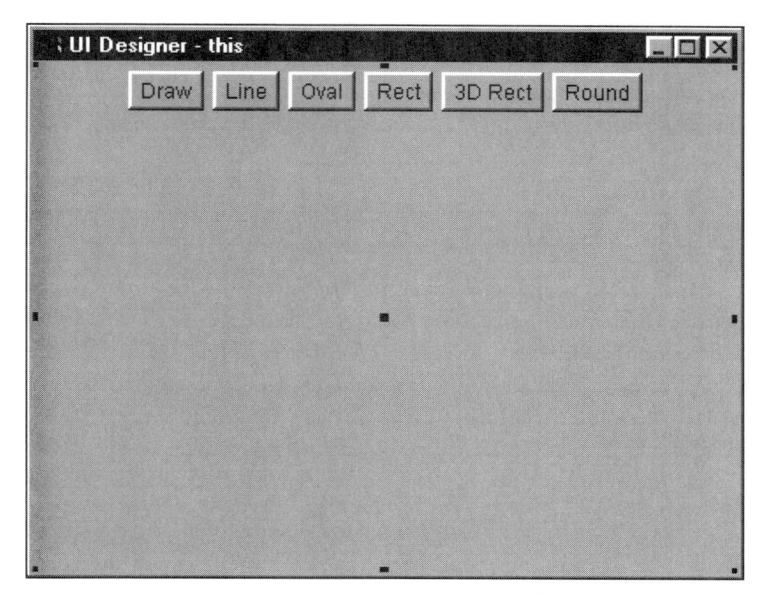

FIGURE 8.5 DESIGNING THE PAINTER APPLET.

We add the Boolean flags we'll need now:

```
public
class painter extends Applet {

    public boolean isStandalone = false;
    Button button1 = new Button();
    Button button2 = new Button();
    Button button3 = new Button();
    Button button4 = new Button();
    Button button5 = new Button();
    Button button6 = new Button();
    XYLayout xYLayout1 = new XYLayout();

    boolean bDrawFlag = false;          <—
    boolean bLineFlag = false;          <—
```

Chapter 8

```
boolean bOvalFlag = false;        <—
boolean bRectFlag = false;        <—
boolean b3DRectFlag = false;      <—
boolean bRoundedFlag = false;     <—
    .
    .
    .
```

Next, open the event handler connected to our first drawing tool, the Draw (that is, freehand drawing) tool, `button1_actionPerformed()`:

```
void button1_actionPerformed(java.awt.event.ActionEvent e) {


}
```

Here, we want to set the freehand drawing flag, `bDrawFlag`, to true:

```
void button1_actionPerformed(java.awt.event.ActionEvent e) {

    bDrawFlag = !bDrawFlag;       <—
        .
        .
        .


}
```

But note that only one drawing tool flag can be active at any one time, so we set the other flags false:

```
void button1_actionPerformed(java.awt.event.ActionEvent e) {

    bDrawFlag = !bDrawFlag;
    bLineFlag = false;            <—
    bOvalFlag = false;            <—
    bRectFlag = false;            <—
    b3DRectFlag = false;          <—
    bRoundedFlag = false;         <—

}
```

Graphics: A Mouse-Driven Paint Program

Now we do the same for the other drawing tools, enabling their flags as well:

```
void button2_actionPerformed(java.awt.event.ActionEvent e) {

  bLineFlag = !bLineFlag;
  bDrawFlag = false;
  bOvalFlag = false;
  bRectFlag = false;
  b3DRectFlag = false;
  bRoundedFlag = false;

}

void button3_actionPerformed(java.awt.event.ActionEvent e) {

  bOvalFlag = !bOvalFlag;
  bLineFlag = false;
  bDrawFlag = false;
  bRectFlag = false;
  b3DRectFlag = false;
  bRoundedFlag = false;

}

void button4_actionPerformed(java.awt.event.ActionEvent e) {

  bRectFlag = !bRectFlag;
  bLineFlag = false;
  bOvalFlag = false;
  bDrawFlag = false;
  b3DRectFlag = false;
  bRoundedFlag = false;

}

void button5_actionPerformed(java.awt.event.ActionEvent e) {
```

Chapter 8

```
        b3DRectFlag = !b3DRectFlag;
        bLineFlag = false;
        bOvalFlag = false;
        bRectFlag = false;
        bDrawFlag = false;
        bRoundedFlag = false;

    }

    void button6_actionPerformed(java.awt.event.ActionEvent e) {

        bRoundedFlag = !bRoundedFlag;
        bLineFlag = false;
        bOvalFlag = false;
        bRectFlag = false;
        b3DRectFlag = false;
        bDrawFlag = false;

    }
```

At this point, we will be able to tell which graphics figure we're supposed to be drawing, because we can check the drawing tool flags to see which is set to true.

Next, we'll work on handling the mouse.

Handling the Mouse in Painter

We'll need to work with three mouse events in painter: `mousePressed`, `mouseReleased`, and `mouseDragged` (`mouseDragged` is for freehand drawing). Add event handlers for each of those events to the applet new using the JBuilder Inspector, and open the `mousePressed()` event handler:

```
        void this_mousePressed(java.awt.event.MouseEvent e) {


        }
```

When the user presses the mouse button, they are establishing the Anchor point for the figure they want to draw, so we'll record that point and place it in a new Java Point object named `ptAnchor`:

Graphics: A Mouse-Driven Paint Program

```
void this_mousePressed(java.awt.event.MouseEvent e) {

    ptAnchor = new Point(e.getX(), e.getY());        <—

}
```

We also put aside space in our applet for both `ptAnchor`, the Anchor point, and `ptDrawTo`, the Draw To point:

```
public
class painter extends Applet {

    public boolean isStandalone = false;
    Button button1 = new Button();
    Button button2 = new Button();
    Button button3 = new Button();
    Button button4 = new Button();
    Button button5 = new Button();
    Button button6 = new Button();
    XYLayout xYLayout1 = new XYLayout();

    Point ptAnchor, ptDrawTo;                        <—

    boolean bDrawFlag = false;
    boolean bLineFlag = false;
    boolean bOvalFlag = false;
    boolean bRectFlag = false;
    boolean b3DRectFlag = false;
    boolean bRoundedFlag = false;
        .
        .
        .
```

Now we've stored the Anchor point for our figure. Now that the mouse has been pressed, we'll also set two flags: `bMouseDownFlag` and `bMouseUpFlag` to keep track of the mouse state (up or down):

```
void this_mousePressed(java.awt.event.MouseEvent e) {
```

Chapter 8

```
    bMouseDownFlag = true;      <—
    bMouseUpFlag = false;       <—
    ptAnchor = new Point(e.getX(), e.getY());
}
```

We'll use these flags throughout the program. For example, in the `paint()` method, we'll have to make sure the mouse button was released before we start drawing. We put aside space in memory for the two mouse flags as follows:

```
public
class painter extends Applet {

    public boolean isStandalone = false;
    Button button1 = new Button();
    Button button2 = new Button();
    Button button3 = new Button();
    Button button4 = new Button();
    Button button5 = new Button();
    Button button6 = new Button();
    XYLayout xYLayout1 = new XYLayout();

    Point ptAnchor, ptDrawTo;

    boolean bMouseDownFlag = false;        <—
    boolean bMouseUpFlag = false;          <—
    boolean bDrawFlag = false;
    boolean bLineFlag = false;
    boolean bOvalFlag = false;
    boolean bRectFlag = false;
    boolean b3DRectFlag = false;
    boolean bRoundedFlag = false;
        .
        .
        .
```

Now we're ready to start drawing, and we'll start by drawing lines. We'll draw our lines when the user moves from the Anchor point to the Draw To point and releases the mouse.

Graphics: A Mouse-Driven Paint Program

Drawing Lines

For our first drawing task, we'll assume the user has clicked the Line drawing tool. When the user releases the mouse button at the Draw To point, we first set the mouse flags to indicate the mouse is up:

```
void this_mouseReleased(java.awt.event.MouseEvent e) {

  bMouseDownFlag = false;    <—
  bMouseUpFlag = true;       <—
       .
       .
       .

}
```

Next, we record the (x, y) location where the mouse went up in the point pDrawTo:

```
void this_mouseReleased(java.awt.event.MouseEvent e) {

  bMouseDownFlag = false;
  bMouseUpFlag = true;
  int x = e.getX();                <—
  int y = e.getY();                <—

  ptDrawTo = new Point(x, y);      <—
       .
       .
       .

}
```

Now we're ready to draw our line, stretching from ptAnchor to ptDrawTo. We'll do that and all drawing operations in the paint() method, so to make sure that method is called, we call the repaint() method here:

```
void this_mouseReleased(java.awt.event.MouseEvent e) {

  bMouseDownFlag = false;
```

Chapter 8

```
        bMouseUpFlag = true;
        int x = e.getX();
        int y = e.getY();

        ptDrawTo = new Point(x, y);

        repaint();                          <—

    }
```

Next, override the `paint()` method with the **Override Method** item in the Wizards menu:

```
    public void paint(Graphics g) {

        //TODO: override this java.awt.Component method;



    }
```

Here, we first make sure that the mouse is up (with the `bMouseFlag` flag) and that we are supposed to be drawing lines (with the `bLineFlag` flag):

```
    public void paint(Graphics g) {

        if(bLineFlag && bMouseUpFlag){



        }
```

If we are supposed to be drawing lines, we use the Graphics class' `drawLine()` method to actually draw the line, passing it the coordinates of the Anchor and Draw To points:

```
    public void paint(Graphics g) {

        if(bLineFlag && bMouseUpFlag){

->          g.drawLine(ptAnchor.x, ptAnchor.y, ptDrawTo.x, ptDrawTo.y);
        }
```

Graphics: A Mouse-Driven Paint Program

The Graphics class' constructors and methods appear in Table 8.1.

TABLE 8.1 THE GRAPHICS CLASS' CONSTRUCTORS AND METHODS

Graphics()	Constructs a new Graphics object.
clearRect(int, int, int, int)	Clears the specified rectangle.
clipRect(int, int, int, int)	Intersects the current clip rectangle with specified rectangle.
copyArea(int, int, int, int, int, int)	Copies area of component.
create()	Creates a new Graphics object, a copy of this one.
create(int, int, int, int)	Creates a new Graphics object based on this one, but with a new translation and clip area.
dispose()	Dispose of the system resources.
draw3DRect(int, int, int, int, boolean)	Draws a 3-D highlighted outline.
drawArc(int, int, int, int, int, int)	Draws the outline of an arc.
drawBytes(byte[], int, int, int, int)	Draws the specified bytes.
drawChars(char[], int, int, int, int)	Draws the specified characters.
drawImage(Image, int, int, Color, ImageObserver)	Draws an image.
drawImage(Image, int, int, ImageObserver)	Draws an image.
drawImage(Image, int, int, int, int, Color, ImageObserver)	Draws an image that has been scaled to fit in a rectangle with a given solid background color.
drawImage(Image, int, int, int, int, ImageObserver)	Draws an image that has been scaled to fit inside the rectangle.
drawImage(Image, int, int, int, int, int, int, int, int, Color, ImageObserver)	Draws an image, scaling it to fit inside the given area of the destination with a solid background.
drawImage(Image, int, int, int, int, int, int, int, int, ImageObserver)	Draws an image, scaling it to fit inside the destination surface.
drawLine(int, int, int, int)	Draws a line between the coordinates (x1,y1) and (x2,y2).

(continued)

Chapter 8

TABLE 8.1 (CONTINUED)

`drawOval(int, int, int, int)`	Draws an oval in the specified rectangle.
`drawPolygon(int[], int[], int)`	Draws a polygon defined by arrays of x and y coordinates.
`drawPolygon(Polygon)`	Draws a polygon defined by the specified Polygon object.
`drawPolyline(int[], int[], int)`	Draws connected lines defined by arrays of x and y coordinates.
`drawRect(int, int, int, int)`	Draws a rectangle.
`drawRoundRect(int, int, int, int, int, int)`	Draws a rounded rectangle.
`drawString(String, int, int)`	Draws the string.
`fill3DRect(int, int, int, int, boolean)`	Draws a 3-D highlighted rectangle.
`fillArc(int, int, int, int, int, int)`	Fills an arc.
`fillOval(int, int, int, int)`	Fills an oval.
`fillPolygon(int[], int[], int)`	Fills a polygon.
`fillPolygon(Polygon)`	Fills a polygon defined by a given Polygon object.
`fillRect(int, int, int, int)`	Fills the given rectangle with the current color.
`fillRoundRect(int, int, int, int, int, int)`	Fills the given rounded corner rectangle with the current color.
`finalize()`	Disposes of this graphics context.
`getClip()`	Return a Shape object representing the current clipping area.
`getClipBounds()`	Returns the bounding rectangle of the current clipping area.
`getClipRect()`	DEPRECATED: Replaced by `getClipBounds()`.
`getColor()`	Gets the current color.

(continued)

Graphics: A Mouse-Driven Paint Program

TABLE 8.1 (CONTINUED)

`getFont()`	Gets the current font.
`getFontMetrics()`	Gets the font metrics of the current font.
`getFontMetrics(Font)`	Gets the font metrics for the specified font.
`setClip(int, int, int, int)`	Sets the current clip to the rectangle specified by the given coordinates.
`setClip(Shape)`	Set the current clipping area to an arbitrary clip shape.
`setColor(Color)`	Sets the current color to the specified color.
`setFont(Font)`	Sets the font for all subsequent text rendering operations.
`setPaintMode()`	Sets the logical pixel operation function to the paint, or overwrite mode.
`setXORMode(Color)`	Sets the logical pixel operation function to the XOR mode, which alternates pixels between the current color and a new specified XOR alternation color.
`toString()`	Returns a String object representing this object.
`translate(int, int)`	Translates the origin of graphics context to the point given.

The result of our line-drawing code appears in Figure 8.6—now we're drawing lines!

Chapter 8

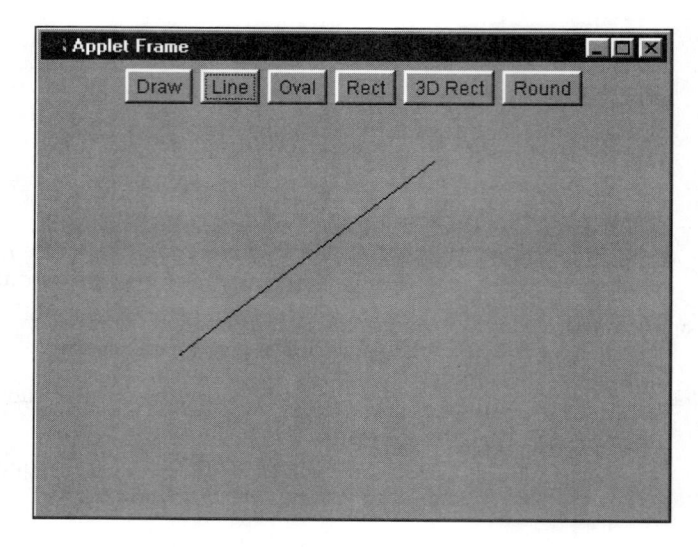

FIGURE 8.6 DRAWING LINES IN THE PAINTER APPLET.

Next, we'll turn to the other graphics figures, starting with ovals.

Drawing Ovals

The code we've put in for drawing lines is fine as far as it goes, but for the other graphics figures (ovals, rectangles and so on) we have to pass the upper left corner at which we want to start the figure and its width and height—not simply the coordinates of two points, as we did when drawing lines. For that reason, we'll order the Anchor and Draw To points so the Anchor point is at top left before drawing any other graphics figures. We order those points in the `mouseReleased` event handler, using the Math class's `Max()` and `Min()` methods:

```
void this_mouseReleased(java.awt.event.MouseEvent e) {

    bMouseDownFlag = false;
    bMouseUpFlag = true;
    int x = e.getX();
    int y = e.getY();

    if(bLineFlag){
```

Graphics: A Mouse-Driven Paint Program

```
                ptDrawTo = new Point(x, y);

            }

            else{

->              ptDrawTo = new Point(Math.max(x, ptAnchor.x), Math.max(y, ptAnchor.y));
->              ptAnchor = new Point(Math.min(x, ptAnchor.x), Math.min(y, ptAnchor.y));

            }

            repaint();

        }
```

To draw an oval or circle in the `paint()` method, we just check to make sure we are supposed to be drawing those figures—that `bOvalFlag` is true—then find the figure's width and height, and call the Graphics class' method `drawOval()`:

```
        public void paint(Graphics g) {

            int loop_index;
            int drawWidth, drawHeight;

            if(bLineFlag && bMouseUpFlag){

                g.drawLine(ptAnchor.x, ptAnchor.y, ptDrawTo.x, ptDrawTo.y);
            }

            if(bOvalFlag && bMouseUpFlag){
->              drawWidth = ptDrawTo.x - ptAnchor.x;
->              drawHeight = ptDrawTo.y - ptAnchor.y;
->              g.drawOval(ptAnchor.x, ptAnchor.y, drawWidth, drawHeight);
            }
                .
                .
                .
```

Chapter 8

That's it—now we can draw ovals, as shown in Figure 8.7.

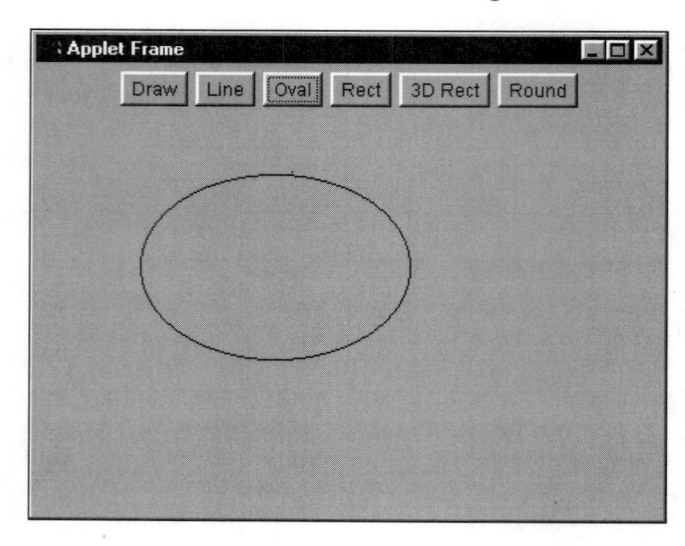

FIGURE 8.7 DRAWING OVALS IN THE PAINTER APPLET.

The next graphics figure we'll draw is rectangles.

Drawing Rectangles

To draw rectangles, we use the `drawRect()` method. In the `paint()` method, all we have to do is check if `bRectFlag` is true, and if so, we draw the rectangle:

```
public void paint(Graphics g) {

    int loop_index;
    int drawWidth, drawHeight;

    if(bLineFlag && bMouseUpFlag){

        g.drawLine(ptAnchor.x, ptAnchor.y, ptDrawTo.x, ptDrawTo.y);
    }
```

```
          if(bOvalFlag && bMouseUpFlag){
              drawWidth = ptDrawTo.x - ptAnchor.x;
              drawHeight = ptDrawTo.y - ptAnchor.y;
              g.drawOval(ptAnchor.x, ptAnchor.y, drawWidth, drawHeight);
          }

->        if(bRectFlag && bMouseUpFlag){
->            drawWidth = ptDrawTo.x - ptAnchor.x;
->            drawHeight = ptDrawTo.y - ptAnchor.y;
->            g.drawRect(ptAnchor.x, ptAnchor.y, drawWidth, drawHeight);
->        }
             .
             .
             .
```

The result of our rectangle-drawing code appears in Figure 8.8.

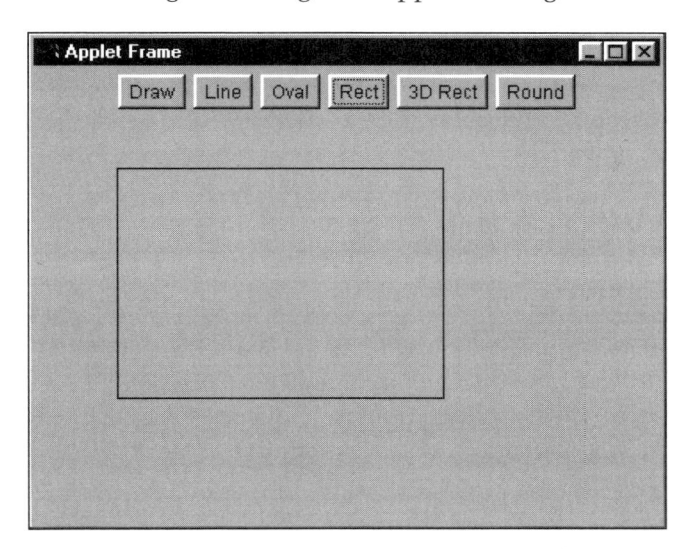

FIGURE 8.8 DRAWING RECTANGLES IN PAINTER.

We can also draw 3D rectangles.

Chapter 8

Drawing 3D Rectangles

The Java 3D rectangle is designed to go around other figures to give them a frame, but as we'll see, it doesn't really look very three-dimensional. To draw a 3D rectangle, we just use the `draw3DRect()` Graphics method:

```
public void paint(Graphics g) {

    int loop_index;
    int drawWidth, drawHeight;

    if(bLineFlag && bMouseUpFlag){

        g.drawLine(ptAnchor.x, ptAnchor.y, ptDrawTo.x, ptDrawTo.y);
    }

    if(bOvalFlag && bMouseUpFlag){
        drawWidth = ptDrawTo.x - ptAnchor.x;
        drawHeight = ptDrawTo.y - ptAnchor.y;
        g.drawOval(ptAnchor.x, ptAnchor.y, drawWidth, drawHeight);
    }

     if(bRectFlag && bMouseUpFlag){
         drawWidth = ptDrawTo.x - ptAnchor.x;
         drawHeight = ptDrawTo.y - ptAnchor.y;
         g.drawRect(ptAnchor.x, ptAnchor.y, drawWidth, drawHeight);
     }

->   if(b3DRectFlag && bMouseUpFlag){
->       drawWidth = ptDrawTo.x - ptAnchor.x;
->       drawHeight = ptDrawTo.y - ptAnchor.y;
->       g.draw3DRect(ptAnchor.x, ptAnchor.y, drawWidth, drawHeight, true);
->   }
          .
          .
          .
```

The result appears in Figure 8.9.

FIGURE 8.9 DRAWING 3D RECTANGLES.

Finally, we can draw rounded rectangles.

Drawing Rounded Rectangles

A rounded rectangle is simply a rectangle with rounded corners. We have to specify the x and y radii of the ellipses that make up the corners, and we'll set each to 10 pixels this way:

```
public void paint(Graphics g) {

    int loop_index;
    int drawWidth, drawHeight;

    if(bLineFlag && bMouseUpFlag){

        g.drawLine(ptAnchor.x, ptAnchor.y, ptDrawTo.x, ptDrawTo.y);
    }
```

Chapter 8

```
        if(bOvalFlag && bMouseUpFlag){
            drawWidth = ptDrawTo.x - ptAnchor.x;
            drawHeight = ptDrawTo.y - ptAnchor.y;
            g.drawOval(ptAnchor.x, ptAnchor.y, drawWidth, drawHeight);
        }

        if(bRectFlag && bMouseUpFlag){
            drawWidth = ptDrawTo.x - ptAnchor.x;
            drawHeight = ptDrawTo.y - ptAnchor.y;
            g.drawRect(ptAnchor.x, ptAnchor.y, drawWidth, drawHeight);
        }

        if(b3DRectFlag && bMouseUpFlag){
            drawWidth = ptDrawTo.x - ptAnchor.x;
            drawHeight = ptDrawTo.y - ptAnchor.y;
            g.draw3DRect(ptAnchor.x, ptAnchor.y, drawWidth, drawHeight,
true);
        }

->      if(bRoundedFlag && bMouseUpFlag){
->          drawWidth = ptDrawTo.x - ptAnchor.x;
->          drawHeight = ptDrawTo.y - ptAnchor.y;
->          g.drawRoundRect(ptAnchor.x, ptAnchor.y, drawWidth,
->              drawHeight, 10, 10);
->      }
            .
            .
            .
```

And that's it—now we can draw rounded rectangles, as shown in Figure 8.10. Now we're drawing rounded rectangles!

Graphics: A Mouse-Driven Paint Program

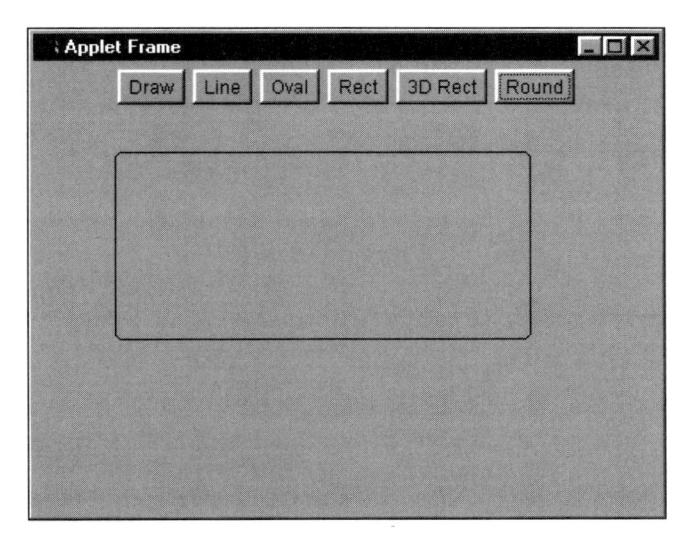

FIGURE 8.10 DRAWING ROUNDED RECTANGLES.

We've finished drawing the graphics figures we'll concentrate on in this chapter. Next, we'll see how to let the user draw freehand objects with the mouse.

Drawing Freehand Objects with the Mouse

To let the user draw freehand objects with the mouse, we'll record the locations over which the mouse travels as the user drags the mouse. We'll record those mouse locations in the `mouseDragged` event handler. We should note, however, that this method is not called for each pixel the mouse travels over; rather, the event handler is called only a few times a second. This means that we will not simply draw every point we get in the `mouseDragged` event handler on the screen. Instead, we'll connect-the-dots by drawing lines from one point to the next. This will give the impression of a smooth freehand drawing on the screen.

Chapter 8

We start by setting aside space for 1000 stored points in an array named `pts[]` and an index into that array named `ptIndex`:

```
public
class painter extends Applet {

    public boolean isStandalone = false;
    Button button1 = new Button();
    Button button2 = new Button();
    Button button3 = new Button();
    Button button4 = new Button();
    Button button5 = new Button();
    Button button6 = new Button();
    XYLayout xYLayout1 = new XYLayout();

    Point pts[] = new Point[1000];                  <-
    Point ptAnchor, ptDrawTo;
    int ptindex = 0;                                <-
       .
       .
       .
```

Next, we record the current mouse location in the `pts[]` array in the `mouseDragged` event handler, if `bDrawFlag` is true:

```
void this_mouseDragged(java.awt.event.MouseEvent e) {

    if(bMouseDownFlag && bDrawFlag){
       pts[ptindex] = new Point(e.getX(), e.getY());
          .
          .
          .
       }
    }
```

In addition, we increment our location in the `pts[]` array and call `repaint()` to make sure the program calls the `paint()` method:

Graphics: A Mouse-Driven Paint Program

```
        void this_mouseDragged(java.awt.event.MouseEvent e) {

            if(bMouseDownFlag && bDrawFlag){
                pts[ptindex] = new Point(e.getX(), e.getY());
                ptindex++;           <—
                repaint();           <—
            }
        }
```

Now we need to draw lines between the various points we've stored in the `pts[]` array, and do that in the `paint()` method:

```
    public void paint(Graphics g) {

        int loop_index;
        int drawWidth, drawHeight;

        if(bLineFlag && bMouseUpFlag){

            g.drawLine(ptAnchor.x, ptAnchor.y, ptDrawTo.x, ptDrawTo.y);
    }

        if(bOvalFlag && bMouseUpFlag){
            drawWidth = ptDrawTo.x - ptAnchor.x;
            drawHeight = ptDrawTo.y - ptAnchor.y;
            g.drawOval(ptAnchor.x, ptAnchor.y, drawWidth, drawHeight);
        }

        if(bRectFlag && bMouseUpFlag){
            drawWidth = ptDrawTo.x - ptAnchor.x;
            drawHeight = ptDrawTo.y - ptAnchor.y;
            g.drawRect(ptAnchor.x, ptAnchor.y, drawWidth, drawHeight);
        }

        if(b3DRectFlag && bMouseUpFlag){
            drawWidth = ptDrawTo.x - ptAnchor.x;
            drawHeight = ptDrawTo.y - ptAnchor.y;
            g.draw3DRect(ptAnchor.x, ptAnchor.y, drawWidth, drawHeight, true);
```

Chapter 8

```
          }

          if(bRoundedFlag && bMouseUpFlag){
               drawWidth = ptDrawTo.x - ptAnchor.x;
               drawHeight = ptDrawTo.y - ptAnchor.y;
               g.drawRoundRect(ptAnchor.x, ptAnchor.y, drawWidth, drawHeight, 10, 10);
          }

->        if(bDrawFlag){
->             for(loop_index = 0; loop_index < ptindex - 1; loop_index++){
->                  g.drawLine(pts[loop_index].x,
->   pts[loop_index].y, pts[loop_index + 1].x, pts[loop_index + 1].y);
->
->             }

          }

          super.paint( g );
     }
```

Now we can let the user draw a freehand object, as shown in Figure 8.11.

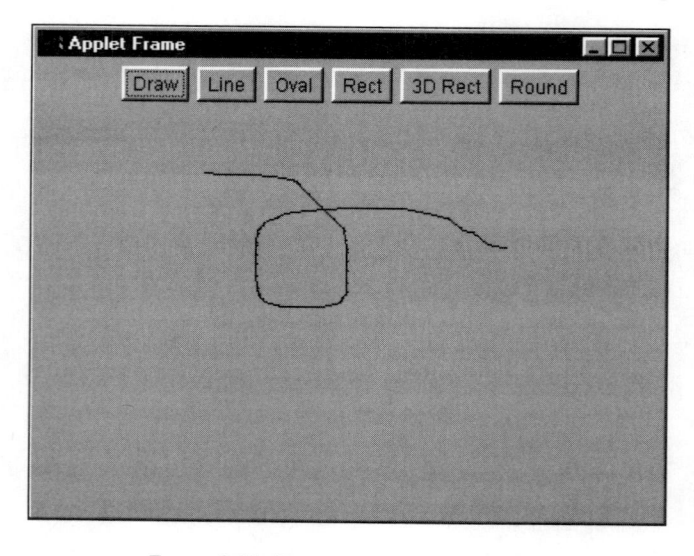

FIGURE 8.11 DRAWING A FREEHAND OBJECT.

Graphics: A Mouse-Driven Paint Program

That completes the painter applet. Now we're able to draw lines, ovals, rectangles, 3D rectangles, rounded rectangles, and freehand objects. We've come a far way in graphics handling. Listing 7.3 shows the painter.java applet.

LISTING 8.3 PAINTER.JAVA

```java
//Title:
//Version:
//Copyright:
//Author:
//Company:
//Description:
//

package painter;
import java.lang.*;
import java.awt.*;
import java.awt.event.*;
import java.applet.*;
import borland.jbcl.control.*;
import borland.jbcl.layout.*;

public
class painter extends Applet {

    public boolean isStandalone = false;
    Button button1 = new Button();
    Button button2 = new Button();
    Button button3 = new Button();
    Button button4 = new Button();
    Button button5 = new Button();
    Button button6 = new Button();
    XYLayout xYLayout1 = new XYLayout();

    Point pts[] = new Point[1000];
    Point ptAnchor, ptDrawTo;
    int ptindex = 0;

    boolean bMouseDownFlag = false;
```

Chapter 8

```java
    boolean bMouseUpFlag = false;
    boolean bDrawFlag = false;
    boolean bLineFlag = false;
    boolean bOvalFlag = false;
    boolean bRectFlag = false;
    boolean b3DRectFlag = false;
    boolean bRoundedFlag = false;

    //Construct the applet
    public painter() {
    }
    //Initialize the applet
    public void init() {
       try { jbInit(); } catch(Exception e) {
e.printStackTrace(); };

    }

    //Component initialization
    public void jbInit() throws Exception{

       this.addMouseListener(new
painter_this_MouseAdapter(this));
       this.addMouseMotionListener(new
painter_this_MouseMotionAdapter(this));
       button1.setLabel("Draw");
       button1.addActionListener(new
painter_button1_ActionAdapter(this));
       button2.setLabel("Line");
       button2.addActionListener(new
painter_button2_ActionAdapter(this));
       button3.setLabel("Oval");
       button3.addActionListener(new
painter_button3_ActionAdapter(this));
       button4.setLabel("Rect");
       button4.addActionListener(new
painter_button4_ActionAdapter(this));
       button5.setLabel("3D Rect");
       button5.addActionListener(new
```

Graphics: A Mouse-Driven Paint Program

```
painter_button5_ActionAdapter(this));
    button6.setLabel("Round");
    button6.addActionListener(new
painter_button6_ActionAdapter(this));
    xYLayout1.setWidth(400);
    xYLayout1.setHeight(300);
    this.setLayout(xYLayout1);
    this.add(button1, new XYConstraints(54, 5, -1, -1));
    this.add(button2, new XYConstraints(102, 5, -1, -1));
    this.add(button3, new XYConstraints(145, 5, -1, -1));
    this.add(button4, new XYConstraints(188, 5, -1, -1));
    this.add(button5, new XYConstraints(232, 5, -1, -1));
    this.add(button6, new XYConstraints(295, 5, -1, -1));

  }

  //Start the applet
  public void start() {

  }

  //Stop the applet
  public void stop() {

  }

  //Destroy the applet
  public void destroy() {

  }

  //Get Applet information
  public String getAppletInfo() {

    return "Applet Information";

  }

  //Get parameter info
```

Chapter 8

```java
    public String[][] getParameterInfo() {

      return null;

    }

    //Main method
    static public void main(String[] args) {

      painter applet = new painter();
      applet.isStandalone = true;
      DecoratedFrame frame = new DecoratedFrame();
      frame.setTitle("Applet Frame");
      frame.add(applet, BorderLayout.CENTER);
      applet.init();
      applet.start();
      frame.pack();
      Dimension d = Toolkit.getDefaultToolkit().getScreenSize();
      frame.setLocation((d.width - frame.getSize().width) / 2,
    (d.height - frame.getSize().height) / 2);
      frame.setVisible(true);

    }

    void button1_actionPerformed(java.awt.event.ActionEvent e) {

      bDrawFlag = !bDrawFlag;
      bLineFlag = false;
      bOvalFlag = false;
      bRectFlag = false;
      b3DRectFlag = false;
      bRoundedFlag = false;

    }

    void button2_actionPerformed(java.awt.event.ActionEvent e) {

      bLineFlag = !bLineFlag;
      bDrawFlag = false;
```

```
    bOvalFlag = false;
    bRectFlag = false;
    b3DRectFlag = false;
    bRoundedFlag = false;

}

void button3_actionPerformed(java.awt.event.ActionEvent e) {

    bOvalFlag = !bOvalFlag;
    bLineFlag = false;
    bDrawFlag = false;
    bRectFlag = false;
    b3DRectFlag = false;
    bRoundedFlag = false;

}

void button4_actionPerformed(java.awt.event.ActionEvent e) {

    bRectFlag = !bRectFlag;
    bLineFlag = false;
    bOvalFlag = false;
    bDrawFlag = false;
    b3DRectFlag = false;
    bRoundedFlag = false;

}

void button5_actionPerformed(java.awt.event.ActionEvent e) {

    b3DRectFlag = !b3DRectFlag;
    bLineFlag = false;
    bOvalFlag = false;
    bRectFlag = false;
    bDrawFlag = false;
    bRoundedFlag = false;

}
```

```java
void button6_actionPerformed(java.awt.event.ActionEvent e) {

  bRoundedFlag = !bRoundedFlag;
  bLineFlag = false;
  bOvalFlag = false;
  bRectFlag = false;
  b3DRectFlag = false;
  bDrawFlag = false;

}

public void paint(Graphics g) {

  //TODO: override this java.awt.Component method;

  int loop_index;
  int drawWidth, drawHeight;

  if(bLineFlag && bMouseUpFlag){
      g.drawLine(ptAnchor.x, ptAnchor.y, ptDrawTo.x, ptDrawTo.y);
  }

  if(bOvalFlag && bMouseUpFlag){
      drawWidth = ptDrawTo.x - ptAnchor.x;
      drawHeight = ptDrawTo.y - ptAnchor.y;
      g.drawOval(ptAnchor.x, ptAnchor.y, drawWidth, drawHeight);
  }

  if(bRectFlag && bMouseUpFlag){
      drawWidth = ptDrawTo.x - ptAnchor.x;
      drawHeight = ptDrawTo.y - ptAnchor.y;
      g.drawRect(ptAnchor.x, ptAnchor.y, drawWidth, drawHeight);
  }

  if(b3DRectFlag && bMouseUpFlag){
      drawWidth = ptDrawTo.x - ptAnchor.x;
      drawHeight = ptDrawTo.y - ptAnchor.y;
      g.draw3DRect(ptAnchor.x, ptAnchor.y, drawWidth, drawHeight, true);
```

Graphics: A Mouse-Driven Paint Program

```java
        }

        if(bRoundedFlag && bMouseUpFlag){
            drawWidth = ptDrawTo.x - ptAnchor.x;
            drawHeight = ptDrawTo.y - ptAnchor.y;
            g.drawRoundRect(ptAnchor.x, ptAnchor.y, drawWidth, drawHeight, 10, 10);
        }

        if(bDrawFlag){
            for(loop_index = 0; loop_index < ptindex - 1; loop_index++){
                g.drawLine(pts[loop_index].x,
pts[loop_index].y, pts[loop_index + 1].x, pts[loop_index + 1].y);

            }

        }

        super.paint( g );
    }

    void this_mouseReleased(java.awt.event.MouseEvent e) {

        bMouseDownFlag = false;
        bMouseUpFlag = true;
        int x = e.getX();
        int y = e.getY();

        if(bLineFlag){

            ptDrawTo = new Point(x, y);

        }

        else{

            ptDrawTo = new Point(Math.max(x, ptAnchor.x),
Math.max(y, ptAnchor.y));
            ptAnchor = new Point(Math.min(x, ptAnchor.x),
Math.min(y, ptAnchor.y));
```

Chapter 8

```java
        }

        repaint();

    }

    void this_mousePressed(java.awt.event.MouseEvent e) {

        bMouseDownFlag = true;
        bMouseUpFlag = false;
        ptAnchor = new Point(e.getX(), e.getY());

    }

    void this_mouseDragged(java.awt.event.MouseEvent e) {

        if(bMouseDownFlag && bDrawFlag){
            pts[ptindex] = new Point(e.getX(), e.getY());
            ptindex++;
            repaint();
        }
    }
}

class painter_button1_ActionAdapter implements ActionListener
{

    painter adaptee;

    painter_button1_ActionAdapter(painter adaptee) {

        this.adaptee = adaptee;

    }

    public void actionPerformed(java.awt.event.ActionEvent e) {

        adaptee.button1_actionPerformed(e);

    }
```

}

class painter_button2_ActionAdapter implements ActionListener
{
  painter adaptee;

  painter_button2_ActionAdapter(painter adaptee) {
    this.adaptee = adaptee;
  }

  public void actionPerformed(java.awt.event.ActionEvent e) {
    adaptee.button2_actionPerformed(e);
  }
}

class painter_button3_ActionAdapter implements ActionListener
{
  painter adaptee;

  painter_button3_ActionAdapter(painter adaptee) {
    this.adaptee = adaptee;
  }

  public void actionPerformed(java.awt.event.ActionEvent e) {
    adaptee.button3_actionPerformed(e);
  }
}

class painter_button4_ActionAdapter implements ActionListener

Chapter 8

```
{
  painter adaptee;

  painter_button4_ActionAdapter(painter adaptee) {

    this.adaptee = adaptee;

  }

  public void actionPerformed(java.awt.event.ActionEvent e) {

    adaptee.button4_actionPerformed(e);

  }

}

class painter_button5_ActionAdapter implements ActionListener

{

  painter adaptee;

  painter_button5_ActionAdapter(painter adaptee) {

    this.adaptee = adaptee;

  }

  public void actionPerformed(java.awt.event.ActionEvent e) {

    adaptee.button5_actionPerformed(e);

  }

}

class painter_button6_ActionAdapter implements ActionListener

{

  painter adaptee;
```

```java
    painter_button6_ActionAdapter(painter adaptee) {

       this.adaptee = adaptee;

    }

    public void actionPerformed(java.awt.event.ActionEvent e) {

       adaptee.button6_actionPerformed(e);

    }

 }

 class painter_this_MouseAdapter extends MouseAdapter {

    painter adaptee;

    painter_this_MouseAdapter(painter adaptee) {

       this.adaptee = adaptee;

    }

    public void mouseReleased(java.awt.event.MouseEvent e) {

       adaptee.this_mouseReleased(e);

    }

    public void mousePressed(java.awt.event.MouseEvent e) {

       adaptee.this_mousePressed(e);

    }

 }

 class painter_this_MouseMotionAdapter extends
 MouseMotionAdapter {

    painter adaptee;
```

Chapter 8

```
painter_this_MouseMotionAdapter(painter adaptee) {

  this.adaptee = adaptee;

}

public void mouseDragged(java.awt.event.MouseEvent e) {

  adaptee.this_mouseDragged(e);

}

}
```

We've seen a good deal of graphics handling in this chapter, but we're not done with graphics yet. In Chapter 9, we'll turn to another very popular graphics topic: graphics animation. In that chapter, we'll see how to make our graphics images come alive with motion.

CHAPTER 9

Making It Move—
Graphics Animation

In this chapter, we're going to take a look at the popular topic of graphics animation. This topic is popular because you can make your Web pages and applications come alive as you move and animate images right before the user's eyes.

Here, we're going to see several different techniques for animation. First, we'll see an easy technique: simply moving an Image control containing an image around the screen. Next, we'll move on the true Java animation as we use multithreaded (multitasking) techniques to create a new *thread*, or execution stream, in our programs and use that thread to animate an image—in this case, a whirling color wheel. The new animation thread will operate by itself, in its own thread (we'll see what this means in detail soon), meaning that you can still handle events and execute code in the program as usual, while the animation thread is working.

After we get a basic animation program going, we'll work on some of the finer points. For example, animation programs can suffer from screen flicker, and we'll see an easy way to reduce this.

Then we'll see another advanced animation topic, double-buffering. This technique lets us develop complex images off-screen. When an image is ready to be displayed, we flash it onto the screen. This way, we do not have to create our graphics images on the screen while the user watches.

Let's get started at once with our simplest animation example, using a JBuilder Image control.

Chapter 9

Using Image Controls for Animation

One of the simplest ways of supporting animation is to place an image into a JBuilder Image control:

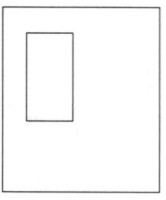

Since JBuilder controls have a built-in `setLocation()` method, we can move the image control as we like, providing simple animation:

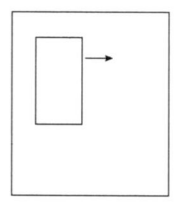

In this example, we'll move the small image you see in Figure 9.1—**ship.gif**—across the screen.

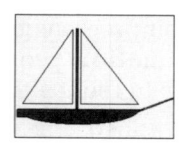

Figure 9.1 ship.gif.

We'll call this new applet sailor. Create that new applet now with the Applet Wizard.

To support animation, we'll have to make this applet *multithreaded*, which means that we will have to implement the Runnable interface.

Making Applets Multithreaded

What does it mean to make an applet multithreaded? As mentioned above, a thread is an execution stream, and an execution stream can execute Java statements. In fact, that's the way an applet works anyway: the main thread of an applet is what executes the statements we've put into it.

However, we can add additional threads to an applet, and they can also execute Java statements. In this case, we'll add a new thread to our applet, and this applet will execute the code that moves the Image control bearing the ship image across the screen.

To make our applet multithreaded, we have to implement the Runnable interface. This interface has one method: `run()`, and that's where we'll put the code that the new thread is to run. We start at the beginning of our applet's code:

```
package sailor;
import java.lang.*;
import java.awt.*;
import java.awt.event.*;
import java.applet.*;
import borland.jbcl.control.*;
import borland.jbcl.layout.*;

public
class sailor extends Applet {
    .
    .
    .
```

Here is where we implement the Runnable interface, in the declaration of our applet's class:

```
package sailor;
import java.lang.*;
import java.awt.*;
```

Chapter 9

```
import java.awt.event.*;
import java.applet.*;
import borland.jbcl.control.*;
import borland.jbcl.layout.*;

public
class sailor extends Applet implements Runnable{     <—
    .
    .
    .
```

Next, we create an object of class Thread named `shipThread`:

```
package sailor;
import java.lang.*;
import java.awt.*;
import java.awt.event.*;
import java.applet.*;
import borland.jbcl.control.*;
import borland.jbcl.layout.*;

public
class sailor extends Applet implements Runnable{

  public XYLayout xYLayout1 = new XYLayout();
  public boolean isStandalone = false;
  ImageControl imageControl1 = new ImageControl();
  Thread shipThread;                                  <—
    .
    .
    .
```

The Thread class' constructors and methods appear in Table 9.1 (we'll see more about this class in Chapter 10).

Table 9.1 The Thread Class' Constructors and Methods

`Thread()`	Constructs a new Thread.
`Thread(Runnable)`	Constructs a new Thread which applies the `run()` method of the given target.
`Thread(Runnable, String)`	Constructs a new Thread with the given name and applies the `run()` method of the given target.
`Thread(String)`	Constructs a new Thread with the given name.
`Thread(ThreadGroup, Runnable)`	Constructs a new Thread in the given Thread group that applies the `run()` method of the given target.
`Thread(ThreadGroup, Runnable, String)`	Constructs a new Thread in the given Thread group with the given name and applies the `run()` method of the given target.
`Thread(ThreadGroup, String)`	Constructs a new Thread in the given Thread group with the given name.
`activeCount()`	Returns the number of active Threads in this group.
`checkAccess()`	Checks if the current Thread is allowed to modify this Thread.
`countStackFrames()`	Returns the number of stack frames in this Thread.
`currentThread()`	Returns a reference to the currently executing Thread object.
`destroy()`	Destroy a thread.
`dumpStack()`	Debugging procedure to print a stack trace.
`enumerate(Thread[])`	Copies references to every active Thread in this Thread's group.
`getName()`	Gets and returns this Thread's name.
`getPriority()`	Gets and returns the Thread's priority.
`getThreadGroup()`	Gets and returns this Thread group.
`interrupt()`	Send an interrupt to a thread.
`isAlive()`	Returns true if the Thread is active.
`isDaemon()`	Returns the daemon flag of the Thread.
`isInterrupted()`	Ask if some Thread has been interrupted.

(continued)

Chapter 9

Table 9.1 The Thread Class' Constructors and Methods (continued)

join()	Waits forever for this Thread to die.
join(long)	Waits for this Thread to die.
join(long, int)	Waits for the Thread to die, with more precise time.
resume()	Resumes this Thread execution.
run()	The executable code of this Thread.
setDaemon(boolean)	Make Thread as a daemon Thread or a user Thread.
setName(String)	Sets the Thread's name.
setPriority(int)	Sets the Thread's priority.
sleep(long)	Causes the currently executing Thread to sleep for the given number of milliseconds.
sleep(long, int)	Sleep, in milliseconds and additional nanosecond.
start()	Starts this Thread.
stop()	Stops a Thread by tossing an object.
stop(Throwable)	Stops a Thread by tossing an object.
suspend()	Suspends this Thread's execution.
toString()	Returns a String representation of the Thread.
yield()	Causes the current Thread object to yield.

Now we've declared a new thread, `shipThread`. However, this thread doesn't actually do anything until we start it, so we'll do that now.

Starting a Thread

We use the applet's `start()` method to create and start our new thread. Add the `start()` and `stop()` methods to the applet with the **Override Methods** item in the JBuilder Wizards menu now. We create the new thread with the Java new operator:

```
public void start() {

    shipThread = new Thread(this);                    <—
```

Making It Move—Graphics Animation

```
        .
        .
        .
}
```

This creates the new thread object. Next, we set its priority to `Thread.MIN_PRIORITY`, which means that it has minimum priority—threads with higher priority will execute their code before this one does:

```
public void start() {

   shipThread = new Thread(this);
   shipThread.setPriority(Thread.MIN_PRIORITY);    <—
        .
        .
        .
}
```

Finally, we start the thread with its `start()` method:

```
public void start() {

   shipThread = new Thread(this);
   shipThread.setPriority(Thread.MIN_PRIORITY);
   shipThread.start();           <—
}
```

Calling the thread's `start()` method starts the thread executing the code in the `run()` method. That's where we'll place our animation code. Before we do that, however, we will provide some way of stopping our thread.

Stopping a Thread

If we don't stop a thread, it will keep going, even after the Web page that holds our applet has been dismissed in the Web browser. To stop the thread, we simply use its `stop()` method and set the `shipThread` variable to `null` in the applet's `stop()` method:

```
public void stop() {
```

Chapter 9

```
    shipThread.stop();      <--
    shipThread = null;      <--

}
```

`shipThread` is running, which means it will execute the code we will place in the applet's `run()` method.

Running a Thread's Code

In this applet, we will move an Image control across the screen. Add a new Image control to the applet now, as shown in Figure 9.2. Next, set the Image control's `imageName` property to the name of the ship image file, ship.gif. This displays the ship in the Image control, as also shown in Figure 9.2.

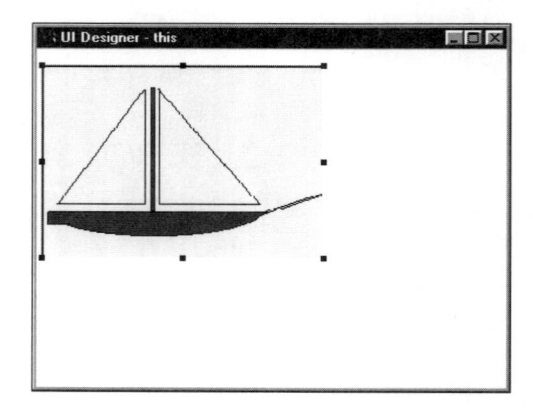

Figure 9.2 Our Image control.

We will move this Image control to the right to animate it, so we need to keep track of its x position. To do that, we'll use a new variable, `xposition`:

```
public
class sailor extends Applet implements Runnable{

    public XYLayout xYLayout1 = new XYLayout();
    public boolean isStandalone = false;
    ImageControl imageControl1 = new ImageControl();
    Thread shipThread;
    int xposition = 0;              <--
```

Making It Move—Graphics Animation

Now we're ready to override the Runnable interface's `run()` method. Add that method to the applet's class now by hand:

```
//Start the applet
public void start() {

  shipThread = new Thread(this);
  shipThread.setPriority(Thread.MIN_PRIORITY);
  shipThread.start();
}

//Stop the applet
public void stop() {

  shipThread.stop();
  shipThread = null;

}

public void run() {          <--

}                            <--
```

This method holds the code that the new thread, `shipThread`, will execute. In this case, we'll simply increment the variable xposition until it reaches a value of 100, in which case we'll set it back to 0 and start all over:

```
public void run() {
  while(true){

     if(xposition++ > 100)xposition = 0;
         .
         .
         .
     }

}
```

Chapter 9

Note that we use a while loop with an argument of true, which appears to means that this loop will keep going forever. In fact, this code will terminate when we execute the `stop()` method, so there is no problem.

The actual code to display the Image control on the screen at the new position will be in the `paint()` method, so we call the repaint method now that we've incremented the xposition variable:

```
public void run() {
  while(true){

     if(xposition++ > 100)xposition = 0;

       repaint();                     <—
         .
         .
         .

  }

}
```

Now we will make the thread pause for a while using the `sleep()` method. This method makes the thread *sleep*—stop executing—for the number of milliseconds we pass to it. In this case, we'll pause for 100 milliseconds, or .1 seconds (since the `sleep()` method can generate exceptions, or errors, we have to enclose it in a try and catch block to handle such exceptions):

```
public void run() {
  while(true){

     if(xposition++ > 100)xposition = 0;

       repaint();
       try {Thread.sleep(100);}              <—
       catch(InterruptedException e) { }     <—

  }

}
```

Making It Move—Graphics Animation

The result of the above code, then, is that the `xposition` variable is steadily incremented, and our applet's `paint()` method is called ten times a second. We will place the code we'll need in the `paint()` method now.

Drawing the Image

Override the `paint()` method in the applet now:

```
public void paint(Graphics g) {

    //TODO: override this java.awt.Component method;

    super.paint( g );

}
```

We won't do any actual drawing in the `paint()` method this time. We'll simply use the Image control's `setLocation()` method to move the Image control in the x direction:

```
      public void paint(Graphics g) {

–>       imageControl1.setLocation(xposition, imageControl1.getLocation().y);
         super.paint( g );

      }
```

Run the applet now. As we see in Figure 9.3, the Image control appears in the applet. The new thread we've set up moves the ship gently along in the x direction—our sailor applet is a success.

Chapter 9

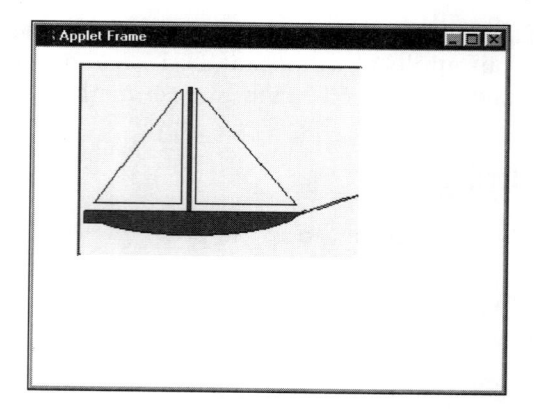

Figure 9.3 Our sailor applet at work.

The code for this applet appears in Listing 9.1.

Listing 9.1 sailor.java

```
//Title:
//Version:
//Copyright:
//Author:
//Company:
//Description:
//

package sailor;
import java.lang.*;
import java.awt.*;
import java.awt.event.*;
import java.applet.*;
import borland.jbcl.control.*;
import borland.jbcl.layout.*;

public
class sailor extends Applet implements Runnable{

  public XYLayout xYLayout1 = new XYLayout();
  public boolean isStandalone = false;
```

Making It Move—Graphics Animation

```
  ImageControl imageControl1 = new ImageControl();
  Thread shipThread;
  int xposition = 0;

  //Construct the applet
  public sailor() {

  }

  //Initialize the applet
  public void init() {

    try { jbInit(); } catch(Exception e) { e.printStackTrace(); };

  }

  //Component initialization
  public void jbInit() throws Exception{

    this.setBackground(new Color(254, 254, 254));
    xYLayout1.setWidth(400);
    xYLayout1.setHeight(300);
    imageControl1.setForeground(new Color(254, 254, 254));
    imageControl1.setBackground(Color.white);
    imageControl1.setBounds(new Rectangle(4, 14, 231, 198));
    imageControl1.setImageName("e:\\jbuilder\\myprojects\\sailor\\ship.gif");
    this.setLayout(xYLayout1);
    this.add(imageControl1, new XYConstraints(4, 14, 241, 172));
  }

  //Start the applet
  public void start() {

    shipThread = new Thread(this);
    shipThread.setPriority(Thread.MIN_PRIORITY);
    shipThread.start();
  }

  //Stop the applet
```

Chapter 9

```java
public void stop() {

   shipThread.stop();
   shipThread = null;

}

public void run() {
  while(true){

     if(xposition++ > 100)xposition = 0;
     repaint();
     try {Thread.sleep(100);}
     catch(InterruptedException e) { }

     }

}

//Destroy the applet
public void destroy() {

}

//Get Applet information
public String getAppletInfo() {

   return "Applet Information";

}

//Get parameter info
public String[][] getParameterInfo() {

   return null;

}

//Main method
```

Making It Move—Graphics Animation

```
    static public void main(String[] args) {

  sailor applet = new sailor();
  applet.isStandalone = true;
  DecoratedFrame frame = new DecoratedFrame();
  frame.setTitle("Applet Frame");
  frame.add(applet, BorderLayout.CENTER);
  applet.init();
  applet.start();
  frame.pack();
  Dimension d = Toolkit.getDefaultToolkit().getScreenSize();
  frame.setLocation((d.width - frame.getSize().width) / 2,
(d.height - frame.getSize().height) / 2);
  frame.setVisible(true);

    }

    public void paint(Graphics g) {

  //TODO: override this java.awt.Component method;
  imageControl1.setLocation(xposition, imageControl1.getLocation().y);
  super.paint( g);

    }

  }
```

You may note that the Image control we're moving is visible when the applet runs, because that control has a border. To avoid showing that border, we can dispense with the Image control altogether and simply draw the image in the applet directly. And that's the basis of animation.

Creating Graphics Animation

In our next example, we'll see true graphics animation. In particular, we'll display a color wheel—half red, half blue—in our applet:

Chapter 9

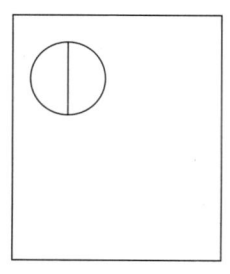

We'll use a new thread to animate this color wheel, spinning it around:

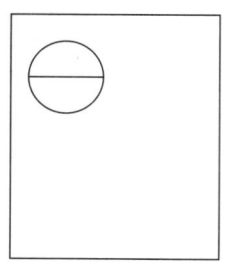

The images we'll animate will be stored in the image files Wheel1.gif to Wheel4.gif. These images appear in Figure 9.4.

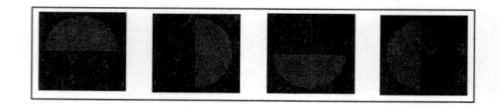

Figure 9.4 Our color wheel images.

Create this new applet, which we'll call animator, now. We'll start our applet by loading those images into an array of images named `wheelImages[]`. We'll also declare an index into that array named `wheelIndex`. As the applet executes, we'll load images from that array into an image object named `nowImage`, and that is the image we'll actually display:

```
public
class animator extends Applet implements Runnable {

    public XYLayout xYLayout1 = new XYLayout();
    public boolean isStandalone = false;
    Image wheelImages[] = new Image[4];          <—
```

Making It Move—Graphics Animation

```
Image nowImage;                          <—
int wheelIndex = 0;                      <—
   .
   .
   .
```

Next, we load the four images into the `wheelImages[]` array in the `init()` method:

```
public void init() {

    wheelImages[0] = getImage(getCodeBase(), "Wheel1.gif");   <—
    wheelImages[1] = getImage(getCodeBase(), "Wheel2.gif");   <—
    wheelImages[2] = getImage(getCodeBase(), "Wheel3.gif");   <—
    wheelImages[3] = getImage(getCodeBase(), "Wheel4.gif");   <—

    try { jbInit(); }
    catch(Exception e) { e.printStackTrace(); };

}
```

We also declare a new thread to handle the animation, `wheelThread`:

```
public
class animator extends Applet implements Runnable {

    public XYLayout xYLayout1 = new XYLayout();
    public boolean isStandalone = false;
    Image wheelImages[] = new Image[4];
    Image nowImage;
    int wheelIndex = 0;
    Thread wheelThread;                  <—
       .
       .
       .
```

We start `wheelThread` in the `start()` method:

```
public void start() {
```

Chapter 9

```
wheelThread = new Thread(this);
wheelThread.setPriority(Thread.MIN_PRIORITY);
wheelThread.start();

}
```

And we stop it in the `stop()` method:

```
public void stop() {

    wheelThread.stop();
    wheelThread = null;

}
```

Finally, we add the `run()` method by hand:

```
public void run() {

}
```

We'll place the animation code in the `run()` method.

Animating Our Images

The main task of the `run()` method is to load images from the `wheelImages[]` array successively into the image object `nowImage` and call the `repaint()` method to draw that image. We start by loading images from `wheelImages[]` into `nowImage` as follows:

```
public void run() {

    while(true){

        nowImage = wheelImages[wheelIndex++];
        if(wheelIndex > 3)wheelIndex = 0;
        .
        .
        .
```

Making It Move—Graphics Animation

Next, we call `repaint()` to draw this new image:

```
public void run() {

  while(true){

    nowImage = wheelImages[wheelIndex++];
    if(wheelIndex > 3)wheelIndex = 0;
    repaint();                              <--
      .
      .
      .

  }
}
```

Finally, we call the `sleep()` method, making the thread sleep for two tenths of a second:

```
public void run() {

  while(true){

    nowImage = wheelImages[wheelIndex++];
    if(wheelIndex > 3)wheelIndex = 0;
    repaint();
    try {Thread.sleep(200);}                <--
    catch(InterruptedException e) { }       <--

  }
}
```

All that's left is to draw the continually reloaded image in the `nowImage` object, and we'll do that in the `paint()` method.

Chapter 9

Drawing the Images

Override the applet's `paint()` method now:

```
public void paint(Graphics g) {

    //TODO: override this java.awt.Component method;


    super.paint( g);


}
```

Here, all we have to do is to draw the `nowImage` object, because each time the `paint()` method is called by the animation thread, `nowImage` contains a new image:

```
public void paint(Graphics g) {

    g.drawImage(nowImage, 10, 10, this);      <--


    super.paint( g);


}
```

That's it—the result of this applet appears in Figure 9.5. Our color wheel appears and spins around—the animator applet is a success. Now we're creating true animation in JBuilder. (Bear in mind, if you're testing this applet in JBuilder, that you might run into the `getCodebase()` bug; to fix that, highlight the **animator.html** entry in the Project window before running the applet.)

Making It Move—Graphics Animation

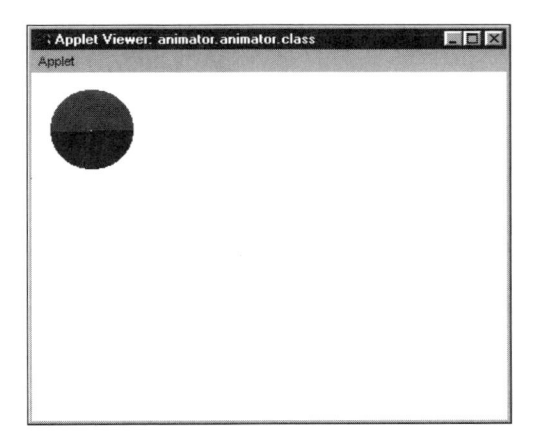

Figure 9.5 Our color wheel spinning around.

The code for this applet appears in Listing 9.2.

Listing 9.2 animator.java

```
//Title:
//Version:
//Copyright:
//Author:
//Company:
//Description:
//

package animator;
import java.lang.*;
import java.awt.*;
import java.awt.image.*;
import java.awt.event.*;
import java.applet.*;
import java.net.*;
import borland.jbcl.control.*;
import borland.jbcl.layout.*;

public
class animator extends Applet implements Runnable {
```

Chapter 9

```java
public XYLayout xYLayout1 = new XYLayout();
public boolean isStandalone = false;
Image wheelImages[] = new Image[4];
Image nowImage;
int wheelIndex = 0;
Thread wheelThread;

//Get a parameter value
public String getParameter(String key, String def) {

  return isStandalone ? System.getProperty(key, def) :
    (getParameter(key) != null ? getParameter(key) : def);

}

//Construct the applet
public animator() {

}

//Initialize the applet
public void init() {

  wheelImages[0] = getImage(getCodeBase(), "Wheel1.gif");
  wheelImages[1] = getImage(getCodeBase(), "Wheel2.gif");
  wheelImages[2] = getImage(getCodeBase(), "Wheel3.gif");
  wheelImages[3] = getImage(getCodeBase(), "Wheel4.gif");

  try { jbInit(); }
  catch(Exception e) { e.printStackTrace(); };

}

//Component initialization
public void jbInit() throws Exception{

  xYLayout1.setWidth(400);
  xYLayout1.setHeight(300);
  this.setLayout(xYLayout1);
```

Making It Move—Graphics Animation

```
  }

  //Start the applet
  public void start() {

    wheelThread = new Thread(this);
    wheelThread.setPriority(Thread.MIN_PRIORITY);
    wheelThread.start();

  }

  //Stop the applet
  public void stop() {

    wheelThread.stop();
    wheelThread = null;

  }

  public void run() {

    while(true){

      nowImage = wheelImages[wheelIndex++];
      if(wheelIndex > 3)wheelIndex = 0;
      repaint();
      try {Thread.sleep(200);}
      catch(InterruptedException e) { }

    }

  }

  //Destroy the applet
  public void destroy() {

  }

  //Get Applet information
  public String getAppletInfo() {
```

Chapter 9

```java
        return "Applet Information";

    }

    //Get parameter info
    public String[][] getParameterInfo() {

        return null;

    }

    //Main method
    static public void main(String[] args) {

        animator applet = new animator();
        applet.isStandalone = true;
        DecoratedFrame frame = new DecoratedFrame();
        frame.setTitle("Applet Frame");
        frame.add(applet, BorderLayout.CENTER);
        applet.init();
        applet.start();
        frame.pack();
        Dimension d = Toolkit.getDefaultToolkit().getScreenSize();
        frame.setLocation((d.width - frame.getSize().width) / 2,
(d.height - frame.getSize().height) / 2);
        frame.setVisible(true);

    }

    public void paint(Graphics g) {

        //TODO: override this java.awt.Component method;
        g.drawImage(nowImage, 10, 10, this);

        super.paint( g);

    }

}
```

Making It Move—Graphics Animation

If you watch our spinning color wheel, you'll see that the screen flickers quite badly. There is a way to get rid of screen flicker, however, and we'll look into it now.

Reducing Screen Flicker

The main reason the screen flickers is that each time we call `repaint()`, the applet is entirely redrawn in the background color before we draw our new image. There is no need for this in our case—each image is the same size and covers the same area on the screen, so we don't have to clear the whole applet before redrawing them. Let's see how to fix this problem.

When we call `repaint()`, the program actually calls the `update()` method, which clears the applet. We can avoid clearing the whole applet by overriding `update()` ourselves, and we do that now:

```
public void paint(Graphics g) {

  g.drawImage(nowImage, 10, 10, this);

  super.paint( g);

}

public void update(Graphics g){          <--

}                                        <--
```

Here, we'll just call the `paint()` method directly:

```
public void paint(Graphics g) {

  g.drawImage(nowImage, 10, 10, this);
```

Chapter 9

```
    super.paint( g );


  }


  public void update(Graphics g){


    paint(g);              <--


  }
```

When we call `paint()` directly like this, we avoid the usual step of redrawing the whole applet. When you run the new version of the applet, the flicker is gone. The new version of this applet appears in Listing 9.3.

Listing 9.3 No-flicker version of animator.java

```
//Title:
//Version:
//Copyright:
//Author:
//Company:
//Description:
//

package animator;
import java.lang.*;
import java.awt.*;
import java.awt.image.*;
import java.awt.event.*;
import java.applet.*;
import java.net.*;
import borland.jbcl.control.*;
import borland.jbcl.layout.*;

public
```

Making It Move—Graphics Animation

```
class animator extends Applet implements Runnable {

  public XYLayout xYLayout1 = new XYLayout();
  public boolean isStandalone = false;
  Image wheelImages[] = new Image[4];
  Image nowImage;
  int wheelIndex = 0;
  Thread wheelThread;

  //Get a parameter value
  public String getParameter(String key, String def) {

    return isStandalone ? System.getProperty(key, def) :
      (getParameter(key) != null ? getParameter(key) : def);

  }

  //Construct the applet
  public animator() {

  }

  //Initialize the applet
  public void init() {

    wheelImages[0] = getImage(getCodeBase(), "Wheel1.gif");
    wheelImages[1] = getImage(getCodeBase(), "Wheel2.gif");
    wheelImages[2] = getImage(getCodeBase(), "Wheel3.gif");
    wheelImages[3] = getImage(getCodeBase(), "Wheel4.gif");

    try { jbInit(); }
    catch(Exception e) { e.printStackTrace(); };

  }

  //Component initialization
  public void jbInit() throws Exception{

    xYLayout1.setWidth(400);
```

Chapter 9

```
    xYLayout1.setHeight(300);
    this.setLayout(xYLayout1);

}

//Start the applet
public void start() {

  wheelThread = new Thread(this);
  wheelThread.setPriority(Thread.MIN_PRIORITY);
  wheelThread.start();

}

//Stop the applet
public void stop() {

  wheelThread.stop();
  wheelThread = null;

}

public void run() {

  while(true){
    nowImage = wheelImages[wheelIndex++];
    if(wheelIndex > 3)wheelIndex = 0;
    repaint();
    try {Thread.sleep(200);}
    catch(InterruptedException e) { }

  }

}

//Destroy the applet
public void destroy() {

}
```

Making It Move—Graphics Animation

```java
//Get Applet information
public String getAppletInfo() {

   return "Applet Information";

}

//Get parameter info
public String[][] getParameterInfo() {

   return null;

}

//Main method
static public void main(String[] args) {

   animator applet = new animator();
   applet.isStandalone = true;
   DecoratedFrame frame = new DecoratedFrame();
   frame.setTitle("Applet Frame");
   frame.add(applet, BorderLayout.CENTER);
   applet.init();
   applet.start();
   frame.pack();
   Dimension d = Toolkit.getDefaultToolkit().getScreenSize();
   frame.setLocation((d.width - frame.getSize().width) / 2,
(d.height - frame.getSize().height) / 2);
   frame.setVisible(true);

}

public void paint(Graphics g) {

   //TODO: override this java.awt.Component method;
   g.drawImage(nowImage, 10, 10, this);

   super.paint( g );
```

Chapter 9

```
    }

    public void update(Graphics g){

        paint(g);

    }

}
```

We've already come far in this chapter on graphics animation. However, there certainly is more to cover in animation. Let's take a look at the process of double-buffering now.

Double-Buffering

When you create your own images rather than reading them in from disk, there is an additional concern. It may take some time to create those images, and rather than drawing those images piece by piece directly on the screen, we can draw them off-screen and display them only when they are ready. This technique is called *double-buffering*, because you develop your graphics in a buffer in memory.

In this case, we'll present the user with an applet that has a button in it, labeled *Start the animation*:

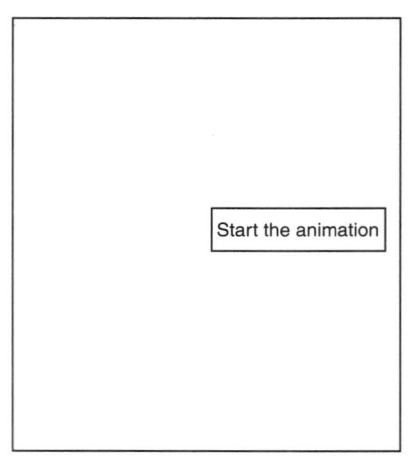

Making It Move—Graphics Animation

When the user clicks the button, we'll start the animation, which consists of successive images flashes on the screen. In this case, each image will consist of colored cascading rectangles, increasing in size as they stretch from upper left to lower right:

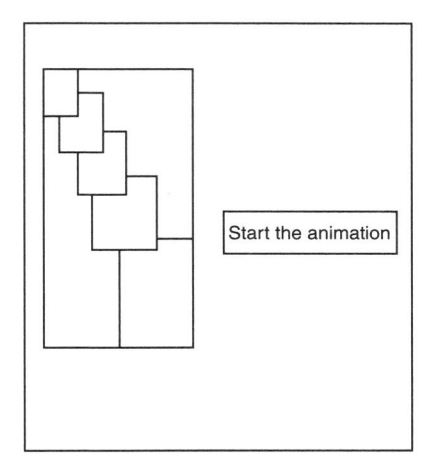

As the animation proceeds frame by frame, we'll display this cascade of rectangles in steadily brightening colors, going through the whole spectrum from light to dark. In this way, each frame will be different from the last, and because each contains a number of elements, we'll draw each frame off-screen before showing it on-screen.

Let's write this applet, which we'll name `doublebuffer`, now. Use the Applet Wizard to create this applet now, and add a button to the applet in the Designer, giving that button the label **Start the animation**. Connect an `actionPerformed` event handler to the button as well.

Now we declare a new thread, `doublebufferThread`, to support our animation:

```
public
class doublebuffer extends Applet implements Runnable{

    public XYLayout xYLayout1 = new XYLayout();
    public boolean isStandalone = false;
    Image nowImage;
    Thread doublebufferThread;                <--
    Button button1 = new Button();
```

Chapter 9

We create that button in the `start()` method:

```
public void start() {

    doublebufferThread = new Thread(this);
    doublebufferThread.start();

}
```

And we stop the thread in the `stop()` method:

```
public void stop() {

    doublebufferThread.stop();
    doublebufferThread = null;

}
```

Finally, in the `run()` method, we make sure the `paint()` method is called every two tenths of a second:

```
public void run() {

    while(true){

        repaint();
        try {Thread.sleep(200);}
        catch(InterruptedException e) {}

    }

}
```

In the `paint()` method, we'll draw our new image and display it. To do that, we'll set up our buffer for the new image we want to display. That buffer will in fact be a new Image object, `nowImage`:

Making It Move—Graphics Animation

```
public
class doublebuffer extends Applet implements Runnable{

  public XYLayout xYLayout1 = new XYLayout();
  public boolean isStandalone = false;
  Image nowImage;                <--
  Thread doublebufferThread;
  Button button1 = new Button();
     .
     .
     .
```

When the user clicks the button labeled **Start the animation**, we can create the Image object with the `createImage()` method:

```
void button1_actionPerformed(java.awt.event.ActionEvent e) {

  nowImage = createImage(200, 200);         <--
     .
     .
     .

}
```

Next, we get a Graphics object, `nowGraphics`, for the Image object:

```
void button1_actionPerformed(java.awt.event.ActionEvent e) {

  nowImage = createImage(200, 200);
  nowGraphics = nowImage.getGraphics();     <--
     .
     .
     .

}
```

This means we can draw in the Image object `nowImage` directly. Now that our buffer is set up, we call `repaint()` to start the painting process:

Chapter 9

```
void button1_actionPerformed(java.awt.event.ActionEvent e) {

    nowImage = createImage(200, 200);
    nowGraphics = nowImage.getGraphics();
    repaint();                          <--

}
```

We'll draw each image in a successively brighter color, so we have to keep track of the red, blue, and green color values used in drawing the image. We will store those values in the integers red, green, and blue:

```
public
class doublebuffer extends Applet implements Runnable{

    public XYLayout xYLayout1 = new XYLayout();
    public boolean isStandalone = false;
    Image nowImage;
    Graphics nowGraphics;
    Thread doublebufferThread;
    Button button1 = new Button();
    int red, green, blue;                      <--
        .
        .
        .
```

Now we'll create the buffered image and draw it.

Drawing a Buffered Image

We'll draw the new image in the paint() method, and then place it on the screen. First, we'll make sure the user has clicked the **Start the animation** button and our buffer is indeed set up:

```
public void paint (Graphics g) {

    if(nowGraphics != null){            <--
```

Making It Move—Graphics Animation

```
    }                              <-


}
```

If the buffer has been set up, we can draw our graphics image in the `nowImage` object. We do that with a loop, drawing 40 rectangles, each of the same color, and incrementing the color values `red`, `green`, and `blue` appropriately for the next time we drawn the image:

```
public void paint (Graphics g) {

    int loop_index;

    if(nowGraphics != null){
      for(loop_index = 40; loop_index > 0; loop_index--){

        if(red < 255) red++;
        if(red >= 255 && green < 255) green++;
        if(red >= 255 && green >= 255 && blue < 255) blue++;
        if(red >= 255 && green >= 255 & blue >= 255)
          red = blue = green = 0;

        nowGraphics.setColor(new Color(red, green, blue));
        nowGraphics.fillRect(5 * loop_index, 5 * loop_index, 5 *
           loop_index, 5 * loop_index);
      }
            .
            .
            .
    }
```

We've drawn our buffered image in the `nowImage` object, using the `nowGraphics` **Graphics object**. At this point, the image is complete—we've drawn it off-screen—so all that remains is to draw it in the applet:

```
public void paint (Graphics g) {
```

Chapter 9

```
    int loop_index;

    if(nowGraphics != null){
      for(loop_index = 40; loop_index > 0; loop_index--){

        if(red < 255) red++;
        if(red >= 255 && green < 255) green++;
        if(red >= 255 && green >= 255 && blue < 255) blue++;
        if(red >= 255 && green >= 255 & blue >= 255)
          red = blue = green = 0;

        nowGraphics.setColor(new Color(red, green, blue));
        nowGraphics.fillRect(5 * loop_index, 5 * loop_index, 5 *
          loop_index, 5 * loop_index);
      }

      g.drawImage(nowImage, 10, 10, this);     <--

    }

  }
```

That's it—run the program now, as shown in Figure 9.6, and press the button to start the animation. This flashes our buffered images onto the screen—each image has been drawn offscreeen and then placed on the screen to create the animation. Our double buffering example is a success.

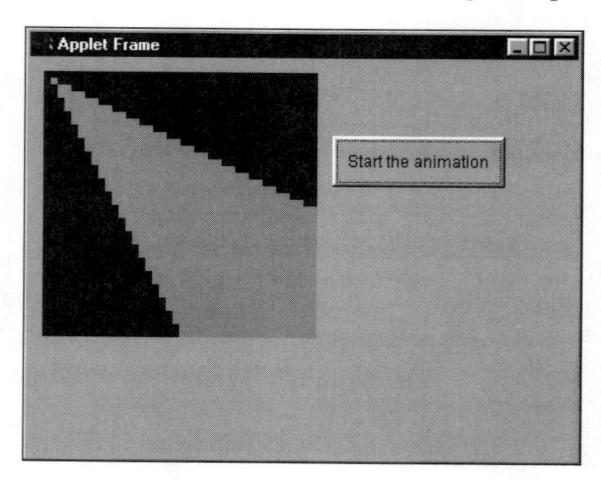

Figure 9.6 Our doublebuffer applet uses double buffering.

Making It Move—Graphics Animation

The code for this applet appears in Listing 9.4.

Listing 9.4 doublebuffer.java

```java
//Title:
//Version:
//Copyright:
//Author:
//Company:
//Description:
//

package doublebuffer;
import java.lang.*;
import java.awt.*;
import java.awt.event.*;
import java.applet.*;
import borland.jbcl.control.*;
import borland.jbcl.layout.*;

public
class doublebuffer extends Applet implements Runnable{

  public XYLayout xYLayout1 = new XYLayout();
  public boolean isStandalone = false;
  Image nowImage;
  Graphics nowGraphics;
  Thread doublebufferThread;
  Button button1 = new Button();
  int red, green, blue;

  //Construct the applet
  public doublebuffer() {

  }

  //Initialize the applet
  public void init() {

    try { jbInit(); } catch(Exception e) { e.printStackTrace(); };
```

Chapter 9

```java
  }

  //Component initialization
  public void jbInit() throws Exception{

    xYLayout1.setWidth(400);
    xYLayout1.setHeight(300);
    button1.setLabel("Start the animation");
    button1.addActionListener(new
doublebuffer_button1_ActionAdapter(this));
    this.setLayout(xYLayout1);
    this.add(button1, new XYConstraints(221, 57, 126, 38));

  }

  //Start the applet
  public void start() {

    doublebufferThread = new Thread(this);
    doublebufferThread.start();

  }

  //Stop the applet
  public void stop() {

    doublebufferThread.stop();
    doublebufferThread = null;

  }

  public void run() {

    while(true){

      repaint();
      try {Thread.sleep(200);}
      catch(InterruptedException e) {}
```

Making It Move—Graphics Animation

```
    }

}

//Destroy the applet
public void destroy() {

}

//Get Applet information
public String getAppletInfo() {

  return "Applet Information";

}

//Get parameter info
public String[][] getParameterInfo() {

  return null;

}

public void paint (Graphics g) {

  int loop_index;

  if(nowGraphics != null){
    for(loop_index = 40; loop_index > 0; loop_index−){

      if(red < 255) red++;
      if(red >= 255 && green < 255) green++;
      if(red >= 255 && green >= 255 && blue < 255) blue++;
      if(red >= 255 && green >= 255 & blue >= 255)
        red = blue = green = 0;

      nowGraphics.setColor(new Color(red, green, blue));
      nowGraphics.fillRect(5 * loop_index, 5 * loop_index, 5 *
         loop_index, 5 * loop_index);
```

```java
        }

        g.drawImage(nowImage, 10, 10, this);

      }

    }

    public void update(Graphics g){

      paint(g);

    }

    //Main method
    static public void main(String[] args) {
      doublebuffer applet = new doublebuffer();
      applet.isStandalone = true;
      DecoratedFrame frame = new DecoratedFrame();
      frame.setTitle("Applet Frame");
      frame.add(applet, BorderLayout.CENTER);
      applet.init();
      applet.start();
      frame.pack();
      Dimension d = Toolkit.getDefaultToolkit().getScreenSize();
      frame.setLocation((d.width - frame.getSize().width) / 2,
        (d.height - frame.getSize().height) / 2);
      frame.setVisible(true);

    }

    void button1_actionPerformed(java.awt.event.ActionEvent e) {

      nowImage = createImage(200, 200);
      nowGraphics = nowImage.getGraphics();
      repaint();

    }
```

```
}

class doublebuffer_button1_ActionAdapter implements

ActionListener{

    doublebuffer adaptee;

    doublebuffer_button1_ActionAdapter(doublebuffer adaptee) {

        this.adaptee = adaptee;

    }

    public void actionPerformed(java.awt.event.ActionEvent e) {

        adaptee.button1_actionPerformed(e);

    }

}
```

That's it for our chapter on animation. We've seen a lot in this chapter—from seeing how to create rudimentary animation by moving an Image control to seeing how true animation works by loading in images and displaying them, as well as eliminating screen flicker. There's a great deal of power here. In the next chapter, we're going to continue to explore multithreading issues, so let's turn to that now.

CHAPTER 10

JBuilder Advanced Topics

In this chapter, we're going to work on handling multithreading. For example, we'll see how to handle the case where we have several threads in a program, not just one.

After we start working with multiple threads in a program, however, that raises several new issues: How do we tell them apart? How do we stop them from trying to work with the same data at the same time? We'll see the answers to these and more questions in this chapter.

Using More Than One Thread

In our next example, we'll see how to set up two threads in a program. In this case, we'll have two text fields, and a button labeled *Start the threads*:

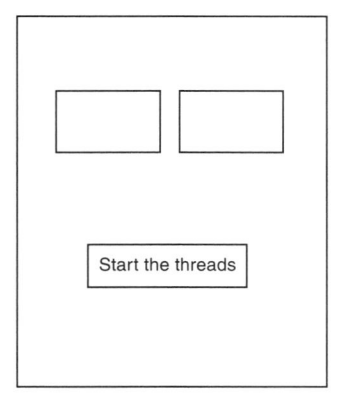

When the user clicks the **Start the threads** button, we'll start two new threads, each of which will display ascending integers from 1 to 1000 in its own text field:

Chapter 10

```
           ┌─────────────────────────┐
           │                         │
           │   ┌─────┐   ┌─────┐     │
           │   │ 897 │   │ 897 │     │
           │   └─────┘   └─────┘     │
           │                         │
           │     ┌───────────────┐   │
           │     │Start the threads│ │
           │     └───────────────┘   │
           │                         │
           └─────────────────────────┘
```

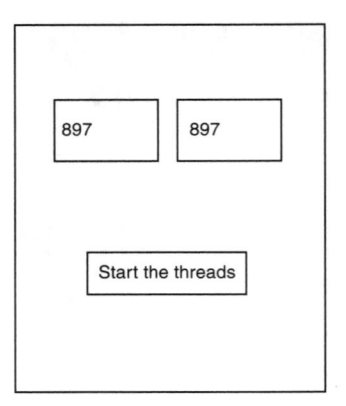

To make this application work, we'll have to be able to tell the two threads apart in the `run()` method so that they display integers in the correct text field. Let's see how this application works now.

Create a new application named integers and open it in the Designer, as shown in Figure 10.1. Next, add two text fields and a button with the label Start the threads, as also shown in Figure 10.1.

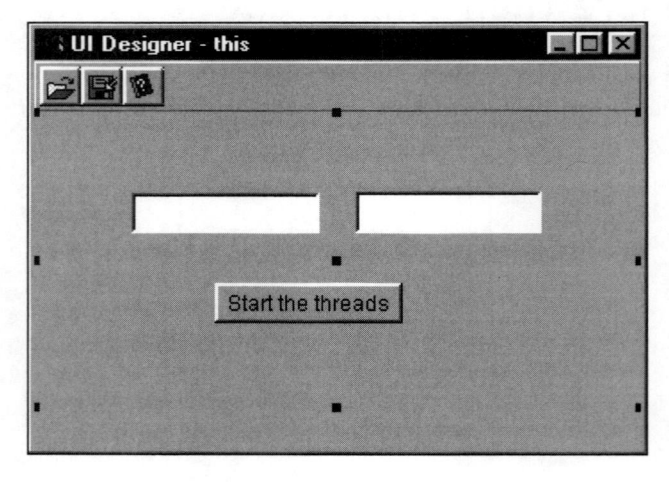

Figure 10.1 Designing the integers application.

Next, we add the two new threads, Thread1 and Thread2, to our application:

```
package integers;
import java.awt.*;
```

JBuilder Advanced Topics

```
import java.awt.event.*;
import java.lang.*;
import borland.jbcl.control.*;
import borland.jbcl.layout.*;

public
class Frame1 extends DecoratedFrame implements Runnable{

  public BorderLayout borderLayout1 = new BorderLayout();
  public Panel panel1 = new Panel();
  public MenuBar menuBar1 = new MenuBar();
  public Menu menuFile = new Menu();
  public MenuItem menuFileExit = new MenuItem();
  public Menu menuHelp = new Menu();
  public MenuItem menuHelpAbout = new MenuItem();
  public ButtonBar buttonBar = new ButtonBar();
  public Label statusBar = new Label();
  TextField textField1 = new TextField();
  TextField textField2 = new TextField();
  Button button1 = new Button();
  Thread Thread1, Thread2;              <--
       .
       .
       .
```

When the user clicks the **Start the threads** button, we'll start the threads. In this case, we will give a name to each thread: *"Thread1"* for Thread1 and *"Thread2"* for Thread2:

```
void button1_actionPerformed(java.awt.event.ActionEvent e) {

  Thread1 = new Thread(this, "Thread1");     <--
  Thread1.start();

  Thread2 = new Thread(this, "Thread2");     <--
  Thread2.start();

}
```

Chapter 10

Note that to be able to use threads, we have to add the **keywords** `implements Runnable` to our frame window class' `class` declaration:

```
public
class Frame1 extends DecoratedFrame implements Runnable{    <-

    public BorderLayout borderLayout1 = new BorderLayout();
    public Panel panel1 = new Panel();
    public MenuBar menuBar1 = new MenuBar();
    public Menu menuFile = new Menu();
    public MenuItem menuFileExit = new MenuItem();
         .
         .
         .
```

Now our two threads are running. They'll both execute code in the `run()` method, so add that method to the application now:

```
    public void run() {


    }
```

But there's only one `run()` method—how do we keep the two threads straight?

Keep Threads Separate

Each thread gets its own copy of the `run()` method, so how do we determine which text field we should place integers in the `run()` method? We'll do that by checking the thread's name. We get the current thread's name with the `getName()` method and store it in the string `ThreadName` this way:

```
    public void run() {

        String ThreadName = new String((Thread.currentThread()).getName());
             .
             .
             .
    }
```

Next, we set up a loop to display the first 1000 integers:

```
public void run() {

    int loop_index;                                      <-

    String ThreadName = new String((Thread.currentThread()).getName());

    for(loop_index = 1; loop_index <= 1000; loop_index++){   <-

    }                                                    <-


}
```

If this copy of the `run()` method is being executed by `Thread1`, we will place the `loop_index` in the first text field, `textField1`:

```
public void run() {

    String out_string;
    int loop_index;
    out_string = new String();

    String ThreadName = new String((Thread.currentThread()).getName());

    for(loop_index = 1; loop_index <= 1000; loop_index++){

        if(ThreadName.equals("Thread1")){                <-

            textField1.setText(out_string.valueOf(loop_index)); <-

        }                                                <-
        .
        .
```

Chapter 10

```
        }

    }
```

If the `run()` method is being executed by `Thread2`, on the other hand, we place the ascending integers into the second text field:

```
public void run() {

    String out_string;
    int loop_index;
    out_string = new String();

    String ThreadName = new String((Thread.currentThread()).getName());

    for(loop_index = 1; loop_index <= 1000; loop_index++){

      if(ThreadName.equals("Thread1")){

        textField1.setText(out_string.valueOf(loop_index));

      }

      if(ThreadName.equals("Thread2")){                          <--

        textField2.setText(out_string.valueOf(loop_index));  <--

      }                                                          <--

    }

}
```

Run the program now, as shown in Figure 10.2, and click the **Start the threads** button. As you can see in that figure, the integers are counting upward. We are using the threads now.

JBuilder Advanced Topics

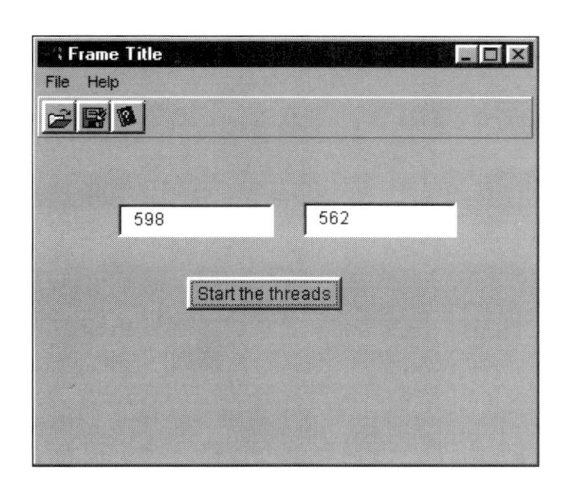

Figure 10.2 The integers application uses two threads.

The listing for this program appears in Listing 10.1, integers.java, and Listing 10.2, Frame1.java.

Listing 10.1 integers.java

```
//Title:
//Version:
//Copyright:
//Author:
//Company:
//Description:
//

package integers;
import java.lang.*;

public
class integers {

  // Construct the application
  public integers() {

    Frame1 frame = new Frame1();
```

Chapter 10

```java
        frame.setVisible(true);

    }

    //Main method
    static public void main(String[] args) {

        new integers();

    }

}
```

Listing 10.2 Frame1.java

```java
//Title:
//Version:
//Copyright:
//Author:
//Company:
//Description:
//

package integers;
import java.awt.*;
import java.awt.event.*;
import java.lang.*;
import borland.jbcl.control.*;
import borland.jbcl.layout.*;

public
class Frame1 extends DecoratedFrame implements Runnable{

    public BorderLayout borderLayout1 = new BorderLayout();
    public Panel panel1 = new Panel();
    public MenuBar menuBar1 = new MenuBar();
    public Menu menuFile = new Menu();
    public MenuItem menuFileExit = new MenuItem();
    public Menu menuHelp = new Menu();
```

```java
    public MenuItem menuHelpAbout = new MenuItem();
    public ButtonBar buttonBar = new ButtonBar();
    public Label statusBar = new Label();
    TextField textField1 = new TextField();
    TextField textField2 = new TextField();
    Button button1 = new Button();
    Thread Thread1, Thread2;
    XYLayout xYLayout1 = new XYLayout();

    //Construct the frame
    public Frame1() {

       try { jbInit(); } catch(Exception e) { e.printStackTrace(); };

    }

    //Component initialization
    public void jbInit() throws Exception{

       this.setLayout(borderLayout1);
       this.setTitle("Frame Title");

       //Add menu bar
       menuFile.setLabel("File");
       menuFileExit.setLabel("Exit");
       menuFileExit.addActionListener(new
Frame1_menuFileExit_ActionAdapter(this));
       menuFile.add(menuFileExit);
       menuHelp.setLabel("Help");
       menuHelpAbout.setLabel("About");
       menuHelpAbout.addActionListener(new
Frame1_menuHelpAbout_ActionAdapter(this));
       menuHelp.add(menuHelpAbout);
       menuBar1.add(menuFile);
       menuBar1.add(menuHelp);
       this.setMenuBar(menuBar1);
       panel1.setLayout(xYLayout1);

       //Add tool bar
```

Chapter 10

```
    buttonBar.setButtonType(ButtonBar.IMAGE_ONLY);
    buttonBar.setLabels(new String[] {"Open", "Close",
"Help"});
    buttonBar.setImageDirectory("borland/jbcl/control/images");
    buttonBar.setImageNames(new String[] {"openfile.gif",
"closefile.gif", "help.gif"});
    this.add(buttonBar, BorderLayout.NORTH);

    //Add status bar
    statusBar.setText("");
    button1.setLabel("Start the threads");
    button1.addActionListener(new
Frame1_button1_ActionAdapter(this));
    this.add(statusBar, BorderLayout.SOUTH);
    this.add(panel1, BorderLayout.CENTER);
    panel1.add(textField1, new XYConstraints(54, 46, 104, -1));
    panel1.add(textField2, new XYConstraints(178, 45, 103, 24));
    panel1.add(button1, new XYConstraints(100, 97, -1, -1));

    //Add center panel
    this.pack();

    //Center the window
    Dimension dimScreen =
Toolkit.getDefaultToolkit().getScreenSize();
    Dimension dimFrame = this.getPreferredSize();
    if(dimFrame.height > dimScreen.height) dimFrame.height =
dimScreen.height;
    if(dimFrame.width > dimScreen.width) dimFrame.width =
dimScreen.width;
    this.setBounds( (dimScreen.width - dimFrame.width) / 2,
(dimScreen.height - dimFrame.height) / 2, dimFrame.width,
dimFrame.height);
    resize(340, 300);

  }

  //File | Exit action performed
  public void fileExit_actionPerformed(ActionEvent e) {
```

```
    System.exit(0);

  }

  //Help | About action performed
  public void helpAbout_actionPerformed(ActionEvent e) {

  }

  public void run() {

    String out_string;
    int loop_index;
    out_string = new String();

    String ThreadName = new String((Thread.currentThread()).getName());

    for(loop_index = 1; loop_index <= 1000; loop_index++){

      if(ThreadName.equals("Thread1")){

        textField1.setText(out_string.valueOf(loop_index));

      }

      if(ThreadName.equals("Thread2")){

        textField2.setText(out_string.valueOf(loop_index));

      }

    }

  }

  void button1_actionPerformed(java.awt.event.ActionEvent e) {

    Thread1 = new Thread(this, "Thread1");
    Thread1.start();
```

```
      Thread2 = new Thread(this, "Thread2");
      Thread2.start();

   }

}

class Frame1_menuFileExit_ActionAdapter implements

ActionListener {

   Frame1 adaptee;

   Frame1_menuFileExit_ActionAdapter(Frame1 adaptee) {

      this.adaptee = adaptee;

   }

   public void actionPerformed(ActionEvent e) {

      adaptee.fileExit_actionPerformed(e);

   }

}

class Frame1_menuHelpAbout_ActionAdapter implements

ActionListener {

   Frame1 adaptee;

   Frame1_menuHelpAbout_ActionAdapter(Frame1 adaptee) {

      this.adaptee = adaptee;

   }

   public void actionPerformed(ActionEvent e) {

      adaptee.helpAbout_actionPerformed(e);
```

```
        }
    }
    class Frame1_button1_ActionAdapter implements ActionListener{
        Frame1 adaptee;

        Frame1_button1_ActionAdapter(Frame1 adaptee) {
            this.adaptee = adaptee;
        }

        public void actionPerformed(java.awt.event.ActionEvent e) {
            adaptee.button1_actionPerformed(e);
        }
    }
```

We have two threads working now, but as you can see in Figure 10.2, they don't necessarily work at the same rate—instead of the same integer in each of the text fields in that figure, we see the values 598 and 562. This points out an interesting facet of threads: their operation is controlled or *scheduled* by the operating system, which means that we can't count on knowing the order in which separate threads perform their actions. This is particularly problematic when both threads try to access the same data, as we'll see next.

Synchronizing Multithread Functions

Let's say that we want two different threads to work on the same data item—for example, we might have a new class named Data with an internal data member, `internal_data`:

```
    class Data{
        public int internal_data;     <—
```

Chapter 10

}

We can set that data member, `internal_data`, to 0 in the class' constructor:

```
class Data{

    public int internal_data;

    public void Data(){

        internal_data = 0;        <--

    }

}
```

Then we create an object, `dataObject`, of the Data class in an application:

```
public
class Frame1 extends DecoratedFrame implements Runnable{

    public BorderLayout borderLayout1 = new BorderLayout();
    public Panel panel1 = new Panel();
    public XYLayout xYLayout1 = new XYLayout();
    public MenuBar menuBar1 = new MenuBar();
    public Menu menuFile = new Menu();
    public MenuItem menuFileExit = new MenuItem();
    public Menu menuHelp = new Menu();
    public MenuItem menuHelpAbout = new MenuItem();
    public ButtonBar buttonBar = new ButtonBar();
    public Label statusBar = new Label();
    Thread Thread1, Thread2;
    Data dataObject;                <--
        .
        .
        .
```

JBuilder Advanced Topics

If we have two threads that access the internal data member, there could be problems. For example, we might have each thread increment the `internal_data` member of `dataObject` and print the result. Since this takes two separate steps—incrementing `internal_data` and printing it—there is the chance that the other thread could slip in between those two steps, increment the same variable, and print out its version of that variable. In this way, the two threads interfere with each other, and when they print out the values in `internal_data`, we'll get a mix of values rather than a smoothly ascending sequence:

```
data value = 122
data value = 121
data value = 124
data value = 123
data value = 125
data value = 127
data value = 126
data value = 129
data value = 128
data value = 130
data value = 131
data value = 134
data value = 133
data value = 132
data value = 135
data value = 137
data value = 136
data value = 138
data value = 139
```

Let's see how to coordinate the two threads now—this process is known as *synchronization*. To see this at work, create a new application named synchronized1 now. (The word *synchronized* is a keyword in JBuilder, so we can't call our application that.) Next, place two buttons in the Frame1 window—*Start the threads* and *Stop the threads*:

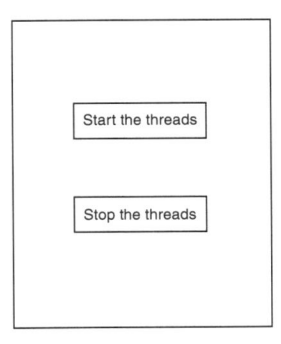

[Start the threads]

[Stop the threads]

Next, add the Data class to the end of the Frame1.java file:

Chapter 10

```
class Data{

  public int internal_data;

  public void Data(){

    internal_data = 0;

  }

}
```

This is the class that will hold our data member `internal_data`. Next, we create an object of that class, naming that object `dataObject`:

```
public
class Frame1 extends DecoratedFrame implements Runnable{

  public BorderLayout borderLayout1 = new BorderLayout();
  public Panel panel1 = new Panel();
  public XYLayout xYLayout1 = new XYLayout();
  public MenuBar menuBar1 = new MenuBar();
  public Menu menuFile = new Menu();
  public MenuItem menuFileExit = new MenuItem();
  public Menu menuHelp = new Menu();
  public MenuItem menuHelpAbout = new MenuItem();
  public ButtonBar buttonBar = new ButtonBar();
  public Label statusBar = new Label();
  Data dataObject;                    <--
     .
     .
     .
```

We'll use two threads in this example, so let's set them up now.

JBuilder Advanced Topics

Setting Up the Threads

We'll name our two threads `Thread1` and `Thread2`:

```
public
class Frame1 extends DecoratedFrame implements Runnable{

    public BorderLayout borderLayout1 = new BorderLayout();
    public Panel panel1 = new Panel();
    public XYLayout xYLayout1 = new XYLayout();
    public MenuBar menuBar1 = new MenuBar();
    public Menu menuFile = new Menu();
    public MenuItem menuFileExit = new MenuItem();
    public Menu menuHelp = new Menu();
    public MenuItem menuHelpAbout = new MenuItem();
    public ButtonBar buttonBar = new ButtonBar();
    public Label statusBar = new Label();
    Thread Thread1, Thread2;            <--
    Data dataObject;
          .
          .
          .
```

We can start the two threads in an `actionPerformed` event handler we add to the *Start the threads* button:

```
void button1_actionPerformed(java.awt.event.ActionEvent e) {

    Thread1 = new Thread(this);         <--
    Thread1.start();                    <--

    Thread2 = new Thread(this);         <--
    Thread2.start();                    <--

}
```

In addition, we implement the `Runnable interface` in the Frame1 class:

```
public
```

Chapter 10

```
class Frame1 extends DecoratedFrame implements Runnable{   <--

    public BorderLayout borderLayout1 = new BorderLayout();
    public Panel panel1 = new Panel();
    public XYLayout xYLayout1 = new XYLayout();
    public MenuBar menuBar1 = new MenuBar();
    public Menu menuFile = new Menu();
    public MenuItem menuFileExit = new MenuItem();
    public Menu menuHelp = new Menu();
          .
          .
          .
```

We stop the threads in an event handler attached to the *Stop the threads* button:

```
void button2_actionPerformed(java.awt.event.ActionEvent e) {

    Thread1.stop();
    Thread2.stop();

}
```

Now we're ready to write the `run()` method.

The Synchronized1 Application's run( ) Method

The `run()` method will be executed by both threads, and we'll have to make sure that only one thread has access to the `internal_data` member of `dataObject` in that method. Add that method now to Frame1.java:

```
public void run() {

}
```

We'll increment the `dataObject`'s `internal_data` member 500 times, so we set up a loop for that purpose:

```
public void run() {
```

JBuilder Advanced Topics

```
        int loop_index;                                          <--


        for(loop_index = 1; loop_index < 500; loop_index++){     <--



        }                                                        <--



}
```

Next, we increment `dataObject.internal_data`:

```
    public void run() {

        int loop_index;


        for(loop_index = 1; loop_index < 500; loop_index++){


            dataObject.internal_data++;        <--


        }


    }
```

After incrementing `dataObject.internal_data`, we will display its new value. We can do that with the `System.out.println()` method. This method can print out a string in the DOS window that appears with the synchronized1 application; to send output to the DOS window, select the **Project Properties** item in the File menu, select, the **Run/Debug** tab in the Properties box that opens, then click the box marked **Send run output to Console Window** and click **OK** to close the Properties window. We'll hope to see an ascending sequence of values there as our two threads increment the `internal_data` member in a coordinated fashion.

Chapter 10

```
data value = 121
data value = 122
data value = 123
data value = 124
data value = 125
data value = 126
data value = 127
data value = 128
data value = 129
data value = 130
data value = 131
data value = 132
data value = 133
data value = 134
data value = 135
data value = 136
data value = 137
data value = 138
data value = 139
```

Now that we've incremented the `internal_data` member in the `run()` method, we want to display that value with `System.out.println()`. We first set up a new String object named `out_string`:

```
public void run() {

    String out_string;                           <-
    int loop_index;
    out_string = new String();                   <-

    for(loop_index = 1; loop_index < 500; loop_index++){

        dataObject.internal_data++;

    }

}
```

Finally, we display the new value in `internal_data`:

```
public void run() {

    String out_string;
    int loop_index;
    out_string = new String();
```

```
        for(loop_index = 1; loop_index < 500; loop_index++){

            dataObject.internal_data++;
            System.out.println("data value = " +
    out_string.valueOf(dataObject.internal_data));    <—

        }

    }
```

That's fine as far as it goes—but what if Thread1 is suspended after it has incremented `internal_data` and is in the process of displaying the new value? When Thread1 is suspended, Thread2 takes over, and Thread2 will increment `internal_data` again and print out the newer value. Then Thread1 takes over again, completing the printing out process—but it prints out the value it had incremented `internal_data` to before Thread2 took over—and that value is out of date. In this way, we get a sequence like *581, 583, 582, 585, 584* and so on.

We can fix this problem, giving access to the `internal_data` member to only one thread at a time. Let's see how to do this now.

Synchronizing Data Access

To synchronize access to the `dataObject` object, we only need to enclose the sensitive code in a synchronized block, indicating which data item is the sensitive one (`dataObject`) this way:

```
        public void run() {

            String out_string;
            int loop_index;
            out_string = new String();

            synchronized(dataObject){          <—

                for(loop_index = 1; loop_index < 500; loop_index++){

                    dataObject.internal_data++;
                    System.out.println("data value = " +
            out_string.valueOf(dataObject.internal_data));
```

Chapter 10

```
            }                       <--
        }
    }
```

Now only one thread can be in the synchronized code block at a time, not both. This makes the operation of incrementing `internal_data` and displaying it one operation. When the new program runs, the two threads no longer interfere with each other. After clicking the **Start the threads** button, we get the result shown in Figure 10.3 in the DOS window—now we've coordinated the actions of two threads. Our program is a success.

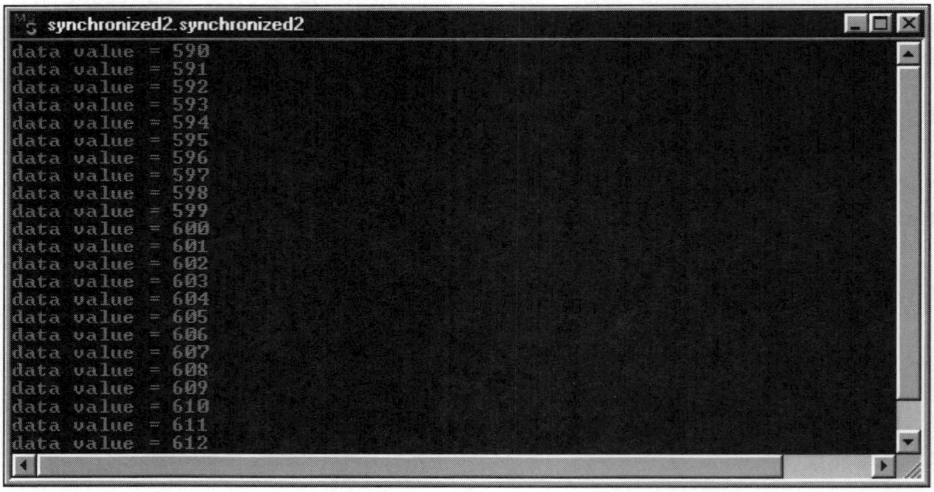

Figure 10.3 We synchronize two threads.

The code for this application appears in Listing 10.3, synchronized1.java, and Listing 10.4, Frame1.java.

Listing 10.3 synchronized1.java

```
//Title:
//Version:
//Copyright:
//Author:
//Company:
```

```
//Description:
//

package synchronized1;
import java.lang.*;

public
class synchronized1 {

  //Construct the application
  public synchronized1() {
    Frame1 frame = new Frame1();
    frame.setVisible(true);

  }

  //Main method
  static public void main(String[] args) {

    new synchronized1();

  }

}
```

Listing 10.4 Frame1.java

```
//Title:
//Version:
//Copyright:
//Author:
//Company:
//Description:
//

package synchronized1;
import java.awt.*;
import java.awt.event.*;
import java.lang.*;
```

Chapter 10

```java
import borland.jbcl.control.*;
import borland.jbcl.layout.*;

public
class Frame1 extends DecoratedFrame implements Runnable{

  public BorderLayout borderLayout1 = new BorderLayout();
  public Panel panel1 = new Panel();
  public XYLayout xYLayout1 = new XYLayout();
  public MenuBar menuBar1 = new MenuBar();
  public Menu menuFile = new Menu();
  public MenuItem menuFileExit = new MenuItem();
  public Menu menuHelp = new Menu();
  public MenuItem menuHelpAbout = new MenuItem();
  public ButtonBar buttonBar = new ButtonBar();
  public Label statusBar = new Label();
  Thread Thread1, Thread2;
  Data dataObject;

  Button button1 = new Button();
  Button button2 = new Button();

  //Construct the frame
  public Frame1() {

    dataObject = new Data();
    try { jbInit(); } catch(Exception e) { e.printStackTrace(); };

  }

  //Component initialization
  public void jbInit() throws Exception{

    this.setLayout(borderLayout1);
    this.setTitle("Frame Title");
    //Add menu bar
    menuFile.setLabel("File");
    menuFileExit.setLabel("Exit");
    menuFileExit.addActionListener(new
```

JBuilder Advanced Topics

```
Frame1_menuFileExit_ActionAdapter(this));
    menuFile.add(menuFileExit);
    menuHelp.setLabel("Help");
    menuHelpAbout.setLabel("About");
    menuHelpAbout.addActionListener(new
Frame1_menuHelpAbout_ActionAdapter(this));
    menuHelp.add(menuHelpAbout);
    menuBar1.add(menuFile);
    menuBar1.add(menuHelp);
    this.setMenuBar(menuBar1);

    //Add tool bar
    buttonBar.setButtonType(ButtonBar.IMAGE_ONLY);
    buttonBar.setLabels(new String[] {"Open", "Close",
"Help"});
    buttonBar.setImageDirectory("borland/jbcl/control/images");
    buttonBar.setImageNames(new String[] {"openfile.gif",
"closefile.gif", "help.gif"});
    this.add(buttonBar, BorderLayout.NORTH);

    //Add status bar
    statusBar.setText("");
    button1.setLabel("button1");
    button1.addActionListener(new
Frame1_button1_ActionAdapter(this));
    button2.setLabel("button2");
    button2.addActionListener(new
Frame1_button2_ActionAdapter(this));
    this.add(statusBar, BorderLayout.SOUTH);

    //Add center panel
    panel1.setLayout(xYLayout1);
    xYLayout1.setWidth(400);
    xYLayout1.setHeight(300);
    this.add(panel1, BorderLayout.CENTER);
    panel1.add(button1, new XYConstraints(68, 82, 129, 55));
    panel1.add(button2, new XYConstraints(70, 168, 135, 59));
    this.pack();
```

Chapter 10

```
    //Center the window
    Dimension dimScreen =
Toolkit.getDefaultToolkit().getScreenSize();
    Dimension dimFrame = this.getPreferredSize();
    if(dimFrame.height > dimScreen.height) dimFrame.height =
dimScreen.height;
    if(dimFrame.width > dimScreen.width) dimFrame.width =
dimScreen.width;
    this.setBounds( (dimScreen.width - dimFrame.width) / 2,
(dimScreen.height - dimFrame.height) / 2, dimFrame.width,
dimFrame.height);

  }

  //File | Exit action performed
  public void fileExit_actionPerformed(ActionEvent e) {

    System.exit(0);

  }

  //Help | About action performed
  public void helpAbout_actionPerformed(ActionEvent e) {

  }

  void button1_actionPerformed(java.awt.event.ActionEvent e) {

    Thread1 = new Thread(this);
    Thread1.start();

    Thread2 = new Thread(this);
    Thread2.start();

  }

  void button2_actionPerformed(java.awt.event.ActionEvent e) {

    Thread1.stop();
```

```
    Thread2.stop();

  }

  public void run() {

    String out_string;
    int loop_index;
    out_string = new String();

    synchronized(dataObject){

      for(loop_index = 1; loop_index < 500; loop_index++){

        dataObject.internal_data++;
        System.out.println("data value = " +
out_string.valueOf(dataObject.internal_data));

      }

    }

  }

}

class Frame1_menuFileExit_ActionAdapter implements

ActionListener {

  Frame1 adaptee;

  Frame1_menuFileExit_ActionAdapter(Frame1 adaptee) {

    this.adaptee = adaptee;

  }

  public void actionPerformed(ActionEvent e) {

    adaptee.fileExit_actionPerformed(e);
```

Chapter 10

```java
    }
  }
  class Frame1_menuHelpAbout_ActionAdapter implements
  ActionListener {
    Frame1 adaptee;
    Frame1_menuHelpAbout_ActionAdapter(Frame1 adaptee) {
      this.adaptee = adaptee;
    }
    public void actionPerformed(ActionEvent e) {
      adaptee.helpAbout_actionPerformed(e);
    }
  }
  class Frame1_button1_ActionAdapter implements ActionListener {
    Frame1 adaptee;
    Frame1_button1_ActionAdapter(Frame1 adaptee) {
      this.adaptee = adaptee;
    }
    public void actionPerformed(java.awt.event.ActionEvent e) {
      adaptee.button1_actionPerformed(e);
    }
  }
  class Frame1_button2_ActionAdapter implements ActionListener {
```

```
    Frame1 adaptee;

    Frame1_button2_ActionAdapter(Frame1 adaptee) {

        this.adaptee = adaptee;

    }

    public void actionPerformed(java.awt.event.ActionEvent e) {

        adaptee.button2_actionPerformed(e);

    }

}

class Data{

    public int internal_data;

    public void Data(){

        internal_data = 0;

    }

}
```

That's it for our synchronized thread example, and that's it for our book. In this book, we've learned a great number of new JBuilder skills: from building applications and applets with JBuilder to using buttons, lists, scroll bars, text fields, Image controls, and other controls. We've also learned how to use tools like the JBuilder Designer, Inspector, and Menu Designer, and how to create windows, menus, and dialog boxes with those tools. We've also seen how to support animation, image-handling, fonts, and other graphics in this book. Now all that remains is to put all this programming power to work for yourself—happy programming!

INDEX

<!> comment tag, 4, 5
3D rectangles, drawing, 376, 377

A

<A> anchor tag, 18-20
Abstract Windowing Toolkit. *See* AWT
action listeners, 95, 96
add(Menu), MenuBar, 250
add(MenuItem), Menu Class, 251
add(String)
  Choice, 197
  List, 189
  Menu Class, 251
add(String, int), List, 189
addActionListener(ActionListener)
  Button, 92
  List, 189
  TextField, 72
addActionListener() method, calling, 94
addAdjustmentListener(AdjustmentListener), ScrollBar, 219
addItem(String)
  Choice, 197
  List, 189
addItem(String, int), List, 189
addItemListener(ItemListener)
  Checkbox, 136
  Choice, 197
  List, 189
addNotify()
  Button, 92
  Checkbox, 136
  Choice, 197
  Java window, 234
  List, 189
  Menu Class, 251
  MenuBar, 250
  PopupMenu, 205
  ScrollBar, 219
  TextArea, 80
  TextField, 72

addSeparator(), Menu Class, 251
aligning, images and text, 20-22
allowsMultipleSelections(), List, 189
animation, 395. *See also* graphics animation
  drawing image, 405
  moving image control, 405
  overriding paint method(), 405
  graphics animation, 409
    animating color wheel, 410
    animating images, 412, 413
    animator applet, creating, 410, 411
    animator.java listing, 415-418
    avoiding clearing whole applet, 419
    buffered image, drawing, 428-430
    color wheel displaying, 409, 410
    declaring thread to handle animation, 411
    double-buffering, 424-431
    doublebuffer.java listing, 431-435
    drawing images, 414
    loading images, 411
    no flicker version of animator.java, 420-424
    screen flicker, reducing, 419, 420
    storing images, 410
    wheelThread, 411, 412
  Image controls, using for, 396
    moving image across screen, 396
    moving image control, 396
    placing image into, 396
  multithreaded applet, 396, 397
    creating object of class Thread, 398

    Runnable interface, implementing, 397, 398
  sailor.java listing, 406-407
  Thread Class's constructors and methods, 399, 400
  thread, starting, 400
    creating with Java new operator, 400, 401
    setting thread object priority, 401
    starting thread with start() method, 401
  thread, stopping, 401, 402
  thread's code, running, 402
    calling repaint method, 404
    executing new thread code, 403
    moving image control, 402, 403
    overriding Runnable interface's run() method, 403
    pausing thread, 404, 405
Anchor point, 356, 357
append(String), TextArea, 80
appendText(String), TextArea, 80
applet wizard. *See* applet
applets
  <APPLET>, 39
  check box, adding to, 135
  creating
    opening JBuilder, 42, 43
  descriptive string, returning to browser, 63-65
  destroying, 62, 63
  embedding in Web page, 39, 40
  init() method, initializing data using, 58-60
  loading in Web page, 40, 41
  main() method, 65, 66
  multithreaded applet, 396, 397
  paint() method, 66-68
  parameter, obtaining information about, 63-65
  purpose, 39

Index

starting, 61, 62
stopping, 61, 62
testing, 48, 49
wizard, writing with, 43
  class, naming in applet wizard, 45
  Java Codes, 43, 44
  package, naming in applet wizard, 45
  project files, creating, 45-47
ASCII text, .html files and, 3
AWT (Abstract Windowing Toolkit), 48

B

<B> bold tag, 18
background color, specifying, 9
base class, interface similarity with, 96
<BASE> tag, 5
bevel panels, using, 110
  action listener, setting up for buttons, 115
  adding buttons to panel layout, 115, 116
  adding to applet, 114
  arranging buttons in bevel panel, 114
  at work, 118
  buttons, adding to, 111
  color, changing, 112, 113
  fPanel.java listing, 119-123
  indicating button clicked, 117
  layout, selecting new, 113
  method for buttons on main applet class, 116
  reporting button clicked, 112
  textfield, adding to, 111
<BODY> tag, 7, 8
border layout, scroll bars
  setting up, 217
  using, 216

 break tag, 14, 15 adding interface to class, 96
buffered image, graphics animation, 428
  drawing image in applet, 429, 430
  graphics image, drawing in nowImage object, 429
bulleted lists, 30
Button(), Button, 92
button(s) and text fields, 87.
  See also radio buttons

action listeners, 95, 96
addActionListener() method, calling, 94
adding to applet, 87-89
bevel panels, using, 110
  action listener, setting up for buttons, 115
  adding buttons to panel layout, 115, 116
  adding to applet, 114
  arranging buttons in bevel panel, 114
  at work, 118
  buttons, adding to, 111
  color, changing, 112, 113
  fPanel.java listing, 119-123
  indicating button clicked, 117
  layout, selecting new, 113
  method for buttons on main applet class, 116
  reporting button clicked, 112
  textfield, adding to, 111
button bars, 123
  bBar.java, 128-132
  creating buttons in, 125
  handling button bar buttons in code, 125-128
  placing buttons in, 123, 124
  reporting button clicked, 124
button.java listing, 100-103
constructors, 92, 93
control
  adding to applet, 94
  events, handling, 90, 91
  properties, setting, 89, 90
  using in code, 92
Java interfaces, 96
  actionPerformed() method, 98, 99
  adding interface to class, 96
  button click method, sending to main applet class, 99
  class constructor derived, 97
  message, displaying, 99, 100
  reference, saving to main applet object, 97, 98
  this keyword, 97
jbcl buttons, using, 104
  adding, 105

ButtonControl, adding to programs, 104, 105
ButtonControl constructors, 105, 106
ButtonControl methods, 105, 106
  image, adding to, 106, 107
  jbButtons.java listing, 107-110
  jbInit(), button installed in, 93
  label, setting, 93, 94
  methods, 92, 93
  summary, 103, 104
  text field, adding, 91
button bars, 123
  bBar.java listing, 128-132
  creating buttons in, 125
  handling button bar buttons in code, 125-128
  placing buttons in, 123, 124
  reporting button clicked, 124
button.java listing, 100-103
Button(String), Button, 92
bytecode, 40.bmp file format, IE and, 10
bytesWidth(byte[ ], int, int), FontMetrics, 330
ButtonControl(), ButtonControl, 105
ButtonControl(Image image), ButtonControl, 105
ButtonControl(String path), ButtonControl, 105
ButtonControl(URL url), ButtonControl, 105

C

C++, Java similarities with, 41
CELLPADDING, 25
<CENTER> tag, 12-14
charWidth(char), FontMetrics 330
charWidth(int), FontMetrics 330
check box groups, radio buttons
  adding check boxes to group, 146
  creating, 145
  event handler, connecting to radio button, 146, 147
  radios applet, designing, 145
  reporting item clicked, 147, 148

Index

handling
  displaying in group, 144
  reporting button clicked, 144
  radios.java listing, 149-154
  Retailer2, creating in Application Wizard, 166
    menu, toolbar, and status bar, setting up, 167-170
    retailer2.java, running on application start, 167
  Retailer2, customizing, 170
    checking checkboxes, 171
    customizing user selections, 174, 175
    examining all checkboxes, 171, 172
    price, placing in text field, 172
    setting price to match checks, 170
    totaling price, 172, 173
  Retailer2 listings
    Frame1.java, 175-184
    Retailer2.java, 184, 185
Checkbox(), Checkbox, 136
Checkbox(String), Checkbox, 136
Checkbox(String, boolean), Checkbox, 136
Checkbox(String, boolean, CheckboxGroup), Checkbox, 136
Checkbox(String, CheckboxGroup, boolean), Checkbox, 136
checkboxes, 133
  adding to applet, 135
  checks.java. listings, 139-143
  connecting to code, 136
    displaying message to indicate box checked, 137, 138
  constructors, 136
  methods, 136
  radio buttons, putting together with check boxes, 154-156
    buttons creating new, 156, 157
    check box group for radio buttons, adding, 156
    event handler, adding to radio button, 157
    placing information in text field, 158
    retailer.java listing, 160-166

    settings check to record information, 157
  using
    displaying in applet, 134
    indicating box checked, 134
    textfield, adding, 134
Choice(), Choice, 197
choice controls, 187
  choices.java listing, 200-203
  constructors, 197, 198
  filling with items, 198
  displaying text field, 196
  displaying user selection, 196, 197
  methods, 197, 198
  presenting options on clicking button, 196
  user's selection, obtaining, 198
  user's selection, placing in text field, 199
circle, drawing, 372. *See also* mouse-driven paint program
  checking shape to be drawn, 373
  setting Anchor and Draw To points, 372, 373
class, Java, 54
  extending, 56
  purpose of, 55, 56
clear(), List, 189
closing tags, 6, 7
colors, setting for pages and text
  background color, specifying, 9
  browser predefined colors, 8
  color values, defining, 8
columns, adding to tables, 26
constructor, 58
container, 118
controls, 39
  adding to applet, 94
  events, handling, 90, 91
  properties, setting, 89, 90
  using in code, 92
countItems()
  Choice, 197
  List, 189
  Menu Class, 251
countMenus(), MenuBar, 250
createScaledImage(int, int, int), Image Class, 289

D

data member, class, 56
decode(String), Font Class, 315
deleteShortcut(MenuShortcut), MenuBar, 250
delItem(int), List, 189
delItems(int, int), List, 189
deselect(int), List, 189
dialog boxes, 231
  caller variable, setting up, 276
  closing on user click, 275
  data, sending form dialog box to applet, 277
    code, adding to Cancel button, 278
    hiding dialog box, 277, 277
    passing typed text to applet object, 277
  dialogs.java listing, 279-283
  displaying new dialog box on screen, 277
  frame window object, communicating with applet object, 275
  Frame1 class, creating new object of, 276
  Frame1.java listing, 283-285
  placing on screen, 274
  reference to applet object, saving, 275
directory lists, 30
dispose(), Java window, 234
double-buffering, graphics animation, 424
  buffered image, graphics animation, 428
    drawing image in applet, 429, 430
    graphics image, drawing in nowImage object, 429
  calling paint() method every two seconds, 426
  creating button in start() method, 426
  creating Image object, 427
  declaring new thread to support animation, 425, 426
  doublebuffer.java listing, 431-435
  drawing and displaying new image, 426, 427
  Graphics object, obtaining for Image object, 427
  painting process, beginning, 427, 428

Index

starting animation, 425
stopping thread, 426
tracking color use, 428
Draw To point, 357
drawing. *See also* mouse-driven paint program
  Anchor point, 356, 357
  circle, drawing, 372
    checking shape to be drawn, 373
    setting Anchor and Draw To points, 372, 373
  Draw To point, 357
  freehand object drawing, 359, 360, 379, 382
    drawing line between stored points, 381, 382
    incrementing location, 380, 381
    mouse location recording, 380
    setting aside space for, 380
  lines, drawing, 367
    drawing line, 367, 368
    indicating mouse is up, 367
    making sure mouse is up, 368
    overriding paint method, 368
    recording mouse up location, 367
  oval, drawing, 372
    checking shape to be drawn, 373
    setting Anchor and Draw To points, 372, 373
  rectangle, drawing, 358, 359
    3D rectangles, drawing, 376, 377
    checking shape to be drawn, 374, 375
    rounded rectangle, 377-379

E

echoCharIsSet(), TextField, 72
email, enabling, 31, 32
equals(Object), Font Class, 315
event, 89

F

FACE, 23
file transfer protocol. *See* ftp
flush(), image Class, 289
font
  size in web page, 23, 24
  typeface, setting, 24
Font(String, int, int), Font Class, 315
<FONT> tag, 22
FontMetrics(Font), FontMetrics, 330
four scroll bars, adding to applet, 215
  adding to applet, 216
frame windows, 231, 239
  controls, adding to window, 235
    button, adding to, 236
    code to hide window, placing, 236
  designing frame window, 235
  frame1.java, listing, 244, 245
  new frame, displaying on clicking, 232
  new frame window, 233
    constructor for, 234, 235
    DecoratedFrame class, extending, 234
    Java window class's constructors and methods, 234
    Object Gallery, opening, 233
  two-button applet, displaying, 232
  window methods, overriding, 236
    placing string in window on painting, 237
  windows, displaying and hiding, 237
    event handlers, connecting to buttons, 238
    hiding window, 238
    placing window on screen, 238
    showing window, 238
    using frame window, 237
  windows.java listing, 240-243
freehand object drawing, 359, 360, 379, 382. *See also* mouse-driven paint program
  drawing line between stored points, 381, 382
  incrementing location, 380, 381
  mouse location recording, 380
  setting aside space for, 380
ftp (file transfer protocol), 3
full menus, 259. *See also* menu system
  check menu items, adding, 262
  checkmark, placing with user selection, 260
  frame1.java, 266-273
  fullmenus.java, 266
  grayed menu items, adding, 262
  items displaying checkmark, creating, 259, 260
  Menu Designer, opening, 261
  menu separators, adding, 262
  submenu items, adding
    alerting users of changes state of check item, 264
    changes to check menu items, determining, 264
    event handler, connecting to submenu items, 263
    opening, 260
    placing message in text field on user clicking, 263, 264
    reporting item selected in, 261
    running programs, 264, 265
function overloading, 73, 74

G

getActionCommand(), Button, 92
getAscent(), FontMetrics 330
getBlockIncrement(), ScrollBar, 219
getCheckboxGroup(), Checkbox, 136
getColumns()
  TextArea, 80
  TextField, 72
getDescent(), FontMetrics, 330
getEchoChar(),TextField, 72
getFamily(), Font Class, 315
getFocusOwner(), Java window, 234
getFont(), FontMetrics, 330
getFont(String), Font Class, 315
getFont(String, Font), Font Class, 315
getGraphics(), Image Class, 289
getHeight(), FontMetrics, 330
getHeight(ImageObserver), Image Class, 289
getHelpMenu(), MenuBar, 251
getImage(), ButtonControl, 105

Index

getImageFirst(), ButtonControl, 105
getItem(int)
  Choice, 197
  List, 189
  Menu Class, 251
getItemCount()
  Choice, 197
  List, 189
  Menu Class, 251
getItems(), List, 189
getLabel()
  Button, 93
  ButtonControl, 105
  Checkbox, 136
getLeading(), FontMetrics, 330
getLineIncrement(), ScrollBar, 219
getLocale(), Java window, 234
getMaxAscent(), FontMetrics, 330
getMaxDescent(), FontMetrics, 330
getMaximum(), ScrollBar, 219
getMenu(int), MenuBar, 251
getMenuCount(), MenuBar, 251
getMinimum(), ScrollBar, 219
getMinimumSize()
  List, 189
  TextArea, 80
  TextField, 73
getMinimumSize(int)
  List, 189
  TextField, 73
getMinimumSize(int, int),TextArea, 80
getName(), Font Class, 315
getOrientation()
  ButtonControl, 106
  ScrollBar, 219
getPageIncrement(), ScrollBar, 219
getPeer(), Font Class, 315
getPreferredSize()
  List, 189
  TextArea, 81
  TextField, 73
getPreferredSize(int)
  List, 189
  TextField, 73
getProperty(String, ImageObserver), Image Class, 289
getRows()
  List, 189
  TextArea, 81

getScrollbarVisibility(),TextArea, 81
getSelectedIndex()
  Choice, 197
  List, 189
getSelectedIndexes(), List, 190
getSelectedItem()
  Choice, 197
  List, 190
getSelectedItems(), List, 190
getSelectedObjects()
  Checkbox, 136
  Choice, 197
  List, 190
getShortcutMenuItem(MenuShortcut), MenuBar, 251
getSize(), Font Class, 315
getSource(), Image Class, 289
getState(), Checkbox, 136
getStyle(), Font Class, 315
getToolKit(), Java window, 234
getUnitIncrement(), ScrollBar, 219
getValue(), ScrollBar, 219
getVisible(), ScrollBar, 219
getVisibleAmount(), ScrollBar, 219
getVisibleIndex(), List, 190
getWarningString(), Java window, 234
getWidth(ImageObserver), Image Class, 289
getWidths(), FontMetrics, 330
global data members, 56
graphics. *See also* animation; drawing; graphics animation; Image class; mouse-driven paint program
  file formats
    .gif, 10
    .jpg (.jpeg), 10
  inserting in Web page, 10
  storing, 11, 12
graphics animation, 409
  animating color wheel, 410
  animating images, 412
    drawing new image, 413
    loading images, 412, 413
    sleep, invoking in thread, 413
  animator applet, creating, 410, 411
  animator.java listing, 415-418
  buffered image, drawing, 428
    drawing image in applet, 429, 430

    graphics image, drawing in nowImage object, 429
  color wheel displaying, 409, 410
  declaring thread to handle animation, 411
  double-buffering, 424
    calling paint() method every two seconds, 426
    creating button in start() method, 426
    creating Image object, 427
    declaring new thread to support animation, 425, 426
    doublebuffer.java listing, 431-435
    drawing and displaying new image, 426, 427
    Graphics object, obtaining for Image object, 427
    painting process, beginning, 427, 428
    starting animation, 425
    stopping thread, 426
    tracking color use, 428
  drawing images, 414
    drawing nowImage object, 414
    overriding paint() method, 414
  loading images, 411
  screen flicker, reducing, 419
    avoiding clearing whole applet, 419
    no flicker version of animator.java, 420-424
    paint() method, calling directly, 419, 420
  storing images, 410
  wheelThread
    starting, 411, 412
    stopping, 412
Graphics constructors and methods, 369-371

H

hashCode(), Font Class, 315
<HEAD> tag, 5, 6
hello.html listing, 52
hello.java listing, 49-52
  defining applet class, 53
  jbcl package, 53
horizontal scroll bars, creating, 216, 217

Index

HTML (Hypertext Markup Language), 1
  tags, 4
    <!> comment, 4, 5
    <A> anchor, 18-20
    <B>, 18
    <BASE>, 5
    <BODY>, 7, 8

 break, 14, 15
    <CENTER>, 12-14
    closing tags, 6, 7
    <FONT>, 22
    <HEAD>, 5, 6
    <HTML>, 4
    <I>, 4
    <IMG> image, 15-17
    <LI> list, 30
    <P> paragraph, 17, 18
    <RANGE>, 5
    <TABLE>, 25
    <TH> table header, 25
    <TITLE>, 6, 7
    <TR> row, 25
    <UL> bullet list, 30
.html file, 3
<HTML> tag, 4. *See also* HTML Hypertext Markup Language. *See* HTML

I

<I> italic tag, 4
IE (Internet Explorer), .bmp file format and, 10
Image(), Image Class, 289
Image class. *See also* graphics
  CODEBASE Web page parameter, 289, 290
  creating Image object in imager applet, 288, 289
  drawing image
    in object named image, 291
    overriding paint() method, 291
  Image class's constructors and methods, 289
  Image control, using, 299
    image.gif file, copying to source code folder, 300
    imagecontrol applet, creating, 300
    imagecontrol.java listing, 301-303
  Image controls, using in animation, 396

moving image across screen, 396
moving image control, 396
  placing image into, 396
image.gif, loading into image object, 289
imager.java listing, 292-294
reading image from disk, 288
scaling images, 295
  drawing image at different locations, 296
  reading image, 295, 296
  scaler applet, creating, 295
  scaler.java listing, 297-299
storing image, 290, 291
images. *See also* Image class
  aligning, 20-22
  animating, 412
    drawing new image, 413
    loading images, 412, 413
    sleep, invoking in thread, 413
  inserting into Web page
    <IMG> image, 15-17
    setting text next to, 22, 23
  <IMG> image tag, 15-17
inheritance, 56
insert(MenuItem, int), Menu Class, 251
insert(String), int), Choice, 197
insert(String, int), Menu Class, 251
insert(String, int), TextArea, 81
insertSeparator(int), Menu Class, 251
insertText(String, int), TextArea, 81
insertion point, 68
interfaces, Java, 96
Internet Service Provider. *See* ISP
isBold(), Font Class, 315
isIndexSelected(int), List, 190
isItalic(), Font Class, 315
isMultipleMode(), List, 190
ISP (Internet Service Provider), 3
isPlain(), Font Class, 315
isSelected(), List, 190
isStandalone, 56, 57
isTearOff(), Menu Class, 251

J

Java, 39
  applet

descriptive string, returning to browser, 63-65
destroying, 62, 63
init() method, initializing data using, 58-60
main() method, 65, 66
paint() method, 66-68
parameter, obtaining information about, 63-65
starting, 61, 62
stopping, 61, 62
testing, 48, 49
C++, similarities with, 41
class, 54
  extending, 56
  purpose of, 55, 56
  constructor, 58
controls, 39
inheritance, 56
interfaces, buttons and text fields, 96
  actionPerformed() method, 98, 99
  adding interface to class, 96
  button click method, sending to main applet class, 99
  class constructor derived, 97
  message, displaying, 99, 100
  reference, saving to main applet object, 97, 98
  this keyword, 97
object, 54
program types
  applets, 39
  applications, 39
text, displaying in, 47, 48
text areas, handling, 78, 89
  placing control in applet, 81
  placing text in text area, 82
  text areas applet, creating, 79, 80
  TextArea constructors, 80, 81
  TextArea methods, 80, 81
  textareas.java, 83-85
text fields, using, 68, 69
textfields Applet, creating, 70
  constructors, 72, 73
  controls, adding to applet, 71, 72
  function overloading, 73, 74
  initializing text in, 75, 76

Index

JBuilder designer, using, 70, 71
  methods, 72, 73
  placing textfield in applet, 74, 75
  textfields.java listing, 76-78
jbcl buttons, using, 104
  adding, 105
  ButtonControl, adding to programs, 104, 105
  ButtonControl constructors, 105, 106
  ButtonControl methods, 105, 106
  image, adding to, 106, 107
  jbButtons.java listing, 107-110
jbInit(), button installed in, 93
JBuilder
  designer, using, 70, 71
  opening, 42

L

label, setting button, 93, 94
<LI> list tag, 30
lines, drawing, 367. *See also* mouse-driven paint program
  drawing line, 367, 368
  indicating mouse is up, 367
  making sure mouse is up, 368
  overriding paint method, 368
  recording mouse up location, 367
List(), List, 189
list boxes, 187
  list controls, filling, 191
  constructors, 189, 199
  displaying option clicked, 188
  displaying list of options, 188
  list.java listing, 192-195
  methods, 189, 190
  user's selection obtaining, 194, 192
List(int), List, 189
List(int, boolean), List, 189
lists. *See* list boxes
lists, creating, 30, 31

M

MAILTO, 31
makeVisible(int), List, 190
Menu(), Menu Class, 251
menu bar. *See* Menu system

Menu(String), Menu Class, 251
Menu(String, boolean), Menu Class, 251
menu system, 231. *See also* full menus
  applet, running, 253
  frame1.java listing, 257-259
  menu bar, adding, 247, 248
    adding object to menus main class, 252
    connecting actionPerformed method to menu item, 252
    designing menu system, 249
    event handler, connecting to new menu item, 249
    reporting selection to user, 252
    to menu bar window, 249
  menu bar class's constructors and methods, 250, 251
  menu class's constructors and methods, 251, 252
  menus.java listing, 254-257
  displaying new window on button clicking, 246
  file menu, opening, 246, 247
  reporting user action, 247
  Show and Hide window buttons, making active, 253
  window buttons, creating, 246
MenuBar(), MenuBar, 250
minimumSize()
  List, 190
  TextArea, 81
  TextField, 73
minimumSize(int)
  List, 190
  TextField, 73
minimumSize(int, int), TextArea, 81
mouse, using in Writer applet, 308
  allowing space for mouse coordinate integers, 309
  inString variable, setting aside space for, 310
  reading mouse clicks, 308
  mouse click location clicking, 308
mouse-driven paint program, 339. *See also* mouse handling
  3D rectangles, drawing, 376, 377
  Anchor point, establishing, 356, 357

circle, drawing, 372
  checking shape to be drawn, 373
  setting Anchor and Draw To points, 372, 373
Draw To point, 357
  drawing line between Anchor and Draw To points, 357, 358
freehand object drawing, 359, 360, 379, 382
  drawing line between stored points, 381, 382
  incrementing location, 380, 381
  mouse location recording, 380
  setting aside space for, 380
Graphics constructors and methods, 369-371
lines, drawing, 367
  drawing line, 367, 368
  indicating mouse is up, 367
  making sure mouse is up, 368
  overriding paint method, 368
  recording mouse up location, 367
oval, drawing, 372
  checking shape to be drawn, 373
  setting Anchor and Draw To points, 372, 373
painter programs user interface, designing, 360
  Boolean flags, adding, 361, 362
  creating painter applet, 360
  Draw tool event handler, opening, 362
  enabling remaining drawing tool flags, 363, 364
  setting remaining drawing tool flags false, 362
painter.java, 383-394
rectangle, drawing, 358, 359
  checking shape to be drawn, 374, 375
rectangle, drawing rounded, 377-379
mouse handling, 340. *See also* mouse-driven paint program
  displaying user prompt, 340
  Frame1.java listing, 350-356
  handling mouse in painters, 364

473

Index

adding event handlers for mouse events, 364
Anchor points, recording, 364, 365
memory space for Anchor and Draw To points, setting, 365
memory space for mouse flags, setting, 365
tracking mouse state, setting flags for, 365, 366
messages placing on screen, 340
mouse events, adding to application, 343
mouse movement
 indocating, 341
 reporting exit, 342
mouseDragged event, 346
mou*See*ntered event, 344
 indicating mouse has entered client area, 345
 intercepting event, 344
mou*See*xited events, 348
mousePressed event, 346, 347
mouser application, designing, 343
mouser.java listing, 349
mouseReleased event, 347, 348
reporting mouse button click location, 341
reporting mouse button release location, 341
multithreaded applet, 396, 397
multithread functions, synchronizing, 449
 adding Data class to Frame1.java file, 451, 452
 coordinating two threads, 451
 creating object of Data class in application, 450
 Fame1.java listing, 459-465
 setting data member in class' constructor, 450
 setting up threads, 453
  naming threads, 453
  Runnable interface, implementing, 453, 454
  starting threads, 453
  stopping threads, 454
 synchronized1 application's run() method, 454
  dataObject.internal_data, displaying new value, 455, 456

dataObject.internal_data, incrementing, 455
 displaying new value in internal_data, 456, 457
 setting up loop, 454, 455
 string object out_string, setting up, 456
synchronized1.java listing, 458, 459
synchronizing data access, 457, 458

N

numbered lists, 30
newline code, 82

O

object, 54
ordered lists, 30
oval, drawing, 372. *See also* mouse-driven paint program
 checking shape to be drawn, 373
 setting Anchor and Draw To points, 372, 373

P

<P> paragraph tag, 17, 18
 ALIGN, 18
pack(), Java window, 234
package, Java, 45, 53
paint() function, 47
paint program. *See* mouse-driven paint program
painter.java, 383-394
panels, scroll bars
 placing panel, 217, 218
 using, 216
<PARAM> tag, 41
paramString()
 Button, 93
 Checkbox, 136
 Choice, 197
 List, 190
 Menu Class, 251
 ScrollBar, 219
 TextArea, 81
 TextField, 73
popup menus, 187
 constructors and methods, 205
 displaying applet, 203
 displaying popup menu, 206

determining button pressed, 206
event handler, adding to code, 206
 at mouse location, 203, 204, 207
examples, 209
placing items in, 204, 205
popups.java listing, 210-214
user's selection
 displaying, 204
 indicating item selected, 208
 obtaining, 207, 208
PopupMenu(), PopupMenu, 205
PopupMenu(String), PopupMenu, 205
postEvent(Event), Java window, 234
preferredSize()
 List, 190
 TextArea, 81
 TextField, 73
preferredSize(int)
 List, 190
 TextField, 73
preferredSize(int, int), TextArea, 81
processActionEvent(ActionEvent)
 Button, 93
 List, 190
 TextField, 73
processAdjustmentEvent(AdjustmentEvent), ScrollBar, 219
processEvent(AWTEvent)
 Checkbox, 136
 Choice, 198
 List, 190
 ScrollBar, 219
 TextField, 73
processItemEvent(ItemEvent)
 Checkbox, 136
 Choice, 198
 List, 190
program types
 applets, 39
 applications, 39
project, JBuilder, 42, 43
properties, control, 89

R

radio buttons, 133
 check box groups

Index

adding check boxes to group, 146
creating, 145
event handler, connecting to radio button, 146, 147
radios applet, designing, 145
reporting item clicked, 147, 148
checkboxes, putting together with radio buttons, 154-156
buttons creating new, 156, 157
check box group for radio buttons, adding, 156
event handler, adding to radio button, 157
placing information in text field, 158
retailer.java listing, 160-166
settings check to record information, 157
handling
displaying in group, 144
reporting button clicked, 144
radios.java listing, 149-154
Retailer2, creating in Application Wizard, 166
menu, toolbar, and status bar, setting up, 167-170
retailer2.java, running on application start, 167
Retailer2, customizing, 170
checking checkboxes, 171
customizing user selections, 174, 175
examining all checkboxes, 171, 172
price, placing in text field, 172
setting price to match checks, 170
totaling price, 172, 173
Retailer2 listings
Frame1.java, 175-184
Retailer2.java, 184, 185
<RANGE> tag, 5
rectangle, drawing, 358, 359. See also mouse-driven paint program
3D rectangles, drawing, 376, 377
checking shape to be drawn, 374, 375
rounded rectangle, 377-379
remove(int)

Choice, 198
List, 190
Menu Class, 252
MenuBar, 251
remove(MenuComponent)
Menu Class, 252
MenuBar, 251
remove(String)
Choice, 198
List, 190
removeActionListener(ActionListener)
Button, 93
List, 190
TextField, 73
removeAdjustmentListener(AdjustmentListener), ScrollBar, 219
removeAll()
Choice, 198
List, 190
Menu Class, 252
removeItemListener(ItemListener)
Checkbox, 136
Choice, 197
List, 190
removeNotify()
List, 190
Menu Class, 252
MenuBar, 251
replaceItem(String, int), List, 190
replaceRange(Sting, int, int), TextArea, 81
replaceText(Sting, int, int), TextArea, 81
Retailer2. See also checkboxes; radio buttons
creating in Application Wizard, 166
menu, toolbar, and status bar, setting up, 167-170
retailer2.java, running on application start, 167
customizing, 170
checking checkboxes, 171
customizing user selections, 174, 175
examining all checkboxes, 171, 172
price, placing in text field, 172
setting price to match checks, 170
totaling price, 172, 173

listings
Frame1.java, 175-184
Retailer2.java, 184, 185
review.html, 33-37
rows, adding, adding to tables, 25

S

screen flicker, reducing, graphics animation, 419
avoiding clearing whole applet, 419
no flicker version of animator.java, 420-424
paint() method, calling directly, 419, 420
scroll bars, 187
applet with four scroll bars, 215
adding to applet, 216
border layout
setting up, 217
using, 216
constructors and methods, 219, 220
horizontal scroll bars, creating tow, 216, 217
matching user moves, 215
panels
placing panel, 217, 218
using, 216
panels.java listing, 224-230
user actions determining, 220
changing buttons caption on clicking, 223
coordinating scroll bar movement, 222, 223
matching button movement, 221
Scrollbar(), ScrollBar, 219
Scrollbar(int), ScrollBar, 219
Scrollbar(int, int, int, int, int), ScrollBar, 219
scrolling lists. See list boxes
select(int)
Choice, 197
List, 190
select(String), Choice, 197
setActionCommand(String), Button, 93
setBlockIncrement(int), ScrollBar, 219
setCheckBoxGroup(CheckboxGroup), Checkbox, 136
setColumns(int)
TextArea, 81
TextField, 73

Index

setEchoChar(char), TextField, 73
setEchoCharacter(char), TextField, 73
setHelpMenu(Menu), MenuBar, 251
setImage(Image image), ButtonControl, 105
setImage(String), ButtonControl, 105
setImage(URL url), ButtonControl, 105
setImageFirst(boolean first), ButtonControl, 105
setLabel(String 1), ButtonControl, 106
setLabel(String)
  Button, 93
  Checkbox, 136
setLineIncrement(int), ScrollBar, 219
setMaximum(int), ScrollBar, 219
setMinimum(int), ScrollBar, 219
setMultipleMode(boolean), List, 190
setMultipleSelections(boolean), List, 190
setOrientation(int)
  ButtonControl, 106
  ScrollBar, 220
setPageIncrement(int), ScrollBar, 220
setRows(int), TextArea, 81
setState(boolean), Checkbox, 136
setUnitIncrement(int), ScrollBar, 220
setValue(int), ScrollBar, 220
setValues(int, int, int, int), ScrollBar, 220
setVisibleAmount(int), ScrollBar, 220
shortcuts(), MenuBar, 251
show(), Java window, 234
show(Component, int, int), PopupMenu, 205
stringWidth(String), FontMetrics, 330
synchronizing multithread functions, 449
  adding Data class to Frame1.java file, 451, 452
  coordinating two threads, 451
  creating object of Data class in application, 450
  Fame1.java listing, 459-465

setting data member in class' constructor, 450
setting up threads, 453
  naming threads, 453
  Runnable interface, implementing, 453, 454
  starting threads, 453
  stopping threads, 454
synchronized1 application's run() method, 454
  dataObject.internal_data, displaying new value, 455, 456
  dataObject.internal_data, incrementing, 455
  displaying new value in internal_data, 456, 457
  setting up loop, 454, 455
  string object out_string, setting up, 456
synchronized1.java listing, 458, 459
synchronizing data access, 457, 458
synchronization, 451

T

table header, adding to tables, 25
<TABLE> tag, 25
tables, creating 24
  adding adding to, 25
  columns, adding, 26
  ending, 27, 28
  example, 29
  rows, adding, 25
  table header, adding, 25
tags. See HTML tags
text. See also Writer applet
  adding to Web page, 17
  aligning, 18, 20-22
  colors, setting
    browser predefined colors, 8
    color values, defining, 8
  displaying in Java, 47, 48
  setting next to images, 22, 23
text areas, handling, 78, 89
  placing control in applet, 81
  placing text in text area, 82
text areas applet, creating, 79, 80
  TextArea constructors, 80, 81
  TextArea methods, 80, 81
  textareas.java, 83-85
text fields. See also buttons and

text fields
  button, adding to, 91
  check box, adding to, 134
  using, 68, 69
text, justifying, 328
  adding location integers to applet, 332, 333
  centering string in applet, 333
  creating new applet, overriding paint() method, 328
  declaring font in applet, 329
  determining string dimension, 329
  displaying
    message, 331
    string in applet window, 331, 332
    text string at coordinated, 332
  drawing justified text, 328, 329
  FontMetrics class's constructors and methods, 330
  justify.java listing, 335-337
  justifyFontMetrics object, declaring, 330, 331
  placing
    text at different window locations, 328
    text string at bottom of applet, 334
  string width, determining, 333
TextArea(),TextArea, 80
TextArea(int, int), TextArea, 80
TextArea(String), TextArea, 80
TextArea(String, int, int), TextArea, 80
TextArea(String, int, int, int), TextArea, 80
TextField(),TextField, 72
TextField(int), TextField, 72
TextField(String), TextField, 72
TextField(String, int), TextField, 72
textfields Applet, creating, 70
  constructors, 72, 73
  controls, adding to applet, 71, 72
  function overloading, 73, 74
  initializing text in, 75, 76
  JBuilder designer, using, 70, 71
  methods, 72, 73
  placing textfield in applet, 74, 75

Index

textfields.java listing, 76-78
\<TH\> table header tag, 25
threads, using more than one, 437
　creating integers application, 438
　　adding new threads to it, 438, 439
　　Frame1.java listing, 444-449
　　implementing threads, 440
　　integers.java listing, 443, 444
　　naming threads, 439
　　run() adding to application, 440
　　separating threads, 440
　　determining and storing thread name, 440
　　loop, setting up to display integers, 441
　　placing ascending integers in second text field, 442
　　placing loop_index in text field, 441, 442
　starting new threads, 438
　synchronizing multithread functions, 449
　　adding Data class to Frame1.java file, 451, 452
　　coordinating two threads, 451
　　creating object of Data class in application, 450
　　Fame1.java listing, 459-465
　　setting data member in class' constructor, 450
　　setting up threads, 453, 454
　　synchronized1 application's run() method, 454-457
　　synchronized1.java listing, 458, 459
　　synchronizing data access, 457, 458
thumb, 187
"tile", 9
\<TITLE\> tag, 6, 7
toBack(), Java window, 234
toFront(), Java window, 234
tool tip, 79
toString()
　Font Class, 315
　FontMetrics, 330
\<TR\> row tag, 25
typeface, setting, 24

U

\<UL\> bullet list tag, 30
Universal Resource Locator. See URL
unordered lists, 30
URL (Universal Resource Locator), 18

V

validators, Web page, 6, 7
void setImage(String path), ButtonControl

W

W3. See WWW
Web page, 2
　body, finishing, 33
　colors, setting
　　browser predefined colors, 8
　　color values, defining, 8
　example, 2
　listing, review.html, 33-37
　graphics, inserting into, 11
　　\<IMG\> image, 15-17
　outline, 5, 7
　text, adding to, 17
　validators, 6, 7
Window(Frame), Java window, 234
windows. See frame windows
World Wide Web. See WWW
Writer applet, 304. See also text
　font, selecting, 313
　　default values, setting, 313
　　Font class's constructors and methods, 315
　　font object, creating new, 314, 315
　　installing new object in Graphics object, 315, 316
　　modifying options to match user selections, 313, 314
　keystrokes, recording, 310
　　drawing text in applet, 311
　　making button keyboard target, 311, 312
　　obtaining character typed, 311
　making text appear at location clicked, 304
　mouse, using in Writer, 308
　　allowing space for mouse coordinate integers, 309
　　inString variable, setting aside space for, 310
　　reading mouse clicks, 308
　　mouse click location clicking, 308
　text, displaying in inString, 316, 317
　type characters, storing, 309
　overview, 304
　writer.java listing, 318-328
　Writer applets' flags, setting, 305
　　assigning font flags, 307
　　assigning format flags, 307
　　Boolean flag setting up, 306
　　buttons adding, 305
　　resetting flags to plain text, 307, 308
　　setting Boolean flags to match user clicks, 306
WWW (World Wide Web) address, 18

477

Important Note Concerning the CD

As this book was going to press, Borland renamed its proprietary class library, originally named "baja" to "jbcl." If you encounter compilation errors when compiling a specific Java source file (i.e., a file with the extension .java), change all references in that file from "borland.baja" to "borland.jbcl" and recompile.